TO ADV

I10643484

DATE DUE

DEMCO 38-296

To Advance Knowledge

Riverside Community College
Library
4800 Magnolia Avenue
Riverside, CA 92506

TO ADVANCE KNOWLEDGE

The Growth of American Research Universities, 1900–1940

ROGER L. GEIGER

New York   Oxford
OXFORD UNIVERSITY PRESS
1986

Riverside Community College
Library
4800 Magnolia Avenue
Riverside, California 92506

AUG   '94

For Derek Lewis Geiger

Oxford University Press

Oxford   New York   Toronto
Delhi   Bombay   Calcutta   Madras   Karachi
Petaling Jaya   Singapore   Hong Kong   Tokyo
Nairobi   Dar es Salaam   Cape Town
Melbourne   Auckland

and associated companies in
Beirut   Berlin   Ibadan   Nicosia

Copyright © 1986 by Oxford University Press, Inc.

Published by Oxford University Press, Inc.
200 Madison Avenue, New York, New York 10016

Oxford is the registered trademark of Oxford University Press

All rights reserved. No part of this publication may be reproduced,
stored in a retrieval system, or transmitted, in any form or by any means,
electronic, mechanical, photocopying, recording, or otherwise,
without the prior permission of Oxford University Press, Inc.

Library of Congress Cataloging-in-Publication Data
Geiger, Roger L., 1943–
To advance knowledge.
Includes index.
1. Research institutes—United States—History.
2. Science—United States—History. 3. Universities and colleges—
United States. I. Title.
Q180.U5G34   1986   001.4'0973   85-30971
ISBN 0-19-503803-7

2 4 6 8 10 9 7 5 3 1

Printed in the United States of America
on acid free paper

Preface

The formation of the Association of American Universities in 1900 signified that the research universities had become a self-conscious group within American higher education. At that date, though, the rubric of 'research university' would have been considered redundant; the province of a true university was then held to be higher learning, graduate education, and the advancement of knowledge through research. Most of the universities whose histories will be followed in this book were charter members of the Association: California, Chicago, Columbia, Cornell, Harvard, Johns Hopkins, Michigan, Pennsylvania, Princeton, Stanford, Wisconsin, and Yale. Illinois and Minnesota joined shortly thereafter, and Caltech and MIT were admitted during the interwar years. By that era it had become apparent that all American universities were not fulfilling the same functions as AAU members, especially the select group studied here. These sixteen institutions tended to head any list of quantitative indicators of university research—number of PhD.s produced, volumes in the library, or dollars expended for research. More importantly, they led all others in the quality of their faculties as judged by their academic peers. Although the fortunes of individual universities would fluctuate over the four decades of this study, their commitments to academic quality remained salient. At the end of the 1930s, for example, these sixteen universities led all others in the number of distinguished scientists on their faculty.

These sixteen are among the best-known American universities, and included in their reknown is an appreciation for their numerous contributions to the advancement of knowledge. Yet, while much of their experience in the twentieth century has been recorded, comparatively little is known of the way in which they developed their most fundamental attribute—that of being research universities. Institutional histories at best signal major discoveries or publications by the university faculty, but they generally fail to elucidate the complex antecedents that made those accomplishments possible. And even where major advances have been closely scrutinized, as in the growing literature on the twentieth-century history of American science, it is seldom possible to appreciate how developments at one institution are like or unlike those taking place at other research universities. The nature of the American university discourages would-be investigators from posing such questions. The nurturing of university research has depended upon a complicated nexus of events stretching from the domain of the individual department to the actions of university trustees. It has also depended heavily upon actors entirely outside the university. In this welter of activities, however, there are three arenas that are crucial to the institutional development of research.

The first concerns the acquisition of social resources, a process historically shaped by the nature of the American university. The bane of American higher education from the perspective of would-be university builders has traditionally been its large teaching burdens. Compared with their counterparts in European universities, American professors have been condemned to provide extensive basic instruction to large numbers of relatively poorly prepared undergraduates. Those who have deplored this situation have generally failed to acknowledge that these duties have allowed the universities to grow and diversify. American society has chiefly rewarded its universities for the undergraduate education that they provided, and the research universities too have heeded this maxim. On the eve of World War I the research universities enrolled one of every five American college students and also managed to claim a disproportionate amount of the total resources available to higher education. To varying extents a part of these resources has also been used to foster research.

The second crucial set of issues faced by research universities, then, involved converting some of the resources they received into a capability for conducting research. Above all this required recruiting and retaining research-oriented faculty; but it also implied providing those faculty with the conditions needed to pursue their investigations—the time, the facilities, and the services to support their research. Transforming educational resources into a research capability has been a process fraught with tension. The particularistic purposes for which each university derived its support scarcely coincided with the universalistic values of national communities of scholars and scientists, the groups that monitored the advancement of academic knowledge. But these two sets of goals were not necessarily incompatible. The complications inherent in this relationship nevertheless made the institutionalization of research commitments proceed somewhat differently at each institution.

Despite the gradual symbiosis of education and research, the increasing direct costs of university research could not for the most part be diverted from educational funds. Research in the American university ultimately had to depend upon external sources of patronage for these direct costs. Thus the third important arena for the constitution of American research universities comprised the extramural supply of resources earmarked for research. Before World War I, American universities were largely on their own when it came to finding patrons to support their research aspirations. After the war, the large general-purpose foundations led the way in providing voluntary philanthropic support explicitly for university research. Most important, over the long run the extramural support for university research tended to flow to those institutions that had most successfully developed their research capabilities.

The account of the growth of American research universities that follows will move freely among these three critical arenas. The initial chapter presents the emergence of the research universities as a distinctive type by the turn of the century. It then examines the factors tending to make them alike—the separate organization of academic disciplines having intellectual sovereignty over their respective subjects—and the factors tending toward diversity—the different ways in which they related to American society to secure the support upon which they depended. The second chapter places the universities within the national system of research institutions, and then concentrates on the ways in which they developed their research capabilities in the period prior to the war. Next are depicted the extraordinary experiences of universities during the war and the far-reaching consequences that ensued. World War I hastened the expansion and differentiation of American higher education, and also produced a glorification of collegiate, as opposed to university, ideals. But another legacy of the war was a national, privately funded university research system. Chapter 4 describes how the foundations assumed leadership in encouraging the expansion of university research. Largely as a result of their efforts, the research universities matured greatly during the course of the 1920s. The fifth chapter examines the different paths followed by eight of these universities as they evolved during the 1920s and 1930s. It then looks across institutions at important changes in student recruitment, faculty careers, and arrangements for research. It concludes by assessing the rise of American university-based science to parity with the best existing elsewhere in the world. The Depression then dealt the research universities a painful blow, but their research efforts, as described in the final chapter, were largely able to sustain the momentum acquired during their golden age. It became quite apparent, however, that the university research system of the interwar years, based as it was upon private patronage, would no longer suffice. New and more ample sources of support would be required if the research universities were to lead the next thrust forward in the advancement of knowledge.

This book could not have been written without the generous assistance of many others. The Yale Program on Non-Profit Organizations provided a congenial and stimulating environment for this project. I am particularly grateful to John Simon and Paul DiMaggio for their confidence in this endeavor and their help in its realization. For occasional hospitality that considerably assisted my research I would like to thank Martin Trow and the Berkeley Center for Studies in Higher Education as well as Burton Clark and the UCLA Comparative Higher Education Research Group. I appreciate the help I received in all the archives in which I worked, but especially the friendly assistance of the staff of Yale's Seeley G. Mudd Library, where many of my sources were housed.

In addition, numerous individuals have helped me to see further, understand more, and avoid errors of fact or interpretation. Robert R. Palmer and Minor Myers, Jr., deepened my comprehension of Princeton, while David Riesman did the same for Harvard; Walter Metzger, Stanley Katz, Richard Nelson, and John Servos provided useful comments on my drafts; discussions with David Breneman and Jon McKenna were useful in formulating this project, while Barry Karl and George Pierson warned me of some pitfalls to avoid; Peter Dobkin Hall, David Levine, Leroy Foster, Seymour Sarasohn, Robert Kohler, John Stanfield, and Alexandra Oleson supplied otherwise unavailable materials; and Sheldon Meyer offered strategic editorial advice. I am also indebted to the many scholars who have elucidated areas of this broad territory: a score of them are acknowledged in the text and many more in the notes. In addition, I owe a particular debt of gratitude to two individuals: Minor Myers, Jr., by giving me unlimited use of his personal collection of source materials on university history, immeasurable furthered by investigations; and Hugh Hawkins, through close reading and judicious comments, made this manuscript much better than it would otherwise have been. I am sincerely grateful for the generosity of the Andrew W. Mellon Foundation, whose grant made possible the inauguration of this study, and of the Earhart Foundation, whose timely support made possible its conclusion. And for support of a different kind during the frustration, uncertainty, and inconvenience that attend a prolonged project of this sort, very special thanks to my wife, Marijane.

Old Saybrook   R.L.G.
May 1986

Contents

I

The Shaping of the American Research University, 1865–1920

The American research university assumed something like its present form in the half-century prior to 1920. In this respect it was scarcely different from many other American economic and cultural institutions that evolved during these decades from small localized concerns with parochial interests and clienteles into bureaucratic organizations integrated with national communications networks.[1] Many of the colleges, institutes, normal schools, and universities remained even by 1920 quite restricted in the scope and the spread of their activities, just as did a multitude of commercial and industrial establishments. But the major research universities had become the corporations of the education industry—organized to gather the lion's share of social resources available to higher education, and committed to produce the most valued educational products for the most important national markets. The evolution of research universities over these years was anything but even. Between the Civil War and 1890 a series of scattered, discrete events provided precedents and stimuli for subsequent developments. The pace of change accelerated abruptly in the 1890s, reaching a peak around the turn of the century. A second surge of expansion in university undertakings and the means for their fulfillment was interrupted by the Great War. In its aftermath science, technology, and an attendant belief in human progress through rational, systematic investigation occupied a permanent niche not only in the major universities of the country but in the national consciousness as well.

The "emergence of the American university" was a multifaceted phenomenon. The book of that title by Laurence Veysey stands at the head of a rich literature dedicated to this subject.[2] The changing position of research in these emergent institutions was largely determined by four interrelated processes within this overall development. The first was structural, in that it concerned the relationship of different institutions: how their activities were coordinated, whether through competition or cooperation; how the actions of one university impinged upon those of others. The very notion of a distinctive set of research universities implied a far-reaching transformation of the structure of American higher education. The second process was intellectual, involving changes in the organization of knowledge in the country. The cognitive growth of university subject matter, both at home and abroad, gradually produced a corresponding change in the way academic scholars received training, taught others, organized themselves, and communicated with one another. Together these changes affected the treatment of knowledge in the university. The curriculum soon reflected the existence of both specialists and their specialties, and the academic disciplines assumed responsibility for the sanctioning of new knowledge. The third process was driven by the proliferation of institutional resources. On the eve of the Great War the research universities were all radically larger in terms of students, faculty, and departments, but they had grown even more in laboratories, libraries, and the kind of financial backing necessary to sustain their activities. The fourth strand in this development was support for the research role of the university. As one important university priority, research derived some benefit from the vast expansion of university resources. However, as a subsidiary of the main university function of teaching, research remained remarkably dependent upon ad hoc arrangements that, with a few exceptions, differed from field to field and from one year to the next.

By 1920, then, American research universities had established patterns of structure, intellectual organization, and financing that are still recognizable today. Yet, the manner in which they sustained their commitment to research was inchoate at best. The major universities thus had a philosophical commitment to the advancement of knowledge but lacked a secure institutional means for meeting that commitment. Despite the great expectations of many, heightened especially by the experience of war, the status of university research remained doubly problematic: within the university it was one priority in competition with other institutional goals, while to a considerable extent its feasibility depended upon the eleemosynary impulse of external patrons.

By this date probably fewer than twenty-five universities were seriously committed to research as an institutional goal. In the discussion that follows the focus will be primarily upon the fifteen whose credentials for this status were most secure. There is a curious symmetry to this group, which in itself is testimony to the diverse heritage of American higher education. Five are state universities from the Middle and Far West—Illinois, Michigan, Minnesota, Wisconsin, and California. Five began as colonial colleges of the Eastern Seaboard and thus are among the nation's oldest institutions of higher learning—Columbia, Harvard, Penn, Princeton, and Yale. And five are private foundations of the latter nineteenth century—MIT, Cornell, Johns Hopkins, Stanford, and Chicago.[3] These institutions fully embody the emergence of research as a fundamental goal in American higher education.

1. Toward a National System of Universities

The myriad small colleges of different religious denominations that dotted the American landscape before the Civil War contrasted thoroughly with twentieth-century notions of higher educations. From a present-day perspective the bare facts of their existence seem bleak indeed.[4] The typical established college of this era consisted of fewer than one hundred students and perhaps five teachers. Students were admitted whenever they were deemed to know enough Latin, Greek, and mathematics to do college work, and often the college itself was overshadowed by an associated academy that performed this preparatory task. The colleges taught a single, fixed curriculum based upon classical languages and mathematics. To this would be added some moral philosophy, history, and a fairly general coverage of the natural sciences. The intellectual potential that these subjects did possess was largely vitiated by memorization and classroom rote recitation. Prevailing pedagogical theories justified these exercises in terms of mental discipline—the capacity to expand the powers of the mind, in the words of the widely respected "Yale Faculty Report of 1828." If the content of college study—"the furniture of the mind"—was less important than the discipline imparted, it was nevertheless expected to produce a man of balanced tastes and Christian morals.[5]

Recently, American historians have viewed these facts in a more favorable light by taking pains to examine the "old-time" college in its proper nineteenth-century milieu. Many of these colleges developed strong local roots by serving cultural and economic needs, thus making them far less ephemeral than has been alleged. And, among the leading eastern colleges at least, science offerings were expanded and upgraded throughout this period.[6] Nevertheless, their nineteenth-century critics were not entirely wrong in seeing the colleges as fundamentally limited. Their small size and fixed curriculum were both part of the problem. The fact was that no matter how eloquently they might defend the existing system of curricu-

lum and pedagogy, the old-time colleges lacked the personnel and resources to offer anything else.

Discontent with the antebellum colleges was evident chiefly among
those who wanted to augment the content of their curriculum. Three clear
themes—occurring together, singly, or paired—were articulated by critics and would-be reformers: that the colleges must give greater scope to
new kinds of knowledge, particularly that being formulated in the natural
sciences; that they should offer some forms of practical training which
would prepare students directly for careers; and that they should incorpo-
rate advanced study similar to what could be found in European, and
especially German, universities. For each of these themes advocates could
muster persuasive arguments. By mid-century the conspicuous advancement of science clearly merited larger and more specialized treatment in
the curriculum. Education for careers held the promise of attracting new
classes of students and contributing to the economic development of the
country's untapped resources. In addition, proponents of advanced study
could appeal to nationalist sentiments by pointing out that the United
States did not yet have a single true university. The last of these themes
was most closely linked with the desire for university research.

It was generally assumed that advanced study could be provided only
by someone with advanced knowledge of a subject, acquired in part
through original investigations. More concretely, people acquainted with
European patterns of education recognized that the offerings of the American college corresponded in large part with the classical regimen of the
gymnasium or lycée. It seemed clear to them that advanced study, such as
that cultivated in the German universities, ought to follow the completion
of an American bachelor's degree. From this perspective advanced instruction and original investigation could be linked only at the graduate
level. Thus, from the first, university research in America was tied to issues of graduate education.

In general, antebellum reformers made grudging progress in areas
where they did not directly challenge the dominance of the classical curriculum, and were largely discomfited where confrontation occurred. The
natural sciences established their most significant permanent footholds
when the combination of internal pressures and timely endowments led to
the establishment of first the Lawrence Scientific School at Harvard (1847)
and then the Yale/Sheffield Scientific School (1854). Serious graduate education also gained a permanent, though somewhat premature, position
when Yale awarded the first American Ph.D., in 1861. A decade would
intervene, however, before others would follow this lead.[7] These innovations succeeded in part because they were separate programs that left the
traditional curriculum intact. Antebellum reformers discovered that conditions were not yet ripe for its overhaul. One of the most forceful critics

of the American college, Brown's president Francis Wayland, attempted to initiate the teaching of practical subjects in the early 1850s. His efforts, however, chiefly attracted ill-prepared students, alienated faculty and trustees, and lost any hope of redemption when they failed to be self-supporting. Henry Tappan, as president of the University of Michigan (1852-63), attempted to implant the scholarly ideals of a German university in the American Midwest but, like Wayland, was ultimately forced from office, his reforms repudiated, although not entirely forgotten.[8]

By the eve of the Civil War some cracks had appeared in the edifice that was the old American college, but it still possessed the resilience that would allow it to endure well into the age of the university. Nevertheless, the entering wedges of science and scholarship were clearly portentous. They signified a commitment to the advancement of knowledge that was incompatible with a fixed curriculum and a pedagogy based on rote learning. It was hardly accidental, then, that the most prominent university builders of the next generation had important associations with these first fruits of reform. Charles W. Eliot and Daniel Coit Gilman were, respectively, faculty members in the Lawrence and Sheffield scientific schools, and Andrew D. White taught at Michigan under Tappan. They would soon bear much responsibility for the permanent establishment of first utilitarian and then scholarly goals in American higher education.

The notion that colleges should teach subjects that would have some practical utility for their students entered the mainstream of American higher education from two different sources.[9] It was most directly embodied in the Morrill Act of 1862, which authorized a substantial grant of federal land to each state for the purpose of maintaining "at least one college where the leading object shall be, without excluding other scientific and classical studies, . . . to teach such branches of learning as are related to agriculture and the mechanic arts."[10] More indirectly, the idea of utility was connected with the gradual spread of the elective system, which allowed students to choose the courses that best fit their own future needs. As a philosophy of undergraduate education the elective system is indelibly associated with Charles W. Eliot, who instituted it and defended it during his forty-year presidency of Harvard (1869-1909). Encompassing both of these developments was the opening of Cornell University in 1868, under the presidency of Andrew D. White. Dedicated to offering any person instruction in any subject, Cornell had an inherent commitment to student choice from the outset, while also being designated as the land-grant school for New York State. Each of these occurrences played a significant part of the utilitarian reorientation of American higher education.

By putting federal money behind the cause of agricultural and mechanical education, the Morrill Act galvanized tendencies in American higher education that were by the Civil War still largely inchoate. The states quickly accepted these grants in principle and only later faced the problem of fulfilling their terms. In the East this was largely done through existing institutions, particularly eccentric ones like the Sheffield Scientific School and the Massachusetts Institute of Technology (f. 1865).[11] However, in the developing states of the Middle and Far West the intentions of Senator Justin Morrill dovetailed neatly with the pragmatic and populist tone of statehouse politics. These funds led directly to the founding of state universities in both Illinois (1867) and California (1868). The land-grant revenues were also used to strengthen fledgling and impoverished state colleges in Minnesota and Wisconsin. The stipulated practical programs may well have made higher education more palatable to state legislators, who were certainly not well disposed toward high culture. In Wisconsin, for example, regular state support of the university began only after the reorganization inspired by the act.[12] It would take the remainder of the century for the brand of higher education championed by the Morrill Act to develop fully in state universities. By then these institutions had become utilitarian universities, accepting students without preparation in classical languages and including a variety of vocational specializations in their offerings.[13]

Cornell University forced utility into the consciousness of American educators in a more dramatic and decisive fashion. Ezra Cornell's desire for accessible, practical education in engineering and agriculture was there combined with Andrew D. White's vision of a modern university—a union made possible by the bounty of the Morrill Act. It is an interesting reflection of these times that Ezra Cornell was willing to invest a large part of his personal fortune in order to make such studies available at a time when state legislatures were reluctant to commit public funds. His gift of $500,000 toward the founding of the university secured for it the proceeds of New York's federal land grant, thus providing the new institution with an unusually solid financial base for this period. Also vital to its success was the leadership of Andrew White. Patrician, politician, and man of letters, White had been a professor at Michigan under Tappan and had firsthand acquaintance with higher education in Europe. He consequently balanced his disdain for traditional American colleges with a positive conception of a useful university. Cornell was to be a nonsectarian and coeducational institution, where science, humanities, and practical subjects would coexist on equal terms. Unlike previous such departures in American higher education, Cornell was an immediate and lasting success. In only its third year of operation it attracted the largest entering class the country had yet seen. As "the first major university in America . . . to be created on a reformed basis from the ground up," and as "the first spectacular visible fruit of the Morrill Act," Cornell and its president for a time represented a beacon of inspiration for the developing state universities.[14]

The academic program at Cornell allowed students to choose between different groupings of subjects, but by this juncture the fixed curriculum was beginning to be eroded by the inclusion of some elective subjects in many schools. Nevertheless, when Charles W. Eliot became the president of Harvard in 1869 he both implemented the elective system in its most radical form and became its chief symbol and spokesman.[15] The controversy that swirled for decades around Eliot's system of free electives concentrated on the issue of what a student could and should learn—on the coherence, breadth, and depth of different plans of study. Yet, the importance of the elective system for the development of American higher education lies in what it allowed faculty to teach. Elective courses not only permitted new subjects to be taught but also freed traditional subjects like classics to be developed in more specialized and advanced forms. As this occurred, the objective of a college education shifted imperceptibly from that of imparting an established culture to that of instilling increasingly specialized knowledge. When Eliot took the reins at Harvard, it already had the most distinguished faculty in America, and Eliot found the financial means that allowed him to expand it even further. The majority of colleges could make only minor additions to the existing curriculum because of the limitations of their faculty. For that reason the direction taken by Harvard signifies the beginning of a fundamental schism in American higher education, between those schools that could and those that could not pursue advanced knowledge at the highest levels.

Eliot may have been only partially correct in the pedagogical debate over free electives. Certainly posterity—as well as Eliot's immediate successor at Harvard—concluded that students fresh from secondary school need some structure and guidance in their course of instruction. But on the more fundamental issue, the centrality of the advancement of knowledge, Eliot was solidly on the side of history. Conservative bulwarks, like Yale under Noah Porter and Princeton under James McCosh, might preserve what they could of the old collegiate culture; but they could not, without slipping into the intellectual backwaters, repudiate the new knowledge that was increasingly proliferating around them.[16] Moreover, it gradually became evident that the teaching of advanced academic subjects could not be separated for long from the question of contributing to their further advancement.

The mission of research in American universities has been irrevocably associated with the founding of the Johns Hopkins University in 1876: "perhaps the single, most decisive event in the history of learning in the Western hemisphere," as it has been extravagantly, but not unreasonably, described.[17] Although it can safely be regarded as inevitable that the ideals of the world-leading German universities would eventually affect American higher education, and as no less certain that on this side of the Atlantic Germanic conceptions of scholarship would have to be assimilated into the unique context of American universities, Hopkins was nevertheless the first to crystallize these influences into a viable institutional form. Credit for this accomplishment belongs to the farsighted and painstaking efforts of the trustees of Johns Hopkins's will; to the deft leadership of President Daniel Coit Gilman in choosing men, inspiring scholarship, and coming to terms with the political and social exigencies of an American university; and to the distinctive chemistry of the original group of professors and fellows, who set the tone and established the customs of this institutional experiment.[18] It was their success in creating an American research university that caused Johns Hopkins to have resonance among other major universities.

The foremost objective of Johns Hopkins was not to promote research per se but to provide advanced instruction of a standard comparable to that being set in Germany. Graduate education, in fact, dominated the university from the outset. Until 1890, graduate students outnumbered undergraduates by a wide margin, and the majority of Hopkins A.B.'s actually remained at the school for some graduate work. Hopkins consequently gave an impetus to American graduate education and did much to standardize the American Ph.D. at a credibly high level. Hopkins produced more Ph.D.'s during the 1870s and 1880s than Harvard and Yale combined. By the 1890s these made-in-America scholars were carrying the Hopkins spirit into all the major universities of the country. Graduate education entails research, however, and Hopkins far more than any other contemporary American university actively encouraged original investigations by its faculty. Here, too, the contribution of the university was something more than the sum of the works of its distinguished faculty. The scholars at Hopkins aggressively seized vanguard positions in their respective disciplines, particularly through the organization of scholarly journals. Five of the six original departments sponsored such journals, several of which became the central organ of their discipline. Other periodicals followed, wholly or partly lodged at the university.[19] These publications in turn played an indispensable role in the emergence of academic disciplines.

Perhaps most important, Johns Hopkins enlarged the range of possibilities in American higher education and by doing so also enlarged the consciousness of educators to include a concrete university research role. This was evident most clearly and most significantly in the case of Charles Eliot. Viewing higher education originally from the single perspective of Harvard College, he had said that a German-style university would suit Harvard freshmen "about as well as a barn-yard would suit a whale."

When consulted before the founding of Hopkins, Eliot could not conceive of graduate education except in the Harvard mold—as an appendage to an established undergraduate college that served a well-defined geographical constituency.[20] But the reality of Johns Hopkins changed perceptions and priorities alike. Eliot could hardly ignore the fact that at least five Harvard faculty members had seriously considered, but ultimately declined, offers to join the new university. The challenge posed by Hopkins in fact quickly acted as a stimulus for encouraging research and graduate education at Harvard.[21] Johns Hopkins set the standard for a research university during the 1880s, but by the end of that decade its ideals were shared to a significant degree by several other major universities.[22] A *system* of American universities was taking shape.

When the complex trends just sketched are reduced to their bare essentials, it can be seen that the natural sciences attained a foothold in American higher education around the 1850s, that utilitarian objectives became institutionalized in the 1860s, and that research-based graduate training became a permanent component in the 1870s. Once established, each of these trends developed according to its own internal logic and momentum. Being substantially interrelated, they powerfully reinforced one another once they were in place. As they overcame the status of innovations, they also ceased to be separable elements in the higher-education complex. In contrast to the outlook of the traditional college, these three trends, each in its own way, represented the more general principle of cognitive rationality—knowing through the exercise of reason—that posterity would define as "the core value of the university."[23]

Cognitive rationality was, of course, never entirely absent in the history of American higher education. Before 1890, however, it was subordinated to the overriding cultural values that dominated the colleges. By the turn of the century cognitive rationality was firmly in place as the dominant value, determining more than any other single factor the organization and operation of the research universities. It achieved this position largely because, where accepted criteria of judgment exist, better knowledge will tend to displace inferior knowledge. For that very reason the spectacular advances made by German science forced academic reorganization in all Western countries during this period. But, in terms of the specific academic structure of the United States, cognitive rationality triumphed by becoming a paramount intellectual value in strategically important institutions. In rapidly developing state universities knowledge—at least certain forms of academic knowledge—was associated by state legislators and the public with useful application; and the advancement of knowledge consequently promised enhanced usefulness. In the institutions devoted specifically to science or technology, systematic rationality was axiomatic. The most important newly founded universities, as was just seen, embodied and impelled forward those aspects of the trend toward cognitive rationality that were ripe for institutionalization. Perhaps most significantly, these trends were assimilated by the oldest, wealthiest, and most influential schools in the Northeast. The 1890s therefore mark the definitive transition to a new university-dominated structure in American higher education.

Clark University opened its doors in Worcester, Massachusetts, in 1889, followed shortly by the establishment of Stanford University in California in 1891 and the University of Chicago in 1892. During the same few years major efforts of academic reorganization were undertaken at Harvard and Columbia. Elsewhere at major universities a succession of less conspicuous changes was opening the way for far-reaching transformations in what was taught, how, and to whom. This was the beginning of what Laurence Veysey has called "the academic boom of the 1890s."[24] The quantitative and structural changes that occurred during this decade rested upon an intellectual and institutional foundation that had been slowly maturing for half a century. Moreover, they were abetted by favorable social and economic developments that produced more students to be taught and more funds with which to grow. The change was nevertheless abrupt. Measures like the elective system, programs in applied science, and graduate education, which had previously had the status of reforms or innovations, suddenly in the 1890s became established and ascendant.[25] Now it was the colleges wishing to resist or dilute these tendencies that bore the onus of justifying their stance. The transformation of the 1890s nevertheless transcended these specific reforms, which were adapted to circumstance in any number of ways as they were implemented in different institutions. Rather, it involved more-basic factors of competition, growth, and organization that affected the very nature of the university.

The creation of new and the enlargement of existing universities, first of all, considerably increased the density of the university network. More frequent and numerous points of contact between institutions had the incidental effect of heightening the sense of competition between schools. This was above all competition for prestige—an ineffable combination of publicity, peer esteem, and pride. In the rapid rise of intercollegiate athletics during this period this competition assumed a ritualized, symbolic form, which tended to become an end in itself. Behind the competition for prestige, however, lay a truly vital endeavor to secure the resources necessary for growth and progress. For the academic development of research universities the most significant competition was for research-minded faculty.

The "boom" of the 1890s had several beneficial effects upon the academic profession. Young scholars with German or American Ph.D.'s could readily find positions in expanding faculties, and scholars with distinguished reputations suddenly found themselves in demand at other universities.[26] The change was perceptible to President James B. Angell of Michigan, who commented in 1892, "Whereas formerly it was rather rare that a professor was called from one institution to another, now the custom is very general."[27] That he and others translated the German term *Berufung* to describe this phenomenon is another indication of its novelty. There can be little doubt that one major cause of this new competition was the creation first of Stanford and then, more significantly, of the University of Chicago. It is instructive to compare the initial faculty recruitment of Johns Hopkins with that of Chicago only sixteen years later. Of the six original Hopkins professors, only Ira Remsen of Williams and Basil Gildersleeve of Virginia were drawn from American professorships. However, the University of Chicago opened in 1892 with a faculty of 120, including 5 teachers enticed from Yale and 15 drawn from Clark.[28] Hopkins was influential by the force of its example, but Chicago caused an immediate turbulence in the academic marketplace.

The academic boom did not wane after Stanford and Chicago had filled their faculties, thanks to the numerous efforts of other institutions to keep up with the spreading competition for academic prestige. After the University of Chicago, none aimed higher or succeeded more brilliantly than Columbia. Frederick Barnard, Columbia's longtime president (1864–89), harbored a frequently articulated vision of the school's greatness. The American version of a university, he believed strongly if not entirely correctly, could not be created de novo but would grow naturally out of certain existing colleges. Columbia was uniquely suited for this transition by virtue of its location in the nation's largest and richest city.[29] This prophecy was realized by his successor, President Seth Low (1890–1901). A rather improbable figure to become a university builder, Low was a retired businessman without a firsthand involvement in academic affairs except as a trustee. Perhaps for that reason he consulted his faculty extensively on assuming his post. Apparently he listened, too, because he immediately committed Columbia to goals that could hardly have been more congenial to research-minded faculty. Given the attractiveness of New York City, Low felt, Columbia should seek out "the best man in the world" for any vacant position. He also wanted to guarantee professors "the time in which to make research," and he quickly took a major step in this direction by establishing paid sabbatical leaves. Low was equally dedicated to creating the facilities required for research: he personally contributed more than $1 million to build the library that bears his family name, and he concerned himself as well with the development of its collections.[30] Low's presidency is most remembered for the reorganization of the disparate schools associated with Columbia into a coherent university (officially renamed in 1896) and for the relocation of the campus to Morningside Heights. However, he also fulfilled his commitment to build a prestigious faculty.[31] From just 34 professors in 1890, the faculty had grown to 134 by 1904. After the turn of the century Columbia had clearly attained a position as one of the country's top research universities: at one time or another it was able to claim the largest number of graduate and professional students, the largest faculty, the second (after Harvard) most distinguished science faculty, and the highest per-student instructional expenditures among the large universities.[32]

The last of Columbia's distinctions should serve to underscore the fact that the competition for scholars was, unlike football, a game that only a few institutions could play. Just what level of resources was required is a subject that will be reserved for a later section. The important point here is that by the 1890s, for the first time in American higher education, enough institutions were vying with one another for the services of recognized scholars to create the conditions of decentralized competition that have historically been credited with propelling the advancement of science.[33] This competition, however, was only one facet of the emerging American university, one component of a more complex strategy of institutional development. A second crucial element, in all but a few cases, was the imperative to grow large as well.

In the decade spanning the turn of the century the fifteen pre-1920 research universities increased their enrollments from about 25,000 to 41,000. This was almost twice the rate of expansion exhibited by American higher education as a whole.[34] Each of these fifteen schools contributed something to this growth, and for most of them it constituted the fulfillment of an important institutional objective. There were at least three interrelated reasons why these institutions were motivated to expand.

Given the logic of university development, growth was imperative in order to support a faculty large enough to cover the major disciplines and specialties. Smallness might be reconciled with an essentially Germanic approach to advanced studies, where each subject was dominated by a single professor; and it was the two most Germanic of American universities, Clark and Johns Hopkins, that remained relatively small, selective in their offerings, and largely graduate oriented. The elective system at most universities, however, presupposed an ample supply of students to enroll in advanced, specialized courses.

The second consideration was purely financial. Except at Stanford, California, and Wisconsin, which charged no fees, tuition was a significant source of revenue for most schools. Although its relative weight could vary considerably from year to year, student tuition at Michigan around the turn of the century amounted to about half of the university payroll;

for wealthy private universities like Columbia the figure could be only 63 percent, while for Penn and MIT it hovered around 90 percent.[35] In the short run most university costs were relatively fixed, and institutions had little control over the other sources of their revenues. Thus, additional student payments provided a welcome cushion that could make the difference between red and black in the final budget. Although the marginal cost of an additional student might be negligible, the real expense of educating each student was in every case higher than the amount of tuition charged.[36] In the long run, growth cost dearly by requiring more faculty and more extensive facilities. Nevertheless, university presidents of this era explicitly opted to increase their resources to meet these needs, rather than restricting enrollments to the available means. That this strategy succeeded is due largely to the third, and possibly most compelling, lure of enrollment growth.

A steadily rising enrollment constituted a recognized mark of institutional success. In their annual reports the presidents consistently underscored each year's progress, gave statistics on the geographical extent of the institution's drawing power, made impressive comparisons with the recent past, and infrequently rationalized a temporary reversal. Laurence Veysey associates this pride in numbers with the spreading business mentality in higher education during these years, and this explanation is consistent with both the changing character of university administrators and the temper of the times.[37] Yet, increasing enrollment did plainly signal votes of confidence in universities on the part of their principal clientele. This, in turn, made a powerful argument for greater support from state legislators, university alumni, or local benefactors. In a nation that idealized strenuous competition and demanded success in recreation, business relations, and foreign affairs, the emerging universities harmonized admirably with the spirit of the age.

The enrollment growth seems to represent in part an unspoken accommodation between the universities and a stratum of society that previously had little involvement with higher education. In general, after 1885 more and more families from the middle ranks of society found themselves with sufficient wealth to be able to spare the labor of adolescent sons. At the same time they sought, perhaps instinctively, to buttress their social position against increasingly numerous immigrants. The universities for their part met the needs of this group by offering its members the possibility of proximate social mobility: students could now forgo the arcane rites of the ancient languages, study practical subjects, and prepare for definite careers.[38] In few of the research universities did such vocationally oriented students become the chief clientele, but from the 1890s onward their presence became increasingly visible. They are consequently an important component in the relatively rapid growth of the research universities.

Precise numerical comparisons across all the research universities are made difficult by the fact that almost every institution organized its divisions somewhat differently. Nevertheless, applied sciences or engineering formed one of the most conspicuous growth areas during this period. At the University of Michigan, for example, the rapid increase in the number of engineering students prompted the formation of a separate school in 1895, which then grew from 331 to 1,165 in the next decade. In contrast, the School of Literature added just over 300 students in these years. For the five state universities, plus Columbia, Penn, and Cornell, enrollments in these types of programs rose from 1,800 to 6,800 in the years 1890–1905.[39] These students by themselves constituted a significant portion of the overall enrollment growth, and they can be readily identified with the newcomers to higher education. The president of MIT, whose clientele was predominantly of this kind, noted that "an unusually large proportion of our students come from families of moderate means [who] never consider the possibility of first going to a classical college and then to a professional school."[40] President Eliot perceived a difference between candidates for the bachelor of arts degree and those "young men who know from the start the profession they are destined for" and who thus choose professional undergraduate studies.[41] At a group of seven universities for which figures can be compared, B.A. students grew by 64 percent, while those seeking other undergraduate degrees shot up by 304 percent (1890–1904).[42]

Quite another kind of new clientele was tapped by the research universities through the creation of summer sessions. This brainchild of Chicago's president William Rainey Harper was in some respects a further development of the well-established Chautauqua tradition. Although summer sessions have served a variety of purposes in their checkered history, they originally were a valued addition to the research universities because they attracted serious, mature students who could follow advanced courses. James B. Angell attributed the greater diligence of these students to the fact that they faced "none of the distractions, the hindrances or the excrescences of university life to molest or make afraid."[43] Only Princeton, Yale, Hopkins, and Stanford originally resisted this trend. Columbia soon became the leader in this respect, with an enrollment of over 1,900 in its 1909 summer session, two-thirds of them not regular Columbia students.[44]

Graduate education at the research universities in the aggregate grew apace with enrollments as a whole. It edged forward from just under 9 percent of the total in 1890 to just over it in 1910.[45] This expansion was obviously important for the research potential of these universities. Graduate students accounted for only 2.4 percent of higher-education enroll-ments at the turn of the century, and these fifteen institutions contained more than 60 percent of them.[46] Individual patterns varied considerably at this early stage of development. Using 1910 as a benchmark, one sees that Princeton, Stanford, and Minnesota had comparatively little gradu-ate education, that MIT had hardly any, and that the relatively large grad-uate school of Johns Hopkins was actually shrinking. The remaining private universities had developed graduate education the furthest, while the other state schools were at that date just entering a significant phase of expansion.

The professional schools of these universities exhibit patterns of growth that are less comparable and more complex, thus making specific numerical comparisons rather pointless. Nevertheless, this aspect of the research universities is crucial to the comprehending of their develop-ment. The established medical and law schools grew moderately at most universities, subject to periodic shrinkage when entrance requirements were raised. Most institutions added new professional schools or ex-panded those that had earlier had only a handful of students. The univer-sities that did not yet teach medicine or law created these units (except Princeton, MIT, and, in law, Hopkins). Some universities added educa-tion, business, or pharmacy to their offerings, and a number of smaller units were created in music, art, architecture, forestry, and veterinary sci-ence. These schools made notable contributions to the overall rate of growth—first, because they were net additions and, second, because they themselves sooner or later grew.

The striking expansion of the research universities in the decades span-ning the turn of the century was thus the sum of several processes. Start-ing with an underlying growth trend in traditional B.A. students and the major professional schools, they added a new clientele in the applied sci-ences, an enlarged contingent of graduate students, and further constitu-encies in the summer sessions and the new professional schools. Part of this growth reinforced their research potential in the basic disciplines; part of it brought entirely new subjects within the purview of the univer-sity spirit of rationality, and some of these endeavors were irrelevant to, or perhaps dilutive of, the university's research function. Nevertheless, the essential point is that as the research universities grew, their character changed. The multiplication of different units was inherent in the organi-zational evolution toward a compartmentalized university.

By the first decade of the twentieth century the country's leading uni-versities had by and large embraced all of the major aims of higher educa-tion that had been contested over the preceding half century. They now sought simultaneously and without a twinge of inconsistency to instill both liberal culture and modern science, to pursue both disinterested

learning and practical knowledge, and to graduate bachelors of arts, aspiring professionals, and doctors of philosophy. Administrators who
spoke for the institution as a whole grew adept at invoking whichever
university ideal best fit the occasion and the audience. Faculty and students pursued their particular tasks largely oblivious to the other facets of
the enterprise. Thus, the twentieth-century research university came to
exist on the basis of the "patterned isolation of its component parts."[47]

The division of the research university into a number of separate
schools was part of a larger process of gradual administrative compartmentalization. The deans who were appointed to look after the affairs of
these units constituted the beginnings of a new administrative layer between the president and the operating units of the institution. Soon their
reports began to be printed after the president's annual report, thus reflecting this new reality. A more significant aspect of this phenomenon
was the growing role of academic departments in the main schools of arts
and sciences. Departments emerged in recognizable form in the 1890s, as
university presidents increasingly relied on their faculties to handle,
among other things, the large annual turnover in junior-level appointments. For evaluative tasks like these the expertise of professors was indispensable to the university's research function. Charles Eliot fully
recognized this when he noted in 1908 that the "increasing authority of
those subdivisions, each within its legitimate sphere, is one of the great
gains made of late years in American university administration."[48] Nevertheless, it should also be noted that in the same period faculty complaints about their waning authority were becoming frequent and stri-
dent.[49] This apparent paradox can be clarified by focusing on what Eliot
regarded as the department's "legitimate sphere."

Decentralization and compartmentalization of the university meant
quite simply that the organizational distance between the faculty and the
central administration was increasing. If the faculty's authority was growing in that legitimate sphere defined by their professional knowledge,
their influence was undoubtedly waning with respect to matters outside
it—that is, over those things pertaining to the legitimate spheres of interests of other university constituencies. At the head of this more and more
complex organization were the president and the trustees, who were perforce progressively losing touch with the intellectual matter of the university and the everyday affairs of its burgeoning student population. In
place of the direct involvement in university life that the chief administrators had formerly had, they gradually took their mandate to be assuring that the institution would be run in a businesslike fashion. The
prevalence of this mentality in universities after the turn of the century
has been widely recognized and generally deplored.[50] It stemmed in part
from the growing apotheosis of business in American society, from the

direct influence of businessmen as trustees, and from the sensitivity to and dependence upon wealthy benefactors. But it also reflected the greater complexity of the organization over which they presided.

These three institutional trends—competition, growth, and organizational change—had the net result of making the original group of research universities resemble one another far more closely in 1910 than they had two decades before. To ascribe this standardization merely to somewhat craven instincts of imitation would seem to obscure the relationship between competition and innovation in the crystallization of the American system of higher education.[51] Standardization came about in the case of schools of applied science, or in the matter of administrative decentralization, because institutions independently responded in similar fashion to more or less the same conditions. Alternatively, the inherent competition between institutions caused them to adopt selectively the successful innovations of their peers. Thus, W. R. Harper's summer school was widely replicated, but not his efforts to transplant Oxford- and Cambridge-style colleges. Johns Hopkins led the way in matters pertaining to research and graduate education but found no imitators in its handling of undergraduates. And Eliot's advocacy of the elective system won the day, but not his campaign for a three-year undergraduate degree. The competitive forces inherent in the American structure of higher education seem more significant when one considers that these "standard" features were adopted by only a handful among the hundreds of colleges and universities. These adaptive institutions became the leaders of the emerging system of higher education.

In 1909–10 the science journalist Edwin E. Slosson visited each of the universities considered here, save MIT, and was everywhere told that a period of rapid and momentous change was under way.[52] Some of this was connected with the growing importance of university research, but a good deal more related to rising student numbers, the proliferation of professional schools, and spreading institutional recognition of the extracurriculum. By this date, in fact, at least ten of these schools could be described as multiversities. This list would include the five state universities as well as Harvard, Cornell, Columbia, Penn, and Chicago. All could be said to conform to a similar organizational pattern of compartmentalized units and multiple objectives, despite the distinctive traditions and student cultures, which Slosson vividly described. As for the others, the pull of the dominant organizational pattern was clearly evident. Yale and Stanford were verging on multiversity status, while only Princeton, MIT, and Hopkins retained a discernible unity of institutional purpose.

Stanford relinquished some of the idiosyncrasies of its pioneer days in the decade after 1910. Its trustees insisted on the creation of a medical school, at some financial sacrifice to the rest of the university; its unique system of major professors was dropped in favor of a more commonplace lower division; the quarter system was adopted in order to allow a summer session; student tuition was imposed following the war; and, after an experiment with rugby, standard American football was reinstated in 1919.[53] Yale already possessed all the components of a multiversity, but they would exist for another decade under the hegemony of Yale College.[54]

The three remaining institutions reflect in purest fashion the formerly conflicting ideals of culture, utility, and research. Princeton exhibited the most far-reaching commitment to liberal culture and undergraduate education but combined them with a resolve to stay in the forefront of higher education. It was able to assemble a distinguished faculty, although it imposed religious tests on candidates as late as 1896. From that date—the year Princeton declared itself a university—the faculty took the lead in stressing scholarly development, establishing advanced seminars, and creating a graduate school.[55] The tensions inherent in these aspirations, however, were evident during the presidency of Woodrow Wilson (1902–10). The strengthening of undergraduate education became the first priority for available funds. A sumptuous, Oxonian graduate college was constructed, which added more to the style than to the substance of graduate education. Moreover, Princeton never did move toward professional education by establishing the law school that Wilson desired.[56] At MIT the unambiguous technological orientation undoubtedly precluded straightforward imitation, but the institution was still drawn into the mainstream of scientific research after the turn of the century. The Graduate School of Engineering Research was established in 1903 to complement the research already under way in physical chemistry, and MIT awarded its first Ph.D. in 1907.[57] Finally, Johns Hopkins, with its preponderant dedication to research, experienced standardization in an opposite sense: it was virtually compelled to bring its undergraduate course into conformity with other universities, and the inadequacy of its original endowment eventually caused it to provide service courses for the Baltimore area. These three institutions represent the most significant departures from "the type . . . defined as the standard American university," but they, too, were ineluctably swept along by the academic mainstream.[58]

There was still another channel through which standardization came to American universities—that of deliberate, concerted action. In this regard the founding of the Association of American Universities in 1900 is both a fitting symbol and a concrete embodiment of the emergence of twentieth-century American research universities. The conference call that led to the founding of the AAU listed three important objectives: establishing greater uniformity in Ph.D. requirements, achieving foreign recognition of the American doctorate, and bolstering the standards of the weaker

American universities. Thus, the creation of the AAU was a declaration by the leading American universities of independence and equality with regard to European universities as well as an endeavor to guarantee the value of their product against "cheaper" foreign and domestic competition.[59] The AAU brought together the leading Ph.D.-granting universities of the day—the same institutions considered here except Illinois, Minnesota (admitted in 1907), and MIT (1934); plus Clark and the Catholic University of America. The prestige of these fourteen schools gave them great leverage over those developing institutions that wished to join this exclusive club.[60]

As a standardizing agency, the AAU first tended to regularize practices among current and potential members, but it soon extended its influence over American higher education in general. The initial annual meetings focused rather narrowly on issues relating to graduate degrees, but occasionally they broached fundamental questions like the amount of undergraduate education that should be required for entry into professional schools. It was easier for the members to agree on such practical matters as the publishing of doctoral dissertations than on the latter type of issue. The AAU nevertheless provided a valuable forum where views could be aired, a consensus formed, and arguments garnered for later use at home. The presidents and deans who represented their universities at AAU meetings well knew the realities of American higher education, yet they consistently advocated a general strengthening of academic standards. This viewpoint became all the more important when the AAU was thrust into the role of accrediting agency. As a result of a request from the University of Berlin, the AAU began in 1913 to compile a list of American colleges and universities whose graduates could be assumed to be ready for graduate study.[61] Thus, the AAU came officially to exercise the leadership role that the research universities had clearly come to occupy by the beginning of the twentieth century.

The position attained by the research universities signified the existence of a new structure of American higher education. The success of the university did not totally eclipse the American college, and may well have been responsible for its indefinite survival either in freestanding form or as a component of the university. The colleges might still be admired for the way in which they taught, but what they taught would increasingly be determined by the universities. Eventually, the highest achievement of the college would be to prepare its students for postgraduate study in one of the research universities.

The strength in the new fabric of American higher education was owing to both the institutional warp of the research universities and the weft provided by the emerging academic disciplines.[62] Changes in the organization of knowledge in the United States, in fact, were coeval and coterminous with the emergence of universities.

2. Academic Disciplines

The basic academic disciplines in the arts and sciences were organized into their current associations during the last two decades of the nineteenth century. These groupings were merely formal manifestations of a more fundamental process of professionalization that advanced along three interrelated fronts. The growth and specialization of knowledge created bodies of increasingly esoteric doctrines over which academic disciplines claimed sovereignty; the social organization of the membership through associations, meetings, and journals formed community structures of authority and legitimacy; and the development of the modern university provided the locus where disciplines could be practiced. The foundation and growth of each discipline seemed to involve these three processes in differently weighted combinations. In moving down the road of professionalization, some subjects appeared to be led predominantly by knowledge growth, some by community formation, and others by university sponsorship. Their destinations were nevertheless identical: whatever the original knowledge base of a discipline, the combination of a university setting and professional forms of social organization gave extraordinary impetus to the further generation of knowledge. The process of discipline formation is thus one of the indispensable components in the shaping of the research universities.

Academic disciplines possess most of the attributes of the traditional learned professions, once adjustment is made for their rather special setting. The literature on professions emphasizes at least two core characteristics: "a prolonged, specialized training in a body of abstract knowledge, and a collectivity or service orientation."[1] The Ph.D., which had become the expected credential for academics in basic university disciplines by 1900, represents prolonged, specialized, and abstract training, par excellence; and the objective of contributing to the growth of human knowledge constitutes service of a high order indeed. University teaching, the common activity of the academic profession as a whole, also represents a service commitment. University faculty, however, organized to defend and enhance their professional status as teachers only after the disciplines were solidly established. The founding of the American Association of University Professors in 1915 represented a different facet of professionalization, with an importance of its own.[2] Still, for most active scholars in university settings the psychological and social commitments to their disciplines take precedence under normal circumstances over their ties to fellow academics.[3]

When professions are viewed as part of a larger social environment, their most salient criterion becomes "legitimate, organized autonomy, . . . the right to control [their] own work." This includes the capacity to determine who can practice the profession, the manner in which it should be done, and the ability to declare external evaluation "illegitimate and intolerable."[4] Certainly, the autonomy of disciplines results in part from the characteristics just mentioned: specialized training is necessarily esoteric, and dedication to service suggests an aura of disinterestedness. But more is required to secure professional status: that status must be granted or recognized by strategic sectors of society. Many of the professions have obtained legal sanction from government through an implicitly political process. For the scholarly professions, however, recognition has come from the university. Consequently, although they were organized independently of the universities, the disciplines do not represent truly independent professions. Part of their purpose in organizing was to monopolize authority over a given area of knowledge and simultaneously to have it incorporated into the university curriculum. Thus, the system of social control over practitioners to which the scholarly professions and their associations aspired was unattainable without legitimization by the universities.

The coalescence of academic disciplines followed a natural history not unlike that of the other professions.[5] Professionalization was originally set in motion by the presence of full-time practitioners who gradually acquired predominance over less committed amateurs. These conditions were likely to cause awareness of the need for formal modes of training, which in these cases was met first by European study and then by the American Ph.D. The next stage called for the founding of an association. Most of the primary disciplinary associations that exist today were in some sense the product of earlier associations. Either they were formed by fission, as disciplines separated themselves from more general and inclusive scientific societies, or they resulted from the fusion of local societies into a national entity. In both cases the national association provided more suitable arenas for the progressive, professionalizing elements in the discipline. The weight of these factions tended to be decisive in the continuing effort to define and elaborate the profession and to distinguish it from neighboring fields.

In the advanced stages of professionalization the academic disciplines diverged more markedly from other professions. Instead of appealing to the state to protect their services with legal restrictions, the disciplines have sought the aegis of the university. The creation of departments at important universities effectively guaranteed the practice of a discipline, even though it may have been necessary over the long run for disciplines to prove themselves through intellectual growth and the attraction of students. The need of consumer-oriented professions to place constraints on member conduct through codes of ethics was expressed quite differently in the disciplines. Once the institutions were in place to operate the reward system of science, the scientific ethos could be expected to constrain the behavior of academics.

If there is a single crucial point in the process of academic professionalization, it would be the formation of a national association with its attendant central journal. By giving form and function to an inchoate or potential scientific community, associations enhanced the knowledge-generating capacity of the disciplines. Competent and advanced figures in the field assumed positions of leadership, so that their influence became more widespread in the evaluation of scholars and scholarship. Channels of scholarly communication were also enhanced, thus bringing local networks of scholars into wider, quicker, and more regular contact. These effects were evident in the diverse patterns of discipline formation that occurred after 1880.

A chronology of some of the institutional milestones along the road to discipline formation is presented in Table 1.[6] Although these founding dates have a real importance for this process, they in no case mark the beginning of the subject in question. The proliferation of disciplinary institutions that occurred in the 1880s and the 1890s should be seen as one phase in the constantly shifting patterns of American learned societies. In the preceding period scientific organizations were typically inclusive and heterogeneous, with only loose and occasional links to higher education. They were roughly appropriate for the relatively dispersed and unspecialized learned community of the time, and they also succeeded to some extent in nurturing the growth of more-specialized forms of knowledge.[7] Thus, they might be called "mother societies" (Table 1), although each developed a distinctive pattern of relationships with its offspring. The associations established after the period of discipline formation was completed, in 1905, also had a different character. Many resulted from the inexorable process of specialization, as expanding areas within disciplines felt the need for their own organizations, and a few were conscious attempts to counteract these tendencies by the erecting of federations or the coordinating of agencies. These later associations were obviously aimed at solving another set of problems, created in part by the very existence of strong disciplinary organizations.

At bottom all of the disciplines faced the same essential issues as they professionalized. The split between amateurs with various interests in a subject and full-time practitioners dedicated to advancing knowledge was one impediment they had to overcome. Cognitive growth was an impor-

1842	Am. Oriental Soc.*	
. . .		
1848	Am. Assoc. for the Advancement of Science*	
. . .		
1865	Am. Social Science Assoc.*	
. . .		
1869	Am. Philological Assoc.	(*Transactions* . . .)‡
. . .		
1876	Am. Chemical Society (N.Y.) (1892a)†	(*Proceedings* . . .)‡
1877		
1878		*Am. Journal of Mathematics*
1879	Archaeological Institute of Am.	*Journal of the Am. Chemical Soc.* (1892a)†
1880	Soc. for Biblical Literature and Exegesis	(*Journal* . . .)‡ *Am. Chemical Journal* *Am. Journal of Philology*
1881		
1882	Am. School of Classical Studies at Athens (1879)†	
1883	a) Am. Soc. of Naturalists* b) Modern Language Assoc.	*Science* (*Publications* . . .)‡
1884	a) Am. Historical Assoc. b) Chemical Soc. of Washington (1892a)†	
1885	Am. Economic Assoc.	*Am. Journal of Archaeology*
1886		*Political Science Quarterly*
1887		*Am. Journal of Psychology* *Quarterly Journal of Economics*
1888	a) Am. Mathematical Soc. b) Geological Soc. of Am.	(*Bulletin* . . .)‡ (*Bulletin* . . .)‡
1889	Am. Academy of Political and Social Science	
1890	Am. Soc. of Zoologists	
1891		
1892	a) Am. Chemical Soc. b) Am. Psychological Assoc.	*Philosophical Review* (. . . *Review*)‡
1893	Botanical Soc. of Am.	*Physical Review* (1899a)† *Journal of Geology* *Journal of Political Economy*
1894		
1895	Am. School of Classical Studies at Rome (1879)†	*Am. Journal of Sociology* *Am. Historical Review* *Astrophysical Journal*
1896		*Journal of Physical Chemistry*
1897		
1898		
1899	a) Am. Physical Soc. b) Astronomical and Astrophysical Soc. of Am. c) Am. Soc. for Microbiology	

TABLE 1. (*continued*)

1900		
1901	Am. Philosophical Assoc.	
1902	Am. Anthropological Assoc.	
1903	Am. Political Science Assoc.	(. . . *Review*)‡
		Modern Philology
1904	Assoc. of American Geographers	*Journal of Experimental Zoology*
1905	Am. Sociological Soc.	(*Publications and Proceedings* . . .)‡

* Mother society.
† Subsequently united with the association listed at date in parentheses.
‡ Publication of the association founded in that year.

tant goad to development, and it sometimes forced further organizational adaptations. Moreover, disciplines had to be concerned with their legitimacy or relative standing in the university curriculum. For purposes of analysis these three kinds of issues can best be exemplified in relation to the three major disciplinary groups. The humanities, especially language-based studies, manifested a visible split between those dedicated to scholarly research and others whose interests and actual work centered on teaching. In the "hard" sciences, scientific accomplishments and individual reputations could be gauged with greatest certainty. These subjects consequently best reveal the interrelationship between intellectual growth and organizational change. The social sciences initially faced some serious problems of definition. Their emergence thus involved the separation of social knowledge from social action, the contested establishment of their respective fields of knowledge, and difficulties in gaining legitimacy in the academic world.

The appearance of "scientific" scholarship in the humanities can be accounted for largely by the combination of, first, the weight of classical and religious studies in the college curriculum and, second, the "academization" of these subjects in German universities. Thus, scholars in these areas could hardly ignore the precise and systematic investigations being made by German scholars. Furthermore, once this mode of analysis was adopted, it inevitably spread to other, similar subjects. The creation of professional organizations was a natural part of this process, as scholarly pioneers sought to unite their meager numbers and to take concerted action to raise the standards of their subject in the United States (Table 1: 1869, 1879, 1880).

The American Philological Association took direct inspiration from the Sammlung der deutschen Philologen und Schulmänner. The existing American Oriental Scoiety, though it had a classics section, was too broad

in scope and too lacking in rigor to meet the specific aims of the phi-
lologists. The new APA was a rather small and clublike group of academics, dedicated to classical scholarship of the German type. Their activities
whetted, but could not satisfy, the ambitions of those wishing to promote
and elevate the serious study of modern languages. The founders of the
Modern Language Association (1886) were primarily college teachers of
French or German who wanted their subjects recognized as appropriate
for advanced university study. The problems of language teaching under-
standably assumed a prominent place on the agenda of the early MLA
and persisted even after the English-language section grew to dwarf the
rest of the association. Teaching nevertheless had to remain a distinctly
subordinate concern, because the overriding goals of legitimacy and professionalization could be attained only through the development of recognized scholarship in these subjects. This was reflected in the nature and
the history of the MLA. Membership was kept strictly professional by
being restricted to college teachers and other "invited" individuals; the
leadership was drawn from a small group of professors at leading universities, where the scholarly status of these subjects was secure. In 1903 the
MLA dropped its pedagogical section and emphasized its commitment to
scholarship, and 1920 saw another of its periodic rededications to research in these fields. The MLA established undisputed intellectual leadership, but in doing so it left the many whose sole concern was teaching
these subjects to fend for themselves. A large number of local organizations were founded for this purpose, usually containing both high school
and college teachers; and in 1916 many of these groups combined to form
a national federation that reflected these interests.[8]

The cleavage in the profession between a scholarly elite and a rank and
file of classroom language instructors was more pronounced in the classics. The latest advances of Germanic or American philology could give
little assistance to the many teachers struggling to preserve the eroding
terrain of Latin and Greek at both the high school and the college levels. They responded by organizing local and regional groups, rallying
around *Classical Weekly* (f. 1907) and ultimately merging some of these
associations into the American Classical League (1918).[9] In religious studies an analogous cleavage developed between the research-oriented Society of Biblical Literature and Exegesis and the later, teaching-oriented
American Academy of Religion (f. 1909). It is noteworthy, too, that the
same split emerged in mathematics, where the original American Mathematical Society represented research and the Mathematical Association of
America (f. 1915) met the needs of teachers. The last example suggests
that this situation is not limited to the humanities, but rather develops in
fields where there is considerable intellectual distance between the few
who labor on the rarefied frontiers of research and the many who are

engaged in routine classroom instruction. The comparative isolation of the scholarly elites in these fields was at the same time testimony to their liberation from the occupational conditions of their putative colleagues. Their professional lives were shaped instead by the roles that had been created for the most part in research universities.

Discipline formation in the natural sciences appeared to lag behind the humanities (Table 1), most of the major national associations being organized in the half-decade around 1890 and the remainder just before the turn of the century. Earlier, however, these sciences were grouped within more comprehensive organizations that found it more and more difficult to accommodate the proliferation of disciplinary knowledge. The *American Journal of Science,* for example, met many of the communication needs of American scientists from its inception in 1818 until after the Civil War. It tended to emphasize geology, probably then the most advanced American science; but it also attempted to encompass the other natural sciences, particularly physics and chemistry. The difficulty of this role became apparent with the emergence of a new generation of German-trained scientists exemplified by the Johns Hopkins faculty. When a long, technical paper by Ira Remsen was rejected by the *AJS* as unsuitable for its readership, Remsen was led to create his own publication with the support of the Hopkins trustees. Neither Remsen's *American Chemical Journal,* narrowly focused with high standards, nor the broad and uncritical *Journal of the American Chemical Society* was at the outset an ideal vehicle for the chemistry profession, but both were clearly better suited to advance the discipline than the *AJS* was. The rejection of another paper by a Hopkins appointee was a more egregious error by the *AJS*. An experimental study of magnetism by Henry Rowland was turned down by *AJS* reviewers, who were out of touch with the subject and could not comprehend Rowland's mathematics. Rowland subsequently sent it to a British expert in this field, who arranged for its publication in England. It took the smaller physics community somewhat longer to create its own professional organs, but it was nevertheless inevitable that the *AJS* could not function as the principal outlet for specific disciplines.[10]

Much of the same can be said about the American Association for the Advancement of Science. From its founding in 1848 until the Civil War, the AAAS provided a certain degree of cohesion, leadership, and professionalization to the country's maturing scientific community.[11] Soon after the war, however, it had to begin adapting to the centripetal forces of discipline formation. In 1874 it officially created two sections: one for mathematics, physics, and chemistry, and the other for natural history. Only two decades later the number of sections had grown to twelve, representing the full panoply of scientific disciplines.[12] In addition, the major disciplinary organizations and a host of other science-related groups affiliated themselves with the AAAS. With its single national meeting and its published *Proceedings*, the AAAS was quite limited in its capacity to set intellectual standards and guide research in any particular field. It consequently developed a different role as a holding company for the scientific and scientifically oriented disciplines and as a forum for issues that transcended individual disciplines.

An analysis of the developing scientific communities in mathematics, physics, and chemistry concluded that prior to 1890 these disciplines were inhibited by serious institutional inadequacies. Effective Ph.D. programs existed at only a handful of institutions, and "the small disciplinary elites and larger productive groups were generally situated outside of the graduate training network." Quirks of the recently established learned journals caused the leading practitioners in all three disciplines to publish their most significant work abroad. Professional societies for these fields were divided or nonexistent.[13] Yet, all of these conditions were to change—decisively—during the next two decades. Journals and associations were created or strengthened so that they became effective agents of leadership and control. The number of qualified practitioners grew in each of these fields, largely with graduates of American Ph.D. programs. Compared with that of any other country, the American scientific elite appears to have been dispersed over a large number of universities, but in fact this decentralization yielded several strong departments. Most important, the disciplinary elites that had emerged in each subject now "commanded an institutional framework—the centers of graduate training and research, the national societies, the journals—that had grown up since the Civil War. A common development in the world of learning, such institutional elements were essential for setting standards of quality in scientific disciplines."[14]

In the development of the social sciences, relevance to human affairs was a two-edged sword. It was an important stimulus in attracting interest and involvement in these fields, but it was also a continual distraction from the task of building a cumulative, disinterested knowledge of human behavior. This situation produced a clearly discernible tendency for aspirations to exceed accomplishments. As a consequence, the social sciences tended to reverse the sequence of professionalization just seen in the natural sciences. Whereas in the latter the professional organizations more or less followed intellectual developments, in the social sciences they were expected to lead, and indeed partly to cause, cognitive growth in the disciplines. Social scientists on the whole consciously created the institutions of their disciplines in order to control, shape, and advance their professions.

When the American Social Science Association was organized in 1865, it was scarcely possible to distinguish the present divisions of the social

sciences. Nor did its founders perceive any difference between social science and current issues of social reform—"questions relating to the Sanitary Condition of the People, the Relief, Employment, and Education of
the Poor, the Prevention of Crime . . . the Discipline of Prisons, [and] the
Remedial Treatment of the Insane." [15] The ASSA brought together many
of the nation's rising and ascendant elite of educators, professionals, and
men of affairs in an optimistic quest to decipher and eliminate the social
ills besetting the country. An expression of genteel reformism, the association never altered either its social composition or its social perspectives. It
was consequently unable to prevent the social science disciplines from
breaking away and forming their own organizations. [16]

History was the first discipline to organize under the umbrella of the
ASSA, but it was scarcely representative of the social sciences. Herbert
Baxter Adams of Johns Hopkins, the founder and early leader of the
American Historical Association, was strongly influenced by the German
historical profession. Yet, the organization he created mirrored the amateur, inclusive nature of the ASSA. The historians initially sought legitimacy by appealing to society at large, instead of concentrating on the
university. Thus, they welcomed sympathetic patricians and men of affairs, preferred famous figures to professional historians as their honorific
presidents, encouraged dues-paying memberships among the numerous
amateur local-history societies, and sought official government sponsorship, even managing to be incorporated by an act of Congress. Despite all
of this, the AHA was predominantly operated by and for the roughly one-
quarter of the members who were employed in higher education. [17] The
AHA and the *American Historical Review,* which it eventually took over,
served the common needs of the discipline, but after its inception the
AHA was decidedly complacent as a professionalizing force until after
World War II. [18]

The economists, who organized themselves only one year later (1885),
at first placed social reform ahead of professionalization. Led by Richard
Ely, they explicitly attacked the doctrines of laissez-faire, thereby splitting
the already narrow potential base of their organization. They also left the
association open to anyone supporting their aims, political or professional. The majority of academic economists nevertheless almost immediately steered the American Economic Association into a specifically
professional role. The governing council of the AEA, which was composed of academics, repudiated the association's original statement of re-
formist principles after only two years. By the 1890s the AEA was
decisively oriented toward fulfilling the professional needs of economists
committed to the intellectual growth of the discipline. [19]

It took political scientists and sociologists almost two additional decades to disentangle their distinctive programs of research from the matrix

of activities encompassed by the ASSA, the AHA, and the AEA, but their pattern of organization in some ways followed that of the economists. A program of social action was instrumental in first bringing together a group of individuals committed to the discipline, but then the pressures of "academization" soon caused them to adopt a more neutral and objective stance. It is interesting to note that after consolidation all three of these disciplines experienced periodic bouts of methodological crisis, in which more-rigorous scientific approaches were advocated.[20] This phenomenon seems to be another instance of disciplinary institutions in the social sciences being utilized in a conscious attempt to stimulate intellectual progress.

These divergent patterns of discipline formation in the humanities, natural sciences, and social sciences had in common several essential features. A discipline is, above all, a community based on inquiry and centered on competent investigators.[21] It consists of individuals who associate in order to facilitate intercommunication and to establish some degree of authority over the standards of that inquiry. The particular arrangements that are actually worked out to realize the first two of these goals may vary enormously, but not those of the third. That is, the community embraced by a discipline may be large or small, and fairly inclusive of well-wishers and hangers-on or not, as long as institutional control remains vested with the competent. Similarly, communication patterns through journals and meetings will be strictly functional, as long as the overriding purpose of the advancement of disciplinary knowledge is respected. The collective authority to evaluate contributions to the field is what makes disciplines different from the myriad other voluntary associations that individuals form to pursue shared interests. It is also the basis on which they assert their claims to autonomy. But the collective authority of disciplines cannot be absolute or repressive. The intellectual authority of disciplinary leaders is subject to implicit or explicit challenge as a result of the development of new specialties that do not fit neatly into existing categories, of new schools of thought that challenge existing interpretations, or of new generations of researchers eager for authority in their own right. The authority that lies at the heart of a discipline is thus as dynamic and pluralistic as the cognitive content of the discipline itself.[22]

These fundamental features of academic disciplines largely account for the remarkable organizational isomorphism of fields as disparate as philology and physics. Institutional forms across all disciplines came to resemble one another because they were created to fulfill the same professionalizing functions.[23] Moreover, this process repeated itself in the twentieth century on a subdisciplinary level, at which communities of specialists have continued to come together to form associations, hold meetings, and publish learned journals. This helps to account for another aspect of professions on which all commentators agree: once firmly established, professions, or in this case disciplines, develop according to their inner dynamics with a considerable degree of autonomy.[24] In part, the gradual accumulation of an esoteric knowledge base places increasing distance between the trained scholar's understanding of the domain and lay appreciation of the subject. Also, the institutionalization and consequent depersonalization of practices and procedures make the second generation more tacitly professional than the first generation of the self-anointed—and the third generation more so still. This process is probably most clearly discernible in the development of the social sciences.[25] Most important in this context are the consequences of this disciplinary inertia. The internal dynamics of the disciplines made American science highly impervious to the vicissitudes of university life in general and to the fate of individual institutions in particular.

It is somewhat ironic that those who thought seriously about the authority structure of science in nineteenth-century America generally endorsed some form of unitary control—a single institution dominated by the best scientists, who could set the standards for science as a whole. Thus, there were periodic suggestions to found a national university. The AAAS initially aspired to provide such authority, and its claims were subsequently superseded by the establishment of the National Academy of Sciences (1863), in rather hopeful imitation of the renowned national academies of Europe.[26] The eminent scientists known as the scientific Lazzaroni were involved in both these organizations, but they combined these centralizing aspirations with an essentially individualistic view of scientific progress. Even as they spoke for the promotion of science in general, their grasp of the institutional requirements of regular scientific advancement was rudimentary at best.[27] Had any of these initiatives succeeded in concentrating scientific authority in a single institution, the result would in all probability have been a narrowly based, elitist scientific establishment that in the long run would have inhibited the overall growth of American science.[28] In the absence of central direction scientific authority grew organically. It became decentralized in the many disciplines and diffused throughout the complementary associations and journals. The resulting structure of recognition and prestige was far more suitable for the country's broad and dispersed scientific establishment.[29] It was at once as salient, as ambiguous, and as multidimensional as the prestige structure of American universities in which it was largely lodged. This was scarcely accidental. That the autonomous academic disciplines evolved as a well-matched complement of the university structure was in some measure due to the role of the universities themselves in promoting the formation of disciplines and in ensuring their effectiveness.

The major universities made important direct contributions to the constitution of academic disciplines by assisting the creation of the organs through which disciplines functioned. Such steps were, for the most part, visible and readily documented. More crucial in the long run, however, were the continuous and largely unrecorded interactions between universities and disciplines that resulted in the universities' utilizing and, in effect, legitimizing the professional authority lodged in the disciplines.

The nexus between modern disciplinary organization and the modern research university can be seen most clearly in the early Johns Hopkins University. Its president, Daniel Coit Gilman, was perhaps the first to perceive the necessity of these cross-cutting groupings of subject experts for the purposes of expanding knowledge.[30] It was no accident, then, that the three most important disciplinary associations started in the 1880s were organized by young, ambitious Hopkins faculty—the MLA by A. Marshall Elliot, the Historical Association by Herbert Baxter Adams, and the Economics Association by Richard T. Ely.[31] In taking these initiatives, these men simultaneously intended to further their own career, advance their discipline, and promote the interests of their university. Ely was explicit on this last aim, at least, when he wrote Gilman, "the prospects seem to be very favorable for an influential movement which will help in the diffusion of a sound Christian political economy. At the same time I trust it may benefit the Johns Hopkins."[32] Ely no doubt expected his efforts to contribute some measure of prestige to his still young and in some sense embattled university, but the professionalization of disciplines that he was promoting had a more profound "benefit" for Hopkins. A university based upon certified, specialized scientific competence was what Hopkins, and for the first decade of its existence Hopkins alone, stood for.

Gilman's university was also the first to assist with the publication of scholarly journals, a practice that was soon imitated at other major universities.[33] Some measure of the timing and the extent of the proliferation of university journals can be gained from Table 2. The listing there is by no means exhaustive. Omitted are a large number of ephemeral, sporadic, and discontinued publications, most of which were issued by single departments. Left out, too, are medical and engineering publications. Nevertheless, the titles in this table do indicate something about the development of disciplinary communications.

The periodicals in Table 2 were actually preceded by publications issuing from a few permanent research institutions in the United States. Such series as the *Annals* of the Astronomical Observatory of Harvard College

TABLE 2. Principal Scholarly Publications of Research Universities (1906), and Date
of First Publication [34]

University of California
    Publications in American Archaeology and Ethnology (1903)
    Publications in Classical Philology (1904)
    Publications in Botany (1902)
    Publications in Zoology (1902)

University of Chicago
    Studies in Classical Philology (1895)
    Economic Studies (1895)
    American Journal of Sociology (1896)
    American Journal of Semitic Languages and Literature (1884/92)
    American Journal of Theology (1897)
    Astrophysical Journal (1882/95)
    Biblical World (1883/93)
    Classical Philology (1906)
    Journal of Geology (1893)
    Journal of Political Economy (1892)
    Modern Philology (1903)
    The School Review (1893)

Columbia University
    Studies in History, Economics and Public Law (1891)
    Political Science Quarterly (1886)
    Columbia University Contributions to Philosophy and Psychology (1884)
    Columbia University Biological Series (1894)
    Columbia University Geological Series (1906)
    Columbia University Studies in Romance Philology and Literature (1902)

Cornell University
    Studies in Classical Philology (1887)
    Cornell Studies in Philosophy (1900)
    Philosophical Review (1892)
    Physical Review (1893)
    Journal of Physical Chemistry (1896)

Harvard University
    Harvard Historical Studies (1896)
    Harvard Studies in Classical Philology (1890)
    Studies and Notes in Philology and Literature (1892)
    Harvard Oriental Series (1891)
    Harvard Psychological Studies (1903)
    Quarterly Journal of Economics (1886)
    Harvard Law Review (1887)
    Annals of Mathematics (1889)

University of Illinois
    Journal of English and Germanic Philology (1897/1906)

Johns Hopkins University
    American Journal of Mathematics (1878)
    American Journal of Philology (1880)
    American Chemical Journal (1879)
    JHU Studies in Historical and Political Science (1883)
    Modern Language Notes (1886)
    Beiträge zur Assyriologie und vergleichenden semitischen Sprachwissenschaft
        (1890)

Massachusetts Institute of Technology
    Technological Quarterly (1887)

University of Michigan
    Michigan Law Review (1902)

University of Minnesota
    None

University of Pennsylvania
    Astronomical Series (1895)
    Contributions from the Zoological Laboratory (1893)
    Series in Philology and Literature (1891)
    Series in Political Economy and Public Law (1885)

Princeton University
    (Irregular publications in geology, psychology, and philosophy)

Stanford University
    (Occasional monographs)

University of Wisconsin
    Economics, Political Science and History Series (1894)
    Philology and Literature Series (1898)
    Science Series (1894)

Yale University
    Yale Psychological Studies (1892)
    Yale Studies in English (1898)
    Yale Law Journal (1891)

(f. 1856) or the *Memoirs* of Alexander Agassiz's Museum of Comparative Zoology of Harvard College (f. 1864) were the outlets for research done in those institutions. In this respect they resembled the publications of the institutes associated with chairs in German universities. It was thus quite natural for research-oriented departments in American universities to adopt this same approach. Most of the titles in Table 2 bearing the name of their school, or those called "studies," "notes," or "contributions," were primarily intended to disseminate the scholarship of local faculty and graduate students. An analytical distinction can readily be made between such series and national disciplinary periodicals (for the most part, those listed in Table 1) sponsored by national associations and having boards of editors drawn from many schools. But the differences were in actuality often a matter of degree: Ira Remsen's *Notes From the Chemical Laboratory* of Johns Hopkins (1877–78) was directly transmogrified into the *American Chemical Journal;* and long-lived journals like Columbia's *Political Science Quarterly* at first disseminated the writings of the mother faculty.

When departmental periodicals were discussed at the Association of American Universities Conference in 1904, such undertakings evoked general enthusiasm. It was widely felt that these publications deserved to be subsidized as part of university support for research, although several university presidents expected them to become self-supporting in the near future. With rare exceptions this did not happen, even if one counts the journals exchanged with other universities as income. Thus, the very existence of these publications represented some form of subsidization. Even though it might amount to only a few hundred dollars at this juncture, few universities were able to make such a commitment solely for the sake of scholarship. The willingness of Hopkins to make outright commitments for learned journals was clearly exceptional. At Chicago the journals were subsidized through the financing of the University Press, and Harvard withheld sponsorship until a publication managed to find a separate endowment.[35] Beyond these schools, only Cornell, Columbia, and California had substantial numbers of titles. On the other hand, Michigan, Minnesota, and Illinois were apparently unable to divert any funds for these purposes. Some of the efforts to stimulate scholarly publication were too ambitious. Chicago launched a "studies" series for each department in its early years (1894–96), but most of these faded out of existence. California inaugurated a similar program (1902–4), but only those listed in Table 2 appeared for a time with some regularity. Wisconsin embarked on a somewhat less ambitious scheme (1894–98), but these volumes also trickled out sporadically.

Such examples suggest that departmental publications became rather overextended during this period. Most individual departments did not produce a sufficient volume of high-quality research to justify a separate publication, and their most productive scholars no doubt preferred to send their best work to the national or foreign journals. Departmental publications for a time served an important function by encouraging research and broadening the base of active scholars. But the persistence of such publications, had it occurred, would probably have proved harmful to the development of effective disciplines. It would very likely have produced the kind of fragmentation that seemed to accompany the chair system in certain European countries. In university systems where each chair-holding professor has an institute, and each institute publishes its own journal, strong disciplinary organizations have found it difficult to take root.[36] This did not occur in the United States, largely because the journals endorsed by national disciplinary associations clearly established intellectual hegemony in their respective fields. By 1906—the date of Table 2—purely departmental publications had probably passed their zenith in terms of numbers and usefulness. At this juncture the wave of the future in academic publishing, already dimly visible, was the specialized subdisciplinary journal. These, like the national journals, represented and were supported to varying extents by inter-university communities of specialists who had organized themselves into associations. The early research universities, then, provided a valuable but circumscribed service by assisting in the creation of the organizational foundations of nascent academic disciplines; however, they made a far greater contribution to disciplinary effectiveness as they came to rely preponderantly upon disciplinary authority to evaluate the competence of faculty.

When Charles W. Eliot in later life recalled the transformation of Harvard under his presidency, he noted that the identification of scholars qualified to offer advanced instruction was one of the chief difficulties of the early years: "Then none of the societies organized for the development and mutual support of learned and scientific men existed. By 1885 I could get some assistance . . . from the proceedings of the learned and scientific societies. At the beginning there was no such aid."[37] This statement is rare testimony in the largely unrecorded history of the emerging symbiosis between academic disciplines and research universities. The original recruitment practices of Johns Hopkins or Chicago may be well known, but the more pervasive and gradual alteration in the criteria for faculty evaluation is difficult to document. The practices at Eliot's Harvard are especially significant, because Harvard never slipped from its preeminent position.[38] Some painstaking research by Robert McCaughey seems to corroborate Eliot's recollections on this matter.[39]

McCaughey's study of the professionalization of the Harvard faculty has the great value of specifying the context and the nature of the changes Eliot wrought. When he assumed the presidency (1869), it could be said, faculty members with professional credentials and outlook already constituted a slim majority. During his first decade, however, Eliot tended to counter this professionalizing trend by choosing junior faculty who, not unlike himself, enjoyed established Harvard social connections. He seems by 1880 to have forsaken these practices. Aware of the competition from a vigorous Johns Hopkins, Eliot now sought professors with distinguished scholarly attainments to their credit. He first followed Gilman's example of searching for such talent in Europe. Few European scholars were interested in coming to Harvard, however, and Eliot in fact made relatively few senior appointments from outside. By the mid-1880s he was engaged in the conscious upgrading of the Harvard faculty, primarily through the rigorous evaluation of the scholarly contributions of junior faculty. By 1892, the end point of McCaughey's study, two-thirds of the Harvard professors could claim either a Ph.D. or specialized study in Europe, and a majority of the faculty were Harvard "outsiders."

McCaughey also notes that the adoption of professional criteria for appointment and advancement made it necessary for Eliot to seek and largely act upon the advice of faculty members in the disciplines in question. Over time this practice set the basis for departmental authority concerning appointments not only at Harvard but eventually, and for the same reasons, at all universities that were serious about research. Academic departments in theory embody the scientific authority and specialized expertise of the disciplines in the university. Still, it took some time before that authority could be exercised in a routine and uncontested fashion.

One can readily outline a natural history of academic departments in American universities, but it is virtually impossible to describe accurately their actual development. In the beginning, or at least until the end of the nineteenth century, it was common for a university president to be directly responsible for the appointment, promotion, and salary level of each individual member of the faculty. The department was born only when several instructors became needed in the same subject, and its first political form was autocracy: the powers formerly exercised by the president came to be wielded by the department head. The evolution to the next stage was in the direction of autonomy and collegiality. Departments acquired greater authority over those things that depended directly upon their expertise (teaching, research, and personnel), and decisions about these matters came to be made in a more democratic and egalitarian manner. In reality, however, the stages of this development overlapped considerably both between and within universities. At Princeton, for example, professors remained directly under the authority of the president until World War I. The history of academic departments before 1920 has few fixed points.

Perhaps the first systematic effort to organize a university in terms of departmental units was undertaken by William Rainey Harper during the creation of the University of Chicago. He deliberately accorded his departments considerable independence and vested authority in a recognized head. Even an indefatigable organizer like Harper had to make allowance for the human factors in such small units. After ten years he felt that departments possessed "the supreme advantage of being flexible":

the administration of the different Departments is today almost as varied as the number of different Departments. This is as it should be. The machinery is a secondary matter, and should be as far as possible that which the men most closely interested themselves prefer.[40]

It was Harper's opinion that departments operating in a "democratic fashion" obtained the best results, but in this view he seems to have been ahead of his time. In fact, the first decade of the twentieth century probably represented the age of the autocratic head. Discussions of faculty issues during these years were marked by complaints of the "prevailing system of departmental organization with permanent heads possessing ill-defined powers."[41] Several factors probably contributed to this situation: the influence of the German chair system, with which most American professors had direct experience; the practice among research universities of according distinguished professors considerable power to build departments; and the inescapable inequality within departments in terms of training, responsibilities, and career expectations. But partly for these same reasons the autocratic department head was largely a temporal phenomenon—the hallmark of a single academic generation. Once these men left the scene, their autocracy was seldom replicated, and the authority of heads tended to be exercised in a more collegial and less arbitrary manner. This was a particularly significant development in light of the broadening of the department's role.

By about 1910 most appointments of junior faculty members at research universities were made on the recommendations of the academic departments.[42] Senior appointments were still likely to bring the direct involvement of the president, but the influence of departments was probably increasing here as well. The growing authority of departments, and the professional judgments that they represented, over matters of personnel was a crucial element in the evolution of research universities.

Disciplines and departments in fact had powerful reciprocal effects upon one another. The growing authority of departments in universities proved to be an important factor in promoting the authority and the coherence of national disciplinary organizations. This was crucial early in the century when the trend toward specialization threatened to fragment disciplines that had been unified for less than a generation. Subdisciplinary specialties could and did organize their own journals and societies outside of the university, but without the backing of departments they could do little to attain permanent academic institutionalization. Departments, however, remained wedded, by and large, to the parent discipline. As Robert Kohler has illustrated in the case of biochemistry, departments sponsored those specialties that were consistent with the central discipline rather than those with other applications: "internal disciplinary goals inevitably came first when it came time to allocate limited departmental resources."[43]

Large, vital disciplinary communities operated an autonomous system for evaluating and rewarding scientific merit. The growing authority of departments thus meant increased reliance upon this system. In this way the reward system of science that was lodged in the academic disciplines became more nearly identical with the institutional rewards that the universities had to offer. As a result, the academic marketplace that first became evident in the 1890s in the competition for a relatively few recognized scholars and scientists gradually came to govern most faculty positions. Productive scholars consequently tended, over time, to become more concentrated in a limited number of research universities.

Some measure of the extent of this concentration at the beginning of the twentieth century may be gained from a survey conducted by James McKeen Cattell, the editor of *Science* and an inveterate champion of American science.[44] Cattell attempted to identify the one thousand most eminent American scientists in a dozen fields. Those who were clustered in groups of three or more (that is, affiliated with the same institution) were distributed as follows: 18 percent were in nonacademic settings, including an even one hundred belonging to six federal agencies; of those with academic posts, two-thirds were attached to only thirteen universities (Table 3), and the other third were to be found in thirty-eight colleges or universities of mostly middling reputation. This left the remainder (approximately one-quarter) of America's eminent scientists spread widely and thinly across undisclosed locations. The importance of the first thirteen research universities is further enhanced when one notes that they claimed an absolute majority of the most highly regarded scientists, those who were rated in the top two deciles of Cattell's classification.

The American structure of higher education depended for its intellectual vigor on both decentralized competition and scientific concentration. One can certainly envision the possibility for concentration greater than that revealed in Cattell's figures, even though his survey of established scientists would not reflect the preponderance of young scientific talent at the principal Ph.D.-producing institutions. In fact, the concentration of distinguished scientists at the research universities would increase during the succeeding three decades.[46] Perhaps the most important conclusions to be drawn from Cattell's survey are the most obvious ones. At the top of the list in Table 3 are the same five schools that had become the leaders in journal publication. In all likelihood, then, the conditions for scientific advancement that Daniel Kevles found in physics and chemistry, cited earlier, can generally be assumed to have prevailed in all disciplines: leaders were heavily concentrated at peak institutions, where they now commanded the means and organization to set the research agenda for their disciplines.

TABLE 3. Distribution of the 1,000 Leading
American Men of Science, 1906
(emeritus, joint appt. = ½)[45]

Research universities:		403
Harvard	66½	
Columbia	60	
Chicago	39	
Cornell	33½	
Johns Hopkins	30½	
California	27	
Yale	26½	
Michigan	20	
MIT	19½	
Wisconsin	18	
Pennsylvania	17	
Stanford	16	
Princeton	14½	
Minnesota	10	
Illinois	6	
Other colleges and universities		193
U.S. government		110
Other non-university		24
No location given		270
		N = 1,000

By the first decade of the twentieth century a number of research universities had clearly established themselves and claimed a significant portion of the available scientific talent. An American pattern of multiple centers of intellectual leadership was now set. But why did these particular institutions succeed so decisively in this wide competition to spur the advancement of knowledge?

3. The Wealth of Universities

From the last years of the nineteenth century through World War I, the United States experienced a period of sustained economic expansion. The gross national product tripled in absolute terms from 1895 to 1915, and that represented more than a doubling of national wealth after adjustment for inflation. Prosperity, however, fell rather unevenly across American society. The giant corporations, which contributed to this economic growth by harnessing the twin revolutions in the production and distribution of goods, were among the principal beneficiaries; and the individuals who controlled these financial behemoths acquired personal fortunes of hitherto undreamed-of proportions. By 1916 the wealthiest 1 percent of the population was receiving a larger proportion of the national income than at any time before or since.[1] The new wealth of this era flowed mainly to the "haves" of American society.

Higher education, it has already been seen, was no less a growth industry during these years than steel or oil. In addition, it was an indirect beneficiary of the burgeoning national economy. But here, too, it was predominantly the haves who garnered the fruits of economic growth. At the turn of the century a substantial majority of the nation's seven hundred colleges and universities were still fairly small, even marginal, operations, with annual incomes of less than $50,000. Many faced dismal prospects despite the growing demand for higher education.[2] Not so the research universities. The organizational parallel between them and the large corporations, mentioned at the outset of this chapter, has a financial analogue. During the first two decades of the twentieth century their regular incomes expanded by a factor of five,[3] and they used this economic muscle to enhance their institutional resources and their capacity for research. For both public and private research universities the two decades before the First World War brought far-reaching changes.

In 1894 the research universities were already for the most part the largest American universities, yet only four of them could count more than two thousand regular students (Harvard, Michigan, Penn, Yale: see Appendix A). Harvard, as the country's largest school, also had the most extensive facilities; but even these were inadequate for a student body that had doubled in less than a decade. Chicago was in the process of constructing the most up-to-date university plant. Facilities at the research universities were in general decidedly primitive by twentieth-century standards. These conditions, however, were to improve markedly over the course of the next two decades. The value of buildings and grounds at both the state and the endowed research universities approximately tripled in real terms during these years. The value of endowments at the private universities increased by the same factor. The number of volumes in the libraries—to take but one index of intellectual potential— likewise tripled at the private schools, and increased by a higher multiple at the relatively less developed state institutions.[4] Part of these increases, of course, were necessary to meet the needs of ever-rising student numbers. This growth nevertheless represents the evolution of these already well-developed institutions into even larger, more complex entities, capable of incorporating greater degrees of specialization.

These few figures on physical expansion suggest a rough parallel between the rates of development in the public and in the private sectors. In fact, by the beginning of the twentieth century a kind of financial parity was widely assumed to exist between state and private research universities: state contributions of public funds to the former seemed to be the equivalent of the endowment income enjoyed by the latter. For a time during the first decade of the century, this was a fairly accurate perception. Tuition income, however, differed significantly in the two sectors: private universities (except Stanford) charged from $100 to $160 per year, while state universities typically charged $30 to $40. These three income sources nevertheless provide the key for monitoring and comparing the financial development of public and private research universities. Endowment income plus tuition for private universities and state appropriations plus tuition for state universities funded the core of the university budget—the current expenditures for general and educational purposes. These figures thus offer a basis for comparing university budgets that are otherwise full of incommensurate items.[5]

Among the state universities there is perceptible a convergence toward a common financial standard during the first two decades of the century. State appropriations to these five universities in 1900 varied from 58 percent to 100 percent of the total, but by 1920 the range had narrowed to 72 percent to 87 percent (and by 1930 it had narrowed still further). These state allocations registered a fourfold increase in real terms from 1900 to 1920, thus substantially exceeding enrollment growth. Moreover, this increased income permitted the state universities in general to gain ground on their private counterparts. The discrepancy in income per student between public and private research universities was smaller in 1910 than at any time before or since.

Given the advantageous relative positions of the private universities in 1900 (except for MIT), the growth rates for their endowment income is nothing like the rise in state appropriations. In addition, there was greater variety in their financial patterns. Johns Hopkins and Stanford were distinctive in relying upon their original endowments for more than 70 percent of their educational costs as late as 1920. Subsequently, however, they conformed more closely to other wealthy universities by relying more heavily on tuition. Princeton and Columbia maintained endowment and tuition income near the fifty-fifty point, but Penn saw its endowment income decline to just half of tuition revenues by 1920. Cornell is clearly a special case, because the dwindling of its relative endowment income was more than compensated for by the inception and growth of state subsidies. The remaining four private universities managed to expand significantly the relative contribution of endowment from 1900 to 1920. At Chicago the completion of John D. Rockefeller's benefactions ushered in a period of financial stability in which endowment income exceeded that from tuition. MIT did not enter the ranks of highly endowed universities until after 1910. Yale and Harvard, however, show the most impressive increases in endowment income: for both it rose to nearly double the level of tuition revenues.[6]

Accounting for the steady rise in university nontuition income is more simply done for the public than for the private sector. Although an inescapable political element was continually present in state support for flagship universities, the thinking of state governments on this issue passed over three thresholds. The first occurred near the 1870s, when it became apparent that the state universities could not be self-supporting on the basis of student fees and revenues from past land grants alone—that they would instead require regular annual appropriations of public funds. For the states considered here the solution to this problem was to establish a permanent property tax, the proceeds of which were directly or indirectly earmarked for university operations. A second change in attitude took place when state legislators perceived their state universities to be important assets requiring substantial recurrent investments for the expansion and improvement of their facilities. The growing value of their physical plants suggests that in these five states this threshold was crossed around the turn of the century, and certainly before 1910. After a spurt of rapid growth, however, these universities came to occupy a position similar to that of other state agencies. Because they were permanent responsibilities of state government, their claims came to be balanced more explicitly against other rapidly growing state obligations and, before too long, against other institutions of higher education as well.

Despite the vicissitudes of statehouse politics, state university finances in the long run conformed to quite similar patterns. After the turn of the century state universities in general enjoyed more than a decade of good fortune. The high prestige and growing popularity of higher education gave an intangible impetus to their development, while the economic growth of their respective states provided a most tangible impetus through the property tax. In Michigan, for example, the assessed valuation of property quadrupled in the years 1900–1920; and the university mill tax was raised from one-sixth to one-fourth of a mill in 1899, then to three-eighths of a mill in 1907.[7] During these years, however, other state services were also growing at a rapid rate. After about 1915 the universities' relative shares of state revenues became difficult to maintain.[8] World War I and its aftermath left all these universities with some formidable financial difficulties. They needed simultaneously to resume building programs halted by the war; to make up for inflation, particularly in the matter of faculty salaries; and to accommodate a large and unanticipated jump in enrollments (see Chapter 3). At the same time, postwar conditions put a severe strain on state finances. A potent political reaction set in against high levels of taxation, and, given the importance of agriculture in these states, there were protests against continued reliance on property taxes in particular.[9] As a result, university expenditures once again became a frequently contested political issue. The fact that results for the 1920s were quite alike for all these states—an approximate doubling of budgets for Big Ten universities and a further narrowing of the relative reliance on tuition—is a strong indication that by this time there existed certain norms that guided state governments in the financial treatments of their flagship universities. In the private sector, however, a wide disparity of means precluded any common standard.

The private research universities, no less than the public, benefited from the general esteem of higher education in this period and from the growing affluence of the principal sources of support. Their nontuition income was ultimately derived from voluntary private giving, both current and past. These universities, of course, owed their relative affluence at the end of the nineteenth century largely to the generosity of numerous benefactors. Four universities were indeed the direct creations of individual philanthropy. But after 1900 this bounty became larger and more constant. This development was not accidental. Instead of accepting such benevolence as acts of providence, these universities increasingly employed organization and foresight in order to stimulate, solicit, and channel existing eleemosynary possibilities. The field in which these energies were unloosed can be broken into three components, each of which embodied somewhat different tactics and strategies. They were the great foundations created by Andrew Carnegie and John D. Rockefeller, major individual givers who commanded the vast personal fortunes of the day, and the increasingly numerous and prosperous graduates of these universities. The fruits of these efforts can also be covered in a threefold classification. Some were added to university endowment, either for specified or unrestricted purposes, some became the physical capital needed to expand university facilities, and a smaller portion was consumed directly for a variety of purposes.

There is no adequate history of the development of American philanthropy during this period. Any attempt at such a study would be hindered by the considerable irregularity from year to year in the magnitude and the purpose of gifts. Nevertheless, the scattered literature on this subject does permit a tentative identification of several trends in giving that affected the private universities.

The rising volume of giving. From the 1880s until the onset of the Great

Depression, there occurred a significant secular expansion of philanthropic giving. This was the by-product, quite naturally, of an enormous economic expansion; but it was also tied to the predominance of holders of new fortunes, who had a higher propensity for giving than did inheritors of old wealth.[10] This is evident in the identity of the principal university benefactors of the period.

Higher education's share. The level of annual giving to higher education may have quadrupled between 1895 and 1915. A breakdown of all gifts over $5,000 for these years shows higher education increasing its share, or claiming a majority of these funds, until about 1908. Then colleges and universities appear to lose some ground to other charitable causes.[11] Thus, the situation is not unlike that of the state universities, which increased their share of state revenues during the first decade or so of the century but then encountered increasing competition from other needs. Still, within giving to higher education there were some minor trends that favored the universities.

Gifts versus bequests. After the turn of the century, the available evidence seems to suggest, gifts by living donors began to overshadow bequests in total size, and that trend largely continued, at least until the Depression.[12] This was significant for higher education because a living major donor is to a large extent an informed consumer. He or she is able to influence, or be influenced by, the recipient institution. This undoubtedly became a factor in the last two trends.

Helping the strong instead of the needy. It has already been indicated that giving for charitable purposes appeared to more than hold its own, but within educational giving 1900 seems to mark a shift, to put it crudely, from the weak to the strong. For example, the three educational charities chartered or conceived in the nineteenth century—the Peabody Education Fund (1867), the John F. Slater Fund (1882), and the Phelps-Stokes Fund (designed 1893; established 1911)—were specifically intended to aid the education of blacks. The early-twentieth-century foundations concentrated, more in their actual undertakings than in their broad charters, on assisting established institutions of higher education.[13] This difference seems to be part of a larger change of emphasis in educational philanthropy from starting new ventures or aiding poor students to strengthening universities already in place. This tendency may have been partly induced by the final trend.

The organization of fund-raising. Just as massive charitable giving found a suitable organizational form in the new foundations, university fund-raising also acquired permanent organizational features. One of these centered on the organization of the alumni for regular low- and middle-level giving. Another was the extraordinary campaign or drive, designed to take in large sums to build endowment or capital. Organization thus greatly enhanced the ability of major universities to raise money at the same time that trends in personal income were making such gifts more available than ever before. University fund-raising was not a reaction to institutional penury but rather a consequence of ambition. Once set in motion, it became a process that fed upon itself. The soliciting of gifts became a permanent function of twentieth-century private research universities.

All five of the above trends were evident in the most remarkable philanthropic phenomenon of this era—the giving activities of Andrew Carnegie and John D. Rockefeller. The hundreds of millions of dollars that they, by far the wealthiest exemplars of the Gilded Age, each donated to various causes simply dwarfed all other contemporary efforts. Just to catalog their manifold fields of endeavor would take more space than can be spared here.[14] Suffice it to point out that after 1900 both focused their giving increasingly on higher education and the advancement of knowledge. Furthermore, there were interesting parallels in their activities, even though Carnegie personally developed his own philanthropic strategies, while Rockefeller delegated much authority to trusted lieutenants. Both men were responsible for the development of major universities—the Carnegie Institute of Technology and the University of Chicago. Both sought to advance knowledge directly through establishments devoted purely to research—the Rockefeller Institute of Medical Research (1901) and the Carnegie Institution of Washington (1902). Rockefeller's General Education Board (1902) and the Carnegie Foundation for the Advancement of Teaching (1905) both took upon themselves the burden of effecting major reforms in American higher education. These were followed by the Carnegie Corporation (1911) and the Rockefeller Foundation (1913), both general-purpose foundations explicitly dedicated to the advancement of knowledge. All of these institutions, and particularly the latter two, will figure prominently in subsequent sections of this study. At this point it is appropriate merely to note their influence before 1920 on higher education as a whole and on the research universities in particular.

In 1904 President Henry S. Pritchett of MIT wrote Andrew Carnegie suggesting that pensions for MIT faculty might be an admirable object for the latter's philanthropy. Carnegie's response was to investigate the feasibility of, and then actually to fund, a nationwide system of faculty pensions. The Carnegie Foundation for the Advancement of Teaching (CFAT) took shape the following year with $10 million in initial assets and with Pritchett as president.[15] Since even these sums could provide for only a fraction of the collegiate teachers (and that fraction, it later turned out, had been grievously overestimated), it became apparent that the CFAT possessed great leverage over supplicant institutions. Accordingly, it began implementing the pension scheme with the ulterior objectives of raising academic standards generally and of reducing what was axiomatically regarded as the "chaos" of American higher education.[16] The foundation specifically demanded that colleges, to be eligible, must, among other things, limit admission to certified high school graduates, meet certain minimal standards of fiscal health, have only Ph.D.'s as department heads, and be free of denominational ties. Although this phase of foundation activity lasted little more than a decade before actuarial realities forced its transformation into the contributory Teachers Insurance and Annuity Association, during these years its standards exerted considerable influence on American colleges.

Also in 1905 the General Education Board, which had originally been chartered to treat educational problems in the southern states, received $10 million in permanent endowment from John D. Rockefeller to use "as the Board may deem best adapted to promote a comprehensive system of higher education in the United States."[17] Operating on the same premises as the Carnegie Foundation, the board set about by different means to attack the "waste and confusion" in American higher education. It carefully screened colleges according to criteria that, although unstated, were somewhat more flexible than the Carnegie Foundation's and that took local conditions into account.[18] Those colleges deemed most likely to survive and prosper by virtue of their central location, prudent management, and "rootedness" in a community were selected for assistance. The predominant form of help was a grant for permanent endowment that had to be matched two, three, or four to one by the recipient institution. The purpose was to strengthen the institution for the future, not just monetarily but also by mobilizing the active commitments of a community of supporters.

The private research universities were quick to join the Carnegie pension scheme, and a few received endowment grants from the General Education Board. Until 1920, however, the foundations had little discernible impact upon these institutions. Influence, in fact, should be seen as flowing in the opposite direction. The standards the foundations wished to impose—concerning who was qualified to teach and who qualified to study—were those already developed by the major universities over the preceding two decades. The conservative financial norms, and especially the preoccupation with adequate endowment, were likewise those of the private research universities. Finally, the injunction to solicit contributions from graduates and local boosters was an adaptation of practices that had recently been developed in the old eastern universities.

The foundations also manifested interest in education for the professions, and this brought them more directly into contact with the research universities. The CFAT contained the "Division of Educational Equity," and it was from there that Abraham Flexner issued his devastating critique of medical education in 1910.[19] This was followed by other investigations of legal, engineering, and teacher education. The General Education Board seized the initiative on Flexner's report by making a series of grants intended to lead the way toward improving the quality of medical education. The Carnegie Corporation also joined in these efforts after the war. Before that, however, its giving to higher education was concentrated almost exclusively on the Carnegie Institute of Technology. Nevertheless, outside of medical education the foundations before the war played no significant part in the philanthropy that multiplied the wealth of the private research universities. Soon this would change, but for this period credit belongs to individual givers.

One of the few strong conclusions emerging from an analysis of late-nineteenth-century philanthropy is that it was overwhelmingly local in character.[20] Indeed, this was true for most universities. "When Harvard needs money she seeks it on State Street" was a dictum largely accurate before 1900. Yale had to appeal to the city of New Haven to salvage its first fund-raising drive.[21] The University of Chicago succeeded in raising donations from local magnates before it even had any alumni. Indeed, the local nexus as a source of donations has to this day remained critically important to most endowed urban universities.[22] Still, propinquity is only one of several prominent motives for giving to universities.

The expanding scale of university activities naturally required greater university revenues. Growing numbers of students created a need for additional faculty and facilities, university commitments to advancing knowledge continually raised overhead costs, and proliferating professional schools demanded buildings of their own. The rising tuition revenues that came from rising enrollments actually covered only a portion of these costs. According to recommended financial practices of the period for private institutions, tuition income was expected to approximate the half of the university budget that was devoted to faculty salaries.[23] This left the other half of operating expenses, plus whatever capital costs were incurred, to be financed by the return on permanent endowment and current gifts. During the 1890s only Johns Hopkins and Stanford attempted to rely predominantly upon their endowments, and both had to weather severe problems stemming from the concentrated nature of their assets.[24] Harvard, perennially the wealthiest American university, saw its endowment grow from $7 million to $13 million in this decade, but even this scarcely matched its burgeoning needs. It and all the other older private universities were constrained in their ambitions by the kinds of support they received.

Deeply rooted institutions like Harvard and Yale each year received hundreds of benefactions, including in-kind gifts of books, specimens, and artworks; money for immediate uses; and donations or bequests ear-

marked for permanent purposes. Before the twentieth century the institutions themselves exerted comparatively little influence over what these
purposes might be, especially since the most significant sums came
through bequests. Charles Eliot, for example, was probably typical in his
disdain for direct presidential solicitation of funds.[25] Such attitudes left
donors largely free to exercise a kind of consumer's prerogative by designating the precise purposes of their gifts. As a result, the Harvard endowment at the turn of the century consisted of more than 450 separate
"funds," for the most part bearing the name and serving the intent of the
original donor. More than 100 of these funds were designated for the
university or Harvard College; almost as many were intended for scholarships; 13 were for prizes and 40 for the library; and some 200 supported
different facets of the university's other schools and research units.[26]
Many of these funds endowed professorships, supported departments, or
otherwise contributed to the core purposes of the university. A significant
portion of them, however, were committed to what university officers
could only regard as less than optimal usage. Thus, Harvard and the other
older universities faced the same fundamental problem as they evolved
into modern research universities—that of securing large amounts of
unrestricted endowment to fund the growing general needs of the institution.

It took almost a generation for these universities to educate their benefactors to give for general rather than specific purposes, and some succeeded better than others. As late as 1914 the Columbia trustees felt
compelled to endorse the resolution

> that for the present it is the policy of the Trustees not to invite gifts of new
> buildings . . . or new gifts for special purposes, but to secure funds the
> income of which shall be applicable to the general educational purposes of
> the University.[27]

But at Yale by 1921 President Arthur Twining Hadley could report that
donors "have learned that the old habit of tying up gifts for specific purposes may result in making them less useful rather than more so."[28] The
fund-raising patterns of these two institutions provide an interesting contrast. Yale met its needs by harnessing altruism through organization, and
the techniques it developed were later imitated widely by other institutions. Columbia became "the Colossus on the Hudson" by tapping the
great fortunes of the New York City area.[29] Between them they exhibit
the principal factors that allowed established universities to accumulate
the wealth to underwrite their expanding activities.

Yale, like many other institutions, had maintained relationships of
some sort with its graduates throughout much of the nineteenth century.[30] In 1871 six places were created for alumni on the Yale Corpora-

tion, and shortly thereafter graduates and friends of the college were canvassed quite systematically in a disappointing attempt to raise $150,000 as a memorial to President Woolsey (1846–71).[31] Still, in 1890 President Timothy Dwight could state matter-of-factly, "Yale University, like all our collegiate institutions, must depend very largely for its success on the generosity of men who have not themselves participated in its undergraduate life during their early years."[32] Only thirteen years later, though, President Hadley declared that "nearly all" the gifts in recent years had "been made either by alumni . . . or by their immediate family connections." Moreover, this situation was sufficiently unusual that he regarded it as "Yale's distinctive position."[33]

The most important single event contributing to this transformation occurred contemporaneously with Timothy Dwight's comment—the establishment of the Yale Alumni Fund in 1890. The initiative for this step came not from the institution at all but from several Yale graduates in New York City.[34] The loose alumni association existing there, like other groupings of its kind, served essentially to provide an opportunity for members to meet socially. In 1890 it occurred to several of them that there ought to be a closer connection between the university and its graduates and that some means should exist for ordinary alumni to be of service to their alma mater. "At that time," one of the founders later recalled, "no Yale graduate ever thought of giving $5 or $10 or any inconsiderable sum to the college, all appeals for money having been made for contributions of considerable amounts, usually from rich men." To this end they therefore proposed the creation of a fund with the modest expectation that, "while it might not accomplish much, it certainly could do no harm."[35]

The Yale Alumni Fund tapped a wellspring of loyalties, and its accomplishments were anything but modest. In the first year 385 graduates contributed over $11,000, and soon the fund was turning over a like amount each year to the Yale treasurer for use as unrestricted income. A small excess of contributions allowed for the creation of a principal fund that became a separate part of Yale's permanent endowment. After the turn of the century this fund grew rapidly, thus providing an annual interest income to the steady flow of contributions. In 1905 the principal fund exceeded $100,000, and the fund's annual gift to Yale was doubled to $23,000. Within a dozen years the principal fund exceeded $1 million, and the annual gifts came to more than $100,000.[36] But the importance to Yale of this support surpassed even these impressive values. First, the unrestricted nature of this income allowed it to be devoted to the general development of the university. Second, the relative importance of its contribution increased over time: between 1910 and 1920 the principal fund grew from about 4 percent to almost 8 percent of the total university endowment, and the fund's annual gift to university income rose from about 10 percent of tuition revenues in 1910 to around 20 percent under normal conditions in the mid-twenties. Third, the fund constituted a reserve protecting the university against financial adversity. When wartime enrollment shrinkage, along with war-induced inflation, caused persistent large deficits at Yale, it was the alumni fund that supplied the amounts needed to balance the budget.

Considering the great success of the Yale Alumni Fund, it is rather surprising that it found few imitators until after the war. Then postwar financial hardships together with the lure of matching grants from the General Education Board prompted most private colleges and universities to mobilize alumni giving.[37] Before the war, however, the distinctiveness of Yale's alumni fund gave it a special aura. Gifts collected in this way were called "democratic contributions," and they yielded the "most democratic endowment of any university." Such a wide base of support, it was further asserted, guaranteed the intellectual freedom of the university.[38] Yale was not entirely alone, however, in drawing upon organized alumni support. In 1905 the Harvard class of 1880 made a gift of $100,000 for unrestricted endowment, and thereafter every succeeding class followed suit on the occasion of its twenty-fifth anniversary.[39] (At Yale reunion-year class gifts of smaller magnitudes were added to the alumni fund.) Over time these class gifts to Harvard alone approximated the size of the Yale alumni's principal fund. Thus, although the approach was somewhat different, the result was essentially the same: through the organization of their alumni both Harvard and Yale were able to augment significantly the volume of crucial unrestricted income. An organized alumni body could be called on for other needs as well.

A second fund-raising strategy for private colleges and universities was to implement a formal campaign or drive. Here, too, organization was decisive. The chief goals of such drives were usually to increase unrestricted endowment and/or to gather capital for building. An established alumni organization was a considerable asset in such an undertaking, but the ultimate success of most drives often also depended upon just a few major donations. Since the potentially large givers could often be enticed by a building bearing their name, such substantial benefactions were largely responsible for the construction of present university campuses. The armies of loyal alumni, in the meantime, were continually persuaded of the virtues of giving to unrestricted endowment.

It is difficult to say who first used fund-raising drives, since various nineteenth-century antecedents can be cited;[40] but Yale's bicentennial fund does appear to be something of a prototype for twentieth-century university campaigns with respect to the setting of monetary targets, an explicit theme, specific building and endowment objectives, and wide canvass. As announced by the retiring president Dwight, the goal was to raise

$2 million for new university buildings before Yale's bicentennial celebration in the fall of 1901. Another $2 million to $3 million for permanent endowment was to be sought in the following years. It would appear that Yale came up somewhat short of both these objectives, although the record is rather hazy.[41] Nevertheless, these efforts seemed to stimulate, as later drives would, other forms of giving as well. By the latter half of the decade Yale was adding more than $1 million annually to its endowment.[42]

The acceleration of giving to Yale began around 1905, and it was indicative of a dramatic upswing in donations to higher education in general that carried through the 1920s. Universities did much themselves to bring forth this largess by perfecting the techniques of conducting fund-raising drives. In 1904 Harvard initiated an organized campaign of what it termed, in mock self-deprecation, "begging." The goal was endowment to support faculty salaries—tantamount to unrestricted funds—and the means was a sotto voce approach to major givers. Notably, the appeal extended beyond State Street to affluent Harvard graduates in New York City, and they responded by contributing the bulk of the total in just twenty $50,000 pledges.[43]

To appreciate the crucial importance of organization in this endeavor, it is necessary to look beyond these rather crude early efforts to the campaigns of the 1920s. Postwar conditions left every university strapped for funds, and the general response among private institutions (encouraged and abetted by a $50 million Rockefeller addition to General Education Board assets for this purpose) was to seek substantial additions to endowment. The outstanding example among all these efforts was Harvard's $15 million drive of 1919–20. Under the professional direction of the John Price Jones Corporation, this campaign possessed all the essential features that have characterized such drives to this day. With the aid of some three thousand campaign workers spread across seventy geographical regions, Harvard for the first time sought out small as well as large contributors. Income-based giving guidelines were suggested to all alumni, but the wealthier prospects were individually rated and then asked to contribute leadership gifts to build the campaign's momentum.[44] Professionally managed fund-raising drives were also conducted in the early twenties by Stanford, Johns Hopkins, Penn, Cornell, Chicago, and Princeton, among others; but Harvard topped them all in number of donors and amounts pledged: 23,477 contributors, 94 percent of them alumni, promised an average of almost $600 to Harvard, yielding a final total of nearly $14 million.[45]

As the scale of giving increased, however, Yale was able to better Harvard's feat in the last half of the 1920s. On April 20, 1926, a drive for an additional $20 million in endowment was touched off by a simultaneous dinner for fifteen thousand Yalies around the globe. The occasion and the subsequent follow-up induced more than 22,000 pledges in a relatively short time, allowing Yale to surpass its goal by $1 million. The remarkable features of this drive, as of Harvard's, were the extraordinary breadth achieved by thorough organization and the concentration on alumni, who in this case composed 97 percent of the givers.[46] In a longer perspective, however, the organization of alumni giving and strategic fund-raising drives allowed a select few private research universities to surmount their financial limitations by permitting them to stimulate and to control the flow of voluntary support.

Columbia provides an interesting foil to Yale and Harvard. As a conglomerate of new and preexisting schools, the university originally had a diffuse identity for its various alumni, and Columbia College was quite overshadowed by the whole. Instead of depending on alumni generosity, then, it sought donations among the city's wealthiest families. A breakdown of major gifts prior to 1914, for example, shows the bulk of them coming from people unconnected with the institution. In fact, families or individuals contributing more than $1 million—the Vanderbilts, the Dodges, Sloane, Pulitzer, Low, Crocker, Milbank, and John Stewart Kennedy—supplied the majority of these funds.[47] Since large donors are in a much stronger position to assert their own preferences, such gifts were more awkward for universities to control. Columbia's president Nicholas Murray Butler often complained of this situation: "Many of those who make gifts to a university really put upon the university the new obligation of acting without compensation as their own trustees or executors for the purpose of carrying out some plan or purpose of their own."[48] As a result, Columbia was chronically starved for discretionary income to support its academic programs. The problem, however, was rooted in the school's ambitions and its expansiveness.

Columbia's predicament, and its glory, dates from its move in the 1890s from cramped quarters on Forty-ninth Street to its present campus at Morningside Heights. The new site was largely purchased, in typical fashion, with $100,000 gifts from J. P. Morgan, Cornelius Vanderbilt, and William Schermerhorn.[49] This was a mere down payment, however. By the time the original campus was completed, in 1898, its total cost reached almost $7 million. The raising of such sums in the 1890s was beyond Columbia's capacities, despite its wealthy patrons. Only $3 million was financed by gifts, including President Low's $1.1 million for the library. The university thus had to assume an indebtedness of $3.75 million.[50] In the years that followed, interest on this sum constituted a sigificant financial burden to the university, equal to approximately one-quarter of the tuition income, although it naturally was supplied from other accounts. It was a source of some embarrassment as well.

When Nicholas Murray Butler took the reins of Columbia in 1901, he likened the university to a "giant in bonds": "strength, power, zeal for service are all at hand, but the bonds of insufficient funds hold them in on all sides." Butler proceeded to identify building needs of $7 million, but he also emphasized that the "greatest single need" of the university was to expunge its debt.[51] Despite such arguments, frequently reiterated, Columbia's benefactors preferred to support the university's expansion rather than to underwrite a fiscally orthodox, debt-free balance sheet. Thus, Butler's early years saw Columbia enlarge its Morningside site (at considerably inflated land prices), add projected new buildings, and embark upon the erection of a costly medical campus. It would take forty years, however, to repay the debt on the original campus.[52] Columbia was thus set, with the complicity of its benefactors, on a hectic path of development that was tantamount to a permanent fund-raising campaign.[53]

In the matter of fund-raising, as in other activities, major universities imitated each other's successful practices as the twentieth century progressed. Yale benefited from major gifts from the likes of Vanderbilt and Rockefeller no less than did Columbia, and by 1920 Columbia, too, had created an alumni fund. Nevertheless, the relative importance of these different sources of gifts never became quite the same: isomorphism in this respect encompassed the principal forms of fund-raising, but not the magnitudes of it. Furthermore, as voluntary support came to loom large in the destiny of the private research universities, their character tended to be shaped by the amounts that they received and by the sources from which these came. The set of programs that each university offered, the number and type of students it considered optimal, the institutional outlook and priorities—all these were not determined by its donors but were part of a coherent and consistent institutional personality of which the sources of voluntary support were an integral part. As a result, after about 1910 the private research universities, which had seemed to be converging on a common pattern of development, began to become less alike in the ways in which they related to their external environment.[54]

Only Yale, Harvard, and Princeton among research universities succeeded at this early date in mobilizing the generosity of their graduates sufficiently to make it the predominant source of institutional income. Over the long run this type of voluntary support proved to be the most lucrative and dependable. Fund-raising drives fell into disfavor after their widespread exploitation during the early twenties. Alumni funds were established to encourage annual giving at most private institutions during the decade, but it took years for them to engender significant levels of giving.[55] Major donations became more infrequent after the onset of the Great Depression, although bequests appear to have been less affected.

These three schools, however, with alumni bodies that were simultaneously numerous, affluent, and loyal, were among the few private institutions able to sustain a significant level of alumni giving even through the decade of the 1930s.[56]

The importance of their support soon gave the alumni an important voice in university affairs. President Hadley, for one, after declaring that Yale was dependent upon alumni support, proceeded to establish an alumni advisory board "to admit them to the largest measure of control of [Yale's] affairs which conditions will allow."[57] Other institutions, using various mechanisms, followed suit.[58] The Yale alumni played an active part after the war in effecting reorganization into a unified university.[59] In general, however, it is doubtful whether many alumni had the time or the interest to become directly involved in the details of university administration or instruction. Instead, they tended to relate chiefly to the institution as a whole. For the most part this oriented them toward the extracurriculum.

When Edwin Slosson made his grand tour of "the great American universities" in 1908–9, he noticed certain noxious traits that were especially evident in the endowed universities of the East. He was disturbed by the importance accorded to "ritualism" and "athleticism" as well as by what he labeled "the Eastern atmosphere of caste and exclusiveness, of wealth and family pride, of vocational predestination, and of the subordination and segregation of women."[60] It is plausible that these incipient trends were connected with these universities' incessant quest for substantial donations.

Early in the century athletics began to fix the attention of university alumni. The Yale graduate who exclaimed after a notable crew victory that he "would rather see the color of the blue-tipped oars first across the finish line than gaze at the matchless splendor of a masterpiece by Titian" perhaps epitomizes the boundless sentimentality that college sports could evoke.[61] The college athletics movement, however, had a momentum of its own that antedated the period of organized fund-raising. It is by no means clear at what date the intense emotional energies of participant students were transferred to adult spectators, but athletic teams quite soon became the natural focus of alumni interests and alumni publications. At Cornell, where organized fund-raising was slow to develop, alumni supported the athletic program first and were only later asked, by President Jacob Gould Schurman, to consider giving for academic purposes.[62] At most institutions, however, athletics were a natural complement to university fund-raising in that they kept alumni involved in and identified with the fortunes of the school.

The other characteristics mentioned by Slosson bear a more subtle relation to the process of fund-raising. They are, in fact, manifestations of a state of mind that itself affected donor perceptions of the university. The spread of ceremony and ritual on campus betokened, according to Slosson, a widespread spirit of exclusiveness and arrogance. It thus seems to have been connected with the increasingly rigid social divisions existing on campus, which he also noted. These social attitudes arose largely from changing occupational expectations associated with a college education. For the increasing numbers of newly or nearly affluent students that were entering the eastern universities in these years, future careers in the business world were likely to depend more on whom they knew than on what they had learned in college. The fraternity house, or its equivalent, thus became in a sense more central to their college experience than the lecture hall. In a coeducational institution like Cornell, women students were regarded with considerable aversion as professional threats and social inferiors.[63] In this kind of situation the social character of the university took on undue importance. Moreover, it was a feature of university life that could be readily conveyed to prospective large donors by former or current students of similar social station.

Like athletics, the social ossification of the eastern private universities was part of a larger evolutionary process that was only indirectly linked with university fund-raising. Nevertheless, the dependence of these institutions upon a substantial and continuous inflow of contributions from well-heeled alumni and friends could not help giving these matters greater weight in the complex balance of forces that determined university policies. As a result, it became evident by the 1920s that these preoccupations had helped alter the social tone and social composition of university life, and not just in the East.[64] But these developments may well have left the university's research role unaffected. The athletic spectacles, campus social life, and the other preoccupations of alumni relations projected a kind of facade of university life for the benefit of the donor constituency. Behind this facade the everyday activities of the universities could proceed without notice or intrusions. This relative autonomy of the core university functions was further enhanced, in an indirect fashion, by the very nature of the appeals for funds. As the techniques of mass merchandising were incorporated into alumni-solicitation and fund-raising drives, the content of the appeals became increasingly abstract—less related to specific university activities. Alumni were beseeched in terms of duty, loyalty, obligation, and competition. It was continually impressed upon them that the greatest service to their alma mater was the giving of unrestricted funds. Aside from capital funds, much of the giving, especially from alumni, consequently took this form. The most successful private universities thus had by the 1920s far more discretionary income to devote to faculty salaries, departmental support, and the appurtenances of research. The research role may have slipped on some campuses in the ranking of institutional priorities, but it remained an inescapable commitment, given the competitive structure of American higher education. Partly for that reason, the enormous sums that were raised by the private research universities were never deemed to be enough.

"Of the needs of a university there is, indeed, no end," lamented Lawrence Lowell of Harvard,[65] and his words could well provide a motto for any university development office. But although the situation appears to be no different today, the general causes of Lowell's statement in 1920 can be related to some temporal conditions of research universities. Their seemingly insatiable needs were in fact driven by prevailing practices of university finance, by the tempo of campus development, and by the open-ended commitment to the advancing of knowledge.

The expectation, mentioned above, that endowment income should cover about half of a university's instructional budget actually created extraordinary financial pressure for institutions under conditions of rising enrollments. Each additional student, in effect, had to be capitalized not just once but twice: once as endowment to yield income equal to tuition, and once in additional physical facilities. From this perspective it seems remarkable that the private research universities were able to sustain and sometimes increase the ratios of endowment to tuition income. The General Education Board, dealing with a wider range of colleges and universities, had to abandon early in the 1920s the attempt to help them meet a fifty-fifty standard through endowment grants. At the same time the private research universities themselves conceded that they could sustain this pattern of financing only by placing limits on enrollments. Until that time, however, this was a powerful factor in the multiplying of university needs.

It is difficult to designate exactly what facilities are strictly necessary for a major university campus. However, if the types of campus building that took place from 1890 to 1930 could be aggregated by this criterion, the movement over time would probably be along a continuum away from necessities and toward amenities. That is, after classrooms and laboratories were in place, the research universities gradually added ceremonial and recreational structures, football stadiums, carillons, and, usually last, student dormitories. To point this out is not to imply that these investments were frivolous. Over the long run most of them clearly were not. Rather, it illustrates how perceptions of the indispensable accoutrements of a university campus inexorably expanded with time. A similar case could be made for the elaboration of professional schools, with medicine providing the outstanding example, which in expense overshadowed all others. After the Flexner report on medical education (1910), most of these universities embarked upon programs of erecting and reforming their medical complexes. These efforts required very large capital commitments over long periods of time. Thus, the result here, too, was a continual redefinition of need that ineluctably outstripped available funds.

Finally, the commitment to advance knowledge was perhaps the most open-ended of all. Given the implicit competition for excellence, every research university had need for more professors of proven scholarly attainments. Equally important were the direct inputs of research—the equipment, the time, and the assistance that advancing scholarship seemed to demand in ever-greater quantities. Yet, in the pre-1920 research university the provision of such resources was an issue that had not yet been satisfactorily resolved.

2

The Conditions of
University Research, 1900–1920

During the last quarter of the nineteenth century the founding of Johns Hopkins, the flood tide of influence from German universities, and the academic boom of the nineties all contributed to the fixing of research as an indelible commitment of the leading American universities. But if the universities were dedicated to science, broadly speaking, by the beginning of the twentieth century, it was not yet evident that science was or ought to be entirely beholden to universities. Scientific investigation was undertaken in government bureaus and in semi-independent institutions like the Smithsonian, as well as in the universities. Moreover, it seemed to many that some forms of research could be pursued more effectively outside of academe. The first two decades of the century, then, were an important interval in which to sort out the relative responsibilities of different sectors in the nation's research system. The research universities considerably strengthened the material backing for their research efforts; and, perhaps more important, through a process of trial, error, and imitation they underwent numerous small organizational modifications in order to better accommodate these ambitions. Yet, even by 1920 the research universities could not be assured of being the primary locus of basic science.

1. The Research System in 1900 and the Founding of Independent Research Institutions

The federal government at the beginning of the twentieth century was, by one contemporary estimate, annually spending $11 million on all types of scientific activities.[1] Not only was this a considerable sum for what is usually regarded as an era of limited government, but it is colossal in relation to the other resources then available to American science. It is of the same order of magnitude, for example, as the operating budgets of the fifteen research universities being considered here or as the founding benefaction for the Carnegie Institution of Washington. This meant, of course, that the amounts actually available for research in either of these locales were but a fraction of the government's expenditures. Moreover, these federal outlays were about to undergo a sizable expansion in the decades ahead.[2] It seems fair to ask, then, without in any way disparaging the accomplishments of government scientists, why federal efforts did not dominate American science during this era. The answer becomes evident only when one disentangles the combination of scientific and political considerations that determine what kinds of research the government would or would not undertake.

During the last quarter of the nineteenth century the bulk of government research came to be organized in a number of scientific bureaus having rather similar characteristics.[3] Their hallmark was a close identification with a definite class of problems. It was practical need rather than scientific curiosity that could persuade a parsimonious Congress to appropriate funds for research. The need to map the continent and to take stock of the vast federal lands in the West helped to justify the Coast and Geodetic Survey and the U.S. Geological Survey. It was agriculture, however, with its abundant problems touching the welfare of producers and consumers and with its powerful political backing, that sheltered most of the late-nineteenth-century scientific bureaus. The Division (later Bureau) of Entomology battled the depredation of insects on American farms; the Bureau of Animal Industry (f. 1884) was founded largely to combat diseases of livestock; and divisions studying different facets of plant life were combined in 1900 into the Bureau of Plant Industry. In addition, the concern for purity in food and drugs made the Bureau of Chemistry a major locus of Agriculture Department research after the turn of the century. In the same era the Department of Commerce added the Bureau of the Census (1903) and the Bureau of Mines (1912).[4] While all these units possessed their own unique features, their problem orientation tended to determine their scientific character.

The basic approach of the scientific bureaus was to mobilize teams of experts to investigate problems of the moment. As a consequence work was often multidisciplinary in nature, and researchers had to possess the flexibility to move quickly from one project to another. These conditions undoubtedly bred a more practical outlook among government scientists than was common among their academic counterparts, and over time their career patterns diverged as well. Movement between these locales was not frequent in the nineteenth century, and it probably decreased further after 1900 as professionalization occurred on both sides. The relationship between university and government scientists was probably closest in agriculture. The Department of Agriculture recruited its scientific workers from land-grant colleges and essentially trained them on the job. On the whole, though, the nexus between government bureaus and university science was rather sporadic, involving schools of agriculture and a few departments in some research universities but being largely separated from most of university science.[5]

The government bureaus were further distracted from pure research by their very success in furnishing routine services. Being of use to a broad constituency tended to guarantee the flow of appropriations, but often at some cost in time for pure research. This trade-off is most evident in the many tasks that were loaded onto the well-funded Agricultural Experiment Stations.[6] In addition, the ultimate resolution of a bureau's problem lay in the realm of social action. Thus, discovery had to be followed by the formulation and enforcement of scientifically based regulation. In fact, the great growth of government scientific bureaus after the turn of the century was due chiefly to their growing regulatory responsibilities.

In short, the millions that the federal government spent annually on science at the beginning of the century were essentially incommensurate with the sums elsewhere being devoted to scientific research. The actual research done by government scientists was heavily applied in character, and it blended into a larger service mission of introducing and disseminating a rational outlook and superior techniques into mundane economic affairs. The fact that the scientific bureaus of the government did make some fundamental contributions to the advancing of human understanding of the natural world is thus almost incidental. Their essential purpose, and great achievement, was to bring science to bear on the formidable problems facing the nation as it underwent the transformation to a commercialized system of agriculture capable of feeding an increasingly urbanized population. Furthermore, in the early decades of this century the increasing sophistication of basic research and the growing regulatory roles of the bureaus would confirm this direction of development. Hunter Dupree concludes his history of this phase of federal scientific activities with the observation that after 1900 "the split between basic research and the common concerns of society . . . became institutionalized in the division of functions between government and the universities."[7] In the years immediately following the turn of the century, however, contemporaries had to assess the role of yet another alternative to university science—the pure-research institutes created by Andrew Carnegie and John D. Rockefeller.

Given the remarkable progress of American research universities as scientific institutions, it is far from clear why there was any need to create a new form of scientific organization after 1900. Certainly, a skeptic could find some deficiencies in the universities' capacity for research. The multiplication of purposes in the American multiversity, in particular, could only deflect energies away from pure research. Then, too, as will be elaborated below, the means for university research were not at all adequate to meet existing aspirations. Nevertheless, far from being in crisis, the research universities were then in the midst of an extraordinary spurt of growth in students, income, and facilities. On the other hand, foreign comparisons definitely played some part in the genesis of independent research institutions. First, there was a certain frustration with America's continued scientific inferiority to Europe; and second, the current prestige of such recent European innovations as the Pasteur Institute (f. 1888) in Paris, or the Koch Institute for Infectious Diseases in Berlin, gave credence to the apparent efficacy of pure-research institutions.[8] In the final analysis, however, adventitious circumstances undoubtedly played a large part in shaping these American research institutes, including the unspoken competition between America's two greatest philanthropists. The nearly simultaneous creation of the Carnegie Institution and the Rockefeller Institute marks a fleeting stage in the personal philanthropies of these two men—a stage that also coincided with a particular moment in the development of research universities. Despite the later creation of other research institutions in various forms, these two constitute a distinctive institutional type in American science. In no way is this more evident than in their original intention to play a leading role in the advancement of basic science.

The first of these creations, the Rockefeller Institute for Medical Research (RIMR), neither challenged university-based research nor provoked much disquiet in the university community. Outside of Harvard and the new medical school at Johns Hopkins, few American medical schools were significantly involved with research at this juncture (see below). The RIMR thus staked out a claim to an area that was underpopulated and largely uncontested. The cautious gradualism of the original board of directors also helped the institute slowly grow into its own, secure niche. The RIMR was incorporated and made its first grants in 1901, but it was another year before Simon Flexner was installed as its full-time director. Ground was not broken for the institute laboratories until 1904, and then three more years passed before the institute received its permanent endowment. During these years the highly professional board of directors worked with Flexner to establish the major fields of inquiry and the mode of operation. Interestingly, before the institute had its own facilities, it supported the research of promising young scientists in university settings, thereby anticipating later patterns of foundation support for university research projects. But once the laboratories were constructed, the institute concentrated its investigations within its walls and ultimately phased out its external-grant program.[9]

The beginnings of the Carnegie Institution of Washington (CIW) contrast sharply with those of the RIMR in being neither restricted nor gradual, and these differences made Andrew Carnegie's philanthropy an object of keen interest to the university community. Carnegie resolved late in 1901 to found a new institution dedicated to "the advancement of knowledge," but the form of this creation remained to be settled.[10] Early in 1902, after being stimulated by an article attributing America's scientific inferiority to the absence of institutions for pure research,[11] Carnegie launched the CIW with a gift of $10 million. The charter of the institution was very broad: the first two aims, which subsequently dominated operations, were to "promote original research" and to discover and aid "the exceptional man." Other objectives included increasing facilities for higher education, assisting universities, helping students working in the Washington area, and facilitating the publication of research results.[12] The trustees were thus left with considerable discretion to decide which aims would be emphasized and how they might be pursued. During most of 1902 they made inquiries, assessed the country's scientific needs, and formulated plans for approaching their unprecedented task. In the meantime, the universities waited anxiously to find out just how the CIW would augment their capabilities for undertaking research.

Nicolas Murray Butler no doubt spoke for other interested members of the academic community when he expressed the hope that the Carnegie trustees would "see the wisdom and the economy of supplementing the facilities for research already offered by American universities."[13] And hopeful the university presidents might well be. The first president of the CIW was Daniel Coit Gilman, retired from Johns Hopkins, where he had for a quarter of a century presided over the country's most notable marriage of higher education and research. University scientists were no less sanguine. James McKeen Cattell, editor of *Science,* offered his own detailed blueprint of how the institution might best spend its income, and he also opened the pages of his journal to the suggestions of fellow scientists. Cattell recommended that half the funds be devoted to constructing and operating major laboratories in Washington for physics, chemistry, and psychology (his own field) and that the other half be employed to assist university scientists in their own institutions. The other respondents who joined this forum in *Science* produced no simple consensus, but most university scientists advocated some direct support for faculty research time, graduate fellowships, scientific publications, or the purchase of research apparatus.[14] Only one contributor unequivocally urged that all the funds be devoted to a single research establishment in the capital.[15] This was not quite what actually occurred. Nevertheless, the hopes of the university community basically went for naught. Each of the strategic decisions that shaped the missions of the CIW pointed away from any direct ties with university science.

Daniel Coit Gilman proved ineffectual as the CIW's president and withdrew in 1903, before the institution was fully operative.[16] Instead, the CIW came to be shaped and led by three individuals with little appreciation for research in a university setting. Each had begun his scientific career before graduate education became the normal prerequisite, and each had spent an important segment of his career in government scientific bureaus.[17] John Shaw Billings, a physician who developed the Surgeon General's Library, controlled the day-to-day affairs in the early years of the CIW as chairman of the executive committee of the trustees. Charles D. Walcott, secretary of the CIW, head of the U.S. Geological Survey, and "probably the last significant American scientist without formal training in a college or university,"[18] teamed with Billings to outmaneuver Gilman. Most important in the long run, however, was Robert S. Woodward, Gilman's successor as president from 1904 to 1920, who made his reputation in government geological surveys and engineered the institution's early commitment to geophysics. Although they had their differences, all three men were in accord in stressing the first of the charter purposes—the promotion of original research—and in believing that this could best be accomplished in the institution's own laboratories by full-time scientists, undistracted by teaching responsibilities. Under this leadership the portion of CIW research expenditures devoted to large, in-house programs predominated from the outset and increased over time.[19]

Although President Woodward at one point likened the CIW to "a university in which there are no students,"[20] it might more accurately have been called a government scientific bureau unencumbered by government—that is, one without federal procedures, the politics of appropriations, or the burdens of practical service. As Nathan Reingold has observed, the fields to which it committed programs all had American antecedents,[21] and they were largely in existing government bureaus. The Department of Terrestrial Magnetism and the Geophysical Laboratory both pursued research related to the concerns of the Geological Survey and/or the Coast and Geodetic Survey; the Department of Experimental

Evolution (i.e., breeding) and that of Experimental Botany paralleled in purer form research in the Department of Agriculture; and CIW funding for the Mount Wilson Observatory helped transfer leadership in astronomy away from the Naval Observatory. The close congruence with government programs, then, meant that even though these departments would give no succor to university research, for all practical purposes they posed no threat to it either. The in-house research sponsored by the CIW thus tended to be concentrated within a few chosen niches; it was hardly an alternative to university-based investigations in the basic disciplines.

The remaining CIW research funds were dispensed as minor grants or research assistantships, and these might have been used to support university researchers far more than in fact they were. The impediments here were, first, a preoccupation with the chimera of the "exceptional man" and, second, an unfortunate instance of maladministration.

The notion that there were individuals of exceptional scientific talent laboring undiscovered throughout the country had a certain appeal to the romantic individualism of this age; but in actuality the professionalization of science had made this concept almost anachronistic by the start of the twentieth century. The idea was nevertheless central to the worldview of the still-present founder. It consequently became an important commitment of the institution, in spite of President Woodward's increasing exasperation with the difficulties it caused.[22] Partly as a result of this commitment, the CIW early made a policy decision to give minor grants and assistantships directly to individuals, thus cutting off any possible cooperation with the universities. While many of these grants went to professors, there seemed to be some straining to discover the hitherto unrecognized exceptional man.[23] The results of such a variegated program could not help being mixed, but it nevertheless seems evident that the CIW paid for its romanticism in this case with rather meager results.[24] Moreover, a more productive approach was clearly open to them. William Welch, dean of the Johns Hopkins Medical School and a chief organizer of the RIMR, had recommended initially that the CIW choose as grantees

> a) those who have demonstrated by published work their capacity to initiate and conduct original scientific investigations; [and]
> b) those recommended by heads of laboratories who have established reputations as investigators to carry on specified researches under their direction.[25]

These, of course, are the classic pathways of professional recognition. Their incorporation at the outset would have led to a close working relationship between the CIW and the universities and would have promoted the advancement of science through university-based disciplines.

One conspicuous case in which the CIW did work through universities ended badly. Its Department of Economics and Sociology launched an ambitious plan for a social and economic history of the United States and farmed out most of the actual investigations to researchers in universities. When the director died in 1909, however, it was discovered that much of this work was poorly done and generally unreliable. Although the fault lay with the director of the program, this case seemed to confirm President Woodward's convictions about the desirability of separating teaching from research.26 Despite this unshakable belief, however, over the long run Woodward could not keep the CIW entirely separate from the university world.27

It became increasingly clear to Woodward that the wastefulness of the grants to exceptional men or the missteps of the Department of Economics and Sociology fiasco could be eliminated only by a reliance on "investigators of known competence." As early as 1906 he proposed replacing the minor grants and assistantships with "research associates," chosen from among proven leaders in their fields.28 These men, of course, were to be found in the universities. As Woodward gradually implemented this policy over the next ten years, the CIW established closer connections with university research, even as it continued its own major in-house programs. The institution learned, for example, in the case of T. H. Morgan's genetics research, that it had to cooperate with established university research projects rather than foster rivals that would compete with them.29 As for the elusive exceptional man, "by 1916 he had clearly become the proven specialist within an established discipline."30 By World War I, then, a network of university-based research associates, advising the institution in their specialties and occasionally receiving support themselves, had largely integrated the CIW with the university research community. The inexorability of this development says much about the research system existing in the United States at the beginning of the century.

One of the arguments frequently iterated at the time of the founding of the CIW was the need to boost the prestige of American science through the leadership of a central scientific institution in the nation's capital. The astronomer Simon Newcomb, Cattell, and others saw this as the chief contribution that the CIW might make.31 While the institution can by no means be termed a failure, this was an expectation that it clearly did not fulfill. The leadership of science had by 1900 become too entrenched in the research universities to be usurped by independent research institutions. The resources of these new organizations seemed impressive at the outset; however, their reliance upon a single source of capital—even the capital of a Carnegie or a Rockefeller—placed a limit on the role they might fill. Carnegie added gifts of $2 million and $10 million to the initial CIW endowment, and Rockefeller eventually gave a total of $65 million to the RIMR; but the inherent expansiveness of scientific inquiry caused most of these additional resources to be channeled into their established programs. In the final analysis, the large and decentralized university system possessed a resource of even greater value to science in the talents of its numerous faculty. This reality ultimately determined the course of development taken by the independent research institutions.

First, the logic of their situation dictated that the independent research institutions concentrate their efforts in a limited number of specialized areas. Since the basic disciplines were receiving wide coverage in the universities and since the research institutions wished to avoid duplication, there seem to have been few alternatives. In the case of the CIW, the constraints upon basic research in the government and the atypical outlook of its leadership apparently drew it toward topics that originally were similar to the concerns of government scientific bureaus. In these domains the CIW formula for intensive, cooperative research achieved notable results.

Second, the strength of university science made the rapprochement just described inescapable in the long run. The dynamics of scientific knowledge meant that some major projects of the CIW, like the work on heredity at Cold Spring Harbor, would eventually intersect with university research in the same or neighboring fields. For minor grants, dispersed widely over many specialties, the CIW ultimately had to turn to university experts who alone were capable of evaluating competence in recondite fields. The RIMR differed in the sense that it led rather than followed university research in the medical sciences. Its assimilation into university science thus occurred later and under somewhat different circumstances, but the final result was the same. By the 1950s, when research had become the norm instead of the exception in university medical schools, the RIMR dropped its exceptional status by reorganizing as a faculty for graduate training and research in medicine and biological science.

Both the RIMR and the CIW became permanent fixtures in the firmament of American science, able to claim many scientific accomplishments in their chosen fields. Nevertheless, their early histories presaged the fact that independent research institutions would not become the organizational model for American science. Instead, the second decade of the twentieth century witnessed the establishment of the great general-purpose foundations of Rockefeller and Carnegie, which sought to promote the advancement of knowledge by a variety of means. In the 1920s they would make the research universities important adjuncts to their activities. Other independent research organizations would later be chartered, but they would for the most part have rather specific and often practical aims. In addition, they would usually be coordinated with university research.[32] During the first two decades of this century the universities were becoming the predominant homes for basic science. Yet, unlike government bureaus or endowed research institutions, the universities had few resources specifically designated for the support of research. Sustaining their commitments to the advancement of knowledge, then, presented a continual problem.

2. Resources for University Research: The Treatment of Faculty

Universities do not perform research, of course; individuals do. The conduct of research requires time and, depending on the subject, varying amounts of material resources. For a university's capacity to foster faculty research, both of these requirements presented parallel considerations. The inevitable mixture of teaching and research at all American universities meant that a certain portion of the needed resources was simply embedded in the makeup of the institution. With respect to faculty time, the portion available for research was inversely related to the teaching load. With respect to material resources, the research potential was inherent in the physical size and design of laboratories, the collections in the library, or even the provision of faculty offices. Beyond these considerations, however, lay the problem of resources explicitly required for research. These consisted chiefly of incremental expenditures clearly distinguishable from the cost of everyday university operations—faculty time specifically set aside for research, special equipment or collections, travel necessitated by research purposes, or personnel needed for supporting services.

These two types of requirements presented problems of a different order for research universities as they developed. Embedded resources depended heavily, in the long run, upon the overall level of university wealth. This is not to deny that hard choices were often involved—that some universities were more willing than others to sacrifice campus amenities to the goal of the advancement of knowledge. Rather, it is simply to highlight the inescapable fact that low teaching loads, space for faculty research, up-to-date laboratories, and large libraries first required the availability of ample institutional resources, and only then decisions about deployment. Incremental resources were different because they could not be lumped into the general mission of the university and into its general operating budget. Even wealthy institutions were exceedingly wary of making large or lasting commitments of discretionary funds purely for the furtherance of individual research—and for good reason. They lacked income for these purposes; there was an inherent problem of equitable distribution; and such needs had no foreseeable limits. An unspoken understanding consequently existed before the turn of the century that the needs of research-minded faculty would have to be funded from extramural sources. More often than not, this meant that individual professors paid their own extra research expenses, but minor forms of patronage, it will be seen, were commonplace.

With the maturation of research universities early in the twentieth century, the problem of specific support for university research increasingly came to the fore. A latent inconsistency, occasionally noted by university presidents themselves, existed between the ringing endorsements of research as a general university goal and faculty time outside the classroom available to realize that goal. Furthermore, the rising costs of research after 1900, particularly in the natural sciences, placed an ever-growing strain upon the ad hoc means and informal channels of raising such funds. The universities responded to these pressures with a variety of innovations, just as the creation of endowed research institutes outside the universities was also a response to a rapidly evolving research system. Although the theoretical possibilities for accommodating research may have been numerous, they were not all consistent with the realities of the American university. In the first two decades of the century the concrete experiences of the research universities winnowed these possible adaptations down to a few alternatives. This process can be seen first in the treatment of faculty and then, in the section to follow, in the matter of material resources for research.

"The American university is emphatically a teaching university," stated David Starr Jordan in 1906.[1] And, indeed, compared with the emphasis on examinations in British and French universities or with the scope allowed for research in German institutions, this was certainly true. American students entered the university with far less preparation than their European counterparts and were consequently far more dependent upon their mentors for basic instruction. The characteristic American form of certification that emerged in this period reflected the centrality of the teaching imperative: credit hours testified to the volume of instruction received, while letter grades signified the extent to which the material may have been learned.[2] A recurrent dream of American university builders was to jettison a major portion of this teaching burden in order to orient the universities more definitely toward research. During the height of German university influence, it was common to equate "true" university work with the graduate level of American higher education. This spirit was evident at the founding of Johns Hopkins and was explicitly behind G. Stanley Hall's unsuccessful effort to establish Clark as a graduate university. Later university reformers would scheme to separate the freshman and sophomore years from the advanced work of the university, but to no avail. Undergraduate education was too essential to the overall functioning of the university to be sacrificed to the interests of research. Instead, as was seen in Chapter 1, enrollment growth was welcomed as both a sign of institutional success and a necessary means for justifying a larger and more specialized faculty. In addition, growth frequently involved innovations like summer sessions and professional schools that tended to increase faculty teaching obligations. For most faculty at most universities, doing research became possible only after their teaching responsibilities were fulfilled. As a consequence, "one of the most difficult of modern university problems" for President Eliot and other university leaders was "to determine the just relation between instruction and research."[3]

The crux of the problem was the basic teaching load of faculty at research universities. Even when these loads can be determined, however, there is considerable uncertainty regarding their meaning. A 1908 survey by the Carnegie Foundation for the Advancement of Teaching (CFAT) of hours actually spent in classroom teaching noted all the appropriate caveats: classroom hours do not reflect time spent in preparation beforehand or with students afterward; different kinds of classes require varying amounts of work; and classroom hours alone cannot reveal the burden of teaching large numbers of students. Nevertheless, the figures reported by the CFAT still shed some light on this situation.[4]

Most striking is the pronounced disparity in teaching loads between colleges and research universities. Faculty in the latter averaged from eight to ten hours of teaching per week (nonlaboratory subjects), while their counterparts in well-established liberal arts colleges (i.e., Carnegie-accepted) were professing from fifteen to eighteen hours. To the survey's authors this represented "a difference in kind of work" that existed by this date between the two settings.[5] A certain amount of research time was already built into faculty positions at research universities. A second conclusion of this survey was that teaching loads tended to be fairly comparable across subjects in a given institution. The somewhat wider discrepancies between research universities, then, probably represent differences in both the composition of teaching responsibilities and the attitudes toward instruction in different institutions. Johns Hopkins, for example, with its predominance of graduate students, had the lowest reported teaching load among research universities, while conservative Yale had the highest. The University of Chicago was unusual in placing an explicit limit on teaching loads. In the original general regulations of the university, it was specified that each faculty member "shall lecture thirty-six weeks of the year, ten to twelve hours a week; no instructor shall be required to lecture more than this amount."[6] When this policy was promulgated in 1892, Chicago was undoubtedly well in advance of comparable universities, but only a decade and a half later this standard was equaled or surpassed by other research universities.

Another inquiry into teaching loads revealed that by 1920 some differentiation was taking place among research universities. The most prestigious universities that attracted the greatest number of graduate students, which were by and large the wealthiest institutions as well, required their faculty to teach from six to eight hours per week. In other research universities ten to twelve hours was a more likely load. The authors concluded that "to require no more than six to eight hours of teaching from a professor . . . is, therefore, already in the United States a mark of first class practice."[7] Clearly in this class were Columbia, Cornell, and Harvard; California and Chicago met this standard for faculty doing graduate teaching; while Stanford, Yale, and, perhaps, Michigan barely qualified for inclusion. By this juncture, then, these schools were granting their faculty an amount of time for research that other universities were not capable of matching.

Student/faculty ratios offer another perspective on teaching burdens, although some caveats are in order here as well.[8] First, because different institutions represent rather different mixtures of teaching responsibilities, comparisons of any single university over time may be more meaningful than those of different universities for a given year. For example, the existence of large medical schools at Penn and Johns Hopkins (after 1893) certainly helped to lower their ratios; and the same is probably true for the high proportion of technical education at Illinois, Cornell, and MIT.

Second, surges of enrollment do not necessarily coincide in the short run with conditions for faculty enlargement. A good case in point is the aftermath of World War I, when enrollments mushroomed before universities had recovered from their financial problems. The figures for public universities appear to be somewhat more volatile, indicating that they had less control over their resources and student numbers. Finally, because teaching methods change as class size increases, it is by no means certain that the larger classes implied by higher student/faculty ratios necessarily meant greater teaching burdens. A survey of faculty at the University of Chicago reported that classes of twenty to twenty-nine students claimed the largest amount of instructor time, and that the time requirements fell for classes that were either smaller or larger.[9] Nevertheless, the overall change in student/faculty ratios seems consistent with the relatively small teaching loads at research universities.

A significant transformation in the teaching load took place in these universities between 1890 and 1910. Even though enrollments grew enormously during these years, the number of faculty grew even faster. The number of students per teacher was halved at Princeton and Cornell and reduced by a third at Illinois, Michigan, Harvard, and MIT. Reductions were significant at Columbia, Yale, and Hopkins as well; at the others fairly stable ratios implied a large absolute growth in faculty numbers. It is probable that this transformation produced a reduction in the teaching burden of the average faculty member and thus increased the time available for individual research. By 1910, however, this movement was largely completed. In the next twenty years a certain amount of backsliding seems to have taken place, most notably at Columbia and Harvard. More significant, though, is a growing standardization between similar institutions. The discrepancies among public research universities is smaller in 1930 than at any prior time. Among private research universities, more heterogeneous by nature, the 1930 differences are smaller still. Overall, then, this suggests that the basic faculty responsibilities for teaching duties and potential research time were quite firmly established during the first decade of the century. Still, this conclusion does not settle the underlying issue: how much teaching was too much teaching?

From the viewpoint of the scientific community the teaching burden imposed by American universities was a continual obstacle to the pursuit of research. At least six of the disciplinary advisory committees set up by the Carnegie Institution of Washington in 1902, for example, recommended measures for freeing faculty from classroom duties.[10] T. W. Richards of Harvard considered this need so acute that he prepared a minority chemistry report to stress the point. His assessment was as follows:

> In a few great universities some at least of the professors are given time for research. . . . But this freedom is the exception rather than the rule. Not only are most American professors overburdened with routine work, but nearly all are obliged, by the inadequacy of their salaries, to consume time and energy in hack work. . . .[11]

An informed estimate for physics around the turn of the century suggests that professors might expect one-fifth, and assistant professors one-fourth, of their time to be occupied in research. For all categories of personnel, American physicists had significantly less research time than their counterparts in Germany, France, and Great Britain.[12] A sampling of the views of assistant professors in research universities at the end of the decade (1910) revealed a situation that was perhaps less dire than the one portrayed by Richards: the respondents divided evenly over the question of whether their own conditions for research and advanced work were satisfactory or unsatisfactory.[13]

The ambiguity of the assistant professors' responses merely underscores the fact that the problem of adequate faculty research time was only partly resolved in the first decade of the century. Moreover, there was another side to the issue. After the pronounced emphasis on university research in the last decades of the nineteenth century, the years after 1900 saw a recrudescence of a cultural emphasis in undergraduate instruction. "The Ph.D. Octopus," by William James, set the tone for a literature that scorned the pedantry and pretentiousness of the Germanic approach to university research. At the same time the movement for liberal culture gave new purpose and stature to undergraduate education.[14] The first decade of the century, then, witnessed an intermittent debate between those who thought the university should place more emphasis on teaching and scholars who demanded a greater accommodation of research.

The individuals most affected by this conflict were undoubtedly the small fraternity of research university presidents. As a requirement of office they were virtually compelled to embrace both research and teaching ideals. They further believed that the two could and should be united. In reality, however, they were being pulled in opposite directions. In the background stood the new endowed research institutes, representing total dedication to research and occasionally luring away their top scientists.[15] The institutions over which they presided, on the other hand, derived their sustenance from the teaching they supplied. In their discussions together at Association of American Universities meetings, or in the everyday tasks of administering their universities, one of the foremost problems faced by university presidents was to find ways to encourage and support faculty research in "teaching universities."

The crosscurrents surrounding this problem were evident in the controversial issue of research professorships. To create such extraordinary positions amounted to a policy of specialization, although it was never actually phrased that way: have the "research man," in the parlance of the day, devote all his time to investigation; and conversely, though not necessarily, have a corps of "teaching men" fully employed in instruction. Although such an explicit division of function may sound incongruous, there were actually enough innovations of this sort in the first decades of the century for specialization to be considered an experiment performed. The results reveal much about the predicament of faculty research.

As background to this question it should be noted that teaching loads were not generally standardized within institutions or even within departments. President Charles R. Van Hise of Wisconsin took pride in pointing out that teaching responsibilities were adjusted according to the personal capabilities of each faculty member:

> At Wisconsin there is no fixed amount of instructional work required from a professor. The quantity of this work varies greatly. Where in the faculty there is a man who is not a productive scholar, he is likely to have a rather heavy instructional work. Where, upon the other hand, there is a man who is doing things, he has large liberty as to the amount of instructional work he carries.[16]

This undoubtedly reflected the general practice at research universities. In fact, when the subject arose, the presidents strongly opposed the substitution of standards or norms for this kind of individualized treatment.[17] Before the turn of the century pure research positions had been created, but on those occasions they were intended for junior faculty. The rank of "docent"—an approximation of the German *Privatdozent*—was tried at Hopkins, Clark, and Chicago, but did not endure.[18] The post of research professor was more permanent, more conspicuous, and considerably more costly. When such appointments were discussed by the AAU in 1906 the opinion of university presidents was decidedly negative, although not for those reasons. Rather, they felt that research professorships violated the unity of teaching and research to which they were strongly committed.[19] In this light, one might wonder why such positions were created by some of these same men.

In general, the existence of research professorships is explained by the stature of the men who held them—scholars of considerable renown, often sought by more than one institution. Thus, the flamboyant psychologist Edward Titchener was allowed to devote himself exclusively to research and graduate work at Cornell; when Stanford made an offer to the historian Frederick Jackson Turner, Wisconsin countered by allowing him half time free for research; and the biologist Jacques Loeb was lured to California by the offer of a research professorship.[20] Most such appointments, however, seem to have ended badly; and the special treatment the incumbents received appears to be the root cause of this. Two research chairs awarded by Chicago, and one of two at Ohio State, were abandoned by their holders. Turner's favored treatment caused such acrimony with the Wisconsin regents that it prompted his departure for Harvard only two years later (1910). In the same year, Loeb fled to the Rockefeller Institute because, as he put it, his "colleagues, and very soon the community and the newspapers, quickly resented the idea that [he] should receive full pay and do little teaching." Loeb's conclusion—"in a democracy today there is as yet no room in a state university for pure research"—was obviously too sweeping.[21] But research professorships were nevertheless not to be the means for promoting research in American universities. Instead, they were no more than extraordinary arrangements for exceptional individuals and unusual circumstances.[22]

The other side of this coin—specialized teaching posts—also made little headway. Periodic suggestions that pure teaching professorships be created to counter undue emphasis on research were superfluous, since most universities already had numerous faculty of that type.[23] President Van Hise, whose announced policy was to require productive scholarship for appointments and promotions, found when he surveyed his faculty that more than one-third engaged in no research at all. Again, there is no reason to regard Wisconsin as atypical in this respect. A far more interesting application of specialization in teaching occurred at Princeton. The decision by President Woodrow Wilson and Dean Andrew F. West to enlarge the faculty with a special corps of undergraduate tutors, called preceptors, directly contradicted trends at other research universities. The intense and intimate instruction that these arrangements were intended to facilitate suited the distinctive aspirations of Princeton but also had the potential of creating a special class of faculty set apart from the professional community of scholars.[24] This was just the situation that research universities increasingly wished to avoid.

The decisive trend working against the specialization of faculty functions was the development of democratic university departments. As the locus of disciplinary authority in universities, the department represented a unitary system of values shared by all members concerning the advancement of knowledge. As permanent department heads were increasingly replaced by rotating chairmen, and as assistant professors gained a voice in departmental matters, departments were inexorably pressured to treat all members equitably.[25] This implied not that treatment be equal with respect to teaching and research but rather that each member at least be given some opportunity to pursue research. At Princeton, for example, the preceptorial system was quickly made compatible with these imperatives by the requirement that all departmental members serve as preceptors.[26]

The fundamental problem of the American research university thus became that of finding the means for providing every faculty member with some chance to contribute to the advancement of knowledge—not to mention the advancement of his own professional career. Innovations that failed this test of equity were simply not imitated and consequently were relegated to a marginal position in the university system. Thus, research professorships attained only a toehold in universities, either in subjects remote from undergraduate teaching or in those supported by special endowments.

More important, the view that all university teachers were entitled to the chance to do research gradually gave rise to the notion that they all had the responsibility to be productive scholars. In particular this attitude came to be directed against a type found on all research university faculties—the permanent instructor who did much teaching but no writing. In 1910 President Hadley of Yale explicitly warned,

> There is nothing more fatal to the efficiency of a department than the maintenance in its teaching force of a number of reasonably good instructors who are kept because they can teach moderately well, but who have little promise of inspiring either associates or their students to work of really high grade and who keep out from the faculty men of less experience but more promise.[27]

It is clear from these remarks that the old distinction between "teaching men" and "research men" was becoming increasingly untenable in the research universities. Yet, it would be another generation before they would fully put in place the tenure ladder that forced junior faculty to climb up or get out. Before World War I, then, there was a disjunction between faculties as they existed and faculties as research-minded presidents would have liked them to be. There was clearly a need to expand the research opportunities of faculty if these expectations were to be met, and innovations that held promise to do this had a widespread appeal. As these needs became more clearly recognized, by the second decade of the century, such mechanisms as sabbatical leaves, revolving research funds, and graduate assistantships were increasingly adopted by the research universities. They became characteristic American adaptations to the difficulty of reconciling the demands of both teaching and research.

The origin of the modern practice of sabbatical leaves can be traced back to Harvard in 1880. As part of an offer that enticed the philologist Charles Lanman away from Johns Hopkins, Eliot promised him every seventh year off with half pay. By the turn of the century this practice had spread to Columbia, Penn, and at least eight other research universities.[28] Clearly, this was a perquisite that other universities had to match in order to remain competitive in attracting and holding leading scholars. Sabbaticals at this juncture were offered only to certain established scholars and were not an entitlement of all faculty members. They were thus part of the deliberately unequal treatment of faculty condoned by Van Hise. The process by which sabbaticals spread throughout American higher education to become available to faculty in general occupies most of the twentieth century. In the research universities, however, departmental democratization soon created pressures for uniform treatment. At Yale, for example, a sabbatical policy covering all professors was announced at the same time when Hadley denounced unproductive instructors.[29] One factor that certainly impeded the utilization of sabbaticals early in the century was the precarious financial situation of faculty. Those without independent means, particularly junior faculty, could hardly afford to

sacrifice half of their annual income.[30] The widespread adoption of sabbaticals for faculty research was thus dependent upon the availability of
supplemental research funds. Systematic progress in this area began to
occur only near the end of this period.

"When funds are not set aside for special purposes they must be used
for general purposes": President Harry Pratt Judson of Chicago invoked
this principle of university finance in 1919 to argue that separate funds be
earmarked for university research.[31] In fact, the measures he urged were
already being tried. Early in the century the formation of administratively
distinct graduate schools provided one conduit for aiding research. At
Illinois, for example, the graduate school began receiving its own annual
appropriation in 1908, some of which was used for assistants, equipment,
and supplies for research.[32] A more explicit provision for research appeared at California in 1915, when $2,000 was included in the university's
budget for incidental faculty expenses related to research. Even though
this sum was subsequently increased, it remained minuscule in comparison with potential needs. To solve the problem of equitable distribution, a faculty committee was established to allot these funds. This would
seem to be an indication of growing faculty authority on research-related
matters. California's faculty-controlled research fund was clearly a precedent for other universities.[33] Only a few years later August Heckscher
bequeathed to Cornell a $500,000 endowment to be used specifically to
provide faculty with research time. Instead of creating research professorships—an alternative apparently considered—Cornell administered these
funds in much the same manner that California did. Harvard, too, preferred to utilize its research funds in this way.[34] Nevertheless, such arrangements presupposed that separate research funds were available, and
that was not ordinarily the case. An AAUP survey in 1921 could find just
nine universities with such revolving research funds.[35]

The utilization of graduate students to assist with the work of the university seems to have been a natural organizational adaptation. Graduate
students had the potential of serving as cheap, competent, and dedicated
assistants for research; and as teaching fellows they could be used to considerably lighten the most resented faculty burden—instruction in introductory courses. Moreover, students could staff these subordinate
positions without the stigma that marked those permanently relegated to
such posts. In light of these advantages, one has to wonder why graduate
assistantships did not appear sooner.

The idea behind graduate fellowships, as they were first employed at
Johns Hopkins and Clark, was to guarantee their holders the means to
devote themselves exclusively to their studies. Chicago was clearly exceptional when it required its fellows to spend one-sixth of their time in
various forms of "university service," but as a rule this did not include

teaching.[36] The true teaching fellowship is essentially a twentieth-century phenomenon. Harvard employed a large bequest to create thirty such positions in 1899, requiring their holders to teach half time. Penn and Wisconsin soon created similar positions, with teaching obligations of about five hours per week. When the AAU considered the general issue of graduate fellowships in 1906, practices differed widely among member universities. Although G. Stanley Hall castigated the practices at Harvard as a "sweating system," opinion overall seemed to favor the use of graduate students as teachers.[37] Graduate teaching fellowships certainly had practical benefits for the universities, and these undoubtedly accounted for their rapid spread after this date. By 1914 the annual payroll of enrolled students engaged in teaching or research at the University of California exceeded $100,000.[38] The utilization of graduate students soon passed from being an innovation to being an integral practice of research universities.

When all of the factors just discussed are taken into account, there can be little doubt that the trade-off between teaching and research for the average faculty member in a research university changed markedly from 1890 to 1920. First came a progressive lowering of both the number of students per professor and the number of hours spent in the classroom. For the purposes of research the latter seems to have been more important. After about 1910, student/teacher ratios rose slightly, while teaching loads appear to have continued to shrink. Larger classes and the utilization of graduate teaching fellows may have made it possible for professors simultaneously to teach more students and to have more time for research. The establishment of regular sabbaticals gave every professor an opportunity—and an implicit obligation—to do intensive research. At the end of this period the appearance of revolving research funds in several universities provided further potential assistance for faculty research. During these thirty years the American research university evolved, through trial, error, and occasional success, away from the unattainable German ideal of pure research toward a characteristically American amalgamation of university teaching and research. In this way the accommodation of faculty research became embedded in the organizational makeup of research universities. The material resources required for university research, however, remained somewhat more problematic.

3. Resources for University Research: Capital and Project Funds

The material, as opposed to the human, inputs to university research cover a broader and more diverse range of phenomena, and they, too, were crucial in the evolution of research universities. Three types of material resources can be distinguished. First, there are capital inputs to research in the form of either physical structures or special endowments. The role of these university assets was not unlike that of faculty: that is, they were generally used for both teaching and research; and, the more of them that a university had, just as the more faculty it had relative to students, the greater the capability for university research. The second category pertains to capital as well, but capital used in a special way. University research institutes were, in sharp departure from normal university practice, devoted almost exclusively to research. Although some of these units were long established, they became more numerous and prominent after the turn of the century. The third category is reserved for funds intended to be expended entirely in aiding research. Into it would fall all of the nonrecurring forms of aid that professors utilized to cover the incremental costs of investigation. These distinctions will be useful first to explicate the system of support for university research as it existed at the close of the nineteenth century and then to identify the forces of change impinging upon this system after 1900.

In 1880 an anonymous donor offered Harvard $115,000 to construct a physics laboratory, with the condition that a permanent endowment of $75,000 be raised to cover its operating expenses. The stipulated funds were soon collected, and in 1884 the Jefferson Physical Laboratory opened its doors. Harvard thus came to possess one of the country's most up-to-date facilities for experimental physics. Yet, its senior professor of physics and the laboratory's first director, Joseph Lovering, was no researcher. He has been described as feeling "no more called upon to extend the domain of physics than as a preacher he would have felt obliged to add a chapter to the Bible." [1] The Jefferson Physical Laboratory, then, resulted from the initiative and the intellectual preferences of the soon-identified donor, T. Jefferson Coolidge. In a similar step some years later he also endowed a new chemical laboratory, despite the fact that the Wolcott Gibbs Memorial Laboratory for Chemistry was then under construction.[2] Both these structures augmented Harvard's capacity for research in the physical sciences, but both were essentially the products of the initiatives of their donor.

A contrasting example can be found in the early history of the University of Chicago. President William Rainey Harper failed initially to secure the funds needed to construct a biology building, and in 1894 he would describe this lacuna as the university's single "greatest need." During the same interval Harper was courting a major gift from the heiress and philanthropist Helen Culver. Late in 1895, after lengthy behind-the-scenes machinations, she summoned Harper to inform him of her intention to make a substantial gift to the university. Her aim was to endow an art school and gallery at a location well removed from the campus. It apparently required all of Harper's considerable persuasive powers to dissuade her, first from giving such an art school, then from her second preference of creating a music school, and eventually to implant the idea of supporting biology at the University of Chicago. The end result was Hull Quadrangle (after her husband Charles J. Hull), containing ample laboratories for anatomy, physiology, botany, and zoology. In this case it was the priorities of the university, most strenuously advanced by its president, that steered the Culver donation into the service of university biological research.[3]

Private universities essentially relied on gifts for their capital needs. Columbia may have resorted to loans to construct Morningside Heights, and Harvard in 1876 reluctantly tapped its "free capital" in order to extend its library, but such steps were exceptions, to be avoided if at all possible.[4] In general, when gifts were not forthcoming, projects could be postponed: existing facilities, no matter how inadequate, could be made to suffice for the next year, the year after, and so on. The gifts that produced the Jefferson Physical Laboratory and the Hull Quadrangle stand out from the thousands of capital gifts received by American universities in the late nineteenth century chiefly because they fall near the opposite ends of a continuum that might be drawn from donor to university priorities. Most benefactions probably represented a more balanced combination of the desires of institutions and of givers. Nevertheless, universities could and did take special measures to see that particular needs were met. They could, as Harvard did in gathering the stipulated endowment for the Jefferson Laboratory, create a special fund and then solicit contributions from among the university's reliable, heavy givers. Later, in the twentieth century, it became common to include special capital needs in organized fund-raising drives. Such needs, however, included far more than research. The crucial point, then, is that a university's capacity to raise large sums of capital for research-related purposes was tied, above all, to its commitment to research objectives, and after that to the predilections of its donors.

When it came to building needs, the state universities basically had a single patron, one who had limited solicitude for university research before the turn of the century. In order to build a new laboratory, state universities would typically appeal to their state legislature on the basis of teaching needs and, if successful, construct a building that would also accommodate faculty research. State universities also appealed for private gifts, but where capital needs were concerned an implicit division of responsibility seemed to exist. The state, in its fashion, would provide for the essential university facilities, while the university had to rely upon its own exertions and its occasional large benefactors for amenities like gym-

nasiums or ceremonial halls. Capital for research purposes fell somewhere between these two spheres for most state universities in the late
nineteenth century.

Research capital was not confined to buildings, but also included endowments for professorships, laboratories, departmental expenses, and
the purchase of books. Endowed professorships had the advantage of
permitting a university to pay above-market salaries to outstanding scholars or to support esoteric subjects that would not otherwise be offered. In
these, as in nearly all forms of donations, Harvard stood ahead and apart.
In 1902 President Eliot noted that Harvard had forty endowed professorships, ten of which had been given in the preceding six years. Eliot called
these professorships "the most fundamental and permanently valuable
. . . of all University endowments," and they played no small part in
maintaining America's most distinguished faculty.[5] Elsewhere, special endowments played strategic roles in the advancement of specific areas. At
Cornell, for example, the gifts of Henry W. Sage made possible the creation of the School of Philosophy (1890), which rapidly became a major
center for graduate training, home of *Philosophical Review* (1892–), and
a center for research in experimental psychology.[6] Like the buildings just
discussed, these endowments not only served research needs but also
helped underwrite some of the basic operating expenses of the university.
However, a purer form of research capital was responsible for the none-
too-numerous examples of university institutes.

During the nineteenth century university research institutes were created for either of two purposes. One was to establish and operate an
observatory—a type of research institute, centered on an instrument, that
has become commonplace today. The second purpose, defining a more
heterogeneous category, was to preserve and utilize collections of scholarly or scientific value. Although both kinds of institutes might offer some
teaching, particularly at the graduate level, they existed essentially for
purposes of research. They would usually have a faculty member in the
capacity of director, but there would also be assistants concentrating entirely on research. Because these institutes were wholly intended for research, universities expected them to be fully supported through special
endowments and private contributions.

Harvard was far in advance of other American universities in these
kinds of arrangements. The Harvard Observatory was founded in 1844
through a public subscription, "filled largely by the merchant shipowners
of Boston." By the end of the century the various and sundry endowments
it had accumulated allowed it to support close to fifty staff members,
including two full, one associate, and two assistant professors.[7] By this
juncture it had to share the leadership in American astronomy with the
36-inch telescope at California's Lick Observatory (f. 1888) and the 40-

inch refractor at Chicago's Yerkes Observatory (f. 1898). The popular mystique of astronomy allowed university astronomers to appeal to benefactors who otherwise had little interest in science. This was certainly true of James Lick and Charles Yerkes, both eccentric self-made millionaires, but there were also exceptions. Catherine Wolfe Bruce, astronomy's most consistent and generous patron at the close of the nineteenth century, was motivated by an informed concern for the subject.[8]

The donation of collections, the buildings to house them, or endowments to care for them were more often made by individuals who were particularly concerned with their subjects. By accepting such offers, universities could sometimes be enticed into unintended and unforeseen areas. Harvard pretty well represents the gamut of possibilities for such institutions. Prior to 1900 it had established museums or endowed collections in anatomy, archaeology, several areas of botany, mineralogy, comparative zoology, and art. The status of these institutes varied widely. The well-endowed Peabody Museum of Archaeology and Ethnology became an important scientific center from the time of its establishment in the late 1860s. The Bussey Institution, however—Harvard's agricultural college and experiment station—although founded by a bequest in 1835, was by 1890 in so parlous a state that it was forced to board livestock and sell vegetables for needed income. It nevertheless improved its fortunes toward the end of the century, and in 1908 was transformed into a virtual research institute by being made a purely graduate school of applied biology.[9] The timing of this development was not atypical. The years around the turn of the century saw the founding of numerous research institutes at research universities. The University of California at this time began to benefit from an unusually rich and steady stream of research-related private gifts. Phoebe Apperson Hearst's donation established the Museum of Anthropology, and other funds set up Jacques Loeb's physiological laboratory as well as a parallel lab in anatomy.[10] Activities near the close of the century at Penn represent both the old and the new strains of university institute work. In the prestigious field of Semitic studies the Archaeology Museum conducted its most fruitful (and ultimately controversial) Babylonian Expeditions. At the same time the newly organized Wistar Institute (f. 1894) was shifting from specimen collecting to active medical research, thus foreshadowing a burgeoning field of twentieth-century institute research.[11]

The definition of a university research institute employed here has been deliberately loose in order for it to be faithful to the conditions of nineteenth-century science. Essentially, these conditions were intended for the tasks of description (the "old" astronomy), classification (botany, zoology), and preservation (archaeology, paleontology). Significantly, such subjects had both academic and nonacademic followings. They were not central to the university curriculum, so they tended to be studied by relatively few advanced or graduate students. Also, the interest these subjects attracted outside the university was largely responsible for the donations that made them possible. In subjects more central to the curriculum, like physics and chemistry, instruction and research were largely integrated prior to 1900. The nineteenth-century research institute, however, was basically an appendage to the university, made possible by the fact that it could pay its own way. After the turn of the century changes in the conduct and the funding of university research would enlarge the role of institutes but without fundamentally altering these conditions.

In the absence of special endowments, special expenditures for the conduct of normal university research tended to be problematic. Investigation in many disciplines might require expeditions, special apparatus, the purchase of collections, or the hiring of assistants. By the last decades of the century most universities made small regular contributions to their physics and chemistry labs, for example, to pay for materials consumed and the services of a mechanic or a glassblower. The projects of individuals throughout the university, however, at times encountered extraordinary needs. On these occasions an appeal was directed outside the institution to the wider university community.

Small contributions, ranging from one dollar to thousands of dollars, flowed into universities during these years to assist almost any imaginable university activity, but several general purposes were prominent. At the head of the list were donations intended for students as scholarships, prizes, loan funds, or support for extracurricular activities. Also common were gifts to assist research and, closely related, donations of books or money for the library. The following gifts are representative:

$2,500 to the history professor Charles K. Adams to buy, books (Michigan, 1883).

$1,500 for assistants' salaries, Department of Semitic Languages (Yale, 1890)

$395 for fossil fishes (Columbia, 1893)

$1,850 (four gifts) for apparatus in electrochemistry (Penn, 1900)

$250 to the physics professor Trowbridge for magnetism research (Harvard, 1900) [12]

The key to understanding this kind of support seems to be in the relationship between the university and its surrounding community. The initiative for such gifts lay predominantly with the university. There were several means by which some special need might be made known. Mention in the president's annual report or some other official utterance was a standard way of publicizing large needs and small; department heads commonly raised donations through their contacts in the community.[13] Subscriptions were sometimes organized so that small gifts from large numbers of people could accomplish some objective. On most subscription lists one would find the names of university officers along with many regular supporters of the university. This strongly suggests that the leadership of prominent citizens acting through existing social networks was the true basis of this kind of fund-raising. It follows that the size of the university-connected community would be an important factor in the amount of support that might be tapped in this fashion. Harvard clearly outdid all other universities in this respect, and by the turn of the century California was also receiving a broad array of research-related gifts. Columbia, Penn, and, later, Chicago capitalized on their metropolitan locations to find numerous benefactors as well, whereas the comparatively small number of gifts to Cornell and Michigan may indicate the limitations of small college towns.

The voluntary support received by university libraries deserves special mention. They were for all practical purposes the laboratories of the humanities, and gifts to augment their collections served to enhance the university's capacity for scholarship. Although large capital gifts were occasionally made to libraries, most giving was of the same small, piecemeal character as the donations to research just mentioned. The preferences of donors were frequently evident in library gifts: people gave collections of books that they had accumulated, acted as patrons to their special areas of interest, or memorialized the intellectual tastes of their departed kin. For those without such guidelines, a common form of giving was simply to provide a sum for the purchase of books. University libraries also organized subscriptions to purchase collections that were particularly sought. Private universities depended heavily upon donations to build their collections. For example, two-thirds of the book purchases at Columbia in 1903 were financed through eleven donated funds. In addition 319 individuals gave books or pamphlets to the library that year. The largest university library, Harvard's, was completely supported by donated funds during the first half of the 1890s, and even after that endowments and gifts managed to finance all book purchases.[14]

When the material resources funneled into university research at the end of the nineteenth century are viewed as a whole, it becomes apparent that credit should be extended far beyond those individuals whose names are emblazoned over the doors of university laboratories and institutes. The university research role in fact enjoyed widespread grass-roots support from the middle and upper classes of the communities in which they were located. Some of these benefactors were alumni; others might be acquainted with university officers or department heads through local social or service organizations; and members of the university who could afford it were themselves frequent contributors. It would go well beyond the scope of this study to attempt to re-create the web of social relations that lay behind this type of giving. Nevertheless, it seems safe to hypothesize that such donations were based on informal personal suggestions or requests, rather than on the kind of organized fund-raising that developed in the twentieth century. These two forms, in fact, are fundamentally incompatible, since organized fund-raising largely preempts the philanthropic potential of large donors. It will become evident later, however, that this was only one reason why the nineteenth-century pattern of individual voluntary support for research was inadequate for twentieth-century research needs. More serious was the fact that such support flowed into the universities at irregular intervals and in uncertain amounts. How, then, could such a system support the expanding needs of modern science and scholarship? In actuality, the answer to this question was long masked by the spectacular prosperity of the research universities.

The years around the turn of the century witnessed a subtle yet significant shift in the arrangements for university research that have just been described. Perhaps the principal underlying cause was the steep escalation in the cost of conducting research in the natural sciences. Through the 1880s there was relatively little disparity between the needs of science and humanities departments, but this began to change in the 1890s, and dramatically so in the twentieth century. The sciences required greater space for laboratory instruction, numberous assistants, and increasingly expensive materials and apparatus.[15] In some cases research came to be conducted on an unprecedented scale. The term *Grosswissenschaft* was coined in Germany in the 1890s, and by 1900 it would certainly apply to America's three leading university observatories.[16] The Carnegie Institution would soon extend Big Science into geological research as well. The appearance of independent research institutes at the beginning of the century was in fact symptomatic of this shift, since their inspiration sprang from serious doubts about the scientific capacity of American universities as then organized. These trends provoked an ongoing concern with the organization and finance of university research.

In 1911 President Hadley reviewed the spiraling costs of science at Yale during the preceding decade. Yale's scientific units, which had formerly been nearly self-supporting, were now presenting significant and increasing charges to general university revenues. For the Sheffield Scientific School these costs rose from zero in 1901 to $25,000 in 1911; for the Peabody Museum the increase was from $5,500 to $16,000; and for the Medical School, from $1,500 to $24,000. The reasons Hadley gave for this spiral were familiar—more assistants and more costly equipment were required, while scientists were demanding higher salaries and greater relief from classroom duties. In particular, Hadley believed that "competition for the services of scientific men [was] more acute than it [had been]," chiefly because the western state universities and the independent research institutes had bid up salaries. Given the mode of research support then prevalent, only one solution to this problem seemed possible: "the research of a university should be as far as possible endowed research."[17] Yale would have to increase its endowments for these areas.

During the first decade of the century the presidents of the other research universities had independently come to the same conclusion. Charles Eliot in 1901 stated, "It is clear that men of means, who reflect on the uses and results of educational endowments, are more and more inclined to endow research" (his exemplar was T. Jefferson Coolidge). He then proceeded to describe the current needs of Harvard for philosophy, psychology, astronomy, Latin American research, archaeology, Semitic studies, mineralogy, and the art museum.[18] This approach was by no means restricted to the private universities. President Van Hise in 1905 looked forward to private donations sustaining research in state universities. Noting that the great gifts to private universities were a phenomenon of only the past generation, and mindful of California's recent success, Van Hise felt that it was just a matter of time until state universities had a numerous and, in part, wealthy body of alumni, as well as large local accumulations of capital, from which to draw support.[19]

Probably the most ambitious and explicit plan for endowing research was formulated in 1910 by President Jacob Gould Schurman of Cornell. Complaining that "the demand for scientific investigators, for laboratories, and for the instrumentalities of research come to the president from all departments," he invited contemporary millionaires to contribute $1 million to $3 million in endowment for each of seven departments.[20] In effect, he was asking for a sum greater than twice Cornell's existing endowment (approximating, in fact, the entire Harvard endowment of 1910) for what would substantially be support for departmental research. Schurman concluded his report by adding that Cornell also needed dormitories, a gymnasium, and an auditorium. Similarly, Eliot had followed his earlier plea for research endowment by specifically requesting endowments for several new buildings under construction. The research universities needed funds for more than just research, and that seems to have been the crux of the problem.

Schurman failed to line up obliging millionaires for his grandiose plan, although the $500,000 Heckscher Research Fund donated almost a decade later may have been an echo of his aspirations. Wisconsin benefited from some private giving, but nothing like the amount Van Hise had envisioned, and considerably less than other state research universities.

Even at Harvard, the flow of philanthropy could not always be directed toward the immediate needs of the university. After the turn of the century its two reiterated research-related needs were for a new library to house Harvard's incomparable holdings, and a chemical laboratory to replace overcrowded Boylston Hall. It was not until 1912, however, that the gift of Mrs. George D. Widener made possible the construction of the long-awaited library, and an adequate chemical building had to await the campaign of 1926.[21]

It was inevitable that the need for research capital would eventually be crowded by the other needs of the university. Although the organizational success of the research university depended heavily upon its being all things to all people, there was a point at which choices had to be made concerning which needs would be publicized in the annual report, emphasized in pleas to state legislators, or urged upon a wavering Helen Culver. University initiatives were important for channeling some research-related gifts before 1900, as has been seen, but they became more important after that date as fund-raising became increasingly organized. University presidents periodically took up the cudgel for research in their appeals, but the demands stemming from the university's paramount teaching responsibilities could hardly be ignored. The steady growth of student numbers required more faculty, facilities, and, for private universities, unrestricted endowment to support them. University presidents were more likely to make their appeals for campus buildings, or for unrestricted income, than for research per se.

The negative implications of this situation for university research were nevertheless long offset by the trends in university finance described in the preceding chapter. The first fifteen years of the century were in general a period of spectacular prosperity for the research universities. The private ones found large donors in ever-increasing numbers, even as their alumni became more numerous and more devoted to alma mater. The state research universities benefited from a rapidly expanding tax base as well as from good relations with their state legislatures. During these years research universities were consequently able to build the new laboratories demanded by their scientists, to reduce the teaching burden on their scholars, and to compete with one another, as Hadley had complained, by offering "scientific men" higher salaries and better conditions for research. As a result, the research imperative was more irrevocably entrenched in these universities by the outbreak of World War I than it had been in 1900. It was only then that the existing system of research support began to show evidence of strain.

The building boom that took place in the research universities during the first decade and a half of this century brought substantial additions to laboratories, libraries, and other basic university resources that increased their capacity for research.[22] The expansion of facilities was most spectacular for the state universities, amounting to more than a quadrupling of physical assets in these fifteen years. The private universities were on the whole more fully developed in 1900, but they still increased the value of their buildings and grounds by some 200 to 350 percent. A more direct indication of research resources might be the value of books and scientific equipment. For this the state universities showed a fivefold increase from 1900 to 1915, while the private universities averaged a threefold rise. Although these figures are obviously imprecise, there can be no doubt about the meaning of such quantum jumps in embedded university research capital, especially during a period of relatively stable prices. The existing system of university financing worked admirably in these years to augment the means available for faculty research.

University research institutes continued to be established after the turn of the century in much the same manner as before. They were adventitious in the sense that they relied upon large supporting endowments, and their focus was generally on areas distant from the undergraduate curriculum. The University of California in 1912–13, for example, was the recipient of two such institutes. The Scripps Institution of Oceanography, which had been organized at La Jolla in 1901, was transferred to the control of the university; and the donation of more than $1 million worth of timber lands established the George W. Hooper Foundation for Medical Research.[23]

One university research institute founded in this period differed significantly from the others, but its unusualness, like the unsuccessful innovation of research professorships, tended to confirm the dominant American pattern. The chemist Arthur A. Noyes sought to relieve his heavy teaching burdens at MIT by creating a German-style research institute. In 1901 he offered to finance personally half of the expenses of an institute if MIT would contribute the rest. In a major policy reorientation in favor of basic research, MIT agreed in 1903 to the establishment of the Research Laboratory of Physical Chemistry. A catalyst in this decision seems to have been the promise of project support from the newly organized CIW (one of its infrequent early contributions to university-based research). From then until the war the laboratory derived about equal thirds of its budget from Noyes's personal funds, from the operating budget of MIT, and from other benefactors (chiefly the CIW).[24]

From the perspective of research funding the result was a curious anomaly. The Research Laboratory of Physical Chemistry was at once ahead of its time in looking to foundation support, behind the times with respect to personal investigator financing, and against its own times in its dependence upon regular institutional support. In many respects Noyes's laboratory was more like a German than an American institute. It was

financed through an annual flow of contributions and appropriations instead of from endowment income. The circumstances of its creation made
it very much like a personal institute rather than an institutional fixture,
and its subject was close to the undergraduate curriculum. In the long run
these factors made it vulnerable to departmental and institutional politics.
It and other research institutes at MIT eventually conformed to the standard pattern of complete reliance on external funding.[25]

Even while the research universities were gaining strength and maturity
in the years before the First World War, the competition was intensifying
for both research captial and current research support. Furthermore, this
competition emanated from within the university itself.

In no single area was the rise of university research so swift and so
dramatic as in the medical schools.[26] At the beginning of the century
almost all of the 160 existing medical schools in the country existed formally or practically as proprietary institutions. Whether nominally affiliated with a university or entirely independent, they relied upon tuition
fees from their fairly numerous students, not all of whom stayed the
course, to cover their expenses and to provide some extra income for the
practitioner-teachers who controlled them. Students were admitted with
high school diplomas or less, and the schools were wholly devoted to
instruction.

The opening of the Johns Hopkins Medical School in 1893 was almost
as portentous for medical education in the United States as the Johns
Hopkins University had been for American higher education in 1876. It
required a bachelor's degree for admission, offered laboratory work with
full-time faculty in both preclinical and clinical subjects, and emphasized
medical research. At this juncture only the Harvard Medical School was
in a position to match these standards, and it soon imitated the Hopkins
admissions requirement. This example graudally set off a wave of reform
at other university medical schools that had two mutually reinforcing
themes. There was a widespread desire to raise entrance requirements to
the level of one or two years of college work. It was equally imperative to
strengthen instruction by offering laboratory courses in basic preclinical
subjects, such as anatomy, physiology, and biochemistry.

In general, the process of reform proceeded rapidly through three pha-
ses. Higher entrance requirements coupled with preclinical laboratory
courses taught by full-time scientists destroyed the financial viability of
the old-style medical schools. Enrollments plunged, while expenses rose.
The resulting financial crisis then precipitated a struggle for control of the
schools. The clinical practitioners who had hitherto governed the schools
and controlled appointments were challenged by the younger research-
oriented faculty in the preclinical disciplines, whose cause was generally
seconded by the research universities. Many university medical schools

had reached or surpassed this stage by 1910, when Abraham Flexner issued his Carnegie Foundation *Report on Medical Education in the United States and Canada*. The report, and Flexner's subsequent activities at the General Education Board, further hastened the evolution of the medical schools. By this time, however, the implicit competition between research universities, particularly their reflexive emulation of higher intellectual standards, had already brought them to the final phase of this process. As the price of financial rescue, the practitioners relinquished control of the medical schools and hospitals to the universities, which were committed to consummating the reform program. The universities thus undertook the responsibility of reorganizing medical education on an unprecedented scale. All of the preclinical medical subjects would henceforth be organized as research-intensive departments and staffed primarily by full-time faculty. An immense amount of capital was suddenly needed to provide the laboratories, hospitals, faculty, and their corresponding endowments, all necessary to teach medicine on this new basis.

The transformation of medical education thus brought all those research universities having medical schools to the same moment of choice. As President Hadley described Yale's situation in 1912,

the time has come for definite decision of the question whether Yale Medical School is to be an effective center of medical teaching and research, or a group of a few inadequately endowed laboratories and casual students. If Yale is to go on teaching medicine, she ought to teach it well.[27]

Yale took the plunge in 1913 by taking over control of New Haven Hospital and pledging to raise $2.5 million in endowment to place its future on a solid financial base. Other schools made similar commitments as circumstances, and some notably large benefactions, permitted.[28] Only where a medical school was not yet a part of the university could there be serious doubts about this course. At Stanford the incorporation of Cooper Medical College was perceived as likely to overburden the financial resources of the university. Its development was nevertheless pursued by the trustees, despite the unanimous opposition of the faculty and President John Caspar Branner. The trustees ultimately emphasized their resolve in this matter by making the medical school dean, Ray Lyman Wilbur, the next president of the university; but the upshot of this episode was to force Stanford for the first time to seek to expand its income.[29]

The battle lines at Stanford in part attest to the strong and growing support that medicine was capable of generating outside of the immediate academic community. Prior to reform the medical schools were the province of groups of well-to-do physicians and thus were not, as Charles Eliot had noted, appropriate objects for public philanthropy.[30] After 1910, and in some cases sooner, reformed and research-minded medical schools became the most attractive single area for major university gifts. Strategic million-dollar gifts played an essential role at most of the private universities by permitting the reorganization of the medical school on an endowed basis, furnishing needed facilities, and forging a link with a teaching hospital. Medicine also stands out as one area where public universities have consistently been able to attract significant amounts of voluntary support. Finally, much of the money donated to university medical schools was designated specifically for research. The Hooper Foundation at California (1913), the George Crocker bequest to Columbia for cancer research (1911), and the Joseph DeLamar bequests to Harvard (1919) and Johns Hopkins (1920) all stand out because of their magnitude, but they were by no means alone.

The research universities played a crucial role in the evolution of American medical schools by providing the academic leadership, the cadres of scientists, and the means for raising necessary capital. All these factors were needed to transform medical schools from loosely affiliated proprietary institutions into academic units of the universities. The completion of this process in the second decade of the century produced a new and different entity. University medical schools became perhaps the most self-contained compartments in already compartmentalized universities. They also maintained the highest research overhead of all teaching units. Henceforth, their insatiable needs for capital and income would have to be factored into university fund-raising plans.

Something like the opposite seems to have occurred with respect to the numerous small gifts for research-related purposes. These donations appear to have accelerated after 1900 along with other forms of university giving. If anything, the first decade of the twentieth century was probably the heyday of this kind of piecemeal support for university research. The growing size and affluence of the greater university community, together with the high prestige of the universities themselves, are probably sufficient to account for this. Although evidence for this kind of a phenomenon is difficult to interpret, it seems likely that the importance of grass-roots support for university science steadily declined after about 1910. The number of individual gifts seems to have decreased, even though a few of them assumed larger magnitudes. Gifts in kind to libraries and museums were somewhat less affected. At Harvard a significant number of donors continued to support research, along with everything else. Overall, however, it seems safe to conclude that this type of income failed to keep pace with university giving in general, the expansion of the greater university community, or the needs of university investigators.

Changes in the nature of the university itself probably account for this development. The increasingly organized character of university fund-raising may have helped to squeeze out those ad hoc, idiosyncratic appeals. The most highly organized university in this respect, Yale, had correspondingly low contributions to research. In 1912–13, for example, none of the individual gifts to income was designated to support the university's research role, but 3,605 individuals did contribute to the alumni fund. This pattern clearly suited the Yale treasurer, who remarked,

> A comparatively small number of [graduates], perhaps, can interest themselves actively in some particular phase of the University's work or attempt to endow or finance any single project. No graduate, however, is excluded from participation in the great work of the Alumni University Fund Association. . . .[31]

The research universities were undergoing a subtle transformation of their social relations during these years. As departments became larger, more self-contained, and more professionalized, it indeed became more difficult for outsiders to "interest themselves actively" in departmental affairs. At the same time it seems likely that the social networks linking faculty and community leaders were slowly deteriorating between the 1890s and World War I. President Wilbur of Stanford, addressing a different matter in 1921 (faculty housing), unwittingly testified to this development:

> It is wise . . . that [faculty] and their children are not brought in social competition with those of a less wholesome but more florid type of living. It is well to have communities where brains and not money set the pace and win the prizes.[32]

As the social distance between faculty members and community elites widened, special departmental needs ceased to be a part of the ongoing matrix of community philanthropy. The university continued to benefit in many small ways from the diffuse support of its surrounding community, but the significance of this kind of assistance for university research was on the wane by the second decade of the century.

A 1920 survey by the National Research Council of "funds available in the U. S. for the encouragement of scientific research" provides a fairly comprehensive account of the resources specifically available for research among the major universities.[33] In general, the expectations voiced earlier by university presidents for the massive endowment of university research were fulfilled in perhaps only two respects. Charles Eliot might well be pleased that Harvard's patrons had created forty-one separate funds providing three-quarters of a million dollars annually for research alone. (This actually understates the total, since much of the income for laboratories and institutes at Harvard, and elsewhere, was not included in these totals.) Similarly, proponents of medical research might take some com

TABLE 4. University Funds Available for Scientific Research, 1920

	Budgetary Appropriation	Special Funds	Institutes	Medicine	Agriculture*	Engineering	Number of Research Fellowships
California	$36,000	$19,500	$100,300	$87,870	$7,080	$26,946	21
Illinois	25,000		3,000	3,500			18
Michigan							28
Minnesota	14,420			[1,693,000]**			5
Wisconsin	23,000			19,200	1,000	3,000	10+
Caltech		18,350					9
Chicago		35,860	32,000	3,250			12
Columbia		465		97,701		2,250	32
Cornell		20,514		2,571	44,550		15
Harvard		8,343	118,644	612,603			50
Johns Hopkins	?			207,730			13
MIT	100,000	2,150				330	5
Pennsylvania			?	?			37+
Princeton	21,200						54
Stanford	2,000		[700,000]**	1,185			13
Yale		88,740		960			15

SOURCE: Compiled from "Funds Available in 1920 for the Encouragement of Scientific Research," *Bulletin of the National Research Council*, no. 9 (1921): 21–54.

* Not including state or federal funds.
** Principal.
? Funds indicated, but amounts not given.

fort in the large and growing sums available for research at California, Columbia, Harvard, Johns Hopkins, and Minnesota. Otherwise the picture seems to be one of irregularity and incompleteness. Seven of these universities had regular appropriations for departmental research, and five of the private universities (Caltech, Chicago, Cornell, Harvard, and Yale) had corresponding amounts in endowed funds, although usually limited to designated departments. Michigan, Columbia, Penn, and Stanford appear to be clearly deficient in this respect.

Whether the sums reported are interpreted to be a lot or a little depends upon whether one looks for reference to the past or to the future. The primary reliance upon ad hoc individual philanthropy succeeded in the first two decades of the century in greatly augmenting the research capacity of these universities. In the midwestern state universities, where this approach had less success, legislators had at least partly recognized the need to support some university research directly. In 1920, however, American universities faced considerable demands on their existing resources. A near doubling of price levels since the outbreak of the war had squeezed budgets badly, and an enrollment explosion following the war greatly increased their paramount teaching responsibilities. Research by this date was no longer a discretionary expenditure for this set of universities. Given the trends just indicated, however, it appeared unlikely that existing forms of research support could expand in step with the needs of science. In the preceding thirty years the American research universities had devised the basic organizational machinery to accommodate both teaching and research; yet, as they entered the 1920s, the funds needed to drive that machinery were by no means assured.

3

Research Universities
from World War I to 1930

The experience of waging total war, which had a visceral impact on the citizenry of the beleaguered European combatants, had a more cerebral significance for Americans, who were far more fortunate in terms of its duration and distance. Nevertheless, the intensity of the American involvement, physical and emotional, accelerated the pace of social, economic, and cultural change. The exigencies of war jarred individuals out of the trajectories of their anticipated life patterns, caused institutions to accept hitherto unimaginable arrangements, and spawned new organizations for previously unforeseen purposes. In the span of less than two years, individuals and institutions alike were subject to a richness and variety of experience that profoundly affected their perceptions and interpretations of the world in which they lived. In the longer term, however, the novelties and innovations of wartime had consequences that could not be predicted. Many of the specific agencies of the war mobilization were quickly deflated after the armistice. But other wartime arrangements provided powerful precedents that persisted in the postwar world. Certainly, all of these reactions were evident in the impact of the war on American universities.

1. Science and the University Go to War

World War I induced a period of extraordinarily rapid technological development, but of more significance for American science was an even

94

more rapid transformation in the general perception of science. To scientists, educators, statesmen, and the lay public, the role of research in winning the war symbolized the marriage of pure and applied science. Applied industrial research had already taken root before the outbreak of hostilities. The nation's great industrial research laboratories were founded early in the century at AT&T (1912), Du Pont (1902), Eastman Kodak (1912), and General Electric (1900). In 1911 the Mellon Institute for Industrial Research had also been established to allow smaller firms in less concentrated industries to drink from the fount of scientific knowledge.[1] Basic science in the universities, although also well established, was shackled with some stubborn popular stereotypes. One of these pictured the academic scientist as an ivory-tower pedant, entirely out of touch with everyday affairs. Another exalted the abilities of the practical inventor—a Thomas Edison or a Luther Burbank—who could solve everyday problems without recourse to abstract scientific theory. The war gave the lie to both these images. A call to the general public by the Naval Consulting Board for suggestions and inventions elicited 110,000 responses, but only 110 of those merited investigation and only one ever went into production. Moreover, Edison's own wartime activities were not very fruitful.[2] In contrast, the academic scientists mobilized to assist the war effort made conspicuous contributions. The altered conception of the role of science was to have direct consequences on the postwar development of American science both in and out of the universities. This was primarily because the same core group directed the organization of science during the war, strenuously articulated the relevance of science as revealed by the wartime experience, and occupied strategic positions in the postwar research system.

The locus of these activities was the National Research Council, an offshoot of the somnolent National Academy of Sciences. Although the NRC both antedated and survived the actual war mobilization, it owed its existence to the conjunction of the hothouse conditions for scientific organizations created by the war with a vision of the proper role of science in America propounded by one man—George Ellery Hale.[3]

By the second decade of the century, the forty-year-old Hale was firmly established as one of the country's leading astronomers. He had pioneered the development of astrophysics after receiving just a bachelor's degree from MIT, and he had then become the driving force behind the creation of first the University of Chicago's Yerkes Observatory and then the Carnegie Institution's Mount Wilson Observatory. His vision of the future of science both reflected and transcended his own unorthodox career as an astronomer. A practitioner par excellence of Big Science, he stressed the importance of organization and cooperation in scientific research. Combining astronomy, physics, and chemistry in his own specialty, he consistently lauded the virtue of interdisciplinary research. Also, as a son of a wealthy Chicago family and as a scientist whose own work depended heavily upon private patronage, he regarded philanthropy as the appropriate basis for the support of science. From Hale's vantage point, however, American science was underdeveloped and unappreciated. Before the war the general public failed to recognize either the tremendous scientific progress that had taken place or the practical benefits that science could bring.[4]

Hale grew preoccupied with this state of affairs after becoming, in 1902, one of the youngest members ever elected to the National Academy of Sciences. Established during the Civil War to provide the government with scientific advice, the NAS soon settled into the torpor of being a largely honorific body. Hale was soon convinced that the prestige and public awareness of American science would be enhanced if the NAS could assume a role similar to that of the European national academies. As a preliminary step, he had attempted before the start of the war to arrange for the erection of a suitable permanent home for the academy.[5] The coming of war, however, soon brought together a number of Hale's preoccupations. Wholeheartedly sympathizing with the Allies, he felt that American involvement was both desirable and unavoidable. The conduct of this war, events in Europe had already revealed, would require the full utilization of academic and industrial science. To organize and spearhead this effort was both consistent with the chartered purpose of the NAS and an opportunity for its rehabilitation.

On April 19, 1916, the day following Wilson's ultimatum to Germany regarding unrestricted submarine warfare, the NAS passed a resolution by Hale offering its assistance to the President should diplomatic relations between the two countries be broken.[6] Within two months the National Research Council was born as an independent offshoot of the NAS. Hale played a key role at every stage of its development. By consensus, he became chairman of the NRC and remained so throughout the war. He arranged for its initial private operating support from the Engineering Foundation and then visited England and France in 1916 to observe the organization of science under actual wartime conditions. By skillfully arranging overt presidential recognition in 1916, Hale bolstered the authority of the NRC in the bureaucratic satrapies of Washington; and later, with the war still raging, he obtained an executive order designating the NRC a permanent arm of the academy.[7]

The actual wartime accomplishments of the NRC are somewhat peripheral to the subject of university research, but the way in which the council pursued its objectives is ultimately germane. Its broad mandate was "to coordinate the scientific resources of the entire country and secure cooperation of all agencies, governmental, educational, and industrial, in which research facilities are available."[8] The NRC was organized into divisions on the basis of functional and scientific tasks, while the work of actual scientific projects took place in numerous committees. The most significant research efforts took academic scientists away from their campuses to Washington, to special laboratories, or to the European front. The most crucial single project was probably the work on submarine detection at the New London Experimental Station. Other efforts improved sound-ranging for artillery and communications for the Signal Corps. In conjunction with private industry, the NRC helped achieve large-scale production of optical glass, nitrates, and poison gas.[9] These achievements seemed to reveal the vast potential that could be tapped through organization and cooperation in scientific research.

The NRC was first and foremost a network for joining academic, industrial, and governmental science. Hale began by recruiting from his own, wide circle of associates. Of particular importance were the physical chemist Arthur Noyes, a friend from undergraduate days at MIT, who became chairman of the central Administrative Division; and the physicist Robert Millikan, a colleague from Hale's years at the University of Chicago and a postwar Nobel laureate, who became vice-chairman of the council, director of research, and head of the research committees on physics, submarines, and optical glass.[10] Hale's long association with the Carnegie Institution assured contact with that large cluster of scientists; in fact, Charles Walcott, the CIW's secretary, immediately became a vice-chairman of the NRC. The academy itself was naturally another asset. When assurance of cooperation from the AAAS Committee of One Hundred on Scientific Research was received, access was guaranteed to the whole of academic science.[11] By the time it reached full operation, the NRC research committees read like a Who's Who in American science. They were assisted at the local level by the formation of research committees at major colleges and universities to facilitate cooperation with the war effort.

Bringing about the collaboration of academic science and industrial research was a fundamental goal of the NRC and one that transcended the war effort. From the outset, Hale secured the participation of his friend Gano Dunn of the Engineering Foundation (another NRC vice-chairman) and John J. Carty, chief engineer for AT&T. By 1918, when the NRC was seeking permanent status, Hale clearly foresaw the coordination of science for industrial research as a postwar goal. An industrial relations division was created, consisting of Carty and the most important research heads of major corporations. This was followed by the establishment of a blue-ribbon advisory committee containing the presidents of AT&T, Phelps-Dodge, Eastman Kodak, U.S. Steel, Mellon Banks, Du Pont, General Electric, and Warner-Swasey. Also included were Henry

Pritchett, of the Carnegie Foundation for the Advancement of Teaching, and Elihu Root—senator, CIW trustee, and general deus ex machina.[12] The first two postwar publications of the NRC would be a collection of exhortations on the union of science and industry by many of these same individuals, followed by an inventory of industrial research laboratories.[13] The National Research Council, then, not only symbolized the merging of basic and applied science brought about by the war but also remained an active force for its continuation thereafter.

While the leaders of science-based industries could be expected to assess their interests in research more or less accurately, it is less evident why this utilitarian view of science should have been advocated with such enthusiasm by academicians like Hale, whose own research was as remote from practical application as the celestial bodies he studied. The war experience, however, created an "ideology of science," which gave scientists reason to believe that everyone might benefit from a perpetuation of the wartime organization of science.[14] In the first place, scientists during the war had demonstrated their ability to solve practical problems, and it seemed clear that this capacity ought to be harnessed for peacetime industry: "for the first time in history the world has been waked up by the war to an appreciation of what science can do," Robert Millikan exulted.[15] Second, organization and cooperation had seemingly enhanced greatly the efficacy of science. Third, the experience of coordination appeared to indicate the continuity, rather than a distinction, between pure and applied science. Scientists were consequently confident that the industrial utilization of science in the postwar world could be expected to generate tangible support for pure science in the university. "Industries are more favorably inclined than ever before to the widespread use of research," George Hale concluded; "their greatest leaders, moreover, are unanimous in their appreciation of the necessity of promoting research for the sake of advancing knowledge, as well as for immediate commercial advantages."[16]

The persistence of these widely shared expectations had some tangible consequences for university science. Most generally, the popularity of engineering programs rose right after the war. At the same time, engineering departments redoubled their efforts to provide useful services to industry. The perceived instrumental value of science was undoubtedly a factor in their obtaining crucial foundation support for the NRC. In 1919 the Carnegie Corporation made a grant of $5 million to the NRC to construct a permanent home for it in Washington and to underwrite its continuing activities. The same year, the Rockefeller Foundation provided $500,000 over five years for the NRC to award postdoctoral fellowships in chemistry and physics. Proposals similar to these had been turned down in the past. These resources allowed the NRC to pursue its goals of promoting and coordinating science, while also strengthening basic research through the fellowship program. Perhaps the most concrete and lasting consequence of the postwar appreciation of science was the creation of the California Institute of Technology—the most important addition to the ranks of research universities in the interwar years. This, too, was largely the doing of George Ellery Hale (as will be seen in Chapter 5), and its realization represented most closely his vision of the proper organization of science.[17]

In a larger perspective the wartime precedent of the NRC set a pattern for the organization and direction of American science in the 1920s. That a central agency was desirable became an axiom of the ideology of science. Of course, some people interpreted the wartime experience to mean that the federal government should play a more active role in promoting science. James McKeen Cattell and Willis Whitney of General Electric, for example, independently argued that the federal government should follow the example of other nations by supporting basic research in the universities and, furthermore, that such investments would yield substantial social benefits.[18] Many others concurred. Between 1916 and 1919 Congress intermittently considered measures that would have provided federal funds to each state in order to establish engineering experiment stations in universities. NRC leadership and support for such legislation might well have improved its chances for passage. Instead, the NRC objected to specific features of the legislation, and, lacking direction, the universities failed to agree upon a plan of distribution. As a result, the existing support for the plan was vitiated.[19] For diehard Republicans like Hale, Robert Millikan, and Elihu Root, science needed to be shielded from the inherent partisanship of the federal bureaucracy, above all from the populist proclivities of congressional Democrats.[20] The public interest in scientific progress, in effect, required that the direction of science be in private hands.

Three basic features of the NRC provide a paradigm for private, elite authority over American science in the 1920s. Essentially, the guidance of private elites was relied upon for scientific leadership, financial backing, and what might loosely be termed social control. In these respects, the paradigm for the direction of science was typical of other forms of social action during the 1920s.[21]

The first pillar of this elitism was a "best-science" approach to the allocation of scientific resources.[22] Basically, such a policy meant concentrating scientific decisions among an elite of demonstrated scientific accomplishment. To a large extent, of course, authority within scientific communities is inherently vested in those scientists who have themselves made significant contributions. Considerable latitude, however, exists in putting such a principle into practice. George Hale articulated one extreme of these possibilities: he sought to promote an active role for the scientific elite of the National Academy of Sciences; conversely, he distrusted the intrusion of government into science and advocated the concentration of postwar science in large, privately funded laboratories.[23] The NRC largely reflected these positions, and this best-science tendency was soon powerfully reinforced by the major foundations. One need only recall the oft-repeated intention of Wickliffe Rose of the General Education Board to "make the peaks higher" to perceive the natural thrust of a best-science policy.[24]

The second pillar was provided by the existence of private capital to sustain the nation's scientific development. In rejecting a government role in science, Hale could state matter-of-factly that he would "not be disappointed if we have to rely on private funds for a long period in the future."[25] Remarkably, in the United States, as in no other country in the world, private capital was available for these purposes. The Rockefeller and Carnegie philanthropies, which made possible the NRC's postwar role, held vast potential for the support of scientific activities. Members of the scientific elite saw no reason why America's proliferating millionaires should not continue to recognize the benefits of investing in science. From their point of view industry, too, could be expected to heed the lessons of the war and thus to support pure science in order to guarantee future American industrial competitiveness. Thus, American science could safely entrust its destiny to the private-sector elites in the worlds of foundations and industry who controlled these vital resources.

The final pillar that allowed this system to stand consisted of the social arrangements that brought these different elites together for the common purpose of furthering science. This became one of the peacetime functions of the NRC, but the council was only one link in a chain of interlocking directorates. The same group of individuals encountered one another, in slightly different combinations, in committees of the NRC, on the boards of the Carnegie or Rockefeller philanthropies, and as trustees of recipient institutions like Caltech.[26] Such gatherings brought together the elite of American science, the heads of the philanthropic world, research directors and corporate leaders of the major research-based firms of the day, and certain key figures from public life, like Elihu Root and Herbert Hoover.

The mobilization of American science during World War I, then, had the enduring effect of bringing industry, foundations, and universities into closer cooperation and of consecrating the direction of science policy to a private elite that represented the leadership of those institutions.[27] The federal government, which the NRC had originally been meant to advise, was pushed into the background during the 1920s. The NRC was the tangible embodiment of these changes in American science—at once a symbol, a promoter, and occasionally an active agent of the research system of the 1920s. American colleges and universities were affected by the same forces as science during the war period. As with science, the combination of organization and relevance achieved then seemed for many to be both the panacea for past weaknesses and the promise for future accomplishments. In this case, however, it proved far more difficult to sustain these wartime features under more normal conditions.

According to the Yale historian George Pierson, American involvement evoked "the unprecedented spectacle of eager and even sacrificial participation—by colleges, professors, and students alike—in the great war effort." The enthusiasm of individuals was understandable; behind it lay the responsibilities of citizenship in a democracy. But Pierson wonders "how institutions also got involved, how campuses became parade grounds, how laboratories were militarized and the quiet men of learning turned to teaching the arts of defense and destruction." His questions are perceptive. The disjunction between normal and wartime activities of colleges and universities was far more profound than the scientists' movement from pure to applied research. Institutions that had consistently vowed their dedication to intellectual freedom and the pursuit of truth for their faculties, or to the cultivation of critical intelligence and the development of moral character in their students, allowed these values to be eclipsed with scarcely a word of protest. In fact, Pierson perceives that circumstances rendered the universities doubly disarmed: their evolution during the past generation had made them "secular, all-purpose institutions, as usable for war as any other purpose"; and their reactions revealed "a self-conscious and determined identification with the purposes and welfare of the nation." As a result, it did not occur to the leaders of higher education to question the absorption of campuses in military ends until after the guns were stilled.[28]

American colleges and universities were involved in World War I for longer than the nineteen months of officially declared hostilities. Campuses were particularly sensitive to the call for American preparedness that sounded as the conflict in Europe dragged on. Their involvement in war-related activities then proceeded in stages until it reached an almost total commitment.

During the initial stage, participation was largely a matter of individual initiatives, although some institutional actions were taken on the more bellicose campuses, like Yale and Princeton. Those students and young faculty who craved direct involvement could volunteer to assist relief efforts for Belgium, to do medical work through the Red Cross, or to engage in actual combat with Canadian regiments or the French Foreign Legion.[29] Harvard, Stanford, and other universities organized volunteer ambulance units that served throughout the war. Above all, preparedness meant readiness to fight. Existing training units at land-grant schools, like the Cornell Cadet Corps, began to grow from the onset of hostilities. At Yale, President Hadley took the lead in establishing an artillery battalion. An additional outlet was provided by the War Department in the form of volunteer summer camps for college men, which by 1915 suddenly assumed a new relevance and popularity.[30] Military training acquired even greater urgency in 1916, as relations between Germany and the Unites States deteriorated.

The 1916–17 school year saw first the psychological and then the actual commitment to war. During this stage of involvement the atmosphere on American campuses changed drastically. Military training for students was facilitated by the creation of the Reserve Officers' Training Corps in the summer of 1916. Before America's entry, ROTC units had been rather hastily organized on 115 campuses, but participation for individuals and institutions alike remained entirely voluntary. Nevertheless, the war hysteria that gradually gripped the country prepared the way for more drastic changes. The die was cast by the breaking off of diplomatic relations with Germany in February 1917. Patriotic rallies and a plethora of organizing efforts ensued. The actual declaration of war on April 6 unloosed a pent-up frenzy that affected higher education in three important ways. The intellectual integrity of the university was, as usual, the first casualty of war. An orgy of patriotic rhetoric swept over college campuses, and the chauvinistic consensus was given real force by systematic purges of faculty suspected of German or pacifist sympathies.[31] Second, campuses were significantly depopulated by the rush to volunteer for military service or war-related work. Universities considerably abetted this impulse by granting students full credit for unfinished courses and by guaranteeing the salaries of departing faculty. Third, university presidents in patriotic speeches pledged to place the facilities of their institutions at the disposal of the nation for the duration of the emergency. A bevy of quasi-academic organizations, like the Intercollegiate Intelligence Bureau or the Advisory Commission of the Council of National Defense, sprang up to work toward this end. Particularly interesting in this respect was the Emergency Council on Education, which was strikingly analogous to the NRC. A wartime offshoot of existing organizations (fifteen major educational associations formed the original core), it aspired to mobilize and coordinate the educational resources of the country, and it did not foresee its function as ending with the cessation of hostilities. It consequently soon achieved a permanent status as the American Council on Education.

The last stage of the war for the universities came in 1918, when the War Department essentially accepted the universities' many offers to make use of their facilities. Campuses were nationalized almost as completely as the railroads had been in order to provide training grounds for the Students' Army Training Corps (SATC). Colleges and universities thus attained direct relevance to the war effort, but at a considerable price.

Several conditions combined to bring about this situation. By the end of the 1917–18 school year, colleges and universities in general were in an increasingly desperate position. Enrollments were depleted by enlistments, and faculties were thinned by wartime service. The shortfall in revenues caused by the loss of students had put most institutional budgets far in the red. Furthermore, the emotional preoccupation with the war undermined those academic pursuits that still remained. At the same time, the War Department, having processed and assimilated the initial flood of volunteers, needed a more efficient manpower policy. In the spring of 1918, it began signing contracts with colleges and universities to host the training of technical military units. At the same time, it announced a reorganization of campus-based training into the Students' Army Training Corps. According to the original formula, able-bodied male students were to enlist in the Army and then be placed on furlough status while they attended college and received on-campus military training. They were to go on active duty as soon as they either graduated or reached the draft age of twenty-one. The scare from the final German offensive in the summer of 1918, however, prompted a lowering of the draft age to eighteen. If directly implemented, this policy would have simply shut down most of American higher education, while also cutting off the future supply of officers and technical experts. To avert these contingencies, the SATC was completely reformulated for the start of the fall semester.

On October 1, 1918, some 140,000 college men on four hundred American campuses were simultaneously inducted into active duty in the U.S. Army. The colleges and universities at which they were stationed had become units of the SATC. The student-soldiers consisted not only of each school's regular eligible students but also of qualified volunteers (who thus suddenly became college students) as well as of noncollege trainees who were attached to the technical training sections. They were to live, drill, and study under military discipline, enforced by a commanding officer whose authority awkwardly overlapped with that of the university president. Their education was to be determined "in accordance with the needs of the service." These needs were defined as eleven hours per week of combined drill and military instruction plus about fourteen classroom hours of more or less academic courses in "allied subjects." Nevertheless, the tone was unequivocally military. Student-soldiers wore uniforms, marched to and from classes, and adhered to a rigid daily schedule of activities. Military matters took precedence over academic ones, and many of the ostensibly academic courses were willingly being adapted to military objectives. Besides altering the curriculum, the SATC mandatorily changed the school year to four quarters in order to facilitate the transfer of the oldest group to regular units at the completion of each quarter. Thus, the SATC would have run through the available cohorts within a year. As it was, the armistice removed both the *raison d'être* and the *raison de financer* of the SATC. It was demobilized only two weeks later—one of the first military units to be terminated. The SATC thus constituted a truncated experience in academic organization, lasting in its fullest manifestation less than two months.

In hindsight, it is difficult to imagine a regime more incongruous with the values and mores of the academy than that of the SATC. Normal university instruction was thoroughly undermined as courses were ludicrously foreshortened for soon-to-depart soldiers and as military duties often took priority over class attendance. Faculty members had to show passes to student guards in order to gain admittance to university buildings. "Chaos" and "confusion" are the terms most commonly employed by historians to describe campus conditions during these weeks. The inherent difficulty of organizing such a novel and complicated undertaking on extremely short notice was compounded by shortages of material and personnel. The ambiguous relationship between academic and military authorities in their overlapping spheres was a constant source of aggravation. A difficult situation was made even worse by the worldwide influenza epidemic. The combination of crowded quarters, fatigue, and enforced outdoor activities in fall weather created ideal conditions for contagion. At the University of Michigan, for example, 1,200 were stricken and 58 perished. Despite everything, at the close of the war, academics were on the whole reluctant to condemn this experiment.[32]

Those involved in the military side of the SATC generally regretted that they had not had the opportunity to get the bugs out of the operation. They undoubtedly sympathized with former President Taft's publicly expressed indignation: "The whole academic character of the institutions was abandoned to aid the Government in the war," he wrote; "a year's training of the kind already begun would be good for the boys and good for the country. It would be a useful step in beginning a system of universal training [and] it would save the country from demoralization of its higher educational work."[33] The civilian director of the SATC, President Richard Maclaurin of MIT, perhaps a bit shell-shocked from the ordeal, was less positive. He found "little to be derived from the experiences of the SATC that can throw any light on what should be the permanent policy of the country regarding the relations between the military and academic training. The conditions under which it worked were all exceptional and all abnormal."[34] The New York *Evening Post* editorialized that "this generation hardly need fear the 'militarization' of our institutions of higher learning. The shift to the military system lasted just long enough to accentuate its deficiencies and inconveniences,"[35] Yet, the writer failed to take into account the elixir of relevance and the heady effect it had on many university leaders.

Two books celebrating the university war experience agreed that higher education could not revert to its prewar state of "laissez-faire," "indiscipline," and "near intellectual bankruptcy." President Parke Kolbe of the University of Akron foresaw with undisguised satisfaction an extension of the wartime nationalization of colleges and universities through the coordinating efforts of a projected federal department of education. President Charles F. Thwing of Western Reserve University, in a somewhat more tempered assessment, thought that the SATC had improved the industriousness, efficiency, health, and manners of the students.[36] These sentiments were shared, at least for a time, by many research university presidents. Hadley of Yale and Schurman of Cornell, like Parke Kolbe, endorsed compulsory military training as a permanent feature of a college education. And Nicholas Murray Butler, an unfailing bellwether of the conventional wisdom, condemned the laxity of the prewar college regime compared with wartime organization and discipline.[37] President Lowell of Harvard, however, kept his head during this period somewhat better than his peers did. He drew the firm conclusion from the ordeal that military drill was absolutely incompatible with academic work. He further warned that "after a great war . . . it is wise to beware of a materialist reaction."[38] This was precisely what was occurring around him. The intoxicating effects of the relevance, sense of purpose, and supposed efficiency of the wartime organization produced decided enthusiasm in higher-education circles after the war. These virtues ought to be preserved, most agreed, but how?

The wartime precedents suggested to leaders like Kolbe that a partnership between the federal government and private organizations would best facilitate the postwar coordination of American higher education. There was no consensus in Washington, however, regarding such an enlarged federal role. When the Smith-Towner bill, which would have created a cabinet-level department of education, failed to pass, it became clear that only voluntary organizations could preserve the wartime spirit of coordination. The American Council on Education, as a national federation of educational associations, was the obvious candidate for this role; and its leadership was eager for the task.[39]

Samuel Capen, the first director of the ACE (1919–22), had been a specialist in higher education in the Bureau of Education. His close associate during the war years and successor at the ACE was Charles R. Mann (director, 1923–34), a Chicago physicist who gained prominence for his *Study of Engineering Education,* conducted under the auspices of the CFAT and the Society for the Promotion of Engineering Education. Both men played an important role in the establishment of the SATC through the War Department's Committee on Education and Special Training. Given their backgrounds, both tended to see American higher education from a central, rather than a campus, perspective and to judge college education from the standpoint of efficiency. The attraction of wartime organization, in contrast to the decentralized nonsystem of peacetime, was natural and obvious to them. Capen spoke after the war of a nationalized system of higher education brought about by the "leadership of ideas" of the proposed department of education. This would not be government control, but direction through "the cooperation of the best civilian thought with the established agencies of government."[40] Without a governmental base, however, the leadership of ideas proved far more difficult. As a private, voluntary organization, dependent upon membership dues, the ACE became instead an association in search of a purpose.[41]

The ACE managed to find a role for itself in a number of different areas. It took the lead in bringing together regional accrediting organizations and published a national list of the institutions they recognized. Its visibility allowed it to represent the United States in international educational projects. Somewhat later, the ACE became involved in the educational-testing movement (which antedated the war), and that section of the ACE eventually became part of the Educational Testing Service (1947). In 1926 it published the first of its handbooks of American colleges and universities. Perhaps the role it was most suited for was monitoring the education-related activities of the federal government, which were regularly published in its journal, the *Educational Record*. All of these admittedly useful activities, however, lay closer to the periphery than to the center of the development of American higher education.[42]

The ACE faced an insurmountable problem in its implicit desire to provide a leadership of ideas for higher education as a whole. The natural leadership of American higher education for more than a generation had been provided by the research universities, and they had slight use for such direction as the ACE had to offer. This became evident in the mid-twenties, when A. Lawrence Lowell privately challenged the utility of the ACE. Lowell pointed out that during the war "too many attempts were made by well-intentioned people to coordinate the work of others." Harvard certainly had no need for external direction; by implication, this would apply to the rest of the research universities as well. In the next decade their association, the AAU, would for a time withdraw from the ACE entirely.[43]

The estrangement of the ACE and the research universities seems to be one reason why the coordination of science and the coordination of higher education were quite different matters. Lowell's disdain for coordination indicates that the war-inspired vision of an efficient, centrally orchestrated system of higher education in the United States would prove chimerical. The ACE functioned basically as a trade association for the rank and file of American colleges and universities. It thus served something of a networking function for those institutions that lacked other significant national ties. Without the eager servility on the part of member institutions that existed in wartime, however, the ACE had no chance of implementing the more far-reaching goals of its leadership. Instead, it had to endeavor to develop services that its membership would have the option of utilizing or not. The different social spheres of the ACE and the NRC are symbolized by the fact that the ACE director Samuel Capen moved to the chancellorship of the University of Buffalo, while the NRC director James Rowland Angell became head of the Carnegie Corporation and then president of Yale.

The NRC was a significant institution for the research universities. By 1920 these schools had become national entities that could utilize channels of communication with the major national corporations and foundations. The NRC was predicated on a shared view of science, and the individuals whom it brought into contact represented vast potential resources for the realizing of scientific goals. Nevertheless, the amount of coordination achieved by the NRC should not be overestimated. NRC-university relations pertained only to the universities' research activities, and only to that part of them dealing with certain applied sciences, research fellows, and major externally financed projects. Moreover, the research universities managed an important degree of coordination, although President Lowell might have objected to the term, through entirely different means. They discussed their mutual concerns within the AAU, and their academic departments were connected to similar departments elsewhere through the multiple institutions of the academic disciplines. The research universities conformed to a common academic standard without need of either the NRC or the ACE.

In a longer perspective, then, it becomes clear that the wartime precedents for greater centralization and standardization in American higher education were fundamentally misleading. Such coordination as existed in the system came about from the decentralized interaction of largely autonomous units. Moreover, in a development anticipated by no one, the forces partly engendered by the war acting in such an environment tended to make American colleges and universities grow in some respects considerably more dissimilar in the years that followed.

2. Growth and Differentiation

In 1919, when American colleges and universities reopened under something like normal conditions for the first time in three years, observers of the campus scene were struck by a significant development: there were far more students than anyone had expected. Contemporary explanations for the increased popularity of going to college were ready at hand. The SATC had brought to college many young men who had not previously considered attending, and a significant number apparently remained to pursue a regular course. The wartime record of American colleges, educators flattered themselves, had demonstrated the practical usefulness of college training. The mature and sober-minded generation formed by the war naturally sought to capitalize on these opportunities. In fact, it turned out that postwar students rejected the mordant seriousness of wartime campuses spontaneously and decisively. Also, the jump in enrollment levels soon extended to those who had not been affected by the war. The rapid rise in higher-education enrollments continued into the middle of the 1920s before finally tapering off.

Enrollment growth, of course, had been the norm rather than the exception for American higher education. The emptying of campuses during World War I actually induced an artificial hiatus in one of the most vigorous spurts in a secular trend of unremitting expansion.[1] In rough terms, the college and university population grew by 40 percent in the 1890s and almost 60 percent in the first decade of the century. In the academic year 1919–20, with the postwar expansion already well under way, enrollments were nearly 75 percent higher than in 1909. The next six years saw student numbers increase at an even more rapid pace, adding an additional 66 percent. For the decade of the 1920s as a whole, college and university enrollment doubled.[2]

The causes for this extraordinary expansion may be sought on different levels. Most immediate seems to be the rapid growth of secondary education. While the college-going rate for high school graduates remained roughly constant, just above 30 percent, the number of high school graduates increased from 231,000 in 1920 to 596,000 in 1930.[3] Thus, growing numbers of high school diplomas translated rather directly into more college students. Behind this increase, of course, lay many of the fundamental social changes associated with higher-education growth in other times and places. This was a period of rising national prosperity and increasing personal income. More and more families acquired the means to pursue prolonged educational strategies for their children. Changes in the structure of the economy created a greater demand for educated workers at the same time that educational credentials were being employed more widely as a screen to select employees. Such factors contributed to a 50 percent rise in the college-going rate for those aged eighteen to twenty-one—from 8 percent in 1920 to a plateau level of 12 percent by just 1928. At the same time the demographic increase of college-age cohorts was adding no more than 1 percent annually to the overall growth.[4] Still, such figures describe only the superficial characteristics of this expansion. To obtain a more nuanced view, one must ask where these additional students went to college. It then becomes clear that "higher education" is not an immutable category. As it doubled in size, American higher education changed in composition. The 1920s constitute an important phase in the differentiation of American higher education.[5]

The postwar surge in enrollments flowed largely into institutions that were already in place. The research universities, nevertheless, saw their share of the total decline from 19.0 percent in 1914 to 16.5 percent in 1919.[6] The war seems to have marked a turning point in the evolution of American higher education. During the preceding generation, the research universities had been increasing their proportion of enrollments. In that period there was no doubt that the largest universities were among the best. The year 1915 may have marked the apogee of that trend. In the first half of the 1920s the three types of research universities—the smaller privates, the larger comprehensive privates, and the state universities—all grew considerably; but they still lost ground to the rest of American higher education. Thereafter, they grew more slowly and lost more ground yet. The loss was most dramatic among the "comprehensive" private research universities, and (except for Cornell) it indicates a significant change in institutional mission. The relative decline was less precipitous among the state research universities, but it was all the more unexpected in these large, service-oriented institutions. Other segments of American higher education were growing more rapidly than the research universities. But what were they?

It is quite difficult to answer this simple question in a systematic manner. Whereas certain types of schools specialize in a single type of education, the universities combine many functions and diverse kinds of students. A profile of the growth of higher education in the 1920s consequently requires looking at separate categories of institutions as well as at different programs within institutions in order to identify relative change. No single set of data adequately describes these phenomena, but enough information can be pieced together to provide an adequate depiction. As benchmarks recall that college and university enrollments, narrowly defined, doubled in the 1920s; broadly defined, enrollments increased by 84 percent,[7] and undergraduate baccalaureate degrees increased by 138 percent.

Undergraduate Arts and Sciences. This staple of American colleges and universities suffered a relative decline during the 1920s, as the new clientele of first-generation college-goers gravitated toward curricula related to clearly defined occupations. The percentage of baccalaureate degrees in arts and sciences declined from 71.6 percent to 63.3 percent, the decrease being more marked for women (85.8 to 69.1) than for men (62.5 to 58.8).

An increasing proportion of men chose programs in business or commerce, while women took more degrees in teaching (see below) and, to a lesser extent, in home economics.[8]

Commerce. The most conspicuous boom in vocational curricula occurred in business education immediately after the war. The number of business majors quadrupled between 1915 and 1920, from 9,000 to 36,000. The number of colleges offering business programs roughly tripled in the years following the war. Business enrollments actually grew in line with the rest of higher education in the 1920s (and then accelerated again in the 1930s), but first degrees in business quadrupled for the decade (1,576 in 1919–20; 6,376 in 1929–30).[9]

Engineering. The other obvious vocational track for men lost popularity in the 1920s. The wartime hoopla concerning applied science could do no more than sustain engineering enrollments near their 1910 share of about 8.5 percent of the total (1919–20), or roughly one in five undergraduate males. Expanding rates of participation, however, do not generally favor difficult (i.e., math-based) curricula. By 1930, engineering majors composed 5 percent of total enrollments, or about one in ten college men.[10]

Teachers. In most states of the Union, the transformation of teacher education into a university-level program (four-year degree course for high school graduates) occurred largely in the 1920s. This made teacher education a dynamic—and confusing—element for higher-education bookkeeping. For illustration, in 1900 there were far more men and women studying in two-year normal schools than there were college undergraduates. The comparable magnitude of future teachers was obviously less in the 1920s, when these two categories became jumbled together. Enrollments in normal schools and teachers colleges made up 27 percent of the broad total in 1920 and 25 percent in 1930.[11] Over time, however, teachers colleges expanded their programs into other areas, while a growing number of students prepared for careers in education in regular colleges and universities. Active teachers also formed a large component of the burgeoning population of part-time college students, and they were one of the principal constituencies of summer sessions. Actual and future teachers, then, accounted for much of the absolute growth of American higher education in the 1920s, but their precise share cannot be accurately determined.

Junior Colleges. The trend in junior college enrollment was unequivocally up in the twenties; unlike other components of growth, it tended to gain momentum as the decade progressed. During the decade, junior college students rose from 1.4 percent to 5.0 percent of the total enrollments.[12]

Professional Programs. Although the number of students in professional schools grew 72 percent in the decade, this category combined two different trends. Law degrees outpaced baccalaureates for the decade, growing 171 percent, but degrees in theology and the health professions lagged behind baccalaureates by only doubling.[13] Unlike the latter, law could be studied part-time in night schools in most cities, and these programs undoubtedly accounted for its above-average growth.

Graduate Studies. This was clearly a growth area, although a relatively minor one numerically. The number of graduate students tripled in the decade, but that accounted for only 32,000 additional students in 1930. The number of graduate degrees awarded jumped 246 percent, earned Ph.D.'s alone increasing 280 percent.[14]

Part-Time and Summer Session. Additional students of this type certainly contributed to expanding enrollments, but it is difficult to say by how much. The Bureau of Education failed to distinguish part-time students and excluded summer sessions from its totals. Their incidence is evident when one identifies the country's fifteen largest institutions in 1930:

For the private and municipally sponsored urban universities, the percentage of part-time/summer students ranges from 48 to 78 percent; for the state flagship campuses, it varies from 10 percent in rural Urbana to 33 percent in urban Minneapolis. It should be obvious, then, where the source of this growth lies: the urban service roles pioneered by research universities were imitated and developed in the 1920s by other urban institutions. This allowed New York University to grow in a decade from 10,500 to 29,200; Western Reserve to climb from 3,300 to 12,500; and Pittsburgh to go from 5,900 to 13,500. The four New York schools in Table 5 could alone count 65,500 irregular students. Clearly, by the end of the 1920s largeness could no longer be equated with the research universities.

During the 1920s American higher education became more heterogeneous in terms of the origins and destinations of students and their experience while going to college.[15] The immediate question here is, How did the research universities position themselves in this expanding and changing universe of higher education?

The higher education system changed after 1920 largely the way that the research universities changed before that date: much of the growth came from the addition or expansion of new units, like teachers colleges, junior colleges, and urban service universities, just as the major universities had added new schools during the preceding generation. As mature institutions, however, the research universities added few new schools in the twenties. It is consequently useful to depict their slower evolution in a wider time frame, like that in Table 6. Here the regular fall enrollments of the fourteen research universities (not including Caltech and MIT) are

TABLE 5. The Fifteen Largest American Universities, 1930

		Total Enrollment	Regular Full-Time	Part-Time and Summer	% Part-Time and Summer
1.	Columbia*	33,144	14,958	18,186	55
2.	New York University	29,214	12,147	17,067	58
3.	City College of N.Y.	24,752	5,312	19,440	78
4.	California* †	22,797	17,322	5,475	24
5.	Minnesota* †	18,505	12,490	6,015	33
6.	Hunter College	15,447	4,614	10,833	70
7.	Illinois* †	14,169	12,709	1,460	10
8.	Northwestern	14,152	6,184	7,968	56
9.	Penn*	13,828	7,252	6,576	48
10.	Ohio State†	13,730	10,709	3,021	22
11.	Southern California	13,627	4,369	9,158	68
12.	Pittsburgh	13,515	7,098	6,417	48
13.	Boston	12,713	5,606	7,107	56
14.	Western Reserve	12,450	3,573	8,877	71
15.	Chicago*	11,757	5,679	6,078	52

SOURCE: *School and Society* 32 (1930): 790.
* Research university.
† State university.

broken down into component programs for the state and private universities. From this it is possible to distinguish how enrollments changed, or did not change, for research universities in the 1920s.

Both public and private research universities capitalized on the 1910–20 enrollment boom by expanding the relative size of their undergraduate colleges of arts and sciences (+7 percent). At this point, however, the development patterns of public and private institutions diverged: the state universities continued to expand these colleges by another ten thousand students in the 1920s, compared with about half that number for the nine private universities. This growth resumed in the state universities once again in the late 1930s, while that decade produced almost perfect stasis for the undergraduate colleges of the private universities.

The predominantly professional schools in the research universities did not generally conform with the patterns for American higher education as a whole. Engineering fell off somewhat sooner in private universities but then registered a relative decline similar to the one found elsewhere in the 1920s. With respect to commerce and education, however, the research universities departed significantly from the national pattern. Business enrollments in the state schools declined in absolute terms during the 1920s and did no better than retain their relative share thereafter. Teacher edu-

TABLE 6. Fall Enrollment by Divisions, Five State and Nine Private Research Universities, 1910–1939

	1910		1920		1929		1939	
	State	Private	State	Private	State	Private	State	Private
Arts and Sciences Undergraduate	7,869	9,504	18,450	15,556	28,536	20,445	32,873	20,522
%	36.6	32.9	43.8	39.5	48.0	37.8	42.0	36.1
Engineering	4,481	4,930	7,290	3,602	7,303	3,066	10,879	3,521
%	20.8	17.1	17.3	9.1	12.3	5.6	13.9	6.2
Law	1,532	2,363	1,221	2,425	1,796	3,928	2,142	3,226
%	7.1	8.2	2.9	6.2	3.0	7.2	2.7	5.7
Medicine	1,140	1,842	1,490	2,412	2,317	3,013	2,208	3,200
%	5.3	6.4	3.5	6.1	3.9	5.5	2.8	5.6
Nonprofessional Graduate	1,064	3,631	2,196	4,054	5,339	7,951	9,546	7,847
%	4.9	12.6	5.2	10.3	9.0	14.6	12.2	13.8
Commerce	NM	NM	4,149	4,086	3,619	4,019	4,962	1,948
%	—	—	9.9	10.4	6.1	7.4	6.3	3.4
Education	NM	NM	553	4,039	4,609	7,251	4,672	6,544
%	—	—	1.3	10.2	7.7	13.3	6.0	11.5
Other %	25.3	22.8	16.1	8.2	10.0	8.6	14.1	17.1
TOTAL	21,489	28,936	42,062	39,430	59,468	54,361	78,181	56,786

SOURCE: *Biennial Survey of Education.* Bureau of Education

cation was surprisingly feeble there as well, especially considering that one-quarter of those totals (1929 to 1939) may have been students in the UCLA Teachers College. The comparable figures for the private universities are not meaningful, because they largely reflect enrollments in Penn's Wharton School of Business (2,000+) and Columbia Teachers College (68–88 percent of total). If those two unique units are omitted, the pursuit of these subjects at the private research universities was numerically insignificant or, as at Harvard, concentrated on the graduate level. Commerce and education were newcomers to higher education in the 1920s, and, with the exceptions just mentioned, had low prestige, a practical orientation, and small scope for knowledge enhancement. Their acceptance was consequently restrained, even at the state research universities, and rather unenthusiastic at private ones.

In the traditional professions of law and medicine, research university enrollments seem to have grown somewhat less than the national totals. This reflects restrictions on enrollment in medical schools generally and in most private law schools. A more significant trend is the expanding share of nonprofessional graduate enrollments in the research universities. Graduate education in the academic disciplines was what the research universities were, by definition, best suited to perform. The fact that they were doing more of it relative to other tasks represented an important reinforcement of their research roles.

Finally, the research universities on the whole seem to have contained the growth of their service commitments in the twenties, although their actions were anything but uniform. In 1915 the Association of Urban Universities was formed to link together those institutions that identified themselves with a service mission to their surrounding cities.[16] Penn and Johns Hopkins were charter members; Minnesota and Harvard soon joined; and Columbia later affiliated as well. Chicago, in some ways the original urban university, remained aloof, but all of the other large urban institutions in Table 5 were members. By 1920 the summer sessions of these schools and their programs for part-time students (excepting Harvard) were fully institutionalized. They nevertheless faced the issue of whether or not to exploit these rapidly growing markets the way that NYU, Northwestern, and the other large urban universities did. The financially weaker private research universities, Penn and Johns Hopkins, as well as Minnesota, took this general course. Harvard, Columbia, and Chicago expanded irregular enrollments little or not at all.

A similar pattern existed in the 1930s, when the first three institutions kept their irregular enrollment steady, while Columbia and especially Chicago reduced them in scope. It is interesting, then, that the role of an urban service university that was pioneered by Columbia and Chicago was progressively deemphasized from the mid-twenties onward by those same institutions. They willingly accepted an implicit division of labor in their municipal domains that sent the bulk of this traffic to neighboring urban institutions. Essentially the same process occurred in Philadelphia, even though Penn remained a strong participant in this market.[17]

By the mid-twenties, then, the research universities had largely foresaken growth, and endeavored instead to concentrate their expanding resources upon fewer students. This occurred first in the private research universities, but a similar pattern followed in the state-financed counterparts. These research universities thus became a shrinking segment of American higher education; ceased to be the largest American universities; and focused their energies upon their enlarged graduate schools, their more select "university colleges," and traditional professional schools. How and why this came about, as well as what consequences followed from it, are important features of the development of research universities. They involve, in fact, the complex institutional priorities of the research universities in this era.

3. The Collegiate Syndrome

The postwar years witnessed important changes in the way that university education was thought about, actually experienced, and supported. The German ideal of a university dedicated to pure learning, which had already been questioned before the war, was largely discredited in a wave of Germanophobia. In its stead, American educators looked to the ally England for inspiration. Oxford and Cambridge, the institutions Americans usually visited, offered a different inspiration. Residential colleges, tutors, and honors degrees became the templates for potential innovations, in much the same way that Privatdozenten, seminars, and research institutes had a generation before. A second change occurred with the onset of the Roaring Twenties. Fraternities, athletics, and campus social activities—accoutrements of the undergraduate experience that had evolved naturally—suddenly seemed to occupy center stage. For many, the extracurriculum overshadowed academics. Going to college was evaluated in terms of what one did, rather than what one learned; with whom one associated, rather than by whom one was taught. The financial strengthening of the research universities after their immediate postwar difficulties was a third major development. The private universities, in particular, were buoyed by an unprecedented surge of private gifts, but the state universities also received an extraordinary bounty from the public purse. In both cases, however, the material prosperity of the decade was accompanied by enhanced involvement of outside constituencies in university affairs. Although each of these trends is significant in itself, when taken together they define the university zeitgeist of the 1920s, a set of attitudes that might better be called the collegiate syndrome.

These three developments were clearly foreshadowed in the prewar university, but their power to set the tone of university life in the 1920s probably derived from mutual reinforcement. The Oxbridge ideal, at least as interpreted in America, emphasized the culture, character, and socialization of the undergraduate. The desired qualities were not ordinarily acquired in a classroom. They grew instead out of the entire texture of college life and thus virtually presupposed that students would live on campus. The extracurricular pursuits and the interactions with classmates that they entailed were of central importance for the overall process of socialization. The visibility of these actitivies made them important to the universities' external backers as well. "The society beyond the campus," Frederick Rudolf has noted, "discovered in the athletic field, the fraternity, the college newspaper what could not be found in the classroom: an earnest recognition and cultivation of those traits of personality most useful on the road to success."[1] In addition, these same activities could evoke the combination of nostalgia and loyalty that made graduates identify with the fortunes of their university. The dependence of these schools on gifts, primarily from their alumni, caused them to go to increasing lengths to promote and publicize the university extracurriculum.

Oddly enough, the emphasis upon university life instead of university studies during the 1920s—the collegiate syndrome—seemed to run counter to the quantitative trends just described, which showed rapidly growing numbers of students in urban universities, teachers colleges, and junior colleges—in those settings where higher education consisted of classroom learning and little else. In fact, the collegiate syndrome can be interpreted in part as a reaction to the loss of exclusiveness in higher education that the spread of such institutions implied.[2] Then, too, these amorphous tendencies could be and were reconciled rhetorically with other hallowed values, including intellectual excellence. The crucial point is that the collegiate syndrome grew in influence at most of the research universities, and these institutions were in many respects the effective leaders of American higher education. The cultivation of college life was only one facet of these complex institutions, but during the 1920s it often appeared to be the rudder that was steering the ship. It is important, then, to determine how collegiate values did and did not affect the research universities in the 1920s.

During the late-nineteenth-century emergence of the American university, a struggle had taken place between proponents of the new university and defenders of traditional collegiate ideals. The logic and vigor of university development repeatedly called the existence of the four-year undergraduate college into question. Early university partisans like Daniel Coit Gilman and G. Stanley Hall would have preferred to organize the university without one altogether; Nicholas Murray Butler and Charles Eliot seriously proposed cutting it down to two or three years.[3] The college party, for its part, rallied around the standard of liberal culture and ridiculed the extremes of specialization, pedantry, or utilitarianism that were not difficult to find in the burgeoning universities.[4] In the years following the war, this timeworn debate entered a new and distinctive stage. In part as a result of the rise of the junior college, there now seemed to be a realistic possibility of splitting undergraduate education in half. Basic preparatory work could be done during the freshman and sophomore years, either in a separate section of the university or at a junior college. The junior and senior years could then be devoted to true university work in academic subjects or professional schools.[5] The only loss under such a system would be the traditional undergraduate college.

For university-minded administrators this would scarcely be a drawback. Chicago had always been committed to a cleavage between junior and senior colleges—a division that Robert Maynard Hutchins would later attempt to make even more radical. Johns Hopkins inaugurated a similar plan in the mid-twenties that allowed study toward the Ph.D. to commence after the sophomore year. Before 1910 Edwin Slosson had felt that universities would one day eschew junior college students entirely and concentrate their resources on upperclassmen who were prepared for advanced work. President Ray Lyman Wilbur of Stanford concluded that rising postwar enrollments and the spread of junior colleges would eventually dictate such a pattern. Clarence Cook Little assumed the presidency of the University of Michigan in 1925 determined to create this kind of arrangement within a state university. His plan to create a separate junior college, which would teach the bulk of students practical subjects and screen the minority that were suited for advanced work, was in the end diluted of any significance by faculty opposition. By 1930 the majority of universities had actually adopted some formal division between the initial and final two years of college. As was true at Michigan, though, most of these were minor administrative measures rather than the restructuring of undergraduate education that had been advocated by university partisans. As a result, the four-year undergraduate college not only weathered this challenge but emerged even more solidly established as the distinctive centerpiece of American higher education.[6]

Collegiate values had their vigorous defenders, particularly in the liberal arts colleges of the East. What was significant for university development, however, was the conscious decision by Ivy League institutions to preserve the college within the university. In the vanguard of this trend were Woodrow Wilson, establishing the preceptorial system at Princeton,

and A. Lawrence Lowell, creating general examinations and college tutors at Harvard. Both men consciously turned to Oxbridge precedents in
conceptualizing and legitimizing their innovations.

A postwar assessment of "European influences on American higher education" identified three principal features of the ascendancy of the English model: (1) insructional methods, meaning tutorials and honors
courses; (2) a focus on the development of the whole person as the objective of higher education; and (3) an emphasis on the importance of university housing for students.[7] The first of these, of course, pertained to the
curriculum, whereas the latter two concerned the extracurriculum. Wilson and Lowell were genuinely committed to both. Their innovations,
they believed, would raise the intellectual content of college while furthering developmental goals as well. Theoretically, this may have been possible; but in reality the curriculum and the extracurriculum tended to pull
in opposite directions, whether it was a matter of students' use of available time or, more important, their whole attitude toward their college
education. By the postwar period, many college and university leaders,
including Lowell, were increasingly stressing developmental goals in their
official and unofficial utterances. And these objectives were invariably
invoked to buttress the inviolability of the four-year undergraduate college. The following statement (1919) by President Hadley of Yale typified
prevailing beliefs: "The moral and social influences of college life are as
important as its intellectual influences; and these influences have proved
sounder and more effective in those colleges which keep their students
four years."[8] If this was the case, as defenders of the college firmly held,
then students ought to reside on campus in order to imbibe in full the
salutary influences of college life. Universities, in short, ought to house
and feed their undergraduates.[9]

College dormitories had long existed, whether out of necessity (where
other housing was unavailable), expediency (where institutions could
profit from them), or propriety (suitable housing for young women).
Early in the twentieth century, however, only a small and dwindling minority of university undergraduates were accommodated in college housing. The notion that such an arrangement was an integral part of a college
education blossomed only after the war. Its precursors were Wilson's ill-
fated quad plan for Princeton (1906) and Lowell's successful campaign to
provide freshman dorms at Harvard (1914). In both cases an important
motivation was the fact that private housing arrangements had over time
led to an alarming social stratification in the student body.[10] Dormitory
construction before World War I was sporadic, but every research university constructed some undergraduate housing during the 1920s.[11] In state
universities these facilities accommodated only a small part of the increased enrollments. Wisconsin in 1930, for example, housed seven hun-

dred of its eight thousand students in university dormitories, while three times that number resided in fraternities and sororities.[12] In the private research universities, however, student housing assumed a more crucial role. This was epitomized at the end of the decade by the construction of the Harvard "houses" (1928–31) and the Yale "colleges" (1930–33).

The completion of these two projects transformed undergraduate life at both universities by bringing the vast majority of students into campus residences for their entire undergraduate career. The houses and colleges were intended principally to break down the large university community into social units that would foster close and formative personal relations. The inspiration, and the enormous sums required for these projects, came from the Yale alumnus Edward S. Harkness. He first approached his alma mater about his desire to promote a regeneration of the social cohesiveness that had characterized the old Yale but that had been diminished by expansion. When Yale's president James R. Angell vacillated, Harkness approached Lowell. The philanthropist's ideas about undergraduate life harmonized perfectly with Lowell's long-standing desire to achieve a closer social integration of the Harvard College student body.[13]

Harkness's remarkable gifts permitted Harvard and Yale to carry the general movement toward residential colleges to an almost ideal realization, which other large universities could scarcely hope to match. Nevertheless, the same impulse, growing as it did out of the contemporary tendency to place developmental goals on the same plane with intellectual goals, was felt in varying degrees among the other private research universities. As the principle gradually became accepted that students ought, if possible, to live in university residences, it also became an implicit constraint upon university development. The implication was that the number of students admitted should bear some relation to the number that could be housed. The supply of dormitory rooms, however, was far more inelastic than the supply of classrooms. And the economics of building dormitories presented greater difficulties than that of adding faculty. As the residential ideal became an integral part of the collegiate syndrome, then, it provided one important reason for the private research universities to place limitations on their enrollments.

A second major way in which the collegiate syndrome affected universities in the 1920s was through the emphasis on extracurricular learning. The term "extracurricular" has been used loosely here to indicate the nonacademic side of college life. In a history of American youth in the 1920s, Paula Fass had made a finer distinction between the extracurriculum per se, which was formally organized through university auspices (athletics, student government, activities, publications), and the effects that students produced on each other through their social relationships. She called the latter the peer society of American youth, and in many ways it was more important than those organized activities that seemed to be the object of student preoccupations and energies. The peer society was actually the true locus of the developmental goals that contemporaries valued so highly.[14]

The distinctive condition of the peer society as it emerged on campuses after the war was its isolation from the social relations of family, community, or workplace that structured the lives of most Americans. This isolation allowed the elaboration of a campus social structure "based on residence, organizational affiliation, extracurricular involvement, and behavioral conformity to peer standards."[15] The value system embodied in this structure gave rise to a distinct hierarchy. The peer society came to be epitomized on most campuses by the fraternities or their equivalent (the eating clubs at Princeton; Harvard's "Gold-Coast" residences on Mount Auburn Street).

While some aspects of the peer society may always have been present in college life, the intensity and notoriety of these tendencies during the early twenties were related to two larger trends in American higher education. The first was the trend toward wider social participation in higher education. This brought students from diverse backgrounds into the colleges and ultimately undermined in part the tacit democracy of the nineteenth-century campus. There seemed to be an understandable propensity to re-create a social order in the college analogous to that prevailing in the country at large. Quite naturally, it was the upper-middle-class values of wealth and breeding that were enshrined in the social hierarchy of the campus. The peer society may nevertheless have been more open than the national society it mirrored. Any student—at least, any Caucasian student—with the will to conform and the talent to succeed had a chance to win a place of esteem. The more a student differed, however, in terms of family income, ethnicity, and the like, the more difficult acceptance into the peer society was likely to be. The relatively privileged, and those who cared to emulate them, thus set the standard for the peer society; in the process they also re-created some of the sense of social distinction that was being lost from merely going to college.

The peer society was, second, a partial response to changing social relations in the university caused by the professionalization of the faculty. As their professional communities increasingly dominated their outlooks, faculty willingly forsook the thankless task of overseeing student life. A potential void was left in place of the disciplinary code that faculty had once attempted to enforce and the moral influence that they had tried to exert. This void was actually filled on the part of students by the growth of an autonomous peer society and on the part of the university through the formation of new, nonacademic administrative units. Both these developments had unforeseen and rather unsettling consequences for the research universities.

One problem was that "the peer society neither honored nor rewarded academic work." Students who applied themselves to their studies were stigmatized as "grinds," "grubs," or "wets." The approved attitude was to get by with minimal effort, if not by resort to outright dishonesty. The issue was not merely anti-intellectualism "but that in the youth world of the twenties campus, studies were only a small part of a social learning environment in which peers played as significant a role as professors." [16] Moreover, the type of developmental learning that was derived from the highly stratified peer society was often considered more valuable, not just by students but also by adult society. Indeed, this was the crux of the matter. With faculty influence confined to the classroom and generally distrusted, there were no compensating forces to encourage serious academic work. "An incentive for achieving high rank in college," according to President Lowell, "has not existed in this country"; and President Angell likewise attributed the low regard for scholarship to its lack of connection with any monetary reward.[17] The research university of the 1920s thus had no immediate answer to the pervasive anti-intellectualism of the peer society.[18]

The university response to faculty withdrawal from student supervision was to create separate deans for students, admissions, student activities, and the like. This was the logical course of action in a compartmentalized university. As this occurred, however, important aspects of university policy slipped away from direct academic control and became lodged with administrators of a somewhat different outlook. The deans that specialized in the affairs of students were not at this date specialists in a professional sense. They tended to be graduates of the university who retained a strong identification with the collegiate culture and its symbols. They consequently supported many of the features of peer society culture—probably not the overt disdain for the classroom or extremes of social snobbery, but certainly the high valuation of athletics and student activities, and especially the importance of developmental learning from one's peers. These administrators would become another constituency in the compartmentalized research university, one with important responsibilities for determining the tone of undergraduate education.

The implications of the peer society obviously varied from campus to campus. At the institutes of technology, scientific courses could not be regarded too cavalierly. The large state universities were microcosms of a sort of their regional societies. Those who identified with the peer society may have opted for the competitive whirl of fraternities and activities, but there were sizable bodies of commuters, working students, or outright iconoclasts who rejected and sometimes resented that definition of the college experience. The result was a laissez-faire administration in the state universities—the only possible basis on which these heterogeneous institutions could function. This allowed students to make of their college experience what they would and led to a conspicuous social cleavage in the student body. At the private research universities, however, such consequences were less acceptable. They generally wanted their undergraduate colleges to offer similar experiences and similar opportunities to every matriculant. It was precisely this impulse that had motivated Wilson and Lowell before the war. In the twenties this objective became more explicit as these schools officially endorsed developmental learning as a goal of undergraduate education. In doing so, they assumed responsibility for shaping and nurturing the peer society in which such learning took place. Since the peer society of the twenties placed great importance on social background as well as on campus interaction, the final implication of this entire situation was unmistakable. The private research universities had to monitor and possibly screen just who attended their colleges if they were to preserve the intended benefits of the extracurriculum.

The collegiate syndrome of the 1920s also had an important bearing on the external relations of the research universities. During this era, college life attained a degree of notoriety that has probably not been equaled since. The image of higher education that for a time enchanted the American public had less to do with libraries and laboratories than with various manifestations of the extracurriculum. Concurrently, the 1920s were also a decade of extraordinary expansion of the capital resources of higher-education institutions in general. American society provided resources for higher education on a generous, and at times even lavish, scale. This generosity, of course, was not unrelated to the general public perception of higher education. Thus, besides triggering an emphasis on college residence and a preoccupation with the extracurriculum, the collegiate syndrome had a third major effect on university development: it was a key factor in the relations between universities and certain benefactors on whom they depended for capital resources.

The popular appeal of college life in the 1920s has been fully documented.[19] Contemporary periodicals continually fed the apparent public curiosity about colleges and universities. Campus stories were routinely covered by regular newspaper reporters and circulated by the wire services. Magazine pieces concerning colleges and their students burgeoned during these years; many universities took to the airwaves with their own radio shows. Fiction and movies dealing with collegiate themes also flourished, and advertisers were quick to capitalize on this interest by associating their clothing or other items with the student culture. In this latter respect, the preoccupation with things collegiate resembled a fad, but it was a fad rooted in the spirit of the times. College life, above all, projected the image of youth: students were in the cultural vanguard of a new social order. They exemplified a relaxation of traditional moral standards and social conventions, as well as a sanguine endorsement of material progress. Higher education represented social progress too. The rising enrollments could be interpreted as evidence both that the opportunity for material success was opening ever more widely and that the economic system was requiring ever more highly trained manpower. American society in the 1920s, then, held for higher education a reservoir of unalloyed admiration, and the universities were able to translate these attitudes into the resources for capital growth.

The 1920s were a decade of unprecedented expansion in both the capital and the income of the research universities. In the public sector, state legislators increased their appropriations to the five universities considered here by 130 percent, while student enrollments were climbing by only 40 percent. The Michigan legislature, for example, in 1921 increased its appropriation for the university by more than 50 percent and at the same time voted $5.1 million for capital expenditures—a sum almost equal to all such state spending in the entire history of the institution.[20] At most private research universities, tuition income and endowment income both more than doubled, while enrollments increased even less than in state schools. In addition, a building boom greatly expanded campus facilities at public and private universities alike. The broad-based support enjoyed by American colleges and universities during this period was reflected particularly in the flow of voluntary support.

In the 1920s more than $1 billion was donated to American colleges and universities.[21] Questions of who gave the money, who the recipients were, and how these funds were utilized are tightly interrelated. Nevertheless, the decade witnessed some new departures on each of these matters.

Donations to colleges and universities during this period came from three main sources: foundations, philanthropists, and ordinary individuals. Although there is no clear line separating major philanthropists from the rest of the human race, these individuals tend to be commemorated on college campuses by the buildings that bear their names. The very rich played an especially important role in university development, even if it defies precise quantification. Before the war, major gifts from the wealthy were chiefly responsible for the growth of university capital; broad-based giving, such as occurred in the Yale Alumni Fund and the Harvard class gifts, was a distinct exception. In the postwar period this would no longer be true. Organized fund-raising drives and widespread efforts to simulate Yale-Harvard practices made less wealthy individuals into another significant source of university capital.

A contemporary attempt to fathom the annual fluctuations of philanthropic giving during the interwar years found that giving levels were
likely to correlate with fluctuations in the national income.[22] Rising personal income seemed to have fueled individual giving during the 1920s, in
part because income was distributed so unevenly. In 1928 some 511 tax-
payers reported incomes of over $1 million, compared with only 67 just
six years earlier. But they were just the tip of a steep income pyramid.
When all income brackets are compared for those two years, the higher of
the bracket, the greater the proportionate increase in the number of tax-
payers. More important, the higher the income, the larger the percentage
of philanthropic donations.[23] By the latter years of the decade, there were
not only more millionaires capable of very substantial gifts but also more
relatively affluent individuals in the upper-middle income brackets than
ever before. Appeals to the multitude could clearly be more lucrative than
in the past. The foundations played a strategic part in assisting higher
education to tap this potential.

In the postwar years American foundations became more numerous
and more actively involved in higher education. Whereas the first fifteen
years of the century saw the creation of eighteen foundations, the next
fifteen years witnessed the birth of fifty-four.[24] Still, the sheer size and
clout of the Carnegie and Rockefeller philanthropies overshadowed all
others. This was particularly evident when John D. Rockefeller, Sr., chose
to bolster college and university finances after the war. Concerned about
the sorry state of faculty salaries, he gave $50 million to the General Edu-
cation Board in 1919 to be used to enlarge private-college endowments.[25]
The board followed its previous policy of making its awards conditional
upon the recipient's themselves raising several times the value of the
grant. Chicago, Caltech, Stanford, and even Harvard ($500,000 toward
$10 million) benefited from these grants, but the basic intention was to
buttress the finances and the fund-raising capacities of a broad spectrum
of private institutions. Soon, more than 100 institutions were engaged in
endowment drives similar to the postwar efforts already instigated by
Harvard, Yale, Princeton, Cornell, and MIT. By 1924 the board had
pledged $36 million to 170 colleges and universities, which had them-
selves received commitments to raise $83 million.[26]

The first half of the 1920s was a period of fund-raising campaigns for
colleges and universities, not only because of the policy of the GEB but
also because of the general need to redress wartime financial damage and
to take advantage of the wide public esteem for higher education. These
drives, moreover, had a noticeable impact upon overall patterns of giving.
In the first decade of the century, the research universities were receiving
about one-half of all reported gifts to colleges and universities;[27] but
throughout most of the 1920s, their share fluctuated between one-quarter

and one-third. Thus, the decade was initially a period in which financial resources were being spread more widely, allowing some other colleges and universities to gain a little ground on the wealthy research universities.

TABLE 7. Value of Private Gifts to Colleges and Universities by Use, 1920–1930 (in thousands of dollars)

	Physical Capital	Endowment	Current Expenditures	Total
1919–20	7,274	50,907	7,105	65,286
1921–22	13,597	53,720	10,084	77,401
1923–24	22,633	46,727	12,375	81,735
1925–26	29,473	72,375	16,296	118,144
1927–28	42,847	50,145	21,690	114,682
1929–30	54,662	67,246	26,493	148,401

SOURCE: Bureau of Education, *Biennial Survey of Education.*

Several trends become evident when aggregate gifts to all colleges and universities are broken down for the period.[28] The GEB's emphasis on endowment clearly had an impact early in the decade but steadily waned thereafter. From 74 percent of total giving at the beginning of the decade (1920 and 1922), giving for endowment dropped to 59 percent in the midtwenties and to 45 percent in the latter years of the decade. The GEB itself partly caused this trend by abandoning its endowment-building efforts. It had adopted as a desirable standard a level of endowment income of about $250 per student—roughly equal to the prevailing cost of tuition. The GEB soon realized that the sheer size of American higher education made this an unattainable goal. Despite the large sums added to endowment in these years, in 1924 only 8 percent of all students were attending institutions that could meet the $250 criterion.[29] Because of the large number of endowment campaigns, the total college and university endowment grew more rapidly during the decade than did the endowments of the research universities, although the "Big Four"—Chicago, Columbia, Harvard, and Yale—continued to claim almost one-quarter of the total.

The relative decline of giving for endowment corresponded to the upsurge in gifts for physical capital and current expenditures. The sevenfold increase in the former is an adequate corroboration of the building boom mentioned above. The rise in the general category of "current expenses" actually conceals an even more important trend. As foundations became disillusioned with providing general endowment, they became increasingly supportive of science and scholarship. Although this sometimes involved earmarked endowment grants, it also produced an increasing level of grants designated directly for research. This was a development of utmost importance for the research universities, one that will be taken up in the next chapter. It nevertheless also contributed to still another trend in higher-education philanthropy. At the end of the decade the relative share received by the research universities turned sharply upward, attaining a level of approximately 43 percent of the total. The supplementary resources available for higher education, in other words, again began to be concentrated in the research universities. This was due partly to the role of the foundations in supporting research and partly to the generally superior fund-raising capacities of the research universities themselves.

The nature of the voluntary support that the research universities could tap can be gathered from the results of the following campaigns conducted in the early 1920s (Table 8). All except Wisconsin's were managed by professional fund-raisers. A conditional foundation grant was an important factor in only the Chicago, Johns Hopkins, and Stanford campaigns. Three different patterns of fund-raising are evident here. The state universities appealed chiefly to their alumni for numerous small gifts. Chicago and Johns Hopkins depended on relatively few large givers. Their support networks sprang largely from their respective metropolitan areas. The Ivy League universities relied primarily upon their alumni for small and large contributions. Both state and Ivy League universities, then, looked to their loyal alumni for philanthropic support. And, as has already been argued, alumni tended to relate to their schools through identification with extracurricular activities. Interestingly, of the two institutions that relied instead on community patrons, Johns Hopkins never embraced the collegiate syndrome, and Chicago repudiated it rather decisively in the 1930s. There is thus an evident connection between the alumni support that was so essential to the development of research universities and the collegiate life of the universities that transfixed the attention of most outside sympathizers.

For the state universities and several of the private ones, it was enthusiasm for the extracurriculum that made it attractive to large numbers of contributors. The objects of these appeals were auditoriums, student union buildings, massive football stadiums, and dormitories. The University of Michigan, which was in the vanguard of state universities in organizing its alumni, provides a good example of this process.[30] Alumni Memorial Hall, an art museum, was the first structure to be built largely through alumni contributions (1910). The fact that it was a memorial to Civil War dead testifies to the languid pace of giving before the Great War. Afterward, though, alumni efforts raised more than $1 million for a commodious building for the men's student Union (1920). A corresponding structure for the women's League was erected with do

TABLE 8. Fund-raising Campaign Results for 11 Research Universities 1919–25 (in thousands of dollars)

	Total Raised	Source (%)			Number of Givers	Number of $1,000+ Givers	% of Total $1,000+ Gifts
		Alumni	Public	Foundations			
Illinois	1,994	90.9	9.1	—	18,761	207	12.1
Michigan	1,530	96.4	3.6	—	23,000	n.a.	n.a.
Minnesota	1,626	84.2	15.7	0.2	15,164	143	23.9
Wisconsin	810	67.6	6.5	25.9	11,500	n.a.	n.a.
Chicago*	8,665	19.6	51.8	28.6	7,855	324	55.8
Cornell	6,413	84.5	15.5	—	10,475	n.a.	n.a.
Harvard	13,932	86.7	13.3	—	23,477	2,515	80.1
Penn*	5,344	65.6	17.6	9.3	8,858	1,061	61.2
Princeton	9,903	74.6	25.4	—	11,682	1,022	59.2
Stanford	1,480	48.3	30.8	20.9	7,055	n.a.	n.a.
Johns Hopkins	4,505	11.0	56.0	33.0	2,699	296	61

SOURCE: John Price Jones Corporation, A Nation-Wide Survey of Fund-Raising (New York: John Price Jones Corporation, 1926).
* Still in progress (January 1926).

nated funds in 1927. The first dormitories at Michigan, both for women, resulted from large individual gifts (1915), but when the university committed itself to housing men as well, in the 1930s, alumni groups donated the funds for several units. Various groups of university supporters also united to fund a bell tower when a carillon was offered as a gift (1936). The huge Michigan stadium that was completed in 1927—the only larger university stadium was Stanford's (built in 1921, enlarged in 1927)—was financed largely through a bond issue.[31] It followed the construction of the present-day football stadiums of California (1923), Illinois (1924), Wisconsin (1925), and Minnesota (1925), all of which involved substantial public fund-raising drives. Once completed, these stadiums proved to be an unanticipated bonanza to their respective athletic boards. The revenues they generated not only quickly eliminated any indebtedness but also provided funds for baseball stadiums, field houses, and golf courses.

The Michigan pattern of broad-based, alumni-led fund-raising for extracurricular structures was replicated in the 1920s at the other state research universities. It is more difficult to discern a pattern at the private universities, though, because of the prevalence of large individual gifts for these purposes. At Cornell, for example, a lavish union and theater was donated by Mrs. Willard Straight, and a similarly well appointed set of women's dormitories was given by Allen Balch; but broad appeals were utilized to build the men's dormitory complex and the football stadium.[32] Where such buildings were not provided for, it would seem, they could become rallying points for the energies of the university's supporters. These donations strengthened the university activities that alumni could most easily relate to; in addition, they provided some direct use to the university's benefactors. Returning alumni could attend athletic contests, stay or dine in the union, and attend events in the auditoriums. The mass of contributors thus seemed most willing to support those activities that strengthened their own ties with the university. They consequently became in the 1920s more than ever before a valued constituency of research universities.

The presence of the donor constituency on campus, physically or in the consciousness of university officials, had several effects on the course of university development. Without doubt, the extracurricular structures that they funded allowed a fuller efflorescence of these activities than would otherwise have occurred. More specific influences are also evident. Individual philanthropists produced some notable effects by themselves. Edward Harkness certainly altered the nature of Yale in ways that had not been foreseen by the school's leaders; and Michigan in the 1920s had to be chary of the sensitivities of William W. Cook, aware that his considerable fortune was willed to the university's law school.[33] More predictably, the organized alumni carried great weight on campus during this era, for good or for ill. The Yale alumni in 1919 forced a long overdue reorganization of the university upon a reluctant administration. At Penn, however, a similar alumni intervention produced an unfortunate presidential choice, who never assumed the office, as well as recommendations that were at odds with the financial realities of the university.[34] More important in the long run, the alumni of the twenties could be counted upon to respond in rather predictable ways to issues involving the social and extracurricular side of campus life. The Stanford alumni, for example, unanimously rejected any disruption of the four-year undergraduate course, even though it seemed logical to President Wilbur that the university ought to concentrate on upper-level work.[35] Ultimately, however, the influence of the donor constituency should be sought in terms not of conflict but of concord.

To a considerable extent university leaders of the 1920s internalized the values and the outlook of the donor constituency upon which they depended for additional resources. They tended to agree about the educational value of the extracurriculum, to accept the desirability of university-sponsored housing for students, and to see the importance, where possible, of cultivating the peer society in the undergraduate college. This consensus did not extend, or for that matter need to extend, to all facets of university activities. The saving grace for the research universities may well have been that university boosters in general were nearly oblivious to such things as faculty research and graduate education. But alumni concerns did extend to the question of who would attend the universities' undergraduate colleges. And the shared views of university leaders and university boosters on this vital issue shaped the development of American research universities in this decade.

4. Who Shall Go to College?

In the fall of 1922 Ernest M. Hopkins, president of Dartmouth, caused a stir in educational circles with a speech averring that "too many young men are going to college." Hopkins was concerned that public and private resources were inadequate to accommodate the college enrollment boom still in full swing and that existing resources were being wasted on men who "spend their time profitlessly in idleness." He consequently called for a "working theory" to select those individuals worthy of the privilege of getting higher education. Rejecting a limitation of college to the wealthy and the well-born, Hopkins advocated instead the recognition of "an aristocracy of brains, made up of men intellectually alert and intellectually eager, to whom increasingly the opportunities for higher education ought to be restricted." [1] He seemed to be proposing, in short, a meritocratic approach to college admissions.

For a college president's address to incoming freshmen, Hopkins's remarks generated exceedingly wide comment in the popular press and educational periodicals.[2] While many commentators could agree with one or another of his points, his overall suggestion definitely went against the prevailing grain. He was critical of the increasing popularity of going to college, although others generally equated this with greater democracy and social progress. Restricting higher education to an "aristocracy of brains," on the other hand, was a well-understood attack upon the collegiate syndrome.

There was a clear reason why Hopkins's unexceptional sentiments had such reverberations at this time: he had, in fact, touched upon a more fundamental issue than he had realized. By the early 1920s, it had become apparent to most private research universities that they would have to limit their enrollments for reasons inherent in their fiscal structure and physical facilities. Once they decided on this step, however, they faced a second and more controversial decision about determining whom to admit. On this point there was a latent conflict between the ascendant mentality of the collegiate syndrome and the entrenched values of the research university. Further complicating this issue was the perceived threat presented by the large enrollments of Jewish students. As the private research universities resolved these issues during the course of the 1920s, they furthered in a significant manner the continuing differentiation of research universities from the rest of American higher education—and from each other as well.

At the beginning of the 1920s the presidents of both Columbia and Harvard announced that the past proliferation of university functions was at an end: "there would appear to be no reason for the university to expand beyond its present limits," stated Butler; while Lowell felt that "the task of the University for the immediate future should be the perfecting of its existing departments rather than branching out into new fields of work." Actually, research universities had difficulty delimiting their activities then and ever since—both men soon violated their stated convictions as Columbia accepted the new School of Library Science and Harvard the School of Public Health. This nevertheless represented a turning point in the history of private research universities. No longer would biggest be best. Instead, they would commit themselves, in general, to developing the work of the university "intensively rather than extensively"—to utilizing "all the possible resources of the university . . . to keep its existing departments at the highest level." [3] The most momentous change signaled by this new state of mind undoubtedly was the limitation of undergraduate enrollment. In 1919 an effective ceiling was placed on

Columbia College's entering class; in 1920 the Cornell faculty voted to limit enrollment; Stanford adopted a fixed class size in 1921; Princeton established class limitations in 1922, followed by Yale (1922), Harvard (1923), and Chicago (1928).[4] Since the circumstances of these schools varied widely, why did they all take these steps when they did?

Two recent histories have provided an exceptionally detailed picture of the motivation behind admissions policies at Columbia, Harvard, Yale, and Princeton. Harold Wechsler's analysis of the implementation of selective admissions at Columbia and Marcia Synnott's treatment of the "Big Three" both document an unmistakable intention to hold down the number of Jewish students at these schools.[5] Yet, that motivation clearly would not apply to all the universities that instituted restrictive admissions policies. Cornell and Stanford, which were the first to follow Columbia, had no "Jewish problem"; and Chicago implemented selective admissions without any evidence of discrimination against Jews.[6] A logic of consolidation and concentration seemed to be at work among the private research universities, irrespective of the Jewish question. It arose, primarily, from the basic financial structure of endowed institutions.

Although the limiting of admissions was widely discussed at the time, the justifications given seemed to avoid the underlying issue. Lowell said that Harvard had sufficient faculty for more students but that housing was a constraining factor. Angell of Yale argued the need to preserve small classes and personal instruction.[7] Stable enrollments would ultimately be a boon to research-minded faculty, but this was not a motivating factor in the early 1920s. Dormitory space was an issue at these schools, but many students still lived off campus. Essentially, it was a problem of the amount of capital available for educational purposes.

The research universities had been severely punished by the war-induced inflation (79 percent from 1915 to 1920), which caused a corresponding diminution of the real value of their endowments and a considerable shortfall in income. The postwar endowment drives were aimed principally at redressing this situation, so that endowment income could be restored to something like its prewar purchasing power. The postwar enrollment boom, however, again diluted the amount of university capital per student. Despite increased tuition, it should be recalled, each research university student cost about twice what he or she paid. Added to this were long university wish lists for new buildings. The conclusion, then, seemed inescapable: enrollments could not be allowed to climb as they had in the recent past. This does not mean, however, that the Jewish question was irrelevant. The evidence Wechsler and Synnott have presented shows the persistent preoccupation of presidents, college deans, and admissions officers at those schools with the numbers and possible consequences of their Jewish enrollment. This issue thus had a determinative influence not on the limitation of enrollment but on the kinds of selective admissions policies that were put into effect.

The antipathy toward Jewish students at private colleges and universities was explored in a remarkably fair-minded contemporary essay by Ralph Boas.[8] The alleged faults of the Jewish students arose directly from qualities that might otherwise be considered admirable: an ingrained desire for education, ambition to attain successful positions in American society, undoubted powers of application, and conspicuous scholarly attainments. The difficulty stemmed rather from the nature of the American college:

> [It] is not, and never has been, an institution primarily for the acquisition of knowledge or the attainment of degrees. It is a social organization, with a very highly organized social structure . . . [and] with unwritten rules more rigid than those which govern the most exclusive society, administered with all the relentlessness of youth.

A sufficiently large contingent of Jewish students, then, would threaten to bring "disunion and strife within the social life of the college"; to trouble "deans and presidents, who want unity above everything"; and to interfere with the ties that bind alumni to this social organization.

Boas held no doubts that it was easier to exclude the offending group, despite some protest, than it would be to change the social nature of the college. He went on, however, to pose the alternatives in stark terms. American colleges might aim "to find the sharpest brains in the country and to cultivate them"; in this case "the problem of the limitation of enrollment would be simple," and "Jews would have nothing to fear." Or, they could emphasize the "careful selection of students to form a type." This would mean "the abandonment of scholastic achievement as the criterion of collegiate success [and] the creation of 'gentlemen's' colleges." Harvard, Yale, Princeton, and Columbia might have the prerogative, as private institutions, to opt for such "social homogeneity," but Boas doubted the wisdom of that course. It would amount to "abandoning the side of the angels in the perpetual fight against bigotry, superstition, racial intolerance and inverted nationalism." It might be difficult for many to accept social mixing on campus, Boas recognized, "but it is harder to see one's college the fostering mother of hates and racial dissensions, the parent of bitterness which for years will be a canker in the minds of men."

For research universities the Scylla of strictly meritocratic admissions was as unthinkable as the Charybdis of being a gentlemen's college. Established traditions of academic research, the prevalence of serious, professionally minded faculty, and the need to furnish competent recruits to their own graduate and professional schools—all militated against overt social selection. On the other hand, the strength of the collegiate syndrome and the sentiments of contributing alumni, whether voiced or anticipated, precluded placing scholarship ahead of "character." What they were groping for in their admissions policies was a middle course—a "tilt" that would encourage the recruitment of desirable social types, while screening out others, particularly the local Jewish candidates—an approach that might be described as bigotry without the tears of bitterness against which Boas had warned.

Before the war American colleges and universities had essentially been open to all who were adequately prepared to do college-level work. Adequate preparation was determined in the West by graduation from an accredited high school (the certificate system), but the eastern private schools clung to an earlier system of entrance examinations conducted independently by each institution. Before 1920 Harvard, Yale, Princeton, and Columbia were eager to broaden their area of recruitment and to improve the quality of incoming students. Columbia facilitated applications from the City and New York State, while the others agreed in 1915 to use the comprehensive examinations of the College Entrance Examination Board as a way to qualify for admission (called the "New Plan").[9] All four universities had well-established recruitment routes with elite preparatory schools, and they were careful not to disturb these mutually advantageous relationships. These schools tailored their curricula to the university entrance exams, and the prep-school students were important socially to the universities.[10] These "Old Plans" of admission consequently remained in force. The new criteria for admission that were introduced were thus intended for the other category of admittees.

The prevailing sentiment during the 1920s was decidedly against an explicitly meritocratic selection for admission to college.[11] Ingrained collegiate attitudes were probably most responsible, but it should also be recognized that reliable means for evaluating academic merit had yet to be established. Existing entrance examinations were designed to determine only whether candidates were prepared, unprepared, or prepared enough to do college work with "conditions." The quality of secondary education was so uneven from school to school that high school grades could not be trusted by themselves.[12] "Psychological" or intelligence tests received a tremendous boost from their wartime applications; but, although many schools adopted them in some form, they were reluctant to entrust their lifeblood of new students to such novel and uncertain means. All this, however, cannot gainsay the fact that the eastern colleges were adamant about denying academic achievement priority over "character" as a criterion for admission.

The first major university to develop the means for resolving the admissions dilemma was Columbia.[13] By the second decade of the century its leaders were clearly concerned, as Wechsler has shown, with preserving the social character of Columbia College.[14] Columbia was becoming too attractive for the multitude of bright and ambitious Jewish students graduating from New York City high schools, and it faced a perpetual problem of retaining the loyalties of the New York City social elite. The solution announced in 1919 combined a ceiling on enrollments and selective admissions based in part on social characteristics. Applicants were henceforth required to supply extensive personal data (family background, religion, school activities, interests, and future occupation), a picture, and three letters of reference, as well as to be interviewed (if possible) and take intelligence tests or the College Board examinations. The essential purpose of this plethora of information was to transform an objective decision into a subjective one: no longer could any single attainment, such as passing an examination, qualify a candidate for admission; but an unsatisfactory showing on any particular item *might* mean disqualification. It would be up to the office of admissions to make multiple evaluations of each student, and ultimately to combine these disparate criteria into a single judgment. The implementation of selective admissions eventually reduced the percentage of Jewish students from a peak of 40 percent of a class to about half that level. Wechsler notes that meritocratic criteria continued to carry considerable weight and also that Columbia was dealing with a finite applicant pool from which to construct its freshman classes.[15] But the great advantage of selective admissions was precisely its flexibility. For this reason it was soon imitated in one form or another by other eastern schools.

The road to selective admissions at Harvard, as portrayed by Marcia Synnott, reveals the inherent conflict between collegiate and university values.[16] By 1920 A. Lawrence Lowell had become convinced that the number of Jewish students at Harvard had become excessive. Here again, the concern was to preserve the social character of the undergraduate college. With his usual bluntness, Lowell sought faculty endorsement in 1922 of a new admissions policy that would have established an effective quota for Jewish entrants. The issue came to public attention and provoked widespread comment (including the article by Boas). The result, however, was an explicit repudiation by the Harvard faculty of discrimination against Jews, and their decision seems to have been generally supported by the greater Harvard community. Clearly rebuffed, Lowell persisted with more circumspection. A limit on freshman-class size was instituted in 1923; greater discretion was gradually given to the admissions committee; and in 1926 a new policy of selectivity that included examining the personal and academic qualities of each applicant was put in place. The meritocratic preferences of the faculty were respected by assurances that candidates with the highest academic qualifications would be accepted without further scrutiny. Harvard's experience made it clear to other schools that overt quotas could not be publicly admitted; and Harvard seems to have learned from others that discrimination required a cloak of ambiguity.

Other eastern research universities developed their own distinctive solutions to the admissions question. At Yale a president with a university outlook, personally opposed in principle to discrimination, was largely outmaneuvered by collegiate-minded officers of the school who seemed to have the larger Yale community behind them. Nevertheless, the gradual elaboration of a selective admissions policy caused no sharp drop in the proportion of Jewish students at Yale (as it did at Columbia and Harvard), but rather kept the number stable at a level of about 10 percent.[17] Princeton, on the other hand, was probably the only research university that could also be comfortable as a gentlemen's college. Synnott has concluded that it enforced a rigid—and low—quota for Jews and Catholics. Moreover, Princeton's admissions procedures blatantly gave priority to social over intellectual qualifications. Princeton first categorized its students according to the social information contained in the application form and references and then admitted only the desirable categories on the basis of their examination scores.[18]

The University of Pennsylvania provides an instructive contrary example on the issue of selective admissions. With a limited pool of applicants, a tradition of serving the population of Philadelphia, and implicit obligations arising from its state subsidies, Penn was in no position to tailor its undergraduate college to conform with the collegiate syndrome. Yet, that is essentially what its alumni demanded in the 1920s. An alumni committee actually recommended that Penn drop its extension and evening courses, eschew state subsidies, and dedicate itself to "education for leadership." In 1926 a serious movement was begun to relocate the college in rural Valley Forge, where it presumably could attempt to become another Princeton. In Penn's case alumni and local backers did not provide sufficient voluntary support to allow them to dictate the course of university development.[19] The situation was otherwise at Columbia, Harvard, Yale, and Princeton.

The establishment of selective admissions at these four schools was basically an incremental process of institutional learning and adaptation. Outright innovations were applied tentatively at first and copied selectively by other schools as the situation warranted. Class-size restrictions, for example, were initially set above current levels of intake in order to minimize discontinuity. Discrimination probably increased over time as the machinery of selective admissions was perfected. There was good reason, however, for the basic conservatism of admissions policy. The highest priority of admissions was not the negative task of exclusion but the positive one of recruiting the preferred clientele from the leading private preparatory schools.

At Yale the proportion of private school graduates in incoming classes rose from 70 percent in the mid-twenties to a peak of 79 percent in 1931. At Harvard the private-school contingent declined from 60 percent in 1920 to 50 percent at mid-decade, before selective admissions boosted it back to around 55 percent. Princeton was most exclusive, with private-school concentrations as high as 90 percent.[20] The children of alumni, no matter where they attended secondary school, were also an important constituency. The fund-raising efforts of the twenties, Synnott notes, made alumni feel entitled to places for their sons. Immediately after Yale limited its class size, it added this qualification: "limitations of numbers shall not operate to exclude any son of a Yale graduate who has satisfied all the requirements for admission."[21] And apparently it did not. The proportion of alumni children in freshman classes doubled in the first decade of selective admissions, from 15 percent to 30 percent. It thus becomes evident that, given the social bias arising from collegiate goals and from dependence upon voluntary support, these four schools had little room for anyone else besides their preferred constituencies. In addition to discriminating explicitly against Jewish students, they were, to a considerable extent, closed to the bulk of American society as well.

In light of the pronounced social bias of the private eastern universities, it is interesting to compare the development of selective admissions in the absence of eastern class rigidities and prejudice against Jews. Stanford was, in fact, the first university to confront the problem of selecting students from among a surplus of qualified applicants. Mrs. Leland Stanford, fearful that women might displace men at the university created to honor her son, in 1899 placed a permanent limit of 500 on total female enrollment.[22] The university's first response was simply to establish a numbered list for each class, but soon eager parents were signing up their girls at birth. Scholastic criteria were then employed, but it was concluded that information on "personality, physique and other personal qualities" ought to be considered too. Thus, in 1921 when rising applications and physical constraints required that male class size be limited as well, Stanford was already experienced in selective admissions. Its approach was nevertheless avowedly "experimental," based upon a continual analysis of "the achievement records of students in relationship to their apparent abilities for admission." By 1925, admissions decisions were being based upon high school records, College Board examinations, intelligence tests, and references given on a personal rating form. Women by this date had to be "quite exceptional" on several criteria in order to be among the 20 percent of the successful applicants. Competition among men was less severe, but to be assured of admission an applicant needed to be in the upper fifth of his graduating class or score above average on the College Board exams.[23]

Stanford gathered more or less the same information as the eastern universities, but instead of employing it to produce a social "tilt" to admissions decisions, it organized the decision-making process so as to strive for meritocratic results. It attempted to make subjective decisions more objective through standard quantitative procedures. The admissions committee that rated applicants consisted of five faculty members, rather than a nonacademic admissions staff, and their independent ratings were combined to reach a final decision. Anomalies like the priority granted to children of faculty and alumni, "because of previous implied obligations," were scheduled to "expire within a few years." Finally, given "the fallibility of human judgment in forecasting the possibilities of youth . . . a personal interview with each student as part of the test is not at present emphasized." In short, while recognizing that perfect evaluation of merit might be impossible, Stanford proceeded pragmatically, scientifically, and evenhandedly to "have its choices made on the ascertainable qualities of the applicants and upon no other basis."[24]

Placing the development of selective admissions at Harvard, Yale, and Princeton in a larger social context, Jerome Karabel has concluded that status-grup struggle between the "Protestant Establishment" and an insurgent Jewish population was the dominant factor behind these policies. These institutions should consequently be seen, he believes, "as organizations so tied at that historical moment to the outlook and interests of the Protestant upper class that they readily volunteered for service on behalf of its interests and eagerly embraced its fundamental goals."[25] Nevertheless, it should also be recognized that these undergraduate colleges were components of larger universities, and that these universities were themselves part of a national system of research universities. Within these universities there existed another constituency that upheld—and had vested interests in—the universalistic ideology of science and scholarship. As universities in implicit competition with other universities, they could not entirely ignore academic merit in their admissions decisions. The approach that evolved at Stanford in the first half of the 1920s furthermore suggests that, in the absence of status-group antagonism, universalistic criteria will tend to predominate in research universities. The conflict between these different sets of values, representing respectively the social and the cognitive functions of higher education, are in fact responsible for the ambiguous legacy of selective admissions.

In the long run the limiting of admissions proved an advantage to private research universities in two respects. Faculty eventually had fewer students to teach, and before long they had better students to teach. This assuaged their perpetual complaints about teaching large classes of elementary subjects to poorly prepared students. It allowed for more advanced instruction and freed time for professional activities. On the other hand, selective admissions as practiced by the eastern schools—"bigotry without tears"—was more than just a blot on their historical traditions. Their admissions policies were partly provoked by the prevailing collegiate syndrome but certainly served when in operation to condone the anti-intellectual implications of those collegiate values.

The implementation of selective admissions in the 1920s was an important step in the differentiation of American higher education because it marked the existence of a recognizable quality gradient. It also brought a nonqualitative differentiation between different types of research universities based upon their mode of selection. The state research universities of this era were nonselective upon intake, but then exercised a significant post-admission selection on the unimpeachable basis of course grades. A few institutions were oriented toward selection primarily upon scholastic abilities. The remaining private universities attempted to build their incoming classes on a shifting foundation of social, personal, and academic criteria.

These same essential categories have persisted over time. The pluralism of admissions criteria has been at the same time one of the strengths of the American system and also its Achilles' heel. By avoiding a single, decisive entrance examination, the United States has been spared the emergence of an extensive and minimally productive cram-school industry, such as exists in France and Japan. On the other hand, the subjective balancing of many incommensurate criteria has produced a changing, but inescapable, "tilt" in the admissions process. Despite the growing emphasis over time on meritocratic criteria, these tilts have continued to reflect the relative status of groups in American society. Although conflicts have flared over just these issues, they have been mitigated by the decreasing importance of undergraduate admissions. In contrast to the situation in the 1920s, the most significant and most direct rewards available through higher education are now bestowed as graduate-level credentials. It was this development that would eventually change the relationship between the research university and what would come to be called the university college.[26]

By the end of the 1920s the research universities differed markedly from the expectations of them held in the immediate postwar period. Nicholas Murray Butler had confidently announced in 1919 that a new "university center of gravity" had emerged: "the political, economic, and purely business developments of the past decade, especially as these have been influenced by the war," had combined to make business and engineering the future focus of university activities.[27] The great influx of additional students, however, soon brought different kinds of values into ascendancy.

The cultivation of a social elite in a residential college became more crucial to Columbia, and to many other research universities, than the dissemination of usable knowledge. The collegiate syndrome consequently held sway through the first half of the 1920s, supported by a powerful constituency in American society that valued college more as an agency of socialization than as an institution of learning. The campus atmosphere engendered by these attitudes supplied little encouragement to the advancement of knowledge. It did help to elicit, however, an unprecedented level of donations to American colleges and universities from philanthropists, foundations, and alumni. University research, although often obscured by the collegiate comedy, was nevertheless able to utilize this largess to make gains that became increasingly apparent in the last half of the decade. Marching to a different drummer, academic research adapted to challenges all its own concerning growth, differentiation, and relations with the rest of American society.

4

Foundations and University Research

Early in the 1920s the major philanthropic foundations significantly altered their standing policies toward higher education: instead of attempting to strengthen and sustain a broad spectrum of American colleges and universities, they committed themselves above all to furthering the advancement of knowledge, chiefly by facilitating the conduct of research.[1] Although this reorientation reflected only a small number of actual decisions, taken at a few major foundations, they represented a substantial portion of the philanthropic resources potentially available to higher education. Some fundamental developments on both sides of the relationship between foundations and higher education had presaged this change. On campus the unanticipated spurt in attendance was producing a higher-education system that was too large and too diverse to be decisively shaped by the actions of one or several foundations. In the foundations the passing of the original donors permitted general objectives to be determined by experienced and knowledgeable professional staffs. All evidence indicates that these new foundation leaders were completely earnest in their desire to fulfill their broad mandates to work toward the "welfare of mankind," as they understood it, and, at least by implication, toward the improvement of American society. Their challenge consequently became to formulate programs that held at least the promise of broad and significant benefits to society, while also being commensurate with the means available.[2] After 1920 these criteria dictated a policy of what was then called "concentration": a trend over time to focus foundation resources upon objectives that were strategically important and carefully delimited.

Outside of the possibilities in medicine and public health, the general goal of advancing knowledge was particularly amenable to such criteria.

Major shifts in institutional orientation like these usually have negative as well as positive causes. Behind the growing needs of university investigators, exciting opportunities on the frontiers of science, and the vision of foundation leaders, it is possible to detect a certain disillusionment among foundation professionals with the prevailing course of undergraduate education in the United States. Henry Pritchett of the Carnegie Corporation stated bluntly that foundation support for higher education had contributed to "an army of youth pressing into the colleges," many of whom would be better off elsewhere. On the other hand, he felt that "to aid fruitful research is, in the estimation of a great body of intelligent people, perhaps the best use of trust funds." [3] The Rockefeller expert on college finance, Trevor Arnett, translated this attitude into practical advice. Whereas at the beginning of the decade he had held that half of the cost of a college education ought to be met through endowment income, by the mid-twenties, despite sharp increases in tuition charges, he argued that undergraduates should be made to pay the full cost of their education. Students were going to college for the economic advantages it brought them, he reasoned, and should therefore not be subsidized beyond the extent of scholarships and loans for the needy. Philanthropy should instead concentrate on the advancement of knowledge, with universities, in particular, devoting their donated funds to the support of graduate education and research. [4]

Foundation officials, it seems, were dismayed by many of the aspects of American higher education that were described in the preceding chapter—the collegiate syndrome, the unrestrained growth of some institutions, and the prevalance of shallow vocationalism among students and institutions alike. Discouraged by the quantitative trends, the major foundations still provided selective support for programs that might strengthen the quality of the American college. Abundant funds were channeled into the general area of testing and selecting students for admission to college. Experimental programs that promised to improve quality also received support, most notably several large grants that allowed the establishment of honors programs. Later, foundations supported considerable research concerned with the transition from secondary to higher education. [5] Foundations were nevertheless quick to accept such unalterable realities of American higher education as the bifurcation between graduate and undergraduate study and the increased differentiation within the system. Whereas late-nineteenth-century university reformers had clung to the possibility that learning would permeate the entire academy, foundation officials of the 1920s seem to have concluded that serious inquiry was destined to thrive at the graduate level.

Over the course of the decade the reorientation of the major philanthropic foundations toward support for research and scholarship proved enormously beneficial to the research universities in particular. This process was nevertheless neither immediate nor automatic. It involved a considerable amount of institutional learning on both sides. As events unfolded, however, the natural advantages of the research universities created over the preceding decades brought them gradually to the fore as the most effective agencies for the achievement of foundation purposes.

1. Ways and Means: Defining the Foundations' Role

The amelioration of the human condition through the advancement of knowledge was one of the original and abiding goals of twentieth-century philanthropic foundations. Yet, the arrangements for pursuing this goal were from the outset problematic. The trustees or directors of a foundation might be able to determine in a general way which facet of human understanding they would like to see broadened, but only the disciplinary expert, working at the frontiers of discovery, possessed the capability of realizing—if indeed realization was possible—these intentions. The challenge of translating the financial assets of a philanthropic trust into human knowledge, and of doing so in a creditably creative and efficient manner, thus became a problem of devising institutional forms that could link those who would stimulate discovery and those who could accomplish it. Simplistic approaches, like Andrew Carnegie's efforts to identify the "exceptional man," demonstrated that the problem would not yield to frontal assaults. Rather, solutions had to be found that were compatible with existing configurations of relevant knowledge-bearing institutions and consistent with the organizational technology of the period. For this reason, the foundations continued to experiment with different arrangements for facilitating research during the entire period of this study.

Prior to the First World War, foundations generally utilized the most direct apporach: for the most part they organized and conducted research under their own auspices. The research institutes described in Chapter 2 were the most obvious exemplars, but even with them it took some time to work out successful strategies. In fact, the Carnegie Institution of Washington and the Rockefeller Institute for Medical Research developed rather different approaches during their formative years. The CIW entered relatively well worked fields, and consequently had to choose with care the specific areas of inquiry on which it would focus. The form of the free-standing research institute was quite appropriate for the choices they made. Such undertakings as the solar telescope, the marine biology station, or the geophysical laboratory required expensive fixed facilities that were best utilized by at least a nucleus of full-time scientists. The RIMR, facing the open vista of a field relatively undeveloped in this country, proceeded by carefully choosing the people it would support. Relying on recognized experts to assemble the best available scientists, it then allowed them free reign to investigate those topics that they considered most likely to yield significant results. Priority and leadership assured the continued recruitment of talented researchers, thereby ensuring the effectiveness of the RIMR.

The "reform" foundations, dedicated to the betterment of a specific social problem, also tended to sponsor occasional in-house studies.[1] Their underlying purpose in these cases was primarily enlightenment: the conviction that if the actual facts of a situation were established and publicized, the proper course of action would become evident. In this view the Carnegie Foundation for the Advancement of Teaching (f. 1906) commissioned a number of studies. Among them, Abraham Flexner's exposé of medical education constitutes a classical success in this rather tendentious form of enlightenment.[2] The Russell Sage Foundation (f. 1907) was dedicated to the more traditional charitable objectives of improving social welfare. Its directors decided, however, that they could contribute most effectively toward this end by studying the root causes of "social maladjustment." It gradually developed a program of in-house investigations into issues of social services, working conditions, and community development. In particular, Russell Sage pursued a vision of public enlightenment through the relatively noncontroversial means of the social survey.[3] To the foundation world there seemed to be little discernible difference at this juncture between discovering social facts and disseminating them: effecting social change by affecting public opinion, after all, required getting the word around. The foundations would soon learn, however, to be aware of the fine line that separated enlightenment from advocacy.

The appearance of the Carnegie Corporation in 1911 and the Rockefeller Foundation in 1913 permanently changed the landscape of American philanthropy. Not only were these the largest benefactions ever made available for charitable purposes, but they were deliberately designated for very general purposes. The Carnegie Corporation ($125 million) aspired "to promote the advancement and diffusion of knowledge and understanding among the people of the United States"; the Rockefeller Foundation ($182 million) sought "to promote the well-being of mankind throughout the world."[4] These arrangements placed enormous resources in the hands of the trustees and staff and gave them great latitude to determine just how these broad purposes might be served. While Andrew Carnegie (d. 1919) was present, the corporation largely supported the phalanx of philanthropic institutions that bore his name. At the Rockefeller Foundation, however, there was from the beginning an eagerness to define and inaugurate significant new projects. The first initiatives were exemplary. In the unimpeachable areas of medicine and public health, the foundation implemented projects in which it had both extensive experience and background knowledge and which also had potential for tangibly improving the welfare of many individual representatives of mankind. One effort sought to duplicate on a worldwide scale the success of the Rockefeller Sanitary Commission in combating hookworm in the American South; another endeavored to introduce modern medical practices to China.5 However, there was also a desire at the foundation, backed by John D. Rockefeller, Jr., to address social and economic problems currently plaguing the United States.6

Their first impulse was to create an economic institute in the mold of the RIMR. Plans to this effect were shelved, though, when the advising academic economists, who welcomed the general idea, fell out over specifics. The absence of consensus was exploited by the longtime Rockefeller counselor Frederick T. Gates, who had different ideas about attacking the social question. A former Baptist minister, noted for his quick judgments and incisive arguments, Gates represented the first generation of philanthropic specialists. He reasoned that the true need of the moment was not economic research but rather the conveying of elementary principles of economics to "all reading and thinking people": "even a low stratum, viz., the sort of men who have the capacity to get elected to Congress, and demagogues, laborites, socialists, editors, ministers and other people who know little of practical life and live in a dreamland."7 More appropriate for this course would be the model of the reform foundations—commissioning in-house studies of particularly timely issues. When this approach was adopted, however, the timely issue addressed was closely involved with the personal fortunes of the Rockefellers.

The public reputation of the Rockefellers was at a low ebb in the years before the war.8 A congressional charter for the foundation had been refused in 1910 and the donor's motives besmirched in the process. In1914 a bitter strike at a Rockefeller subsidiary in Colorado erupted into the "Ludlow massacre," just after John D. Rockefeller, Jr., had staunchly defended the rights of employers in public testimony before a congressional committee. In a transparent effort to improve the family image, Mackenzie King was commissioned by the foundation to conduct a study of industrial relations. King, in fact, functioned as a personal adviser to the Rockefellers and thus seemed to support the widely bruited accusations that the foundation was merely a front for family interests. The following year the U.S. Commission on Industrial Relations used this pretext for a wide-ranging muckraking inquiry into Rockefeller philanthropic activities, which ended by condemning foundations as means through which philanthropists tried "to become the molders of public thought."[9] As for Mackenzie King, a far better adviser than scholar, his eventual study of industrial relations neither advanced knowledge nor swayed opinion.[10] Once again, a frontal assault upon a complex social issue had proven naive; only in this case the consequences were potentially detrimental to the whole world of foundations. The lessons were accordingly well learned.

The Rockefellers quickly realized that a formal and effective separation would have to be made between the philanthropic activities of their foundation and the personal interests of the family. As they took the appropriate steps to accomplish this, and as the Carnegie Corporation also became free of its founder's influence, the modern general-purpose foundation under the direction of professional staff emerged as a permanent institution in American society.

A second lesson of this episode seemed to be that social research was inherently too controversial for the activities of foundations. The Rockefeller Foundation confined its activities to medicine and public health in the following years, and the enormous needs of war relief also absorbed considerable funds and energies for the remainder of the decade. When the Commonwealth Fund was formed in 1918, for example, it initially wished to shed light on the industrial question but soon concluded that "the question is so controversial that it seems impossible to enter the field without being suspected of taking sides."[11] Even afterward, it remained clear that foundations could not engage directly in social research without casting doubt on the legitimacy of their undertakings. Henceforth, they would have to pursue their goals in this sphere through other institutions, ones whose independence and credibility were beyond reproach.

This episode turned out to be a crossroads in the development of foundations in another important respect. By the beginning of the 1920s, it had become conventional wisdom among foundation leaders that they should support enlightenment rather than advocacy of the sort that Gates had championed. The new generation of foundation leaders, in particular, would not repeat the error of the Rockefellers. Frederick P. Keppel, on taking direction of the Carnegie Corporation, explicitly rejected "the deliberate and conscious propagation of opinion" as a policy; he favored instead "the discovery and distribution of facts from which men and women can draw their own opinion." And Beardsley Ruml, as he prepared to direct Rockefeller funds once again into the perilous waters of social inquiry, established as guiding principles that no support would be given for efforts to secure reform legislation, that no in-house social research would be conducted, and that no attempt would be made to influence the conclusions reached by researchers.[12] Generalized throughout the foundation world, the attitude shown by Keppel and Ruml in effect conceded to the professional experts who would actually be conducting research a substantial power to determine what and how knowledge might be advanced. This situation obviously benefited the academic community. The institutional arrangements by which this nexus might be made, however, were still in an amorphous state at the beginning of the 1920s.

In their study of the development of American foundations, Barry Karl and Stanley Katz have noted that the foundations operated in a far more congenial environment following the war. Maturation and professionalization were only some of the reasons for this. More crucial was the fact that numerous wartime boards and agencies had set a precedent for voluntary collaboration between government, industry, and nonprofit institutions. "The war . . . transformed the country's sense of the role of American philanthropy": in the aftermath a national consensus seemed to accept the appropriateness of private voluntary organizations fulfilling vital public services.[13] Not surprisingly, then, some of the ad hoc institutional arrangements of the war years persisted as models for this role.

The National Research Council, it was seen in the preceding chapter, was just such a combination of private initiatives for public ends. It was at a pinnacle of public esteem as a result of its wartime accomplishments. The NRC was therefore a natural magnet for foundation support, as well as an alluring organizational model for other fields of knowledge. The American Council on Education (f. 1918), the American Council of Learned Societies (f. 1919), and the Social Science Research Council (f. 1923) each in its own way took inspiration from the NRC. Despite their differences, all three sought to coordinate relevant activities, sponsor certain projects of general usefulness to their constituencies, and facilitate research. The latter two active functions, however, were made possible only by the availability of foundation grants. The NRC was the most fortunate, receiving $5 million from the Carnegie Corporation for a permanent home and endowment (1919). All of the councils, with the exception of the ACE, represented channels through which foundations could pursue their avowed goals of advancing knowledge. Since the councils were dominated by academics, these foundation gifts largely redounded to the advantage of university research. This pattern became evident immediately after the war.

The Rockefeller Foundation was interested at this time in aiding the development of the physical sciences. Its original impulse was once again to create another research institute like the RIMR. A polling of leading scientists, however, turned up some misgivings about this course. Robert Millikan and George Hale, in particular, eventually came to the conclusion that the physical sciences ought to be strengthened within university settings. Working through the NRC, they initiated a counterproposal to the foundation for the creation of a program of postdoctoral research fellowships. In 1919 the Rockefeller Foundation appropriated $500,000 for the first five years of such awards in physics and chemistry.[14] Committees of experts organized by the NRC took care of the delicate task of nominating promising young scientists. The opportunity for these chosen scientists to embark immediately upon intensive, advanced research and study made a strategic contribution toward augmenting the manpower of American science.[15] The NRC research fellows program was soon expanded to other disciplines and became a permanent fixture among Rockefeller Foundation programs until the 1950s. Similar programs were soon initiated in medicine through the NRC and in the social sciences through the SSRC. The mechanism of the research fellowship, mediated through the collective expertise of the councils, proved to be an effective and timely means for foundations to channel support to promising university researchers at critical junctures in their careers.

The existence of foundation patronage could be a threat as well as a boon, since it created the possibility of cultivating basic research outside of the universities. Before the war a number of private institutes had sprung up to serve the research needs of industry, but there was little overlap between these efforts and academic research.[16] One exceptional institution did provide a new model with rather different implications. The Institute for Government Research was chartered in 1916 for the purpose of promoting efficiency and effectiveness in government through the scientific study of administration. The IGR was an endeavor typical of the period, which aimed to compensate for perceived failures in the public sector through private voluntary action. This initiative was prompted in part by the lack of congressional action on the recommendations of President Taft's Commision on Economy and Efficiency (1911–12). The Rockefeller Foundation played a central role in the preliminary organization of the IGR but felt compelled to abstain from direct financial support for fear of stigmatizing the organization.[17] Instead, the foundation sought an entity that would be broadly representative of industry, education, and philanthropy. A subscription campaign among wealthy supporters induced forty-three donors to contribute the initial operating funds. A board of trustees was assembled from leaders of corporations, universities, and foundations. The institute thus attained the stature of a scientific institution, free of the taint of special interests. By avoiding the outstanding impediment to social research, the IGR soon became a paradigm for other undertakings.

Economics, more than government, was the field in which current issues were most sensitive and guidance was most urgently sought. The National Bureau of Economic Research was founded in 1920 by Professors Edwin Gay of Harvard and Wesley Mitchell of Columbia in order to utilize economic science for just such ends.[18] To ensure impartiality it was governed by a board constructed to represent the gamut of contemporary opinion and economic interests. Full freedom of inquiry was guaranteed to its staff. Support came primarily from the Carnegie Corporation, although the Commonwealth Fund, which had specifically rejected direct involvement in research of this nature, contributed as well. The NBER exemplified the capacity of an intermediate organization to stand above partisanship. It also provided a bridge between the public and private spheres. On two occasions it conducted research projects for the federal government that were financed by private foundations.[19] The NBER was soon joined by the Institute of Economics (f. 1922) when Robert Brookings, now the guiding hand behind the IGR, founded a sister organization in economics. In this case the Carnegie Corporation backed Brookings's idea with a generous grant of $1.65 million over ten years. His institute became involved in more controversial issues than the NBER did, but, like that of the IGR, its blue-ribbon board of trustees was intended to vouch for the disinterestedness of its work.[20]

The Institute for Economics and the IGR were merged into the Brookings Institution in 1927. The enduring vitality of both Brookings and the NBER should not be allowed to obscure the fact that they were born at a particular juncture in the evolution of the American research system. First, they owed their existence to the great general-purpose foundations. Even the IGR, which was originally supported by old-style subscriptions, was sustained in the 1920s by Rockefeller grants, originally channeled through the ephemeral Brookings graduate school.[21] Second, these research institutes in turn provided the foundations with the means for pursuing their interests in current social issues, while at the same time maneuvering around the Rockefeller-induced prohibition of foundation social research. These independent research institutes were thus deliberately tailored to be intermediaries through which the foundations could pursue the advancement of knowledge in these controversial areas. What is more, here was a development that seemed to challenge the ascendancy of the university as the center of basic research.

During the first part of the 1920s there was a growing concern that the proliferation of research outside of academe was threatening the vitality of university-based research. The expansion of industrial laboratories following the war, it was alleged, had attracted natural scientists from university posts. Foundation support for independent research institutes in the social sciences potentially stood to skim the thin layer of talent in these departments, or so it seemed. To alarmed academics, pure-research facilities seemed to offer advantages that the universities could not hope to match: the chance to devote one's full time to research and writing, research assistance and clerical support, and the opportunity to conduct large-scale cooperative investigations. Fears were expressed that over the next generation this trend could reverse much of the progress that American universities had achieved.[22] These concerns reached a kind of crescendo in 1926: conferences on university research were held in Philadelphia and New York; the AAUP launched an extended inquiry; and Herbert Hoover voiced his official concern that America's flow of scientific talent would dry up at its source.[23] However, as often happens in such matters, public clamor reached its peak after the issue was well on its way to being resolved. Important commitments had already been made, not just to maintain a university research capacity but to augment it appreciably. The most significant initial steps were taken in the Rockefeller group, and they involved the once-taboo social sciences.

2. Foundations and Universities: The Social Sciences

The Laura Spelman Rockefeller Memorial was organized in 1918 in memory of the wife of John D., Sr., and for its first four years it operated out of the office of JDR, Jr., dispensing gifts for quite traditional charitable causes that had been favored by Mrs. Rockefeller herself. This pattern was broken in 1922 when Beardsley Ruml was hired to become the memorial's first (and only) director. A wunderkind of sorts at age twenty-seven, Ruml had already earned a Ph.D. in psychology at Chicago under James Rowland Angell, worked extensively with mental testing, and assisted Angell during his brief tenure at the Carnegie Corporation. Although he retained the memorial's established concern for social welfare, Ruml felt that a more enduring service could be rendered by the promotion of scientific research: "knowledge and understanding of the natural forces that are manifested in the behavior of people and of things," he believed, "will result in the improvement of conditions of life." Here Ruml's own scientific background undoubtedly supplied a crucial element to his vision. In the empirical field of mental testing, he had participated in both the discovery and the application of knowledge. It must have seemed that the key to social welfare lay in an analogous process—in "the production of a body of substantiated and widely accepted generalizations as to human capacities and motives and as to the behavior of human beings as individuals and groups." Under Ruml the memorial would dedicate most of its resources first to building social science, broadly defined, with an eye to later applications of "social technology."[1]

On taking control of the memorial, Ruml wrote a remarkable memorandum describing his perception of conditions in the social sciences and measures that might be taken to improve them. A report that he commissioned, written by Lawrence K. Frank and entitled "The Status of Social Science in the United States," fully corroborated his initial assessment. By 1924, a few tentative initiatives having already been taken, Ruml was able to present to the memorial trustees some general principles that would guide its work in the social sciences. Taken together, these three documents form a keen diagnosis of the inadequacies of contemporary social science and a potent prescription for foundation actions to deal with them.[2]

Essentially, Ruml sought a strategy to resolve four interconnected problems that were obstructing the creation of valid and usable social knowledge: the immature intellectual state of the social sciences, the dearth of scientifically inclined investigators, organizational impediments to actual social science research, and the old Rockefeller problem of insulating social inquiry from foundation sponsorship.

At this date the social sciences seemed on the verge of a breakthrough to a more rigorously scientific practice, similar to that which had occurred only recently in clinical medicine and Ruml's own field of psychology. Traditional historical and a priori approaches, often with polemical slants, still dominated these literatures. A small number of more empirically minded social scientists had become active in their fields, but they had yet to attain real influence within their disciplines. Frank's study had shown that most dissertations were the product of library work; field work and statistics were seldom required of graduate students, and in some major universities these techniques were not even taught. If social science were to be brought into touch with social reality, these conditions would obviously have to change. The problem, Ruml concluded, had to be attacked and resolved in the universities.

Ruml perceived that the universities possessed some inherent advantages as places for research. Their traditions gave them great stability of organization and purpose, they included a wide range of professional opinion, and scholarly or scientific standards were well established. Moreover, considering the current paucity of adequately trained social scientists, only the universities could produce the new cadres that were needed. The memorial was perfectly willing to support those research institutes that were doing empirical investigations (the NBER and the IGR), while recognizing that they were too specialized for training purposes and, if enlarged, would simply drain the universities of their best scientists. Support would thus have to be given for graduate education and research fellowships. Faculty, too, needed to be given the kind of supporting staff to which lawyers and businessmen had become accustomed. In a section on "the mechanics of research," Frank reported that "opportunities and resources for scientific work in the universities are limited." The challenge here, as with fellowships, was to identify those active researchers who were endeavoring to surmount the shortcomings of their disciplines. In fact, it is an interesting reflection on conditions in the research universities that the type of social scientist the memorial wanted to aid was contrasted with heads of departments. Ruml's objectives, then, required bypassing to some extent the superannuated power structure in university social science. Soon his policies would indeed produce a new one.

The key contribution to resolving these issues was the creation of university-affiliated research institutes. Frank's study had already identified those universities doing the most promising work, and the best individual researchers could be identified through personal recommendations. Through such institutes faculty could be relieved of some of the burdens of teaching, and their productivity could be greatly enhanced if they were provided badly needed clerical and statistical assistance. Support for graduate students could be channeled through these auspices and would thereby provide the desired kinds of research opportunities to empirically inclined students. University institutes would also permit Ruml to put into practice his strongly held belief in the efficacy of cross-disciplinary research. Finally, and important for the operations of the memorial, large block grants could be made to universities for the maintenance of these units with confidence that the funds would be expended for the proper purposes. The trustworthiness of universities was an important consideration, since the memorial had neither the capacity nor the desire for close accountability.

Building research centers at those universities with the strongest social and behavioral science departments and providing fellowships to train more researchers in these areas thus became the basis of Ruml's program. A necessary accompaniment, he felt, was some means for coordinating existing work in the social sciences. This expressed need was both a reflection of conditions in the social sciences and an imperative for implementing the memorial's policy. Some means was required for communicating with social science as a whole, rather than with specific departments or individual disciplines. Despite his own credentials, Ruml did not concern himself with the actual content of social science. He preferred to depend upon the qualitative judgments of working social scientists. Social science consequently needed a "head" that could express consensus, communicate, and act. It needed, in short, its own NRC. To this end, the memorial played a crucial role in bringing the Social Science Research Council into existence and then utilized it for the memorial's goal of building social science.

The SSRC, to be sure, had its origins in an indigenous movement among younger political scientists and sociologists, who aspired to deal with some of those same deficiencies that were to be highlighted in the

Frank report.[3] In 1923, representatives of sociology, political science, and economics were able to agree upon the formation of a "Social Research Council" that would confer on such matters of mutual concern as teaching, abstracting periodicals, and gathering statistics. At this point the beginning of financial support from the memorial led the council to assume a far larger role. It first agreed to cooperate in a memorial-funded study of human migration, and this was shortly followed by a small grant for operating expenses. These fiscal responsibilities caused the council to become legally incorporated as the SSRC (December 1924). The resources of the council also served to attract the membership of the more hesitant disciplinary associations of statistics, psychology, anthropology, and, finally, history. In the first decade of its existence, the SSRC received grants of more than $4 million. It rather conspicuously reported that its foundation patrons included the Carnegie Corporation, the CFAT, the Commonwealth Fund, the GEB, the Rosenwald Fund, and the Falk and Russell Sage foundations. In fact, 92 percent of these funds were allocated by the memorial and its successor division of the Rockefeller Foundation.[4] As an active promoter of social research, then, the SSRC was a creature of Ruml's policy.

The council itself consisted of three representatives from each of the seven member disciplinary associations. It had a full slate of officers and soon acquired a permanent staff as well. The real work of the SSRC was done by numerous committees with shifting memberships, which allowed a wide representation of disciplinary expertise. During the 1920s the chief functions of the council were awarding fellowships, making small individual grants-in-aid, funding major research projects, and seeing to the more diffuse requirements of planning, coordinating, and facilitating communication. In its distributive capacities the council attempted to direct foundation funds into those university departments where they would be most effective. It thus functioned as an additional channel for Ruml's policy of bolstering university social science. The SSRC also considered it important to cultivate ties between social scientists and their benefactors outside the university. Starting in 1925, it annually sponsored extended summer meetings, attended by social scientists, prominent university leaders, and representatives of the foundations. These interchanges gave foundation leaders some role in determining the directions of social science research.[5]

By 1924, having laid the groundwork for his social science program, Ruml began to implement it in a major way. For the next five years (1924–28) the memorial appropriated over $20 million for social and behavioral sciences, almost two-thirds of that in the final two years before the memorial was absorbed into the Rockefeller Foundation.[6] This last development did not immediately change policy too greatly. The foundation regarded Ruml's policies as successful and largely continued them for another five years before a major reassessment took place (see below). The sum of $20 million was enormous in itself, and quite unprecedented in terms of the resources then available for these subjects. While it is difficult to categorize foundation giving with any precision, one comprehensive attempt recorded more money flowing to the social sciences during the decade than to the natural sciences (excluding medicine).[7] The grants of the memorial during these five years represent three-fourths of the total for all social science.

Ruml remained faithful to his announced policy of concentration: the allocations indicated in Table 9 represent 94 percent of the memorial's social science appropriations. Concentration was tempered somewhat by the funds channeled through the SSRC (including fellowships), which, although they undoubtedly tended to benefit individuals in strong centers of social science, were still open to competition. Thus, aside from regular

TABLE 9. Principal Recipients of Support for Social Science from the Laura Spelman Rockefeller Foundation, 1924–1928 (in thousands of dollars)

University of Chicago	$3,363
Social Science Research Council	2,719
Fellowships	1,409
Columbia University	1,399
London School of Economics	1,245
Harvard University	1,195
University of Minnesota	965
Vanderbilt University	881
State University of Iowa	879
Brookings Institution	761*
Yale University	490
University of North Carolina	453
University of California	295
Stanford University	262
University of Texas	250
National Bureau of Economic Research	217
Fisk University	194
Cornell University	151
University of Pennsylvania	150
University of Cambridge	150

SOURCE: Adapted from Joan Bulmer and Martin Bulmer, "Philanthropy and Social Science in the 1920s: Beardsley Ruml and the Laura Spelman Rockefeller Memorial, 1922–29," *Minerva* 19 (1981): 387.

* Not including $2 million appropriated as a matching endowment grant but never awarded, for lack of matching donations.

support for the NBER (which was linked to Columbia through Wesley Mitchell) and the Brookings Institution, these funds went primarily to support and develop university-based social science.

The universities that appear in Table 9 include only a bare majority of the research universities as well as some rather unlikely candidates. In fact, the memorial made grants for a variety of purposes, which must be taken into account to explain this distribution. Besides the avowed aim of building social science per se, the memorial also promoted research on child development, race relations, and "social technology." The first of these topics resulted in research centers at Iowa as well as at Columbia, Yale, Minnesota, and California. The second accounted in part for grants to Fisk and North Carolina.[8] Under the rubric of social technology, support went to several schools of social work, some major law schools, and the business schools of Harvard and Penn. Also, given the international outlook of the Rockefeller charities, considerable sums were expended to build foreign centers of social science research.

At the outset of their work, Ruml and Frank had identified Chicago, Columbia, Harvard, Penn, and Wisconsin as leading centers of research and graduate training in the social sciences; and, except for Wisconsin, these were the centers of strength upon which they proceeded to build. An unusual development excluded Wisconsin from this group. In a throwback to prewar anti-Rockefeller sentiment, the Wisconsin trustees in 1925 forbade the university to accept *any* foundation grants. Richard T. Ely, whose Institute for Land Economics was viewed favorably by the memorial, promptly departed for Northwestern, where his transplanted institute was awarded more than $100,000. The Wisconsin trustees soon rescinded their ban, but foundations seem to have been wary for some time thereafter of provoking controversy in Madison.[9] The University of Chicago, on the other hand, was the largest recipient of funds from the memorial, and the showcase for building social science.

The connections between the University of Chicago and Rockefeller charities are too dense to recount, but the memorial's support of Chicago social science involved more than favoritism. Chicago probably possessed more capable, research-oriented social scientists than any other university at the beginning of the 1920s. Moreover, they shared a strong belief in the importance of making social science research empirical, cooperative, cross-disciplinary, and rooted in local communities. There can be no doubt that Beardsley Ruml's aspirations for social science were significantly shaped by the outlook prevailing in the Chicago departments. Chicago was consequently the university most prepared and most eager to undertake the memorial's program.[10]

In 1923 Ruml used Chicago as a test case of his inchoate policy. A small grant of $21,000 was made in support of research intended to further the

development of social science through the study of local community issues. To distribute and administer these funds, the university created the
"Local Community Research Committee" (LCRC), consisting of representatives of five departments. This original grant was largely expended
for projects in sociology by Robert Park and Ernest Burgess, and in political science by Charles E. Merriam and Harold Gosnell. The funds went to
purchase clerical and statistical assistance, hire research assistants, conduct surveys, and pay for released time from teaching. The next year
Ruml would call these efforts "an experiment as to the possibility of a
university assuming intellectual leadership based on scientific investigation in matters affecting the welfare of the community."[11] In the years
that followed, the LCRC would receive extensive regular support from
the memorial in order to continue and expand this experiment. An appropriation was made for 1924–27 that provided $50,000 per year to the
committee, plus up to $25,000 per year in matching funds, should other
donors be found.[12] For 1927–31 these levels were raised to $70,000 out-
right and $30,000 matching. In all, the committee had at its disposal an
annual average of $113,000 during these years to spend as it saw fit on
research. In addition, $138,500 was granted for special appointments;
$725,000 was pledged for the support of the School of Social Service Ad-
ministration; and in 1927 a gift of $1.1 million was made to construct,
equip, and maintain the Social Science Research Building.[13]

The LCRC was one of the most important innovations in the organization of university social science. Roughly a third of the council's research
funds went toward support of services and field work. The next-largest
block of expenditures was for research assistants.[14] The use of funds for
these purposes facilitated three notable objectives. It made possible large-
scale empirical research that would not otherwise have been feasible. It
undoubtedly enhanced the productivity of some of the country's most
talented and advanced social scientists—including Park, Burgess, Merriam, Louis Wirth, Robert Redfield, and William Ogburn. And it assured
that a large generation of graduate students—soon to be known in sociology as the Chicago school—were trained in empirical research methods. In addition, by the end of the 1920s the University of Chicago was
arguably the leading center of social science research in the world. Ruml
could indeed take pride in the memorial's contribution to these achievements. But could this formula be replicated at other universities? He
seems to have been tempted to try.

One of the final acts of the memorial was to launch, in conjunction
with the Rockefeller Foundation, the Yale Institute of Human Relations
(f. 1929). The IHR was in part a result of previous links between Yale and
the memorial. President James Rowland Angell had been Ruml's mentor
at both Chicago and the Carnegie Corporation (Ruml jocularly addressed

him as "chief"), and Angell sat on several Rockefeller boards, including that of the memorial. Ongoing support for Ruml's and Angell's own field of psychology had been granted to Yale by the LSRM and the GEB since the mid-1920s. These programs would continue as components of IHR. The guiding force behind the new institute, however, came from two aggressive professional-school deans—Milton C. Winternitz of the Medical School (1920–35) and Robert Maynard Hutchins of the Law School (1926–28).[15] Both men felt that the study of their respective professions should be integrated with the social sciences. Under their leadership the rationale for the institute was to combine—physically and intellectually—different facets of the study of man at Yale. To be included were not just the behavioral science and social science departments but also the professional schools of medicine, law, divinity, and nursing. This was to be an effort of cooperative, cross-disciplinary research on a grand scale; its aim was no less than to investigate "problems of human welfare and to develop a unified science of individual and social behavior as a foundation for the more effective training of physicians, lawyers, ministers, nurses, teachers and research workers."[16] Little wonder that Abraham Flexner, always skeptical of large research projects, remarked, "As far as I can make out, the Institute is just another name for Yale University."[17] Yale, however, proved resistant to such aggrandizement.

A total of $4.5 million was initially pledged to the IHR—a part of it to build the IHR its own impressive building (after the precedent of the Social Science Research Building at Chicago), and the remainder to support several lines of research over the next ten years. With an annual budget of $250,000 the institute had the capacity to generate a considerable amount of research. Most of these funds, however, were committed to established programs in psychology, psychiatry, child development, and anthropoid research. Partly for this reason, for its first six years there was little convergence, or even coherence, in the welter of activities that took place under its auspices. Within the academic departments IHR funds were largely utilized to support preexisting lines of disciplinary research, while the clinical units became directly involved in the local community through programs dealing with juvenile delinquency, mental health, crime, unemployment, and adaptation to social change. Disciplinary research was undoubtedly congenial to those Yale faculty who were recipients, but it did little to fulfill the original goals of the Rockefeller Foundation. Community action, on the other hand, was little valued by the bulk of the Yale community. President Angell, in fact, was virtually alone among the Yale leadership in believing that a great university had an obligation to provide such services to its surrounding community. But considering Yale's dependence upon its graduates and the paramount importance of Yale College, it is hardly surprising that few shared his Chicago-inspired views. With the departure of Hutchins for the University of Chicago, the focus of the IHR, diffuse as it was, shifted toward the medical school. This development tended to preclude any meaningful interaction with the social sciences and the nonhealth professions. President Angell had felt from the beginning that the IHR would greatly strengthen the behavioral sciences at Yale, even if it could not fulfill its initial ambitions.[18] But once events had taken this course, it remained to be seen whether this consolation would justify the substantial investment of Rockefeller funds.

When the issue of refunding appeared on the horizon the Rockefeller Foundation was of a far less expansive disposition. The IHR faced an incipient crisis in justifying its continued existence. A new director was appointed in 1935 specifically to deal with this situation, and he promptly undertook a major reorganization.[19] The most powerful and autonomous units—psychiatry and child development—were transferred to the Medical School. The funds that remained under the control of the institute were then concentrated into a liquid research fund that was centrally controlled from the director's office. The input of university faculty members into the disposition of research funds, which had operated so effectively in Chicago's LCRC, was largely precluded by this arrangement. Instead, the institute's new orientation echoed Rockefeller Foundation policy: "the finding of better solutions of persisting practical social problems," the director announced, "was dependent upon the development of a more unified and comprehensive theory of human behavior." The institute's resources would henceforth be devoted exclusively to interdisciplinary efforts toward that end.[20]

In its reincarnation as a research institute, pure and simple, the IHR had to abandon most of its original pretensions. No longer could it aspire to integrate the study of man at Yale, nor would it play a part in training practitioners of the humane professions. In the years following reorganization the institute compiled a creditable record of producing academic publications in the areas of learning and behavior, personality development, and cultural anthropology. It made a pioneering effort to reconcile psychoanalytic theory with the other behavioral sciences, although the preoccupation with this controversial subject may have estranged the institute further from the rest of the university. These accomplishments, in any case, did not constitute a unified science of individual and social behavior.[21] The IHR clearly, then, fell far short of its grandiose billings. In fact, after reorganization it became rather isolated from the mainstream of university activities—a condition undoubtedly exacerbated by its location on the medical campus, across town from the rest of the university. In 1949 Yale quietly phased it out of existence.

It is not difficult to recognize the underlying conditions that contributed to the success of the Local Community Research Committee at Chicago and the relative lack of success of the IHR at Yale. The institute's original rationale, besides bordering on the utopian, was incompatible with the principal mission of Yale and inconsistent with the university's organizational structure.[22] The leaders most committed to the original vision, moreover, did not remain in place to work toward its realization. The Chicago committee, by way of contrast, had more modest and attainable goals and a stable and committed group of leaders, and it was integrated with the departmental structure of the university. More interesting in this context, however, are the similarities between the experiences of Chicago and Yale. The widely recognized achievements of the Chicago social scientists, it seems, tended to obscure basic problems in foundation policy toward university social science that were all too evident at Yale. These included the inherent awkwardness of interdisciplinary research and the fundamental tension between university and foundation goals.

In seeking to overcome what he regarded as "the anachronistic categories of history, economics, sociology, psychology and so forth," Beardsley Ruml was fighting against one of the strongest structural features of American research universities: namely, the socioprofessional and cognitive linkages between national academic disciplines and individual university departments. His motivation for this probably reflected in part the meager intellectual progress that the separate social sciences had made to date, the widespread postwar zeal for cooperative undertakings, and the aspiration to use foundation resources to create research opportunities not otherwise available. Nevertheless, in attempting to transcend academic disciplines, the memorial and other foundations met with little success. Ruml later noted with some resignation, "We tried everything to encourage . . . unity in the social sciences. . . . We tried joint studies, numerous organizational devices, encyclopedias and publications, fellowships and . . . [the] social science building at the University of Chicago." Instead, perhaps the greatest success of the memorial's program was to develop the disciplines of sociology and political science, especially at Chicago.[23] This was largely a consequence of the memorial's laissez-faire policy of making block grants, which university faculty then allocated to the projects that they favored. The result, according to Martin Bulmer's analysis, was that "the interdisciplinary character of the Chicago program had more reality in its form of organization than in the research carried out. Relatively few projects were truly interdisciplinary and efforts to promote them did not meet with success."[24]

After the social science programs of the memorial were transferred to the Rockefeller Foundation (1929), a subtle change of emphasis took place. Henceforth, the foundation became more mindful of the practical objectives that lay behind the research it supported. Research areas consequently tended to become more narrowly focused and explicitly cross-disciplinary. Thus, it became difficult for university faculty to pursue their own discipline-inspired interests under these auspices. Focused research of this type was less likely to have theoretical importance for specific disciplines, and it also presented fewer opportunities for subsidizing the training of graduate students.[25] The change in Rockefeller policy soon prompted a reorganization of the LCRC at Chicago in line with these new attitudes. A proud research tradition was continued, but with fewer spin-off benefits for the departments. According to Bulmer, the apogee of Chicago sociology and political science probably came at the end of the twenties—just when this transition occurred.[26] The evolution of research under the Yale IHR was somewhat analogous. During the initial anarchistic period, institute funds at least provided support for a broad range of disciplinary research. After research funds began to be allocated from the director's office with the aim of fulfilling more closely the expectations of the Rockefeller Foundation, however, the IHR became a marginal and isolated research institute.

This predicament essentially stemmed from the divergent aims of universities and foundations. Universities, and the academic disciplines they harbored, were committed to the advancement of knowledge for its own sake; foundations sought social knowledge that might be employed for improving the welfare of mankind. Each needed the other, as Ruml had perceptively realized. The dilemma of university-foundation relations in the social sciences was that stressing the goals of either one meant slighting the goals of the other. Ruml may have been able to rise above this practical dilemma by taking a very long-range view—discipline building today and applications tomorrow. He also optimistically extrapolated from the assumed relationship of basic and applied research in the natural sciences. The result was a policy on the part of the memorial that for a time was extraordinarily beneficial to university social science. It eventually became apparent, however, that juvenile delinquency could not be eradicated like hookworm. That is, the human sciences did not succeed in discovering unequivocal solutions to persistent social problems. As the foundations matured during the 1920s, they naturally evaluated the results of their policies. They later readjusted their stance toward university social science in light of this disappointment with their own overly sanguine expectations. However, they also had to adapt to a changing philanthropic environment.

The onset of the Depression gave added impetus to the general redirection of foundation policy, as the magnitude and the gravity of the problems afflicting American society could not be ignored. The Rockefeller Foundation, while continuing its university-based social science programs, directed resources as well toward critical contemporary problems

like "economic stabilization."[27] In addition, the financial effects of the
Depression on the assets of foundations restricted the scope of their activities. Still, a decisive shift of policy at the Rockefeller Foundation did
not occur until 1934. A committee chaired by Raymond Fosdick (soon to
become foundation president) essentially repudiated the Ruml policy of
giving block research grants to universities for allocation by local research
committees. Instead, the foundation's future emphasis would be on supporting specific fields of research with "the hope of making a realistic
contribution to contemporary problems."[28] This was a significant juncture in university-foundation relations, the implications of which will be
considered in due course.

There were at least two distinctive features of the social sciences that
strongly affected the course of university-foundation relations during this
period. First, the immaturity of these disciplines as empirical sciences at
once made them an uncertain, but potentially rewarding, field in which to
invest research capital. The resources directed through the LCRC at Chicago, through Howard Odum's Institute for Research in Social Science at
North Carolina, or through several other centers were fecund indeed.
There can be little doubt that these appropriations accelerated the growth
of the social sciences. Furthermore, one could argue, it was in large measure because of these accomplishments that the Rockefeller Foundation
was able in 1934 to embark upon a policy emphasizing the utilization
rather than the creation of social science knowledge.

A second source of distinctiveness lay in the nature of the social sciences—in the inherent ambiguity shrouding the connections between
studying, predicting, and affecting human behavior. To be sure, the foundations had progressed considerably from the days of Frederick T. Gates
and Mackenzie King. A major achievement of the 1920s, in fact, was the
use of a whole panoply of institutional arrangements, from Brookings
and the NBER to the SSRC and internal university research committees,
in order to promote the conduct of professional, disinterested social inquiry. Only then did it become apparent that what foundations really
sought was social action rather than social knowledge. The recrudescence
of this impulse, however, did not disrupt the relationship between foundations and university social science that had been so assiduously cultivated. It merely brought to the fore a ubiquitous tension in the funding of
university social science, one that has remained embedded in the complex
institutional structures that were devised during this era in order to link
grantors and grantees.

3. Foundations and Universities: The Natural Sciences

The evolution of foundation policies in the natural sciences exhibits some
immediate parallels with the developments just described in the social

sciences. Once again, it was the Rockefeller charities that dominated the field. Also, the most important initiatives emanated from one individual, who was able to redirect the thrust of an existing foundation. Wickliffe Rose, who assumed the direction of the General Education Board in 1923, was concluding a distinguished career with the Rockefeller philanthropies that had most recently involved directing the International Health Board. He expressed a faith similar to Ruml's in the efficacy of science—natural science in this case—to bring substantial benefits to mankind.

Rose was nominated to head the GEB just as it was concluding its efforts to build college endowments, and he was thus in a position to formulate a new set of programs for higher education. This opportunity by itself, however, seemed insufficient to Rose. After operating on a global scale with the International Health Board, he did not wish to confine his efforts to the United States, as the GEB charter required. He was able to persuade JDR, Jr., to create the parallel International Education Board to overcome this limitation. Assuming the presidency of both foundations, Rose proceeded much as Ruml had, spending the first years of his tenure carefully assessing the situation, and thereafter awarding major grants at an accelerating pace.[1]

Rose began his dual presidencies convinced that the time had arrived to cease assisting the expansion of higher education and to seek instead to heighten its quality.[2] His basic strategy for accomplishing this was to use the resources at his disposal to enhance the capabilities of those institutions or departments that were already doing the best work—or, in the phrase that became affixed to his work, "to make the peaks higher." He thus contributed to the Harvard Law School because it was "the leading institution for the training of lawyers" and the prime source of law-school teachers; and he also helped Frank Aydelotte establish an honors program at Swarthmore.[3] Rose believed, above all, that this was an age of science, and that the rigor of the scientific method would ultimately serve to guide other human endeavors.[4] The combination of these convictions produced an emphatic "best-science" policy, domestically and internationally, which channeled substantial sums into a few carefully chosen centers of research.

During Rose's five years at the GEB (1924–29) almost $12 million was appropriated directly for science in American universities. This sum represented nearly half of the board's disbursements for these years.[5] The majority of these funds could be classified as research capital: grants for either endowment earmarked for support of the natural sciences or buildings and laboratories for scientific research. These capital grants were usually offered on a matching basis, so that the recipient would typically have to raise an equal or double amount. Gifts were quite concentrated; just six research universities claimed more than three-quarters of the total:[6]

Caltech	$2,815,000
Princeton	2,000,000
Chicago	1,798,000
Cornell	1,500,000
Stanford	750,000
Harvard	400,000

Essentially, Rose's program was restricted to those private universities (hence dependent upon private capital) that had eminent science programs and that were also willing to pledge a portion of their own voluntary support toward a strengthening of natural science. The GEB grants listed above were in fact contributions toward $20 million of scientific capital for these six universities. They represent, then, additions to the scientific capacities of these institutions that are to some extent still productive today.

The International Education Board had assets, all told, of almost $28 million. This would place it near the bottom of the top ten American foundations of this period. Rose was given the discretion, however, to dispose of both income and principal during his stewardship. This gave the IEB a grant-making power for a number of years equivalent to that of giant Carnegie Corporation. Despite manifold foreign activities, the IEB was important for American science. In fact, more than half of its entire wealth found its way to just three American universities (see below). Thus, there was a disparity between the most active programs of the IEB and its largest commitments.

In total the IEB also expended about $12 million on the natural sciences. One of its most productive programs, providing international fellowships, was also one of its cheapest (roughly $1 million). These fellowships were designed to allow young scientists who had demonstrated a capacity for productive research to spend a year or more studying in the most advanced foreign laboratories in their fields. By 1926, 126 young European and American scientists were abroad under this program. These fellowships greatly augmented the international contacts of American science. In the indicated year, for example, 30 Americans were studying in Europe and 33 Europeans chose to pursue their research in the United States.[7] The importance of these contacts became all the more evident, in retrospect, after the diaspora of Continental scientists (see Chapter 5).

Capital gifts for scientific research in European universities were somewhat more focused than those made in the United States. Rose had personally investigated conditions in Europe immediately upon assuming direction of the IEB. Soon a succession of grants followed that permitted, for example, the enlargement of Niels Bohr's Intitute of Theoretical Physics at Copenhagen; the equipping of specialized laboratories in Sweden, Norway, Holland, and Switzerland; buildings for the renowned physical and mathematical institutes of Göttingen; and even the hiring of an assistant for Albert Einstein. These and other strategic interventions proved to be relatively inexpensive. Construction costs were apparently lower in Europe, and, more important, no attempt was made to endow these state-controlled institutions.

In comparison, grant making in the United States was done wholesale. Just before his retirement Rose virtually liquidated the IEB through three massive commitments. For a biology building at Harvard, $2 million was given; on the initiative of the indefatigable George Hale, $6 million was promised to Caltech for the erection of the world's largest reflecting telescope. The largest grant of all was in the humanities: $8.4 million for construction and endowment for James Breasted's Oriental Institute at Chicago.[8]

The retirement of Wickliffe Rose, the departure of Beardsley Ruml, and the ensuing reorganization of the Rockefeller philanthropies signaled the end of the era of large capital grants for university research. In large measure these policies had been possible because of the fragmentation of Rockefeller funds among four independent foundations and the free hand given to their directors. For several years sentiment had been growing among the trustees for a more rational arrangement. The fields of activity of these foundations overlapped considerably, and central direction was wanting within the Rockefeller Foundation, the largest and most fragmented of them.[9] The reorganization that took effect in 1929 remedied these conditions by making the foundation responsible solely for activities furthering the advancement of knowledge. It thus absorbed the Laura Spelman Rockefeller Memorial and the IEB, while also claiming the research programs of the GEB.

The Rockefeller Foundation itself was reorganized into four separate divisions, having responsibilities for research in the humanities, the medical sciences, the natural sciences, and the social sciences.[10] The new divisions inherited the commitments of their predecessors, but they possessed neither the freedom for bold undertakings nor the abundant resources of the formerly independent entities. Furthermore, before they could develop definite programs of their own, the effects of the economic crisis began to be felt. From 1929 to 1934 Rockefeller Foundation annual disbursements declined by a third, and appropriations fell far more than that.[11] Moreover, financial hard times changed the economics of endowments. With interest rates steadily declining, much larger endowments would have been required to yield a given level of income.

The half-decade after reorganization was a period of transition for the Rockefeller Foundation and for foundation assistance of university research. Million-dollar appropriations for capital purposes became less frequent, finally disappearing altogether during the depths of the Depression. At the same time the list of recipients grew longer as smaller grants were dispensed more widely.[12] The University of Chicago continued to be the most prominent beneficiary of the Rockefeller Foundation, but by the mid-thirties all of the research universities were regular recipients of grants. Before mid-decade such grants were often in the form of "fluid research funds" to promote unspecified research in a particular area. The foundation also provided funds for the National Research Council to make small grants-in-aid to individual researchers and funded fellowships for Europeans through its Paris office and for Americans through the NRC. European and American science thus received much needed support from the Rockefeller Foundation in a variety of forms during the deepening economic crisis. Within the foundation, however, there was growing dissatisfaction with this role.

During the years of transition controversy smoldered among the trustees concerning the proper role of the foundation, and the issue was definitely heightened by the necessity of scaling back the level of grant making in line with shrinking income.[13] In 1934 a consensus was reestablished by the Committee of Appraisal, chaired by Raymond Fosdick, which confirmed the foundation's emphases on the major special programs and on the application of knowledge. In this way, the same logic of concentration that was apparent in the social sciences had its effect upon the division of natural science, even though applicability to human welfare was quite broadly construed in this context. Ideally, the foundation was to seek to support emerging areas of scientific research in which strategic assistance might produce significant breakthroughs, and where advancing knowledge might also produce benefits for mankind.[14] Such ambitions, however, clearly demanded considerable scientific acumen on the part of foundation leaders. Thus, concentration of foundation efforts inevitably transferred some of the initiative in research away from active scientists into the hands of foundation officers. This arrangement suited the inclinations of the new director of natural science at the Rockefeller Foundation—Warren Weaver.

Unlike the past Rockefeller science czars Ruml and Rose, Weaver exercised his authority as a subordinate to the president of the foundation. He was also far more involved with the actual content of the science that he was supporting. This combination made him a kind of philanthropic technocrat, or what Robert Kohler has called a "manager of science."[15] It was the circumstances of the Rockefeller Foundation in the mid-thirties that shaped this novel role, even if Weaver's considerable talents were needed to make it a success.

Weaver was a classical physicist at the University of Wisconsin when he was offered the directorship in 1931, but he believed that the area of natural science with the greatest immediate potential was biology. He sensed that the biological sciences were poised for a major advance similar to that which had just been occurring in physics. He furthermore felt that breakthroughs might be made through the application to biology of the recent discoveries of the physical sciences. When he presented his first tentative research agenda to the foundation president, he featured these concerns prominently alongside aid for other investigations of the kind that the foundation had until then been supporting in physical science, earth science, mathematics, and psychology. Largely for reasons of economy, these latter areas were stricken by President Max Mason. This left the natural science division program almost entirely concentrated on what came to be called "experimental biology." In 1933 the trustees ratified this new emphasis as the primary field of interest. This was actually a natural choice for the foundation. Basic research in biology held the promise of relevance to human well-being through its links to other established foundation programs in medicine and public health. The natural science program was narrowed even further the following year as a result of Fosdick's Committee of Appraisal. In this case it was the means of support that were restricted. The fellowship program was focused on biology, grants-in-aid through the NRC were abolished, and contributions to university fluid research funds were eliminated. In other words, support was terminated for research that was not under foundation control. Instead, the dominant means for funding research became medium-sized project grants for specified pieces of research.

The adoption of project grants brought the Rockefeller Foundation into a much closer relationship with the science it supported, and also spread its funds more widely than had the former capital grants. As Robert Kohler has pointed out, "every measure of economy approved by the trustees in fact increased the officers' control in promulgating and guiding their programs." Correspondingly, project grants were an ideal form: "Since each grant was made for a specific project, with an eye on its long-term potentiality, it could be carefully selected and could often be discreetly influenced by Weaver." [16] The experimental-biology program was in full swing by 1934, and the last of the former natural science programs were phased out shortly thereafter. The result was a complete transformation of the grants list of the natural science division. In 1938, for example, $1 million was appropriated for twenty-two project grants, all in experimental biology. Another $300,000 went to support fellowships and grants-in-aid that were also almost exclusively in this area. By this juncture it is noteworthy that most of the grants were going to American universities. In fact, all of the research universities, save MIT, received payments from the Rockefeller Foundation for biological research in that year.[17]

From the foundation's point of view, Weaver's program was an outstanding success, and credit for this must be given to the manager of science himself. Weaver's intuition about the situation in biology proved to be correct. The projects he supported yielded significant advances in understanding the physical and chemical nature of biological processes. Their results made fundamental contributions to the knowledge of such things as the effects of vitamins and hormones, the nature of proteins, and the chemistry of respiration. Contributions were also made to the development and utilization of such key scientific procedures as the ultracentrifuge, x-ray diffraction, particle accelerators, and radio-isotope tracers. So pronounced was the preoccupation with the molecular basis of life processes that the program's title was soon changed to "molecular biology."[18] Nevertheless, from the perspective of the research universities, the more important questions were these: To what extent did the evolution of the Rockefeller Foundation represent the drift of foundations generally? What did the concentration of foundation giving portend for university research?

One difficulty with the first issue is that no other foundation played a role comparable to that of the Rockefeller Foundation in the promotion of research. In 1934, for example, its grants constituted 35 percent of the total foundation giving, 64 percent of that in the social sciences, and 72 percent of the total for the natural sciences.[19] The Rockefeller Foundation by itself was a huge presence in the university research system.

The Carnegie Corporation of New York had comparable assets, but because of its substantial obligations to other Carnegie trusts it had much less income for discretionary grants. These same connections created cross-cutting interests on the corporation board that ultimately obstructed its interest in university research. Unlike those of the Rockefeller boards, its interests in science waned rather than grew in the 1920s.

Immediately after the war the Carnegie Corporation for a time epitomized the wartime spirit of scientific cooperation.[20] Under its acting president, Elihu Root, it granted the endowment to the National Research Council and then recruited James Rowland Angell from the NRC to head the corporation (1920). Angell sought to lead the Carnegie Corporation into a permanent commitment to strengthen university research and graduate education. His most notable accomplishment was undoubtedly the grant to Caltech that virtually launched its meteoric scientific development. But Angell was enticed to Yale the following year, and with his departure the fragile consensus behind support for university research evaporated. Angell's eventual replacement, Frederick P. Keppel (1923–41), represented the balance of other Carnegie interests on the corporation board. He accordingly devoted considerable assets to resolving the problems of the CFAT's pension program, and he left scientific research largely to the Carnegie Institution of Washington.

During his long tenure Keppel was perpetually concerned about the proper role of philanthropic foundations: he spoke often on the subject, discussed it in his annual presidential reports, and established an "audit of experience" in order to learn from the corporation's past policies. Somehow, though, he never seemed to find definite answers to the probing questions that he raised.[21] In general he opposed specialization in foundation giving. He kept the corporation officially open to all manner of supplication and supported a broad range of educational and cultural institutions. Thus, there was no discernible theme linking such major areas of support as improving the quality and usefulness of American libraries, developing education in the fine arts, and promoting dental research.[22]

By relying upon the Carnegie Institution of Washington to administer its scientific grants the Carnegie Corporation found a unique solution to the problem of intelligently allocating research support. The corporation provided a substantial part of the funds that the CIW awarded to external, chiefly university, researchers. In this respect the officers of the CIW might claim that they were the first managers of science: their individual programs were structured in this manner almost from the inception of the institution. However, their external research programs generally lacked the strategic focus and active direction that characterized Weaver's approach to experimental biology. The CIW was able, for example, to launch inquiries into cosmic rays at a time when that subject was at a peak of controversy. In general, though, there tended to be a high degree of stability in their external project grants, with support continuing year after year to the same trusted scientists for ongoing investigations. Overall, then, the incidence of Carnegie funds for university research was rather narrow.

It is difficult to generalize about other existing and newly created foundations during this period, but they tended to resemble the approach of the Rockefeller Foundation more than that of the Carnegie Corporation. Surveys of foundation activities note a "contraction of foundation interests": grants tended to be made in fewer fields, and interests became more focused within those fields: "from widely scattered interests . . . foundations are moving more and more toward specialization."[23] To judge what this meant for university research, one must take a longer view of the university research system in this era.

4. Common Goals and Cross-purposes

There can be no doubt that foundation giving had a major impact on the expansion of university research in the interwar years. Yet, not all contemporaries were certain that this impact was entirely positive. The British political scientist Harold J. Laski returned from four years of teaching at American universities with grave misgivings about the foundations' role. He questioned three aspects of the relationship between foundations and universities that had blossomed in the last half of the 1920s:

> I doubt whether the results to be achieved are likely to be proportionate to the labor involved. I doubt, in the second place, whether the effect upon university institutions is likely, in the long run, to be healthy; and I doubt, in the third place, whether the result of the policy will not be to give to the foundations a dominating control over university life which they quite emphatically ought not to have.[1]

These were insightful criticisms that could perhaps have been raised only by a person somewhat removed from the fray. There are nevertheless some good reasons to demur from Laski's first two doubts; in regard to the third, events seem to have proved him wrong altogether.

Laski argued that foundation-sponsored efforts to promote collective research placed the emphasis on the mere gathering of facts instead of on the scholar's responsibility to weigh and interpret facts. While no one would maintain that every foundation research dollar extended the domain of human knowledge, in the longer run the social surveys and abstracts that he disdained largely served their intended effect: the fact gathering of one generation of researchers (often graduate students) provided a body of empirical evidence upon which others could exercise critical judgment. This allowed the development of certain fields of knowledge that would otherwise simply not have been possible. On the second score, Laski charged that foundation influence favored the advancement of the kind of professor "who is active in 'putting goods into the shop window,'" rather than the cultivation of great scholars, and that furthermore it produced an emphasis on research at the expense of teaching. In regard to individual students and professors, this argument must perforce be impressionistic. But in institutional terms it seems that foundation backing of research tended to redress what had long been perceived as the excessive burdens of teaching in American universities. This will be seen explicitly in the next chapter, where the development of individual research universities will be examined.

Finally, was it true that the foundations, through their bountiful gifts to universities, "cannot help controlling them"? It may have seemed so in the golden age of the late 1920s, but fundamental differences in outlook as well as inherent limitations in resources prevented this from happening. By reviewing the principal forms of foundation support for university research and the manner in which they changed over time, one can arrive at a more realistic assessment of the ways in which this support did and did not coincide with university aspirations.

Research Capital. Foundation giving for endowment restricted to purposes of research or for research buildings represented a natural continuation of previous practices of enhancing general endowment and occasionally assisting building programs. Such grants were easily administered by a small foundation staff and readily explained to trustees. Nevertheless, the extent of research-capital commitments to universities in the last half of the 1920s was unprecedented. In large measure this was due to the unusual circumstances existing at the International Education Board and the Laura Spelman Rockefeller Memorial. Both of these trusts had more assets than were strictly needed for ongoing giving requirements, and both liquidated their own endowments by making a number of capital appropriations of over $1 million. One might question in several instances whether such grants represented an optimal usage of foundation resources.[2] As a whole, however, there is no disputing the important contribution of these capital gifts. In addition, as seed capital, some of these grants either directly, through matching requirements, or indirectly, through the effects of competitive emulation, induced universities to commit further funds of their own for research purposes. Moreover, this occurred at a time when institutional priorities were not otherwise strongly inclined toward research. Finally, the existence of this research capital was particularly valuable in the worst years of the ensuing economic crisis, when discretionary resources for research—or anything else—for a time almost disappeared. Buildings and endowment, however, were not the only form of research capital that foundations provided.

Intermediate Organizations. Foundation largess made possible the activities of the National Research Council, the Social Science Research Council, and, to a lesser extent, the American Council of Learned Societies. These institutions in turn fulfilled the invaluable function of providing foundations and other interested parties access to these respective scientific and scholarly communities. Foundations were thus able to delegate tasks, such as choosing postdoctoral fellows and allocating small grants-in-aid, for which they lacked specialized expertise and administrative capabilities. Although the councils had some endowment, their very existence implied that the foundations had an obligation to provide pass-through funds for them to distribute. This was done not only by the major foundations but on occasion by moderate-sized ones as well. Once established, the councils thus provided ready channels through which scientists or scholars might be mobilized for a variety of foundation purposes. It was foundation resources, then, that allowed these organizations to assume a prominent role in the promotion of university research.

New University Units. Conspicuous among foundation activities was capitalizing, and thus essentially founding, new university units that would not otherwise have existed. In this respect they complemented the role that individual philanthropy often played in the establishment of new university schools or institutes. One of the first such postwar initiatives was the Carnegie-funded Stanford Food Research Institite, established in 1921 in order to investigate questions related to the production, distribution, and consumption of foodstuffs. This kind of founding occurred more typically somewhat later, during the era of large capital grants, as with the Yale Institute of Human Relations. Perhaps the most spectacular example of this type was the Oriental Institute at Chicago. Although it was begun through the initiative of Professor James Breasted, who in 1919 solicited a direct gift from JDR, Jr., the fulfillment of Breasted's ambitious plans (six active expeditions employing sixty people by 1928) and the provision of a museum building and permanent endowment were due entirely to gifts from Rockefeller foundations.

Some new professional schools were also founded by foundation initiatives. The long-standing Carnegie interest in libraries resulted in a gift to the University of Chicago for the establishment of the first school of library administration (f. 1928); and a Rockefeller donation made possible the founding of the first university-level nursing school at Yale. These cases, in particular, demonstrate how foundation capital drew research universities into areas quite beyond their normal aspirations.

Fellowships. Possibly no type of foundation program had more profound benefits for university research than postdoctoral fellowships. They were begun in an almost offhand way with a Rockefeller grant made in lieu of a founding of research institutes. Their effectiveness was soon apparent, however, and they were expanded to the medical and the social sciences, as well as implemented internationally through the IEB. Given prevailing conditions for university faculty, fellowship holders received some invaluable advantages. They were freed to pursue their research during the critical postdoctoral years, when most aspiring academics were overburdened with the teaching obligations of starting instructors. Also, the fellowships generally induced scientists to relocate at different research centers. In a period when young academics at best tended to remain at their doctoral institutions, such mobility greatly enhanced the possibilities for both intellectual development and career advancement. A new model for foundation fellowships appeared in 1925 with the creation of the John Simon Guggenheim Foundation. Instead of relying upon the councils or other independent academic bodies to identify promising scholars, it created its own system of evaluating applicants through the use of voluntary referees. Because it specialized in fellowships alone, it was able to surmount the administrative complications that this approach entailed. It also filled a lacuna in the research system by providing more than half of its fellowships outside of the natural sciences and by supporting scholars at all stages of their careers.[3] The admirable record that the J. S. Guggenheim Foundation has compiled to this day is ample testimony to the importance of the niche that it filled in the research system.

Direct Support of Research. These types of grants were made at all levels of magnitude. Small grants-in-aid assisted scientists with the expenses of ongoing research; project grants were intended to fund specific investigations, which usually included full-time research workers and some equipment costs; and large appropriations were also made to support unspecified research in certain departments over a given number of years. The administrative requirements for each sort of grant obviously differed. Grants-in-aid were much like fellowships, in that a close knowledge of the specialty was needed to reach an adequate judgment. For this reason the Rockefeller philanthropies worked through the councils. The Carnegie Corporation, however, preferred to risk making such grants directly—an approach that cost little in terms of assets but that invited an avalanche of applications.[4] Major commitments of fluid research funds to trusted scientists at leading universities were an approach that fitted the administrative style of foundations during this period. It took some time for this approach to be supplanted by project grants, because the latter placed the greater administrative demands upon foundations. Effective project grants required that officers have a good grasp of the fields with which they were dealing and that they keep in touch with active scientists in a number of specialties. In return, however, such a strategy allowed foundations to focus the likely impact of their gifts. This consideration clearly grew more important during the decade of the thirties.

When the interwar period is viewed as a whole, the foundations appear as the most dynamic element in the research system. They warmed to the cause of university research in the mid-twenties, and the volume of such grants then rose to a peak by the end of the decade, being responsible in part for the golden-age conditions of those years. The momentum of these commitments carried through the period of the most precipitous economic decline. Then foundation support for university research dropped off dolefully. From 1930 to 1934, for example, total grants to the natural sciences fell by 77.5 percent.[5] In fact, this is a rather misleading comparison. The level of foundation grant making at the end of the 1920s was unsustainably high. According to one painstaking estimate, disbursements for university research rose from an average of $3.3 million during 1923–26 to $6.4 million in the period 1927–30.[6] The disparity in appropriations would be much greater. At the Rockefeller Foundation—the source of a significant portion of the total foundation giving—appropriations exceeded disbursements for 1929–31 by $17.6 million; but for the next three years disbursements were greater by $12.2 million.[7] (The years that followed saw a rough balance restored.) Thus, the effects of the Depression on university research seem to have been somewhat cushioned as this bulge of appropriations worked its way through the pipeline.

Annual comparisons of aggregate foundation gifts in these years are misleading for another reason. The peak of foundation support represented to a large extent the provision of research capital. The formation of university research capital during the 1920s had been an outstanding achievement, and the efforts of the foundations made a significant contribution. The lower giving totals in subsequent years represented different, and less expensive, forms of support. Changes in the composition of research support, in fact, contributed greatly to the dynamism of the foundation role.

The years from the first Rockefeller forays into social policy until the reorientation of the Rockefeller Foundation in the mid-thirties constitute a generation of experience in the maturation of American foundations. Certainly one of the notable accomplishments in this process was the accommodation that evolved between the foundations and a university-based research system. The first impulse of the foundations had been to seek their social or scientific objectives directly through the sponsorship of in-house research. This approach had succeeded in the earlier era when the CIW and the RIMR were chartered, but it confronted formidable problems of objectivity and vested interest when extended to the social realm. The postwar creation of independent institutes of social research funded by foundation grants filled an immediate but limited need. Basic science and the supply of scientific manpower continued to be dependent upon the universities.

As this situation became apparent to foundations, they began to assist university research in some obvious and noncontroversial ways: money for fellowships would develop scientific personnel; small grants-in-aid would help complete research projects. Both types of support were fuel that supplied additional energy to the existing research system. The transition to a deeper commitment of support did not occur until Beardsley Ruml perceived and articulated that the universities were the true home of basic research—the engines of American science. The audacious program of large capital grants that followed was characterized by a faith in the abilities and motivations of university researchers and by the hope that the long-range results would bring tangible benefits to society at large. It was also based to some extent upon an appreciation of the system of social control that existed in the research universities. Strengthening the universities, one could confidently assume, would strengthen American science.

The research universities, for their part, did not disappoint. Rather, other factors gradually shaped a different foundation mentality after

1930. The very success of academic science widened the ranks of supplicants as more disciplines and subdisciplinary specialties presented reasonable claims on foundation resources. At the same time large prior commitments and shrinking income placed constraints upon foundation undertakings. The manifold problems of the Depression, in addition, eventually shortened the temporal horizons of foundation officials from decades to the months immediately ahead. Committed, in any case, to reduced levels of grant making, foundation leaders sought programs that would contribute in a direct and perceptible way to the benefit of society. Thus, the tension again became apparent between disinterested academic research oriented toward the solution of disciplinary puzzles and the social goals of the foundations.

Superficially, it might appear that foundation attitudes had come full circle, but their position in the mid-thirties, after a generation of experience, was far more sophisticated and had far different implications for university research. Foundation aspirations to advance knowledge were now predicated upon working through the university research system rather than outside of it. The necessity of focusing their commitments, however, now meant that foundation largess would have a more limited incidence. Previously, fellowships, grants-in-aid, and fluid research funds had to a large extent placed in the hands of academics the authority to decide what research merited support. The eventual predominance of project grants, however, shifted the balance of power in research decisions back to foundation officers, who now attempted to match and fit the research potential of academic scientists with the general program goals formulated in the foundation.

In 1925 Frederick P. Keppel had told the American Association of Universities that "any important research project which has the endorsement of a representative group of scholars can find financial support from one or another of the foundations."[8] This interesting statement was patently untrue in 1925—or, for that matter, in any other year. (For example, virtually no state research universities were yet receiving foundation support.) It nevertheless represents an implicit, but unattained, ideal for the interwar research system based upon nongovernmental sources of support. In the years that followed, the vast foundation outlays may have brought this ideal somewhat closer to realization. The change of course in foundation policy during the thirties, however, made it clear that this ideal would never be achieved through the resources of foundations alone. The foundations played an indispensable role during these years in enhancing the capabilities of the research universities. As that role stabilized in the late 1930s, though, it became more apparent than ever that an expanding university research system required a pluralistic resource base.

5

The Privately Funded
University Research System

1. Business and University Research

The ideology of American science that emerged from World War I, and that was enshrined in the National Research Council, foresaw the advancement of knowledge led by a partnership between the universities, private industry, and the philanthropic foundations. Universities and foundations, after a halting start, had joined forces by the middle of the 1920s to provide a powerful impetus to scientific development. The role of industry, however, was somewhat more equivocal. Contemporary rhetoric stressed the continuity and complementarity of the basic research pursued in universities and the applied research utilized by industry. Business was thus presumed to have a vital stake in the research of university scientists, but just how this stake ought to be embodied in institutional relationships was a matter of continual uncertainty. Moreover, this was a fundamental issue underlying the privately funded university research system: there was a significant difference between relying upon the surplus wealth of previous generations and tapping directly into the wellspring of productivity for the private economy. The potential link between private industry and university research that was optimistically posited immediately after the war had in fact a long-range significance for the privately funded university research system that was just beginning to take shape.

Business interacted with science and universities over a broad front. Much of the wealth that flowed into American universities in the form of individual gifts had, of course, been generated in private industry. This individual philanthropy was directed toward diverse ends, especially when transmitted through bequests, by the eleemosynary impulses of widows and heirs, or under the professional direction of organized philanthropy. On the other hand, when substantial gifts were made by active businessmen, they were more often intended to further specific university activities considered strategically important by the donor. Thus, George Baker largely financed the Harvard Graduate School of Business Administration in 1922, much as Joseph Wharton had done at Penn a generation earlier; George Eastman lavishly supported the practical engineering that was taught at MIT; and Daniel Guggenheim gave millions to universities to promote the development of aviation. These and other donors used their considerable wealth to create or enlarge features of the university that they felt would make significant contributions to American society.[1]

In an entirely different sphere the 1920s witnessed an efflorescence of direct industrial research of the kind that had appeared early in the century. Industrial research and development expenditures rose substantially during the decade. In the high technology fields of the day—electricity, communications, and chemicals—industrial laboratories conducted basic as well as applied research. Firms in these industries also tended to maintain close ties with universities. The graduates of university science departments were eagerly sought by private industry; in fact, some companies gave fellowships to increase scientific manpower in areas that were important to them. In addition, professors in critical fields consulted with corporations, and companies in turn assisted science and engineering departments by giving small research contracts and donating equipment.

Somewhere in between these two very disparate kinds of linkages between business and academe lay the issue of general business support for university research. If private industry was deriving substantial benefits from university science, as the national scientific community widely believed, corporations had a responsibility to help meet the manifold needs of university-based research. The modalities of such assistance, however, were problematic. Corporations had vested interests in the research that they supported. Before the tax code was changed in 1935, corporate "gifts" were not deductible from taxable income unless they could be construed as a cost of doing business. University research, on the other hand, was wedded to the ideal of disinterested inquiry. The divergence in these outlooks held potential for conflict. There were important differences between the interested and the disinterested pursuit of knowledge in terms of what problems would be investigated and what use was to be made of the results. This was an arena in which the universities and private industry had to develop means of accommodating their disparate goals.

Industry had varying concern for some university activities, and none at all for many of them. The fields in which university-industry cooperation was most concentrated were engineering and chemistry. For that reason the issues raised by cooperation were most acute at engineering schools, particularly at the two institutes of technology that were also research universities. For both Caltech and MIT the conduct of industrial research was an important institutional commitment. Both were also rapidly developing institutions during this period. And, perhaps most significant, both aspired to conduct basic research in the same manner as other research universities. Their contrasting experiences in the 1920s consequently illustrate the major issues raised by industry support for university research. In addition, during the latter part of the 1920s these issues were projected onto a national scale by the attempt to create a fund for university research from contributions by private industry. By the time that these three episodes had run their course, the limits of corporate support for university research were far better marked.

There are no reliable figures for corporate support before the IRS began tracking these deductions in 1936. An examination of corporate donations to individual research universities during the interwar years nevertheless reveals that they were commonplace by the early 1920s and became more frequent as the decade progressed. The Depression, surprisingly, seems to have had only a minor impact upon these grants, largely because they were small in size and because they originated disproportionately from industries less affected by the economic slowdown. By the mid-thirties the secular expansion of corporate patronage had resumed.[2]

The character of this support was essentially pragmatic: university researchers were granted funds in order to work in areas of interest to the corporation. Often, the topic would concern an industry as a whole, as when lead producers sponsored numerous investigations into the nature of lead poisoning, or when the National Rock and Slag Wool Association financed research on building insulation at the University of Minnesota. Other examples might reflect the interests of particular firms, such as Eli Lilly and Company's funding of arthritis research or the Borden Company's support of investigations in food chemistry.[3] Much of this funding necessarily went to the professional schools of the universities, particularly to those of engineering and medicine. Conglomerate research universities that had many such schools consequently tended to attract the largest numbers of industry grants. In size these awards ranged from a few hundred dollars up to perhaps twenty thousand, the mean probably falling around two thousand. Such sums may appear insignificant in comparison with the munificent Rockefeller grants, but they considerably exceeded the amounts typically doled out through university research committees.

Corporate-sponsored research represented a significant, but rather eccentric, segment of the university research system. Where circumstances were propitious, some universities not surprisingly took steps to stimulate this form of interaction. Penn, for example, established a department of industrial research within the Wharton School in 1919 to perform contracted investigations on problems of labor and management. The Harvard Economic Service was established to forecast business conditions for private subscribers. Michigan established a department of engineering research in 1920 to do contract work for industry, and Minnesota and Illinois followed suit.[4] Nevertheless, the school that pursued industrial research most aggressively was MIT.

As a school with a mission to train engineers, MIT had a natural relationship with firms in which their graduates were employed. Beginning in 1903, however, MIT aspired to have a role in basic scientific research and graduate education as well. Its showpiece in this respect was the Research Laboratory in Physical Chemistry, headed by Arthur A. Noyes, which was discussed in Chapter 2. The desire to join the academic mainstream nevertheless did not inhibit the cultivation of links with industry. The electrical engineering department established in 1902 had close ties with AT&T, which provided regular support for both research and courses. In chemistry a formal vehicle for such linkages was created in 1908 with the founding of the Research Laboratory of Applied Chemistry. Organized like Noyes's lab as a semi-autonomous unit, the RLAC was expected to cover most of its expenses through research contracts with industry. Its director, William H. Walker, was a particularly ardent champion of this form of industry-university cooperation.[5]

Given the presence of some applied research on most university campuses, there was no inherent reason for conflict between what Noyes did in his lab and what Walker did in his. In fact, the compartmentalized nature of the modern research university permitted the coexistence of just such dissimilar activities. MIT, however, was remarkably noncompartmentalized in this era. Since chemical engineering was not yet organized as a separate field, Noyes and Walker had to coexist in the same department. There they disagreed fundamentally over the proper education of chemists and engineers. Noyes valued above all "thorough training in the principles of the fundamental sciences and in scientific method," while Walker contended "that it is a much smaller matter to both teach and learn pure science than it is to intelligently apply this science to the solution of problems as they arise in daily life."[6] Moreover, it would appear that disagreement on this point seriously divided the institution. In 1912, for example, a brilliant young chemist, G. N. Lewis, departed with several colleagues for Berkeley carrying an abiding enmity toward industrial intrusions into university research.[7] As an institution that was rapidly developing beyond its traditional mission, prewar MIT had something of an identity crisis, and it may have been made more acute by the financial anxieties involved in relocating the campus to Cambridge. Unlike other research universities, MIT seems to have been forced to choose between basic research for academic ends and applied research for service to industry. Two postwar incidents indicated the course that would be followed in the 1920s.

Immediately after the war the conflict between Noyes and Walker reached unmanageable proportions. In the spring of 1919 Walker sent an ultimatum to President Richard C. Maclaurin in which he threatened to resign if Noyes was not removed from the chemistry department. Given the strategic importance of Walker for relations with private industry, Maclaurin apparently felt that he had to give in: Noyes was asked to withdraw from the department, and his resignation from MIT soon followed.[8] For an academic institution to treat a scientist of Noyes's stature so cavalierly was quite remarkable. Not only was he one of the country's most renowned chemists, but he had also just filled one of the top posts in the NRC. In addition, he was a past acting president of MIT! His move to Caltech, it will be seen, was the first concrete achievement in that institution's rise to prominence. Maclaurin's capitulation was a clear repudiation of academic science.

To place this incident in perspective, it should be noted that 1919 was a year of frantic fund-raising for MIT. George Eastman had promised the institute $4 million for a badly needed building fund on the condition that $3 million more be raised as matching funds by the end of the year. As late as October the success of this campaign was in considerable doubt.[9] It was under these circumstances that MIT launched its hastily conceived "Technology Plan"—the second telling indication of MIT's commitment to applied industrial research.

The Technology Plan was essentially a device to secure corporate contributions for the endowment drive in return for certain general services provided by MIT. Corporations contracted to pay an annual retainer to MIT for five years. In return MIT gave these firms use of the library and access to its alumni and student files for purposes of recruitment. It also promised to arrange conferences with its staff on technical problems and advise firms on means of securing research assistance. The Division of Industrial Cooperation and Research was created to administer these ties, and, appropriately, William H. Walker was named its first head.[10] The plan appeared to be an immediate success: within months more than $1 million in contracts were signed, and this sum carried the endowment drive comfortably beyond its target.[11] More important, by placing the human and physical resources of the institute at the disposal of private industry, the Technology Plan set MIT upon an uncharted course of development.

Unlike any other research university, MIT in the 1920s was wedded to applied science. Besides its traditional role of training engineers for industry, it was now also committed to that of providing direct services. And the demand was considerable. Sponsored research at MIT exceeded $100,000 in 1920–21 and had risen to more than $270,000 by the end of the decade.[12] The Research Laboratory of Applied Chemistry provided the predominant share at first but accounted for only $100,000 of the latter total. Sponsored industrial research thus had spread widely throughout the institute.[13] The experience of MIT raised at least two compelling issues of university research: could service to private industry provide sufficient resources for the development of a research university, and was this kind of involvement compatible with basic scientific research?

The growing volume of industrial research activity did not in itself contribute appreciably to MIT's prosperity. Arrangements with firms basically covered the costs of the contracted research but yielded few spin-off benefits for the institute. Units like the RLAC still required infusions of institutional funds to sustain their total operations. In addition, the temporary nature of industrial contracts caused the work load and the staff requirements to fluctuate irregularly. In some cases, no doubt, industry supported important faculty research; however, the persistent complaint in the 1920s was that industrial research too often concerned trivial development problems.[14] As for the vaunted centerpiece of industrial relations—the Technology Plan—it turned out to be a one-time windfall rather a model for sustained cooperation. When the institute attempted to sign subscription renewals after the initial five-year period, it found virtually no takers. The original contracts, it seems, had been entered into with widely varying expectations. Some old Tech supporters may have simply regarded their payment as a disguised gift, but others apparently expected MIT to perform routine services for them. Whatever the case, it proved impossible to sell this package again. The plan became transmogrified into simple fee-for-service arrangements, and in 1929 it was terminated entirely.[15] MIT continued during these years to receive contributions from industry for such things as the electrical engineering course, but there seems to have been little industrial support for ongoing institute activities.

During the 1920s MIT nevertheless irrevocably entered the ranks of the wealthy private universities. The postwar endowment drive more than doubled its endowment, to $15 million. By 1930 it had more than doubled again, to $33 million—the fifth-largest university endowment in the country. More than half of this latter increase represented a combination gift-annuity from George Eastman (1925). Other significant gifts came predominantly from large bequests rather than from regular giving. MIT in fact lacked a reliable constituency of benefactors. The increase in the net operating income for the decade was an unimpressive 37 percent (1920–1929).[16] In comparison with other research universities, MIT seemed to need considerably more discretionary income and was particularly lacking the amenities that facilitated basic research elsewhere.

The complaints about low faculty salaries at MIT may resemble a perennial academic lament; however, MIT faculty were in close contact with their better-paid counterparts in private industry, and many of them devoted their nonteaching time to consulting rather than to personal research. In fact, salary levels at MIT were well below those of other East Coast research universities. Also indicative of inferior conditions at MIT was the lack of endowed chairs for outstanding scientists, of an institutional fluid research fund, and—a kind of litmus test for research universities—of any provision for sabbatical leaves. MIT's benefactors showed little interest in underwriting this type of academic support. President Samuel W. Stratton launched an appeal for an institutional research fund in 1926, but potential contributors did not respond.[17] Similarly, the creation of named chairs failed to attract supporting endowments. Perhaps most telling was the absence of any foundation support for research at MIT. During the entire decade the institute received only two grants—both from the Daniel Guggenheim Foundation for aeronautical (1928) and meteorological (1929) investigations.[18] When President Stratton approached the Rockefeller Foundation in the hope of securing general research funds, he was turned down on the grounds that MIT was an engineering school whose chief importance was to industry. In the opinion of the Rockefeller trustees, that was where it should look for support.[19] MIT's predicament seemed to indicate that it could not attain full stature as a research university while relying on private industry for voluntary support.

It was also evident by the end of the decade that MIT's considerable emphasis on applied industrial research was obstructing its desire to be in the forefront of academic science. Loss of faculty in the basic sciences caused the institute's prestige to drop in national comparisons.[20] Troublesome conflicts between industrial and academic practices further alienated academically inclined scientists. On several occasions, for example, researchers were prevented from publishing discoveries made under industrial contracts.[21] Faculty in the basic sciences at MIT during the 1920s had to endure a scarcity of resources and a discouraging atmosphere; meanwhile, their colleagues doing applied industrial research seemed increasingly to be distracted from academic matters by their second task-master. A report to President Stratton from the Division of Industrial Cooperation and Research estimated that 50 percent of the staff depended upon outside income from industrial consulting and research. His exasperated reaction was, "The Institute *can not* help being an interested party. It should know and 'administer' this work."[22] The great success of MIT in industrial cooperation during the 1920s thus not only took place at the expense of basic science but also generated serious administrative problems. The institute trustees ultimately concluded that new leadership was needed in order to steer MIT back into the mainstream of academic science.

The selection of a new president of MIT symbolized the beginning of a new era in the relations of industry and university science. The man chosen to bring about the reorientation of MIT was Karl T. Compton, the forty-three-year-old head of the Princeton physics department. Compton was a widely respected theoretical physicist who, not coincidentally, had played a key role in securing a large General Education Board grant to bolster the natural sciences at Princeton (see below). The decision to offer him the presidency of MIT seems to have come from Gerard Swope, president of General Electric, and Frank Jewett, president of the Bell Telephone Laboratories. It was Jewett who actually persuaded Compton to accept, by stressing the obsolescence of traditional engineering education, locked into teaching immediate practical skills. As the leading institution of engineering education, MIT had a responsibility, according to Jewett, to introduce fundamental science into engineering. Thus, the leaders of the nation's most technologically advanced industries in effect repudiated the approach that had been advocated by William Walker in favor of that espoused by Arthur Noyes. Inspired by this challenge, Compton became president of MIT in 1930 with a clear mandate to strengthen basic science and to rehabilitate the school's sagging reputation.[23]

Compton approached his task with an appreciation of the considerable strengths that MIT already possessed as the largest and wealthiest institute of technology.[24] Accordingly, he set out a program to upgrade undergraduate education by imposing selective admissions and more rigorous academic standards; to create a leading position in the relatively undeveloped field of graduate engineering education; to promote disinterested academic research among the faculty; and to adjust relations with industry to conform with institute's more academic posture. Although Compton's efforts were slowed during the worst years of the Depression, he made progress in each of these areas during the 1930s.

Some of Compton's first actions were directed toward asserting institute control over industrial research. The measures that were taken reveal the problems that had built up during the 1920s. Compton immediately altered faculty contracts so that all faculty promotions or appointments included an agreement to contribute 50 percent of all outside earnings to a "professor's fund." The following year it was decided to use this fund to support sabbatical leaves. Thus, those faculty members who sacrificed their personal research for additional income for a time supported the personal research of their colleagues.[25] The new attitude toward outside work was expressed in a listing of faculty obligations: consulting came last, and it was expected to be "of such important and dignified nature that its carrying on enhances the prestige of the institution, vitalizes teaching, and provides helpful contacts for the students."[26] The next step was to reorganize contract research under institute auspices. All separate units like the RLAC were eliminated in favor of the single Division of Industrial Cooperation. With all industrial relations centralized, it became possible to implement consistent policies regarding secrecy, overhead charges, and the treatment of patents.[27] It became the general policy of the institute that routine scientific work would be directed to commercial laboratories. MIT would undertake only research touching upon important scientific questions that required the special capabilities of its faculty and facilities.

Compton's immediate efforts to institute selective admissions had to be postponed when the Depression caused an unwelcome shrinkage of applications and enrollments. The institute countered this trend with a campaign to solicit applicants through direct mail and alumni contacts. By 1935 it was able to implement an "enrollment stabilization plan." The improving quality of MIT's undergraduates was evident in steps to integrate institute research with the undergraduate curriculum. When Compton became president, MIT was training almost a third of the country's engineering Ph.D.'s. In 1932 a separate graduate school was organized, as in most other research universities, thereby recognizing MIT's special mission in this area.[28]

Progress was more grudging on the matter of stimulating faculty research. This required hard resources in addition to presidential leadership. The Rockefeller Foundation provided a valuable endorsement of the institute's new course by granting $170,000 in fluid research funds over six years (1930–36); but foundation grants would not be sufficient to sustain institutional research at MIT, especially in light of the more stringent grant-making policies that were then being adopted. Compton appealed in vain throughout the 1930s for a $5 million endowment specifically for research. Funds for research consequently had to be sought through other expedients. In 1934 a program of research associates was announced, in apparent imitation of Caltech (see below). To attain this honorific title donors pledged $1,000 per year toward support of research at MIT. By 1936, when the Rockefeller funds ran out, the research associates provided more than $48,000 in sorely needed support.[29] The institute, however, required nearly $400,000 per year for research alone. Throughout the latter half of the decade, Compton complained that MIT was starved for research funds. He likened the institute to a well-trained athlete, "at the peak of condition to perform." Lack of funding, however, was preventing it from undertaking research that ought to have been done.[30] Nevertheless, MIT had accomplished a notable transformation during these lean years.

MIT corrected what was perceived by the scientific community to be an overdependence on private industry. The institute consciously adopted this course before the Depression constricted industrial research activity. This decision was based upon the realization that private industry could not provide sufficient resources to permit MIT to keep up with the scientific progress made at other research universities. At the same time, close industrial ties prevented MIT from benefiting from the resources that foundations were making available for basic research. The new course did not sacrifice the great prowess that MIT had developed in engineering education and research, but instead combined it with a renewed emphasis on basic science. This was a combination with enormous potential. The academic credibility of MIT improved with the arrival of Karl Compton, and the relative standing of its science departments gradually recovered. The turnaround was most dramatic in physics, which Compton had reorganized with a new head and several of his own Princeton students. By 1937 it had become one of the top three departments in the country.[31] In addition, the institute's capacity for doing advanced engineering research was stronger than ever. By 1937–38 the volume of sponsored research, now no longer exclusively from industry, had surpassed its 1930 peak. MIT's transformation, however, was in one way ironic; the balance between engineering and basic science that MIT had attained by the end of the 1930s bore a close resemblance to that existing at the school that had set out to imitate MIT just two decades earlier.

The emergence of the California Institute of Technology as a major center of American science was one of the most remarkable developments in interwar higher education. It was the only institution able to break into the ranks of the major research universities during these years, and it did so starting almost from scratch. The building of Caltech in many ways exemplified the features of American science that emerged from the war-time National Research Council. Its dedication to the advancement of basic science placed it squarely in best-science traditions; it looked to various forms of private patronage for the resources with which to develop; and it was very much part of the network of elites that had assumed responsibility for the leadership of American science. Most of these features were directly transmitted. The genius behind the NRC, George Ellery Hale, was also the driving force behind the founding of

Caltech. It was perhaps more unexpected that the spirit of the NRC would fructify in the academic backwater of southern California.

Before the war the Throop College of Technology, the forerunner of Caltech, was a one-building school that annually graduated about ten engineers.[32] Its greatest asset at this juncture was undoubtedly a devoted board of trustees consisting largely of wealthy businessmen from the Pasadena and greater Los Angeles area. The chairman, the lumber magnate Arthur Fleming, made up the annual Throop deficit out of his own pocket. Other trustees represented interests in banking, oil, real estate, and electric power. On the whole they exhibited a booster enthusiasm for the development of the southern California region that transcended their own vested interests in the region's growth. They felt that Throop had an important part to play by supplying scientific and technological solutions to the natural obstacles that were impeding development. Also a member of the board after 1907 was George Hale. His overriding desire was to have a center of scientific research at the foot of Mount Wilson to augment the work of his observatory. Given Hale's extraordinary influence in the scientific world, this incongruous combination of an astronomer and local businessmen on the Throop board proved highly effective for the development of the institution.

Hale's first coup was to lure his old friend Arthur Noyes to Pasadena, initially on a part-time basis and then permanently.[33] Noyes agreed in 1915 to spend three months of each year at Throop after the C. W. Gates family promised to build and equip a chemical laboratory. He immediately began sending some of his MIT students west, and by 1919, when events at MIT prompted his own departure, a fully staffed research laboratory was operating at Throop. By this time Hale and the Throop trustees had clearly formulated their ambitions for the school: they wished to make Throop into the MIT of the West, a center of science and technology closely linked with the industries of southern California. In 1920, at the suggestion of Noyes, the name of the school was accordingly changed to the California Institute of Technology. They were spurred in part by the hope that the Rockefeller Foundation would choose the institute as the site for a national research center for the physical sciences, but their determination remained even after those prospects faded.[34] To Hale the immediate goal was establishing an advanced research program in physics that would complement his own work and that of Noyes. As far as Hale was concerned, only one man was suited to head such a program—his close NRC colleague, the Chicago physicist Robert A. Millikan.

Millikan had already been recognized as one of the country's top physicists well before he was awarded a Nobel Prize in 1923. In addition, he had demonstrated his leadership and his versatility with the NRC during the war. He possessed the scientific credentials, the personal qualities, and the network of contacts needed to bring Caltech to the forefront of American science. As with Noyes, Hale first persuaded Millikan to spend one quarter of the year in Pasadena after the trustee Norman Bridge promised to donate a physics laboratory and funds for physics research. Then, when the presidency of Caltech fell vacant in 1920, the campaign to secure Millikan's undivided allegiance was launched in earnest.

The package that Hale and the Caltech trustees eventually assembled to persuade Millikan to leave Chicago may well be the most extensive in American academic history. Millikan would become head of the institute but would still have most of his time free for research. He would receive a princely academic salary of $15,000 (approximately double the top salaries at other universities), but most of the inducements proffered were for his science rather than for himself. Norman Bridge increased his contribution toward the physics lab by $100,000, and Robert Blacker added $50,000 for equipment. Arthur Fleming first offered a $1 million endowment for physics and then pledged his entire fortune of over $4 million in trust to the institute. Henry Robinson persuaded the Southern California Edison Company, of which he was a director, to donate a one-million-volt high-tension laboratory to Caltech. And George Hale, besides offering Millikan regular use of his own Mount Wilson laboratory, used his influence with the Carnegie Corporation to secure a promise of a research grant for chemistry and physics. Millikan's new physics department would have an annual budget of over $100,000, more than double that of Chicago. Little wonder, then, that he finally concluded that "he owed it to physics to accept the offer."[35]

With three of the nation's top scientists, Caltech suddenly became one of the important centers of American science. The donations that had made this possible, however, soon turned out to be but a down payment toward the development of scientific research at Caltech. To build upon the promising base that had been established in physics and chemistry would require more buildings, equipment, scientists, and money. The leaders of Caltech were prescient enough to recognize this, and their fund-raising efforts scarcely abated with the arrival of Millikan in 1921. Rather, they continued to exploit the same sources that had contributed to the recruitment of Millikan—local patrons, national foundations, and private corporations. The effectiveness of their appeals was greatly enhanced by an ideology of science that pervaded the Caltech community. It was a rather different spirit from the applied-science mentality that had become dominant at the institution they had originally intended to emulate.

At MIT the considerable emphasis on applied industrial research had the unfortunate effect of creating a dichotomy between engineering and basic science. Extreme statements by partisans like Walker seemed to deprecate the importance of fundamental research. In contrast, it was an article of faith at Caltech that basic science and engineering were inseparable. Nevertheless, at this school run by scientists engineering was expected to "grow out of physics and chemistry."[36] Specifically, the Caltech creed might be reduced to three propositions that were continually invoked in various permutations. The overriding task was to stress basic science in the undergraduate curriculum and in faculty research; basic research and scientific training would yield discoveries in practical matters as well as in pure science; and these practical discoveries would prove to have tangible benefits for the development of the industries of southern California. As articles of faith, these doctrines turned out to have a remarkable degree of validity. Furthermore, this creed proved to be a potent rationale for raising the funds that Caltech needed in order to develop.

Given its outlook, Caltech was able to cooperate closely with private firms without compromsing its scientific programs. The operation of the high-tension laboratory, for example, was governed by a joint committee drawn from both the institute and Southern California Edison. Noyes overcame his misgivings about industrial-sponsored research and acceded to the organization of a laboratory of industrial chemistry (although with tighter controls on contract research than had existed at MIT). The oil industry provided regular fellowships for the training of petroleum engineers. And somewhat later, the Guggenheim Aeronautical Laboratory would be extensively used by the aviation industry.[37] Moreover, there occasionally occurred important interactions between basic and applied research. For example, the investigation of theoretical problems in the high-tension laboratory by Millikan and his colleagues led to the development of the high-voltage x-ray tube. The medical potential of this device became the rationale for a gift from W. K. Kellogg for the construction of a radiation lab. Advances made in the design and completion of this facility, in turn, solved one aspect of the problem of particle acceleration. Millikan could justly claim that "at Pasadena science and engineering were merged in sane proportions."[38]

Private industry provided only a small portion of the donations that built up science at Caltech. The cooperation that was fostered between the institute and private industry, however, engendered something of far greater value in the goodwill of the southern California business community. The concrete scientific accomplishments of the institute gave businessmen good reason to believe that supporting basic science at Caltech would benefit area industries. It was the support of these individuals that provided the resources for further development.

Millikan's Caltech contract specified that he would not be required to participate in its fund-raising efforts, but he soon realized that if the institute was to grow with its surrounding community that notion "was out of the window."[39] Caltech's next step, however, was unclear. It had almost no alumni, and the trustees who had given most generously had already committed much of their wealth. With ingenuity worthy of a great experimentalist, Millikan devised a means for enlarging Caltech's constituency of supporters. With the assistance of the most socially prominent trustees, one hundred wealthy southern Californians were recruited to become "California Institute Associates." Each pledged to give the institute $1,000 per year for ten years, and in return was invited to lectures and social gatherings at the school. It took only a year to find members for this exclusive club.[40] The Associates Plan by itself provided the institute with $100,000 annually in unrestricted operating funds, or the equivalent of $2 million in endowment. Even more important, however, was the increase it brought in the base of Caltech supporters. During the 1920s many of these individuals made substantial contributions for new laboratories, for the Caltech dormitories, and for other buildings. They also made it possible for Caltech to match several large grants from the General Education Board. Thus, Caltech's base of local patronage became an important factor in its securing of foundation grants during the 1920s.[41]

Caltech was in many ways ideally suited to become a recipient of foundation support. Initially, the manifold contacts of Hale, Noyes, and Millikan gave them ready entrée to the highest levels of the major foundations. This was evident in 1921 when John C. Merriam of the Carnegie Institution sweetened the research package that enticed Millikan; and it was evident a few years later, too, when Millikan used influential NRC associates to intervene with the Guggenheims to secure an aeronautical laboratory for Caltech.[42] In the era when Wickliffe Rose was "making the peaks higher," Caltech was the outstanding exemplar of the best-science philosophy. It was a matching grant from Rose's General Education Board that allowed Caltech to lure America's premier geneticist and imminent Nobel laureate, Thomas Hunt Morgan. Finally, when the emphasis in foundation giving swung to project grants, Caltech's scientific prowess was so well established that it naturally received its share. Thus, Caltech succeeded, as MIT had not, in tapping into the largest pool of capital available for research during the 1920s.

Caltech's ability consistently to find the resources needed for its development was no doubt the key to its emergence as a major center of university science. Success ultimately depended, however, upon the effectiveness with which these resources were employed and upon the individuals who formed the scientific community at Caltech.

As a fledgling institution, Caltech had resources that were still rather limited in comparison with those of other research universities. It com-

pensated for this relative weakness by concentrating its efforts, both ped-
agogically and scientifically. As early as 1922 Caltech could claim a
freshman class with the highest average test scores in the country (a distinction it still holds today).[43] Caltech deliberately chose to remain small
and educate students of high ability. Scientifically, physics emerged as the
true center of Caltech's development. By the late 1930s the Caltech physics department was ranked, along with Harvard's, as the most prestigious
in the country.[44] Other important areas of Caltech eminence were closely
related to physics—physical chemistry, microbiology, astrophysics, aeronautics, and geology. By keeping its efforts focused upon a limited number of complementary scientific fields, Caltech was able to become a
major presence in American science.

Accounting for the human factor is less obvious than may at first appear. Caltech recruited three of America's most renowned scientists in
Noyes, Millikan, and T. H. Morgan, but the major scientific accomplishments of each were well behind him by the date that he moved to Pasadena. Under some circumstances such appointments might have been
disastrous. That they were not at Caltech was due to the scientific dedication and acumen of these individuals, and also to the continual expansion
of the institute's activities. Noyes, Millikan, and Morgan all brought
younger colleagues with them to Caltech, and they also used their extensive contacts to recruit other promising scientists. Far from becoming a
gerontocracy, Caltech probably had the youngest scientific staff of any
research university.[45] The youthful element was further enhanced by the
large numbers of National Research Council Fellows who chose to study
physics or chemistry at Caltech.[46]

The success of Caltech naturally involved other factors as well. The
collegial style of managing the institute and its laboratories made it, more
than any other research university, an institution truly run by scientists.
The constant visits of prominent foreign scientists allowed it to quickly
carve for itself a niche in the international world of science. The frequent
travels of Hale and Millikan to maintain communications with their numerous East Coast contacts kept Caltech at the center of developments in
American science. In the final analysis, however, Caltech succeeded in
realizing the vision of science shared by Hale, Noyes, and Millikan largely
because they were able to accomplish two separate tasks. They conveyed
their vision of the promise of basic scientific research to a constituency of
Caltech supporters and thereby managed to attain the resources for the
institute's development. They then effectively employed those resources
toward its institutional fulfillment. It was an impressive, though singular,
achievement. American society in general was more reluctant to place its
faith in basic science.

If the postwar ideology of science proved to be highly effective in stimulating the development of Caltech, then it was not unnatural to think that the American business community in general might be persuaded of the benefits that could result from support of basic university research. For George Hale this notion was an idée fixe. He had worked to bring about closer contacts between business and academe through the National Academy of Sciences and the National Research Council, but the linkages he devised failed to produce any tangible contributions for university research. Early in 1922 Hale began lining up support for a concrete scheme—a public subscription for a fund to finance scientific research in the universities. At this juncture the foundations had not yet made major commitments to underwrite university research, nor had the universities fully recovered from their postwar difficulties. There was much validity in Hale's central argument that the country's impressive achievements in industrial research rested upon a precariously weak foundation of "pure" scientific research. Nevertheless, it was not until mid-decade that Hale succeeded in organizing his network of contacts in science, industry, and public life into an official campaign to gather the National Research Endowment, subsequently renamed the National Research Fund.[47]

The goal of the fund was to secure $20 million in commitments for university research over ten years, or an annual income of $2 million. Its board of trustees, who were to do the actual fund-raising, exemplified the network of elites that Hale believed to be the natural leaders of American science. Secretary of Commerce Herbert Hoover agreed to accept the chairmanship, and he was joined by Secretary of the Treasury Andrew Mellon, Elihu Root, and Charles Evans Hughes from the political realm; from the independent scientific institutions came John C. Merriam (CIW), Simon Flexner (RIMR), and the principal officers of the NRC; Hale, Millikan, T. H. Morgan, and James Breasted were among the distinguished academic scientists; and industry was principally represented by John J. Carty of AT&T, Owen Young of GE, the banker Felix Warburg, and Julius Rosenwald, the philanthropist chairman of Sears & Roebuck.[48] This last group, in fact, was the real target of the drive. The basic strategy was to secure the $20 million through large pledges from major corporations. In part this emphasis stemmed from the rationale behind the fund, that industry derived large but unforeseeable benefits from basic scientific discoveries. An unspoken consideration must nevertheless have been to avoid diverting the assets of foundations and individual philanthropists that were already supporting universities. The essential task of the trustees thus became selling pure science to private industry.

The campaign was launched at the end of 1925 with fanfare, publicity, and a rousing speech from Hoover. A $1 million pledge from Julius Rosenwald was soon announced, and AT&T followed with an expected offer of $2 million. It was not until 1927, however, that the National

Electric Light Association (representing GE, Westinghouse, and others) increased the fund with a $3 million pledge. The fund's momentum was then halted entirely when U.S. Steel refused to contribute.[49] Worse yet, all of the pledges were contingent upon the entire $20 million's being raised. After another stretch of inactivity it became apparent that the fund would have to be either fulfilled soon or scrapped entirely.

The goal of the fund was lowered to a more attainable figure of $10 million, representing income of $1 million per year. In 1929 a concerted effort, largely carried by Robert Millikan, was begun again. U.S. Steel, now under new leadership, was finally persuaded to promise $1 million; and the corporation induced the industry's Iron & Steel Institute, which it dominated, to do the same. A similar pledge from George Eastman brought the fund's pledges up to $900,000 per year. The organizers then turned to the Rockefeller Foundation as a last resort, and it agreed to supply the sum that would fulfill the goal. The fund quickly attempted to call in its pledges as economic conditions worsened in the fall of 1930. But Julius Rosenwald, always a wavering supporter, and the National Electric Light Association, which had also had second thoughts, failed to pay. Other contributors used this as a pretext for withholding their contributions. Just $379,900 of the promised $1 million was received; given the dubious legal status of these funds, nothing was distributed. The Depression extinguished any hopes that pledges would be honored, and in 1934 the books were closed on the National Research Fund.

One might hesitate to pass too severe a judgment on an effort that apparently raised $10 million, only to be swamped in the collapse of the economy. Yet, the National Research Fund deserves to be regarded as a failure in a double sense. It palpably failed, of course, to provide a dollar of support for university research; but in a deeper sense it failed in its original goal to mobilize private industry for the support of pure science. A campaign of five years' duration managed to secure tenuous pledges from just two corporations, two industry associations, two philanthropists, and one foundation. Records of actual solicitations and responses do not exist, but the absence of any commitments of less than $1 million is sufficient indication of the narrow and elitist approach that was taken. The insurance, automobile, and railroad industries were apparently approached unsuccessfully. No mention appears of such industries as chemicals, pharmaceuticals, petroleum, or food-processing, where firms regularly provided direct support for university research.[50]

An analysis of this pattern on the basis of straightforward economic logic has suggested why those few industrial donors were persuaded to support the National Research Fund and why the remainder were not.[51] The industrial contributors represented monopolistic (AT&T) or oligopolistic (U.S. Steel) industries, where the dominant firm could be expected to make the most effective use of any relevant scientific breakthroughs that might occur. For the industrial associations, any scientific benefits would be available to all members. Firms in competititve industries, however, could hardly be expected to use their funds to support pure research when any lucrative findings would be available to their competitors at no cost. This would not necessarily mean that such firms would eschew all connection with university research. A slight extension of this logic, however, can account for the patterns of industrial sponsorship of university research that have been described at the beginning of this section.

While American business in general could not be convinced of its vested interest in pure science, individual firms made thousands of investments in specific aspects of university science during these years. Some followed the lead of Du Pont in funding graduate fellowships to increase the supply of scientific manpower. Others funded specific research projects in areas of special concern to them, secure in the knowledge that they were best situated to profit from any discoveries. This was especially true if the researcher, as was often the case, was also made a consultant to the firm. Geography could also be a factor. The more economically self-contained a region, the more likely that university activities would redound to the particular benefit of local industries. Thus, support for Caltech was successfully equated with support for the development of southern California.

It became evident during the 1920s that investigations too closely tailored to the wishes of private industry had limited scientific or pedagogical advantages for universities. For example, the commercial services that MIT offered provided little in the way of benefit for the institute, while at the same time absorbing the time and energies of its teaching staff and eroding its academic reputation. Obviously, there were cases where a true symbiosis could occur: where industry confronted a problem of real scientific significance and could provide the wherewithal for university researchers to grapple with it. The Caltech high-tension laboratory exemplified this type of conjuncture, but in fact the histories of Caltech and MIT (probably more than those of any other institutions) could supply many others.[52] Nevertheless, on the general relationship between private industry and university research the extraordinary vision of George Hale was for once flawed. Pure science had to find a different patron, at the institutes of technology no less than at other research universities.

2. Institutional Patterns of University Research

The university research system that was in place and functioning by 1930 was quite different from what anyone could have anticipated only a decade before. At the beginning of the interwar years, it might be recalled from Chapter 2, most of the essential organizational features of the research universities had at least roughly taken shape, but the external resources needed to make these arrangements consistently productive could not be assured. While the postwar cooperative euphoria lasted, scientists could hope that business would become the patron of university research. The foundations, insofar as research was concerned, seemed at this juncture inclined to favor the independent research institutes, possibly, it was feared, to the detriment of the universities. Certainly, in 1920 no one could foresee the reorientation of the largest foundations toward support of university-based research, the largess that individual philanthropy would bestow upon higher education, particularly the research universities, or the circumstances that allowed these institutions to concentrate their resources to the advantage of faculty research. The privately supported university research system of the interwar years, in fact, was inherently unpredictable.

There existed in this period no single, monolithic funding agency, such as the National Science Foundation was to become, to which all institutions might appeal on an equal basis for research support. Instead, donor preferences for institutions and for subject areas were an inescapable part of this system. This was seen to be true of foundations: when they were most open about the usage of their grants, they gave to only a small group of universities; but when the competition was widened, the types of projects that they funded were restricted. When universities were fortunate enough to receive large amounts of unrestricted capital, they then faced another problem of preferences. The amounts devoted to research had to be squared with other institutional priorities. Under this privately supported system donors were an important constituency of the research universities. To be snubbed by the foundations, as MIT was, could cause major ramifications. Generally, however, this did not happen. The donor constituency of a university was a consistent part of a larger university personality. And so, too, was the research profile of each university, dependent as it was upon the institution's benefactors. Thus, diversity characterized institutional patterns of university research, primarily because of the heterogeneity that existed in sources of university voluntary support.

This diversity was already evident in the research profiles of MIT and Caltech. The distinctiveness of these two cases, however, was partly due to their specialized nature. The other fourteen research universities were, for the most part, more diffuse and more complex. Nevertheless, the integration of research—the mission they all shared—with other institutional responsibilities had a somewhat different character at each. In the remainder of this section the patterns of research development at six research universities will be examined in order to show, first, just how they differed from each other—that is, how institutional traditions, faculty structure, leadership, and available resources shaped the research profile of each; and, second, to examine how research universities in general advanced during this era. Harvard and Chicago, by consensus the country's two leading universities, are naturally important cases. Princeton and Yale, too, are important in their own right, but their contrasting developments reveal the working of underlying forces. Finally, the different circumstances and strategies of state universities will be traced in the two most successful examples, Michigan and California. These six cases, in addition to the two already considered, illustrate the dynamics of a pluralistic and hierarchical system of university research.

Harvard. Few would fail to agree that Harvard overall had the preeminent university faculty in the country from the turn of the century to World War II.[1] It had this despite the marked change in orientation that took place when A. Lawrence Lowell assumed the presidency in 1909. Charles Eliot's emphasis on research and his relatively permissive attitude toward college studies were supplanted by a new preoccupation with the life and education of Harvard undergraduates. Lowell's administration saw first the establishment of fields of concentration, general examinations, and a corresponding system of tutors. Special dormitories for freshmen, selective admissions, and, finally, the Harvard House system followed.[2] His concern for the collegiate experience was enthusiastically supported by Harvard alumni, who gave on an unprecedented scale during his tenure. This reorientation, however, seemed not to have unduly disturbed the Harvard faculty.

Lowell's program for undergraduate instruction created a need for additional teachers, as large lectures were broken down into discussion sections and tutorials were phased in. These needs were met largely by utilizing graduate students rather than permanent faculty. On the whole this seems to have produced a beneficial division of labor: research-minded professors could concentrate on advanced instruction, while apprentice university teachers handled much of the time-consuming contact with undergraduates. One result of this division was that Harvard never felt the need to divide the faculty into graduate and college divisions, nor did it have to hire a large corps of junior faculty.[3]

The Harvard Faculty of Arts and Sciences was in fact notably top-heavy with full professors. They constituted about half of the faculty in the 1920s, and better than 40 percent during the next decade.[4] The entire faculty expanded inexorably along with the fiscal prosperity of the university, at least until the depths of the Depression. Even in 1934, it was almost 60 percent larger than a decade before. Graduate education expanded as well. It doubled during the 1920s before succumbing to the effects of the Depression, but the number of Ph.D.'s granted—certainly the most crucial figure for research—grew steadily during both the 1920s and the 1930s.

More than any other university in the country, Harvard had the means to call almost whomever it chose to professorships. It generally paid the highest salaries and had more endowed chairs than any rival. Its facilities in most sciences were excellent, and nonscientists benefited from the world's largest university library collection. In addition, a plethora of endowed funds were earmarked for research and graduate fellowships.[5] Besides the great prestige associated with the name of Harvard, no other institution could match the range of advantages it could offer across the board. Yet, Harvard's power to call was exercised sparingly.

During the academic generation of Lowell's presidency most Harvard departments had to be completely reconstituted, but no single formula was employed in making these critical appointment and promotion decisions. A number of faculty managed, particularly in the first part of Lowell's tenure, to work their way through the ranks without leaving Cambridge; other Harvard men proved themselves elsewhere in order to earn an invitation to return; occasionally non-Harvard men were called from other American universities; and sometimes Harvard filled its needs with eminent foreigners. Running through these many decisions are, first, the consciously acknowledged obligation of Harvard's remaining preeminent and, second, the constraint of choosing scholars that fit the Harvard type. Scholarly attainments were expected of Harvard faculty in the Lowell era, but "intellectual excellence alone had never been enough to gain a Harvard post."[6]

Lowell sought to assure that permanent appointments would measure up to his conception of a Harvard gentleman, and this attitude inevitably encouraged a high degree of inbreeding. Harvard's world-famous philosophy department of William James, Josiah Royce, George Santayana, and Hugo Münsterberg, for example, was replaced during Lowell's early years entirely with Harvard products.[7] During this process Bertrand Russell was rejected as too eccentric and Arthur O. Lovejoy (a founder of the American Association of University Professors) as too zealous in the cause of professors' rights. To give this homegrown department more-conspicuous renown, Alfred North Whitehead was called from England (1924). The pattern was similar in the larger and more dynamic economics department during the years that it was probably preeminent in the country:

> No one who had not taken his Ph.D. at Harvard was invited in any other than a visiting capacity between 1903 and 1919. . . . This inbreeding had its

effect during the next decade when the Department found itself saddled with a certain amount of deadwood.

Economics, too, resorted to foreign scholars in order to bolster its slipping prestige, bringing in Joseph Schumpeter and Pitirim Sorokin. It seems that a foreign scholar constituted less of a threat to the homogeneity of Harvard than one from an alien American university.[8]

It is noteworthy that when economics rebuilt in the 1930s it promoted none of its own students to permanent positions. As a result of this approach its most brilliant student—Paul Samuelson, first Nobel laureate in economics—was lost to MIT. Although Samuelson himself found nothing anomalous in this turn of events, his recollections of the department during the 1930s depict a situation that could occur at Harvard but that would be most unlikely anywhere else. Quite simply, Harvard nurtured the dominant economics department in the country while under the leadership of the "deadwood" referred to above. The aura of Harvard, it seems, outweighed specific departmental faults in attracting outstanding scholars. Harvard economists thus spearheaded the introduction into the discipline of Keynesianism, imperfect competition, and econometrics, despite the fact that the department chairman, in Samuelson's words, "stood for everything in scholarly life for which [Samuelson] had utter contempt and abhorrence."[9]

As a meritocracy the Harvard faculty may have been restricted in scope and imperfect in operation, but it was never closed. A powerful sense of academic destiny caused it periodically to search out outstanding scholars with whom to maintain the eminence of its departments. The result was a faculty that was, at once, capable of effectively utilizing the unparalleled resources of Harvard University for the advancement of knowledge and yet comfortable with the prevailing ethos of Harvard College—whose alumni were the principal fount of those resources. By the end of Lowell's presidency (1933), however, this situation was becoming strained.

There were widespread feelings by the time Lowell left office that the Harvard faculty was declining in stature; that his prolonged emphasis on building the college had occurred at the expense of the university. No less a personage than Frederick Keppel of the Carnegie Corporation charged him with favoring "the urbane scholar of the British type, who will charm and stimulate the undergraduate," over "the authority of the multiple footnote variety, who might prove more useful to the candidate for the doctorate."[10] Criticism was even sharper among some parts of the faculty. One member felt that by "filling up the younger ranks with mediocre men whose merit consisted largely in their willingness to be tutors" Harvard was "betraying its trust . . . guilty of almost criminal negligence."[11] The professor of these views was the chemist James B. Conant, who was chosen, significantly enough, by the Harvard governing boards to become the successor to Lawrence Lowell. The priorities of the university thus were redirected once again toward cultivating a preeminent research faculty.

Although Conant is best known for his postwar impact upon secondary education, his actions during the 1930s were consistent with the position stated above. Without departing radically from established Harvard traditions, he consistently worked to reassert the universalistic values of science. He made the object of Harvard's three hundredth anniversary fund the endowment of "university professorships" and "national scholarships." The former were designed to allow scholars of unique talent and breadth to teach what they pleased outside of the departmental structure. The scholarships were meant to leaven the Harvard student body with a group of young men of outstanding ability chosen through competitive examinations. By the end of the decade circumstances forced Conant to deal with the issue of appointments that had been his original concern. The eventual result was a policy of referring tenure promotions to an ad hoc committee made up of Harvard professors outside the department in question and of non-Harvard specialists in the field concerned.[12] No longer would being a proper Bostonian be a factor in appointments. Harvard under Conant, then, pointed the way toward a more rigorous standard of meritocracy among research universities.

Chicago. The tensions between the undergraduate college and the research university assumed a rather different form at the nation's second great university. In 1930 the graduate school dean at the University of Chicago wrote,

> Perhaps the unsatisfactory condition of graduate schools in this country today is ultimately due to the fact that the original plan, which has been followed ever since, of attaching a German system of advanced work to the American college is fundamentally unsound and constitutes an educational hybrid that can never prosper.[13]

This was a curious judgment for one in such a position, particularly at the historical moment when the American university was moving into the forefront of international science. But it was not an altogether unusual opinion to be voiced at the University of Chicago.

William Rainey Harper's university was from its outset dedicated to academic excellence, educational innovation, and community service. By the 1920s most of its innovations were well in the past, and the less prestigious types of service commitments were being attenuated; but Chicago was more single-mindedly dedicated to pure academic inquiry than any other American university. During the twenties, for example, the faculty senate passed a resolution affirming that research was the chief aim of the university, and it was frequently recommended that the faculty teaching load be reduced from two courses to just a single seminar. A 1925 report called for the intensive development of graduate education and research, including the establishment of research units like the Oriental Institute in each academic area. A 1927 report urged that the entire institution be pervaded by the "university spirit" of disinterested inquiry. Chicago's junior college, it was suggested, should be placed on a self-supporting basis and removed from the main university campus.[14] That these sentiments, which hark back to the early Johns Hopkins or Clark, were thriving at Chicago in the 1920s was due to both the strengths and the weaknesses of the university.

Chicago was established and developed with the gifts of John D. Rockefeller, Sr., complemented by many substantial donations from wealthy Chicagoans. The development of the university was propelled in the 1920s by this same combination, except that now Rockefeller money came from the several foundations. Local benefactors tended to provide useful amenities for the campus, besides helping to support the major professional schools. Foundation gifts, however, benefited the academic core of the university and particularly its capacity for research. As was seen in the last chapter, Chicago was the single largest beneficiary of grants from both the Laura Spelman Rockefeller Memorial and the International Education Board. It also received nearly $16 million from the General Education Board.[15] Moreover, almost all of these grants were made in the last half of the decade. Little wonder, then, that during this golden age it seemed to Chicago professors that they were on the threshold of becoming a "pure" research university, encumbered by only a modicum of fairly advanced teaching. Undergraduates in general, and freshmen and sophomores in particular, had little to contribute, according to this scenario. In fact, the undergraduate college carried less weight in the institutional balance scales at Chicago than at any other university.[16]

The Chicago undergraduate colleges (junior and senior) never attained the stature of its graduate and professional schools. Despite the national reputation of its faculty, 60 percent of the undergraduates were recruited from the city of Chicago. Like other private universities, Chicago instituted selective admissions, but its perennial problem was actually too few applicants.[17] If the quality of incoming students tended to rise over time, it was probably due more to self-selection than to anything else. Chicago had a distinct reputation among students for high standards, a heavy work load, and severe attrition. Each year one-quarter to one-third of its freshmen were lost for academic reasons. Instructors, who often graded on rigid curves, were of little help. It was alleged that first-year courses were taught "as though every student in them were planning to devote his life to the subject." [18] Despite rigorous standards—or perhaps because of them—the senior college was a poor feeder for the graduate school. The college alumni, usually a countervailing force against research-minded professors, were weak and fragmented for a number of reasons. The chief concern of local alumni seemed to be the football team, which had increasing difficulty competing against other midwestern juggernauts. Most important, the alumni had provided little of the voluntary support that had made Chicago what it was.

The disjunction between ideals and reality at the university widened even further when Robert Maynard Hutchins assumed the presidency in 1929. One of the most outspoken proponents of pure intellectual inquiry, Hutchins was also convinced that the institutional structure of American higher education was all wrong. [19]

Like other easterners who presided over midwestern universities, Hutchins was dismayed by the inclusiveness of the undergraduate college. Instead of endeavoring, like Lowell of Harvard, to assure that each student received a first-rate education, he believed that comparatively few undergraduates were capable of moving on to advanced work. The rest would be better advised to terminate their studies after receiving a general education in the junior college. The University of Chicago was accordingly restructured early in his administration. The senior college was combined with the graduate school in four separate divisions, while the junior college remained separate. Hutchins then concluded that a period of two years was insufficient to accomplish the ends of the junior college. He therefore tried to extend it downward to include the last two years of high school. Even though this plan worked poorly at Chicago, Hutchins nevertheless claimed that schools of this type were "destined to be the characteristic instruments of popular education in America." He was similarly disdainful of Chicago graduate students; he regarded only a minority as potential scholars, and so the rest constituted a hindrance to the development of this small elite. [20]

Hutchins's performance was inherently contradictory. As an educational philosopher, he wished to address all of American education, but at the same time he advocated an impossibly high standard of intellectual excellence, even for Chicago. In addition, the arena in which he worked was like that of no other university in the country. He complained that his goal of having the Chicago junior college stand as a national model was thwarted because the university was too good: "our standards are so high that we are beaten from the start when we recommend our program to most other institutions." He disbanded the department of home economics, although it was the leading center for training university teachers in that subject, because its standards were low relative to those of the rest of the university. [21] The contradictions might have been more blatant had his scope for action been wider; however, Hutchins took over the university just before the Depression took hold.

Chicago was struck doubly in the 1930s, as its income declined precipitously and its special relationship with its principal benefactor gradually dissolved. From 1930 to 1933 endowment income declined by more than a third; the general budget of the university had to be lowered by this amount; and about half of this reduction occurred in salaries for instruction and research.[22] These latter cuts were accomplished basically by retiring all senior faculty at the age of sixty-five, even though this meant losing many well-regarded scholars. Most of these positions were simply not filled during the 1930s. When appointments could be made, Hutchins's standards were exacting. As conditions improved in 1935, eight professorial appointments became possible: six of the appointees were called from Europe and two from elsewhere in the United States. There were few promotions to tenure from within the university during this period. By the middle of the decade several departments were in near rebellion over Hutchins's refusal to heed their recommendations for appointments and promotions. Continued discontent prompted two critical AAUP studies of academic tenure and departmental authority at Chicago, but Hutchins dismissed both categorically. Faculty complained more and more about their plight of being guided by a philosopher-king.[23]

Although Hutchins continually endorsed the research role of the university, this too was increasingly squeezed during the 1930s. In the first part of the decade the effects of the Depression were cushioned by the continuing flow of appropriations pledged by the Rockefeller Foundation. The reorientation of the foundation in 1934, however, dealt a heavy blow to Chicago. Henceforth, only project grants would be available for the biological and social sciences. The Rockefeller Foundation did grant the university $3 million in 1936 to ease the transition, but once that was committed no additional sources of income were foreseeable. By the end of the decade Hutchins had recommended that the board approve spending a considerable portion of the university's endowment—a fiscal measure that would have been unthinkable at other private universities.[24]

Hutchins's strong personality and brash statements tend to occlude more-fundamental features of Chicago's singular situation. Chicago was decidedly an ivory tower of pure academic inquiry even before 1929, and that mentality was encouraged by the golden-age conditions of the late 1920s. The Rockefeller philanthropies were the chief donor constituency of the university, and they favored, above all, the kind of academic dedication and achievement that Chicago was eager to provide. The otherworldliness of Hutchins accentuated this orientation, even as the Rockefeller Foundation began to withdraw its special sponsorship. Chicago was nevertheless committed to a course that would distinguish it even more sharply from the one prevailing at most other research universities. This made it all the more difficult for Chicago to react pragmatically to its mounting financial problems.

Hutchins's idealism may have appealed to the Rockefeller Foundation, but it probably contributed to his lack of success with other constituencies. Relations with wealthy Chicagoans deteriorated to such an extent that the university was advised against attempting a fund-raising campaign. Hutchins also alienated the alumni at a time—demographically speaking—when they were becoming older, wealthier, and more numerous. Typically, he abolished football in 1939, as the university was preparing its semicentennial fund-raising campaign. Moreover, Hutchins did not seek to reach external constituencies by broadening the teaching mission of the university. He further fragmented undergraduate education at Chicago instead of trying, as other private schools did, to increase social cohesion.[25] And he was, as a matter of principle, disdainful of the service roles that helped to sustain other urban universities. In the name of providing an ideal model, Hutchins chose to ignore much of the reality of American higher education.

For all his dedication to the life of the mind, Hutchins's leadership was not congenial for actual scientists and scholars. His own belief that higher education should be guided by an overriding metaphysic gave him little appreciation for many fields.[26] He was openly contemptuous of mere "empiricism," a rubric that would include much university research. In practical matters he rode roughshod over departmental prerogatives, attempting to concentrate authority in his appointed divisional deans. Chicago's persistence as a leading research university in the 1930s owed much to sheer inertia. Hutchins fortified the inherent idealism of the university and its commitment to excellence—qualities that should not be taken lightly—but these years left Chicago materially weaker. In part this was due to the conscious rejection of the kind of complementary teaching and service roles that all other research universities to some extent fulfilled. By the end of the interwar years Chicago was more precariously financed than previously, but was still the ivory tower among research universities.[27]

Princeton. Yale and Princeton, despite some salient differences, were quite similar as research universities. Yale was larger and wealthier, in part because of the presence of professional schools. Princeton was far from poor, but it enrolled scarcely more than two thousand undergraduates during these years, and just a tenth of that number in its graduate school. Both institutions valued the academic accomplishments of their faculty, but for each the overriding institutional priority was the education—intellectual, social, and moral—of undergraduates. Both schools, as well, owed their growing affluence to their loyal and generous college alumni, whose influence reinforced the paramount position of the undergraduate college. Yale and Princeton thus exemplified, far more than Harvard with its accustomed academic supremacy, the tension between the pursuit of excellence in undergraduate education and its pursuit in academic research. It is interesting that these tensions were worked out somewhat differently at each institution, particularly with respect to research in the natural sciences.

Princeton in a number of ways managed to turn its small size into an advantage. Unlike that of any other research university, Princeton's faculty was concentrated in the arts and sciences. When measured on this basis, it was not small at all; during the 1920s, in fact, it was larger than the Harvard Faculty of Arts and Sciences. The Princeton faculty even outnumbered its graduate students during these years. By 1920 the departments at Princeton had acquired considerable autonomy, including tacit authority over appointments and promotions. Moreover, they harbored a dynamic faculty whose members were for the most part active scholars. In 1920 a regular policy of "up or out" was instituted for all instructors and assistant professors, along with regular salary reviews for senior appointments. In addition to the turnover that this entailed, the Princeton faculty also managed to grow by more than 50 percent during the 1920s.[28]

Princeton's idea of graduate education was an aberration in the American system. At Princeton the graduate dean Andrew Fleming West had prevailed over the opposition of the president Woodrow Wilson in the erection of the imposing Gothic Graduate College, somewhat removed from the main campus.[29] West's insistence that graduate students, too, should benefit from collegiate living meant that the enrollment in the graduate school was in effect restrained by the number of places in the Graduate College. The result was that Princeton's few chosen students enjoyed extraordinary opportunities for close work with faculty and compiled an admirable record. Only Chicago graduates captured more NRC Fellowships in mathematics and physical science during the 1920s, and no Princeton applicant was turned down.[30] Even before concerted efforts were made to strengthen the sciences, Princeton possessed one of the country's finest mathematics departments and well-regarded departments of physics, chemistry, and biology.

Princeton at the beginning of the 1920s was characteristically preoccupied with issues of undergraduate education. A postwar fund-raising campaign was partly aimed at endowing Woodrow Wilson's system of preceptors, which had never been adequately financed. Other important matters included the establishment of selective admissions and a more rigorous upper-class study plan, both of which were instituted in 1923. Not until 1924–25 was President John Grier Hibben able to look beyond these immediate tasks to consider the future needs of the university. The result was the announcement of an ambitious effort designed to raise $20 million in endowment for faculty salaries, to complete Princeton's building needs, and to increase resources for graduate study. Although this heterogeneous appeal encompassed everything from a new chapel to a chemistry lab, it inadvertently proved to be of strategic importance to the development of scientific research at Princeton.[31]

In its desire to raise additional endowment, Princeton naturally turned to the General Education Board. Discovering that the GEB's interests had changed from endowment building to advancing science, Princeton sent a delegation of its leading scientists to meet with Wickliffe Rose.[32] The original Princeton proposal envisioned funds to finance a mathematical institute and concerted research programs on radiation, the cell, and geology. When pressed by Rose, the scientists placed a tentative price tag of $3.5 million in endowment on this endeavor. Rose was favorably impressed by the Princeton science program, but much further clarification was needed, including how these funds would fit into Princeton's announced endowment campaign. Subsequent negotiations between the two parties in the fall of 1925 substantially transformed Princeton's plans.

The final proposal to the GEB requested $3 million, most of which would be used to establish endowed research professorships in mathematics, physics, chemistry, biology, and astronomy. The remainder would be devoted to such things as visiting professorships and graduate fellowships. This sum represented a quantum increase in the resources available to Princeton science and a provision for research professorships that went beyond that of any contemporary rival. Then, late in the negotiations, the GEB informed Princeton that the board could consider only *a contribution toward* this sum. Princeton hastily amended its request, but the addition of these few words committed the university to financing an unspecified part of this program out of its own resources. In November the GEB approved a conditional grant of $1 million to Princeton, leaving the university with the task of raising twice the amount in matching funds.

Fortunately for Princeton, the times were propitious. The necessary funds were pledged within three years, as the trustee Thomas B. Jones and his family provided almost two-thirds of the amount. Nevertheless, one is left with the impression that the lure of GEB money enticed Princeton into making a more extravagant commitment to the natural sciences than it would have made if only Princeton's internal priorities had been considered. In fact, at almost the same moment, President Hibben was proclaiming the "imperative need . . . to enlarge our Faculty in a manner that will adequately correspond to the possibilities of increased effectiveness in teaching, which is our main aim and purpose."[33]

Scientifically, the Princeton program was an outstanding success. The endowed chairs allowed the university to call several top European scientists and virtually guaranteed the eminence of the Princeton departments. During the interwar years Princeton compiled the remarkable record of attracting more NRC Fellows in mathematics and physical sciences than any other institution.[34] In terms of distinguished scientists on its faculty, Princeton enhanced its relative standing more than any other private university in this period (save the neophyte Caltech). The achievements of the sciences, moreover, were a constant goad to other fields at Princeton. The establishment of the School of Public and International Affairs (1929) solidified Princeton's status in that field, and continual efforts were made to create endowed chairs and special research funds for the humanities and social sciences. All this did not fail to elicit criticism from alumni, who feared that the emphasis on research detracted from the "main aim and purpose" of the institution.[35]

President Hibben made a conscious attempt to educate Princeton alumni about the place of research in a leading university. One promotional piece began with the unsubtle heading "What is Research?"[36] In his annual reports Hibben forcefully and effectively linked the advancement of knowledge to Princeton's traditional teaching mission. Continuous involvement in research, he emphasized, was necessary for teachers to remain abreast of their subjects and to sustain their enthusiasm for it. "The best teachers today," he further stressed, "will not be attracted to an institution which does not give them the opportunity for scholarly activity and research."[37] This argument became a part of the ideology of Princeton—an indispensable nexus between the donor constituency of college alumni and an erudite, research-minded faculty.

Yale. President James R. Angell employed much the same language as Hibben to emphasize the importance of research at Yale, but he had a more difficult task.[38] Not only did he need to enlighten the crucial constituency of Yale alumni, but he also had to prevail over certain factions within the Yale faculty. The Yale predicament stemmed largely from its belated integration into a unified university, and it spawned a particularly deep-seated conflict over the values that were to guide its institutional development.

Although the schools of science at Princeton and Harvard had been integrated into their respective institutions before 1900, Yale's Sheffield Scientific School remained a separate, affiliated entity as late as 1919. Then a complete reorganization of the university was instigated by the alumni and carried through by the Yale corporation, despite the disapproval of the faculty and the misgivings of President Hadley. Under the new arrangements the Sheffield School kept its separate identity even though it became, in effect, the science division of the university. A further measure of unification was the establishment of a common freshman year, with its own faculty and dean. The result was an "artificial splitting up of the fabric of undergraduates study" that would never "have been adopted on its merits by any authority when founding a college of liberal arts de novo." Thus, "Yale's peculiar form of undergraduate education was an anomaly due to historical accident."[39] Part of this anomaly was the existence of four different faculties—for the freshman year, Yale College, Sheffield, and the graduate school. To a considerable extent they represented the divergent outlooks prevailing in the university.

When Yale elected James Rowland Angell to its presidency in 1921, it chose a certified insider from the nation's research community. Son of the venerable Michigan president James Burrill Angell, he had worked up the ladder at Chicago, from the post of instructor to being dean of the faculty and later acting president. He then briefly headed the NRC before becoming president of the Carnegie Corporation. The selection of a non-Yale man was further testimony to the corporation's belief that the insularity of the Yale community needed to be broken.[40] Considering the ample resources that Yale had, or was about to receive, the basic challenge that Angell faced was to identify and recruit active scholars to strengthen the Yale faculty. He was obstructed, however, by traditionalists who had a powerful entrenched position in the Yale College faculty.

One area of contention concerned appointments to the freshman year faculty. Some departments saw such positions as the natural starting points for beginning scholars and consequently sought to choose instructors on the basis of their scholarly potential. The freshman dean, on the other hand, stressed the importance of dedication to teaching at this level. In this context one almost had to be a graduate of Yale College in order to be considered an effective teacher. The dean consequently found the departments' emphasis on scholarly productivity to be "inappropriate." From his perspective the departments appeared to be the "natural enemy" of the freshman year.[41]

The ambiguous overlapping of authority between faculties and departments evident in the conflict over the freshman year made it difficult to conduct a coherent staffing policy. Instead, there occurred a drift toward a faculty tailored to student demand:

> In Yale College this meant at the lower-class level a continued emphasis on instruction in small classes by many home-bred instructors. At the upper-class level, the distribution of faculty staffing would be molded by undergraduate elections, and particularly by the relative popularity of the different majors.[42]

In Yale College during the last half of the 1920s more than 50 percent of each class majored in English. This buttressed one of the best and most conservative departments in the university but made it difficult to build other departments through strategic appointments. The result, according to the Yale historian George Pierson, was that before 1930 "comparatively few scholars of outstanding distinction were brought in from the outside and given permanent tenure" on the college or freshman faculties. Thus, Angell's efforts to strengthen these faculties, "by the *direct* infusion of scholarship from the outside, substantially failed."[43]

The Sheffield Scientific School found itself in a distinctly subordinate position in the reorganized Yale, without even the limited degree of independence that it formerly possessed. The Sheffield dean consistently complained that the school did not receive enough students; however, the Yale system was stacked against it. Selective admissions favored prep-school products, who were comparatively less interested in science, and the common freshman year caused some potential science students to be seduced away by the powerful Yale College culture. The Sheffield dean continually requested additional appointments to enlarge and strengthen the faculty, but lagging enrollments made the Sheffield case weak. As Yale's prosperity grew during the last half of the 1920s, the Sheffield budgets increased less than those of the other three faculties.[44] Conceivably, discretionary appointments by the graduate school could have alleviated this situation, but few were made. During the most active decade for appointments (1926–35), only six of forty-three graduate school professorships went to scientists.[45] The contrast with Princeton could hardly be more stark: during an era when extraordinary exertions were often necessary to keep abreast of the rapid advancement of science, the science faculty at Yale was allowed to languish—indeed, to lose an E. O. Lawrence to Berkeley (see below). The reason for this stands out just as clearly: the structural disadvantage of the Sheffield School under the peculiar Yale organization.

The cause of research was not without its partisans at Yale, and they were most effectively represented in the graduate school. Dean Wilbur Cross was an ally of President Angell when it came to blocking weak appointments or engineering the recruitment of noted scholars.[46] It was Cross, apparently, to whom Angell entrusted the discretionary income that Yale's growing endowment made available. During the halcyon years (1925–30) the faculty budget of the graduate school increased at more than twice the rate of those of the other three faculties.[47] Insofar as the actions of the graduate school changed the scholarly balance in New Haven, they helped to build the social sciences: fifteen of the forty-three senior appointments referred to above went to history and political science.[48]

The progress that Yale made as a research university during the 1920s was due largely to extraordinary financial prosperity. Most important for the academic development of the university was the great bequest of John

W. Sterling. Originally estimated to be worth $15 million in 1918, and at that the greatest gift an American university had ever received, it permitted the Sterling trustees to grant Yale more than two and a half times that amount over the next two decades. Almost $23 million went to building such key academic structures as the library, the chemistry lab, and the graduate, law, and medical school buildings (all appropriately named in honor of John Sterling). Another $12.5 million was used to endow professorships, fellowships, and scholarships.[49] Thus, much of the infrastructure necessary to a research university came to Yale without any recourse to formal fund-raising. When Yale did go to its loyal alumni, it was able to ask them for unrestricted endowment. The $20 million endowment fund that was kicked off by a "round-the-world dinner" on April 20, 1927, was therefore intended to generate income to shore up faculty salaries and permit new appointments. "Not one dollar of the new endowment is being sought for the physical expansion of the university," the Yale treasurer could promise the alumni; its purpose was rather "to make a finer, not a bigger Yale."[50]

Yale's ample resources seem in fact to have allowed the research university to develop without altering the spirit that still animated much of Yale College. Angell and Cross felt by 1930 that the graduate and professional schools had been raised to the high standards to which Yale was accustomed; but Cross's successor at the graduate school, Edgar Furniss, found more than vestiges of the old myopia: an English professor who maintained that only a practicing Christian could possibly teach English literature (because of biblical references); an economics professor who alleged that all texts written since his own were the work of Communists; and a sociology chairman who responded to the suggested appointment of a recognized scholar from another university, "I can't be expected to whistle just anybody in from the street and set him to teaching this all-important subject!"[51] At other research universities the departments were usually the champions of disciplinary standards and provided the natural impetus for academic strengthening. But Yale College, with its strong traditions and considerable past accomplishments, may have had the most insular research university faculty. Furniss felt that it would have been "folly" to expect the departments to improve themselves, since "some of them were under the command of senior officers who appeared to be fearful lest they add to their numbers abler scholars than themselves."[52] Organizational adjustments were consequently needed if Yale was to make the most effective use of its resources.

After the reorganization of 1919 it took a number of years for Yale to evolve the administrative mechanism appropriate for a unified university. Probably the most important underlying trend was the gradual centralization of authority in the university administration. This was accomplished largely through the power of the purse. The key administrative officer for this was the provost, who exercised responsibility for the financial affairs of the academic part of the university. It was here that the president could exert financial leverage on a faculty that did not always share his goals. The office became closely associated with that of graduate school dean— the effective spokesman for research interests. Wilbur Cross held both positions, as did Edgar Furniss. The provost during the last half of the Angell administration was Charles Seymour, a noted scholar himself as well as a proponent of scholarship. Seymour was also "the quintessential Yale man."[53] When he succeeded Angell as president in 1937, it may well have signaled the unification in spirit of Yale College and Yale University.

Seymour was able to be a forceful advocate of faculty research without threatening the deeply respected traditions of Yale College. He stressed the necessity of scholarly productivity for faculty members and advocated that Yale search out the best available scholars for its positions. Although he took over in a period of retrenchment, he made the expansion of the faculty his principal goal.[54] Yale may have remained somewhat parochial in its viewpoint, and the sciences would not soon recover the ground lost because of their structural handicap, but by the end of the 1930s the Yale faculty was no longer internally divided. It generally accepted that for Yale College to remain a great teaching institution, Yale University would have to be a great research university.

The five state institutions most closely followed the prewar pattern of research university development. "A state university," Michigan's president Marion Burton exclaimed, "must accept happily the conclusion that it is destined to be large."[55] Strictly speaking, bigger did not necessarily mean better for these institutions, but for a critical period in their history growth seemed to be the inescapable requirement for enhancing academic quality. Each of the five developed somewhat differently. Wisconsin was probably the most highly regarded state university and the most fecund producer of Ph.D.'s for the first two decades of the century, but it fell out of step with the other research universities for much of the interwar period. Its president was not an academic; undergraduate pedagogy was a persistent preoccupation there; and foundation support was initially disdained. It was not until the late thirties that new leadership and substantial contributions from the unique Wisconsin Alumni Research Fund counteracted these tendencies.[56] Michigan quietly made its traditionally strong academic position even stronger during the interwar years. Although no university should be regarded as typical, Michigan exemplifies some of the forces underlying the development of public research universities. California is an important case because of its spectacular rise in university rankings. Illinois built a national reputation in chemistry but achieved recognition in few other subjects. Minnesota's president Lotus Coffman became a national spokesman for state universities, and his leadership helped the university maintain its stature.

On the whole the state research universities made a good showing against their private counterparts. The breadth of their development compensated in part for the fact that the most highly rated departments were almost monopolized by Harvard, Chicago, and Columbia. In fact, conditions for the development of state universities were unusually propitious during the 1920s. The universities were then all severely affected by the Depression, but their recovery was such that by the late 1930s the private research universities felt decidedly defensive toward them.

The state universities underwent a spurt of rapid growth in the decade before the war, but the unsettled conditions that followed largely prevented them from taking the measures needed to accommodate that expansion. The postwar enrollment boom then occurred on top of an accumulated backlog of capital and personnel needs. State governments, however, soon were both willing and able to assist university development. On most campuses the decade began with a building boom that to varying degrees carried through the 1920s. Millage rates, the usual basis of university financing, were raised so that state appropriations outpaced enrollment growth. For the decade state contributions to current expenses at these five schools climbed 130 percent, while enrollments were up just 40 percent.[57] Although they were not as "wealthy" as this single statistic would seem to indicate, they did find the funds to make new appointments, to establish faculty research funds, and generally to allow greater opportunity for faculty research. These five universities were thus probably stronger than ever when fiscal disaster struck. This strength enabled them to preserve much of the academic progress of the preceding decade. Moderate expansion during the last half of the 1930s then alleviated the worst strains caused by the Depression. By 1940 these state universities were more committed to research, and more productive in it, than at any point in their past.

The progress of the state universities depended upon more than budgetary allocations. It in fact required changes in the composition of the faculty, teaching responsibilities, administration, and voluntary support. Events at the University of Michigan illustrate one version of this basic evolution.

Michigan. During the 1920s the Michigan faculty increased by 82 percent, which was remarkable in two respects. This growth was the largest for any state research university, while Michigan's increase in student enrollment was the smallest.[58] Partly, this allowed Michigan to make up for ground lost during the war years, but the large number of new faculty in itself contributed to the intellectual vitality of the campus. As in most state universities, this growth was concentrated in the junior ranks, so that during the last half of the 1920s about two thirds of the faculty in the College of Literature, Science and Arts were instructors and assistant professors. Michigan thus had a youthful and highly mobile faculty during a period in which academic evaluation in general was becoming more rigorous. A candidate had to have some visible scholarly attainments to merit one of the relatively few senior appointments. This process did not create world-famous departments, but it was conducive to broadly based academic strength.

When the Depression struck, these trends promptly reversed. Michigan was the most severely affected state research university. By 1940 the university faculty was smaller than it had been a decade earlier, despite almost 30 percent enrollment growth. The Literature, Science and Arts faculty lost a full sixth of its positions. The faculty structure also changed markedly: Literature, Science and Arts now had forty-seven more senior appointments, which altogether made up 56 percent of the total. As part of this change in faculty structure a much greater share of the teaching load was shifted to graduate assistants. In this manner the Michigan faculty adjusted to the winnowing of the Depression years with minimal damage to its academic standing.

The composition of the student body at Michigan also changed during these two decades. The College of Literature, Science and the Arts evolved much like an eastern college with selective admissions. After a postwar spurt of growth, its enrollments remained on a plateau from 1925 to 1940. As a result the weight of the college within the university declined from 53 percent to 38 percent. Its percentage loss, however, equaled the gain made by the graduate school, whose share of the total enrollment grew from 8 percent to 23 percent. As the university as a whole became more oriented toward graduate education, its teaching became more integrated with research.

Presidential leadership at Michigan was decidedly sympathetic toward faculty research. Marion Burton (1920–24), whose forceful direction inaugurated the building boom, also instituted faculty sabbaticals. His successor, Clarence Cook Little (1925–29), kept up his own investigations as a biologist even while president, and he finally resigned in order to pursue full-time research. The university's next president, Alexander Grant Ruthven (1929–51), came directly from one of the university's research institutes—its museum of natural history. Nevertheless, of longer-range importance than presidential leadership for the academic development of the university was the general devolution of administrative authority away from presidents and regents and toward the deans and departments. Burton initiated this trend by establishing representative executive committees in the departments and colleges, as well as regular presidential conferences with the deans. He also reorganized the regents' committees in order to break the special relations that had developed between individual regents and certain schools. Under President Little the faculty had sufficient power to thwart his plan to split the university into junior and senior colleges. The long tenure of the unassuming Ruthven, however, confirmed this evolution. An effective administrator who believed in delegating authority, Ruthven decentralized the university further by creating a vice-presidential layer of administration, while also distancing the regents from everyday university affairs. By the end of the interwar period, the academic values of the Michigan faculty were a considerable force in the determination of university policies.[59]

Michigan was particularly fortunate among state institutions in benefiting from private gifts. Voluntary support played a different role at state universities than at endowed ones. The latter had need above all for unrestricted gifts that could underwrite the general operating expenses of the institution, but public universities looked to their respective state legislatures for this kind of income. Not wanting their donors to appear to lessen the state's responsibility, they sought restricted gifts for purposes that the legislature would be unlikely to support. President Ruthven was quite forthright about this: he "encouraged donors to attach 'strings' to gifts—the stipulation that they should be used for a specific purpose." During his tenure the university was sufficiently conscious of the importance of such support to make a historical inventory of all donations. Presented en masse, they appear to have had a substantial impact on Michigan's development as a research university, especially during the difficult decade of the 1930s.[60]

By 1939 Michigan had received a total of $44 million in gifts of various types. About 85 percent of this constituted permanent contributions to the university's assets (land, buildings, endowment, or additions to collections). That sum represented about half of the university's total current assets. The university received gifts worth $18 million in the period 1931–39, and probably a comparable amount during the years 1920–31. Many of the larger benefactions were destined for amenities like the stadium, Burton Tower, dormitories, the men's Union, and the women's League; but increasingly during this period voluntary support aided research. In 1929 the university obtained its first substantial grant from a major foundation—$250,000 from the General Education Board for a dictionary of early modern English. Even before this it had been favored by two special benefactors. William W. Cook was the patron of the Law School. He donated several buildings during his lifetime, and left Michigan $15 million for this end upon his death in 1930. Since his objective was to enhance the quality and standing of the school, much of his gift went for research-related purposes. Horace Rackham had funded archaeological investigations by the university during this lifetime, but in 1935 the fund he created gave Michigan $6.5 million for the construction of a graduate school and the endowment of research.[61] In addition, Michigan received during these decades gifts for current research too numerous to list or characterize. From 1920 to 1931 these gifts came to roughly $1.5 million; and in the next eight years they amounted to $1.6 million. These totals do not include more than $1 million in research contracts performed by the Department of Engineering Research.[62] Voluntary support, then, made a substantial contribution to the maturation of Michigan as a research university.

California. The same elements that figured in Michigan's development were even more prominent at the University of California. During these years the official university was spreading itself over the entire state, while the home campus of Berkeley was building the foundation of its future preeminence. The same basic expansion of faculty positions was under way there, with particular emphasis on junior appointments. The increasing weight of graduate education was evident as well. In other respects, however, California was more fortunate than Michigan or any other state university.

In the years immediately following the war, the Berkeley faculty greatly expanded its responsibilities for the governance of the university. Reorganization produced a period of turmoil and conflict, including the resignation of a president, but the faculty gains were largely consolidated during the subsequent presidency of William Wallace Campbell (1923–30), longtime director of the Lick Observatory. Basically a researcher like Ruthven of Michigan, Campbell too believed in administrative decentralization. In addition, he shared the fundamental goals of the research-minded faculty. During the "tranquil, prosperous and comfortable years of his administration," science at Berkeley made great strides.[63]

California consistently received more voluntary support than any other public institution, and from at least the beginning of the century research was a conspicuous beneficiary of this support. These traditions continued into the interwar years, when, for example, the $1.5 million bequest of Edward Searles was used to support research. California was also the first state university to have budgetary appropriations purely for research and a standing faculty committee to allocate them (1915). During the 1920s these funds were increased dramatically, reaching $100,000 in 1929—far more than any other state appropriated directly for research.[64] In addition, California had something else that was lacking in other state universities: a commitment not just to quality but to academic preeminence.

President Campbell wished to place California on the same level as the leading half-dozen institutions in the country, and many of his department heads shared this ambition. The chief obstacle, however, was that neither California nor any other state university was generally able to offer the conditions and salaries to lure the academic stars around which leading departments were usually built. When California did extend such offers in the 1920s, they were generally declined.[65] The university could not, then, pursue the strategy of Caltech or Princeton or adopt the practices that Harvard took for granted. The only alternative seemed to be to attract the most-promising young scholars and scientists available and then to give them the best possible conditions in which to advance their research. This strategy succeeded brilliantly in the California physics department.[66]

Building a nationally recognized academic department requires leaders who can spot and recruit talented investigators, as well as institutional support to make them compelling offers. California already had G. N. Lewis, successor to Alfred Noyes as America's foremost physical chemist, and also an active force in university affairs. Lewis was behind the initial push to develop physics, but most of the later recruiting was done by Leonard Loeb and Raymond Birge, themselves new recruits. The university built a new physics laboratory in 1923 that was admirably designed for research. Even more important, the department during the 1920s received ample support for research, flexible teaching loads, numerous graduate fellowships, and money for travel. California became an increasingly attractive location for ambitious physicists, and, thanks partly to the foresight of the foundations, the latter were in plentiful supply. All of the California appointments in this era were former NRC Fellows; that is, they were judged to be among the best of the nation's science Ph.D.'s, and they had then honed their skills further in the most advanced laboratories. These appointments were particularly significant in light of the fact that both public and private universities in this era staffed most junior positions with home-grown Ph.D.'s, whereas the California department refused as a matter of policy to give its own graduates regular appointments. The Berkeley physics department also showed conviction and persistence when it identified a scientist it wanted. This was evident in its most notable coup, its attracting of E. O. Lawrence from Yale.[67]

Leonard Loeb was impressed by the advanced nature of Lawrence's work when he met him in 1926. He arranged an offer of an assistant professorship the following year, but Lawrence decided to remain in New Haven when Yale matched this promotion. Loeb persisted, however, and was able to offer Lawrence a position at the rank of associate professor the following year. Yale would not accede to such an unseemly pace of advancement, even though Lawrence as an assistant professor at Yale was barred from teaching graduate students. He went to Berkeley in 1928 to advance his research as much as his own career, and his work there earned him a Nobel Prize just eleven years later. The following year (1929) J. Robert Oppenheimer accepted a dual appointment at Berkeley and Caltech. By the end of the 1920s, then, a quite young Berkeley physics department had taken its place in the front ranks of the field.

The individual stories of these six institutions, as well as those of the two institutes of technology examined in the preceding section, suggest no single formula for the successful development of a research university. Nor is it likely that detailed examinations of the other eight research universities would alter this conclusion. Certain tendencies are apparent, but none seems conclusive in itself.

A growing contingent of graduate students appeared to be an important accompaniment to university research at most universities, although this was not true at Princeton. At the state universities and at Harvard, graduate students absorbed much of the burden of introductory teaching; but their presence everywhere created more research manpower and more advanced seminars. Voluntary support played an indispensable role at all of these universities, but because the sources varied so widely it may well have been the factor that made these institutions differ so widely from each other. Only a few institutions directly addressed their benefactors for research-related purposes (Caltech and, to an extent, Princeton and Harvard); some derived research capital from unanticipated bequests (Michigan and Yale); and for several the foundations played a crucial role (Chicago, Caltech, Princeton). Patterns of faculty development also differed, largely in keeping with available means. Harvard, Chicago, and, sometimes, Yale could hope to call the top men in their fields; but the state universities and MIT usually had to find their talent at earlier stages of academic careers. Caltech and Princeton tended to combine these strategies by making only a few strategic calls and otherwise relying upon faculty development. Finally, no prescription for leadership could encompass all these institutions. At California, Michigan, and Princeton the faculty seemed to seize the initiative in critical academic decisions; at Harvard and Chicago research-minded faculties provided a counterweight to presidents with somewhat different priorities; and at Yale and MIT administrative leadership was required to encourage universalistic disciplinary values. Caltech, to complicate the picture further, had strong executive direction from a committee of scientists rather than from a president. Yet, although no specific prescriptions emerge from these examples, some general conclusions are possible.

It should be evident that, whatever the imperfections of a given research university during a particular period, the system of university research functioned effectively during these decades. When inbreeding at Harvard seemed to be weakening the country's premier faculty, when the parochialism of Yale College threatened to retard the effectiveness of Yale University, or when overemphasis on applied research threatened to exclude MIT from the basic research community, steps were taken to reassert fundamental academic values. In part the effective functioning of this system was due to the competitive structure of American universities. The competition was considerably abetted, however, by an infusion of resources that gave universities the encouragement and the rewards to strive for academic distinction.

From the entry of the United States into World War I until the early years of the 1920s, American universities were buffeted by financial uncertainties and enrollment fluctuations, but perhaps unsettled even more in their institutional souls by rapidly shifting expectations about higher education. No sooner had they attained a kind of equilibrium by the middle twenties than change accelerated once again. These changes, however, were welcome ones. A golden age seemed to have dawned. In place of perennial anxieties there was suddenly plenitude. University budgets grew markedly, and the contributions of the foundations guaranteed that much of the expenditure supported research. The advancement of knowledge for the first time became a lucrative undertaking. University faculties, in particular, expanded rapidly in the last half of the 1920s, and unprecedented mobility assured that productive scholars found their way to accommodative institutions. A new generation of scientists who had sampled the best of European and American laboratories on foundation fellowships—Oppenheimer, Lawrence, and Linus Pauling, to mention only widely known figures—entered the most productive years of their careers. Universities like California, Princeton, and Caltech that were poised to make special efforts to enhance their scientific standing did spectacularly well during these years; but all the research universities were to some extent lifted by the tide of prosperity.

In a relatively short period university research made a quantum leap to a new scale of organization and operation. The hardships of the Depression years squeezed, but did not force back, the advancements of the late 1920s. The preceding pages have depicted the various ways in which institutions adapted to this new environment. The section that follows will attempt to gauge some of the effects.

3. Students, Professors, and Research

The golden age of the 1920s marked a subtle but definite watershed in the evolution of the research universities. Material prosperity was conducive to numerous small alterations in the everyday practices and procedures of the universities, in prevailing attitudes toward academic matters, and in expectations about university development. Cumulatively, these changes erased many vestiges of the pre-World War I university; and in retrospect, although somewhat occluded by the general turmoil of the Depression, they foreshadowed some characteristic features of the post–World War II research university. There was no revolution. This transformation lacked a charismatic spokesman or a symbolic event. In fact, those who raised the loudest clamor about American higher education in these years were, with respect to research universities, generally barking up the wrong tree. Nevertheless, by the early 1930s the research universities were operating on an unmistakably higher level of academic seriousness than just a decade before. The difference was perceptible in undergraduate teaching and learning, in graduate education, in faculty career patterns, and in arrangements for research.

Undergraduate Education. The establishment of selective admissions at private universities in the early 1920s was the first step toward a gradual strengthening of undergraduate studies. Barriers to admission, particularly at the eastern colleges, were not intended to inhibit their traditional prep-school clientele, and the emphasis on character at times scarcely veiled ethnic and social prejudices. But while presidents, faculty, and admissions officers might insist that "brainpower" alone was an insufficient qualification, they overwhelmingly agreed that those who lacked the capacity to perform adequately should be the first pared from the admissions list. As soon as applications exceeded openings, which they quickly did, the process of selective admissions acted not to reward merit but to eliminate the most obviously unfit. One result was the rapid desuetude of many traditional admissions customs. The course of events at Yale was typical of these developments.

The last pre-ceiling freshman class, which entered Yale in 1922, was "not merely the largest but one of the most riotous in the history of the University." It also included the largest number of transfer students and repeat applicants in Yale's history (145).[1] These last two categories were particularly likely to contain weak students. As the number of qualified applicants grew, the transfers and repeaters were gradually squeezed out. Yale announced first that its chief responsibility would be to those it had originally admitted as freshmen and then that it would discourage applicants with a year of preparation beyond high school. Transfers and repeaters declined accordingly, reaching a low of just eleven in the freshmen class of 1930.[2] In 1926 the old practice of admitting freshmen with "conditions" was abolished, and in the following year the same fate befell the September entrance examination. Both of these practices had benefited primarily students with deficiencies. Although Yale joined other schools in 1926 in requiring applicants to take the Scholastic Aptitude Test, it did so proclaiming that "what aid it gives the examiners is still problematic." Thus, the principal change of the 1920s was the closing of the routes generally taken by students with weak secondary school records and accomplishments. By the end of the decade official Yale policy still held that character was supremely important; but, in a significant qualification that mirrored changing attitudes elsewhere, Yale now believed that scholastic achievement was the best indication of character.[3]

At Yale and other private universities the elimination of the weaker elements brought a noticeable change in the student body. By the late 1920s fewer students were compiling unsatisfactory academic records, more were graduating in four years, and more were attaining academic distinction. Undergraduates did not suddenly acquire a devotion to learning. When David Riesman entered Harvard in 1927, he found that the approved attitude of his fellow students was insouciance rather than dedication: "it was common . . . to pretend that one did no work."[4] Yet, a variety of literary, artistic, and intellectual interests flourished among undergraduates.[5] Moreover, faculty took advantage of the greater abilities and greater seriousness of their students to impose a more rigorous regimen. Although the details differed on each campus, probably the most widespread curricular change was the adoption of departmental majors in order to counteract the laxity of the prevailing modified elective system. When combined with comprehensive senior exams, or a senior essay, they were intended to assure that every student would face some academic challenge.[6] The establishment of honors programs at some private institutions, on the other hand, allowed highly motivated students to make greater use of the intellectual potential of their universities. When President Lowell created an end-of-semester reading period at Harvard in 1927, he attributed its success to the greater seriousness of current Harvard students: their predecessors of just a decade earlier, Lowell believed, could not have been trusted to make good use of this time.[7]

These same general tendencies were discernible at the state universities, but their impact was far more muted. Steps were taken to reorganize the under-class curriculum and to require upper-classmen to concentrate in a major subject. Improvements in the study body, however, were slight. At Michigan, for example, the proportion of freshmen admitted with "deficiencies" dropped from 15 percent in 1926 to 7 percent in 1930, but academic performance, measured by grades and withdrawals for poor scholarship, remained about the same.[8] The problem was inherent in the large and heterogeneous student bodies that state universities were charged with educating. Whereas private institutions could attempt to impose a single vision of a liberal education upon their preselected students, the state universities had to deal with at least three categories of students—described in contemporary terms as "those who enter upon pre-professional courses, those who will become scholars and men of science, and those who come for a training in citizenship, for what is called general education."[9] Presidents like Lotus Coffman of Minnesota and Clarence Cook Little of Michigan dreamed that the burgeoning junior colleges might relieve them of the burdens of teaching underclassmen, thus allowing the university to focus upon more advanced work.[10] The realities of American higher education, however, made this hope chimerical. Moreover, it was not feasible to differentiate within the university. Alexander Meiklejohn's Experimental College in the midst of the University of Wisconsin proved to be unsupportably awkward (1927–32). The state universities, in fact, did not even establish honors programs until well into the postwar era.[11] During the interwar years they had to seek their salvation instead through the complementarity of graduate and undergraduate education.

In the private research universities the Depression forced a relaxation of admission standards, but the last half of the 1930s witnessed some renewed upgrading. As the effects of the Depression continued to penetrate American society, they diminished the rather small pool of students from which the eastern private colleges drew the bulk of their entering classes. The academic quality of their student bodies consequently underwent a perceptible decline.[12] This slippage did not cancel the gains of the preceding decade, but it did cause a reevaluation of their reliance upon the preparatory schools. There was a clearly recognized institutional need to broaden the applicant pool. At the same time the national mood no longer condoned their explicit social elitism. Both these factors gave an impetus to the efforts of Harvard, Yale, and Princeton to become more "national" and more meritocratic institutions.

President James Bryant Conant wanted to give greater weight to merit in the selecting of students as well as faculty at Harvard. To this end he established a token program of "national scholarships" in 1934. Originally confined to six midwestern states, this program had the parochial purpose of pleasing Harvard's western alumni and lessening its perceived eastern orientation. But the scholarships were also framed to embody Conant's belief that "any man with remarkable talents may obtain his education at Harvard whether he be rich or penniless."[13] Accordingly, the scholarships were awarded through a competitive process that centered upon the SATs. Winners were given financial assistance in accordance with their needs, so that these scholarships would be regarded as academic honors rather than as badges of indigence. As long as they did honors-level work, recipients were entitled to hold their scholarships all the way through Harvard graduate school. Conant's national scholarships were a new departure in university recruitment. For the first time

Harvard endeavored to bring in very high achievers—students who were expected to graduate near the top of their class. Moreover, this approach was a decisive break with what David Riesman has labeled "aristocratic meritocracy": procedures whereby personal judgments, using tacit criteria, are made upon a largely self-selected sample of applicants.[14] It was the first, hesitant step toward an open, "democratic meritocracy," and its reverberations were quickly felt.

Harvard, Yale, and Princeton did not compete significantly for the same prep-school graduates: well-established traditions defined which paths led to what schools. When they began to recruit by merit beyond the Eastern Seabord, however, they quickly found themselves vying for the same highly qualified students. Before this Yale and Princeton were actually engaged in more-extensive national recruitment than Harvard; but they did so largely through their respective networks of alumni clubs, thereby assuring selection by aristocratic meritocracy.[15] They could not, however, ignore Harvard's competitive scholarships, in light of their similar needs for more and better applicants. The competitive pressure to attract bright students from throughout the nation began a trend away from the rigid entrance requirements that had served well for the selection of the traditional eastern clientele and toward greater reliance upon objective aptitude tests. In 1937 Harvard, Yale, Princeton, Columbia, and nine other colleges had all scholarship applicants take a six-hour exam specially prepared by the College Entrance Examination Board. In effect, these schools were in implicit competition for a circumscribed pool of talented secondary school students. In fact, Harvard, Yale, and Princeton found it necessary to confer formally about common applicants in order to avoid bidding against each other. In this context it was no longer possible to disparage brainpower in favor of character; that is, to back away from the explicitly democratic form of meritocracy. This was the beginning, then, of the protracted process by which the student bodies of the eastern private universities were leavened with increasing numbers of scholastic high achievers drawn from the nation at large.

The major impact of meritocratic recruitment upon the student bodies of the private research universities was not evident until the 1950s. The direction of change, however, was clearly established earlier.

The desire to have a bright and motivated body of students can be regarded as ubiquitous among university faculty and administrators in the modern era, but because of the requirements of maintaining large and complex educational enterprises, this wish has seldom been gratified. The decision by the best-situated private institutions to place a cap upon enrollments produced a chain of events that altered this. The concentration of resources enhanced their attractiveness; an excess of applicants made meaningful selection possible; and under these conditions the natural bias toward quality began to be expressed. Once begun, the process of upgrading had compelling logic. In the 1930s it was expressed more powerfully in the active recruitment of high achievers. This was not a natural process, however, like the gradual elimination of weak students in the 1920s; it was, rather, an active commitment, and a costly one as well. Conant had to make National Scholarships a major objective of Harvard's three hundredth anniversary fund. Elsewhere resentment was expressed that students were being paid to attend with funds that might have been used to enlarge the faculty.[16] But the faculty benefited in other ways. A more serious undergraduate student body made a significant contribution toward lessening the tensions between teaching and research. Instructing well-prepared underclassmen in small classes was not terribly burdensome, and often proved stimulating. Then, too, the expansion of advanced courses brought classroom subjects closer to disciplinary specializations. Thus, the movement toward democratic meritocracy in undergraduate recruitment in the private research universities was consistent with the mission to advance knowledge.

Graduate Education. In both state and private research universities the mix of teaching and research was enriched by the rising enrollment of graduate students. Besides permitting the conduct of advanced seminars, an abundance of graduate students allowed considerable flexibility in the handling of teaching loads. Productive scholars in large departments could be favored with graduate instruction, while more-plodding colleagues handled large undergraduate lectures. Graduate assistants could also be utilized to carry much of the burden of introductory courses. This latter practice particularly improved research opportunities for state university faculty. When necessary, however, the use of graduate students could save money almost anywhere. At Cornell in 1920, for example, the postwar enrollment surge caused 55 percent of the graduate students to be pressed into teaching.[17] Perhaps because of these advantages, no research university (save Princeton) restricted graduate enrollments at the same time that it was placing caps on its undergraduate colleges and professional schools. Graduate education was in theory the intellectual and professional lifeblood of the research universities. Actual conditions in the 1920s, however, fell somewhat short of the ideal.

American graduate schools in 1920 were about as open as American colleges had been a generation before. The only recognized requirement was a bachelor's degree from a college accredited by the Association of American Universities; but those with unaccredited degrees were judged upon their records and were almost always admitted. Just as it had formerly done with regard to undergraduate admissions, the heterogeneity of applicants precluded the establishment of standards. Since graduate study was an arduous journey without promise of great reward, it could be assumed that only the dedicated would embark. But ease of entry attracted the uncertain as well. A portion of each fall's new entrants were likely to be June graduates who had failed to find employment during the summer.[18] As inducements for schoolteachers to attain advanced degrees were increased during the 1920s, this less erudite segment of the graduate population also swelled. The observation of the Columbia graduate dean that "the majority of [students] enter the graduate schools for other than scholarly motives" was generally true.[19]

Most research universities found a major part of their graduate clientele in their own undergraduate colleges. At Michigan in 1925 about half of the graduate students held degrees from the university. Of the coeval cohorts at Harvard, 25 percent were from Harvard College. The remainder of the graduate students tended to come from nearby colleges. The research universities, by and large, recruited a relatively small portion of their graduates students from one another.[20] As might be expected, a disporportionate number of graduate students did come from the top of their class, but a dismaying number were undistinguished students. A census done at Wisconsin revealed 25 percent of the graduate students coming from the highest decile of their class; however, 40 percent came from the bottom half. A national study of only the leading graduate schools reported that under one-third of their students had graduated from college with high honors or the equivalent. Little wonder that attrition was high. Even at Harvard only half of the entering graduate students could be expected to enroll for a second year.[21]

The problems of uneven preparation, uncertain motivation, and unproven ability were compounded by the absence of common standards. There was no general agreement on matters of graduate curriculum, requirements for master's degrees, or even the basic objectives of graduate education. At various times in the 1920s it was earnestly suggested that graduate students be given broader cultural education, more thorough language preparation, pedagogical training, stronger religious convictions, and greater social refinement.[22] At the same time it was also widely held that the duration of Ph.D. programs should be shortened. When Henry Suzzallo was commissioned by the Carnegie Foundation to examine graduate education, he found the confusion overwhelming. But he and others like him who wished to find a single formula for rationalizing graduate education were in fact doomed to frustration.[23] In American research universities graduate students were the responsibility of the academic departments. Only they possessed the expertise to judge the requirements of recondite knowledge. Abstract notions of what might be desirable in graduate study had no chance of reforming this decentralized empire. To the extent that a higher degree of orderliness developed in graduate education during the interwar years, it grew largely from within. For that reason it expressed a commonality of interest between the graduate schools and highly independent departmental fiefdoms.[24]

By the late 1920s most major graduate schools believed that the time had come for the selective admission of graduate students. No means to this end seemed feasible, however, in light of the broad variety of applicants on one hand and the diversity of departmental needs on the other.[25] They consequently continued to rely upon attrition despite the inefficiency that this policy entailed. The onset of the Depression finally galvanized the universities into action. As they did with selective undergraduate admissions, the eastern private universities showed the way, and the first measures were aimed at eliminating the most obvious weaklings. Harvard instituted selective practices in 1930 by requiring applicants to show some evidence of scholarly attainment—election to Phi Beta Kappa, graduation with honors, or at least standing in the upper half of their class.[26] The other private universities rather quickly followed Harvard's lead, and the state universities also began screening graduate admissions later in the decade. At first Harvard excluded relatively few applicants, and this was undoubtedly true of other schools too; but once the principle of selection admission was established, intake could be adjusted according to the supply of students and the teaching capacity of departments. Yale's graduate dean Edgar Furniss correctly foresaw that meaningful selection would ultimately depend upon a department's power to draw numerous applicants.[27] By the last half of the 1930s this seemed to be occurring at the leading schools. In 1937 Columbia, Harvard, Princeton, and Yale cooperated in the development of the Graduate Record Examination. The aim was to provide departments with another means for assessing student ability.[28] By the end of the 1930s the thrust of graduate admissions had made a discernible shift from barring the unfit toward identifying and aiding the outstanding student.

Over this period as a whole the amount of support available for graduate students steadily increased. The growing utilization of graduate teaching fellows was one source of support; the need for assistants in prosperous science departments was another. In addition, the research universities explicitly recognized the need for more graduate fellowships. These were a minor but consistent priority in private universities' fund-raising and a legitimate budget item in appropriations for state universities. The obvious result was to provide the strongest kind of encouragement for the most promising students. Largely for this reason the output of Ph.D.'s was not diminished by the abysmal economic environment of the 1930s.[29] By the end of that decade graduate education had transcended the anarchic conditions of the 1920s. Not only were the research universities choosing their graduates students with greater care, but they fully expected to support most of them for much of their Ph.D. program.

For the purposes of research the most significant interwar changes in graduate education came at the end of the student career. The rise of graduate teaching caused a blending of the positions of graduate student and faculty member.[30] For many students, receiving their Ph.D. meant a change of title, but essentially no change of duties. Remaining for a time at a research university permitted, indeed required, that they develop their scholarly prowess. Even more prized were the opportunities for postdoctoral fellowships. Robert Millikan called the fellowships funded by the Rockefeller Foundation and administered by the National Research Council "the most vital influence" upon the rise of American science.[31] From this standpoint, these fellowships were probably the most cost-effective employment of foundation funds during this period. By allowing recipients to work at the immediate forefront of their respective fields, the fellowships tended to assure their continuing involvement in research. The success of the NRC Fellowships encouraged other foundations, like the John Simon Guggenheim Foundation, to invest in the training of young academics. The results of the NRC Fellowships alone, however, were impressive. In their first twelve years, less than a third of the applicants were accepted, but that number still represented one of every eleven Ph.D.'s in those fields. Of 774 fellowship recipients, 80 percent were subsequently employed in educational institutions.[32] Taken together, the availability of instructorships and/or fellowships considerably augmented the research effectiveness of graduate education. Moreover, since these effects transcended the Ph.D., they were ignored by critics who focused on the immediate content of doctoral programs.

Perhaps of greater importance, and equally invisible to critics, was the sorting that was taking place at the Ph.D. level. This amounted to nothing less than a rationalization of postdoctoral careers at a time when, as will be explained below, recruitment patterns for young faculty were in an amorphous state. To illustrate how this development was lost on educators (though not on scientists like Millikan): Henry Suzzallo puzzled over the fate of those young Ph.D.'s "lost sight of" at undistinguished colleges.[33] Their fates had in fact been largely sealed when the research opportunities at their mother university were given to more promising fellow graduates. The variety of postdoctoral opportunities that existed in the laboratories and institutes of the research universities also allowed these institutions considerable flexibility to take care of their best Ph.D.'s, even in the worst of times. For the decade of the 1930s an average of 60 percent of all Ph.D. recipients found employment in higher education; for those receiving their degrees in 1933 and 1934, when there were virtually no academic openings, this percentage fell only slightly, to 58 percent and

56 percent respectively.[34] Being a research assistant in the depths of the Depression not only was better than nothing but also seems to have preserved the prospects of an academic career.

As graduate enrollments rose during the interwar years, interrupted only briefly by the Depression, graduate education underwent a process of differentiation not unlike that which occurred at the undergraduate level. The large graduate schools, in particular, could not help serving the interests of a diverse constituency. By the late 1930s, however, a distinct pathway could be discerned within this untidy category that gave the most able students not only the tools to conduct original investigations but also the postdoctoral opportunities to utilize them.

Faculty Careers. The distinguished chemist Roger Adams embarked upon an academic career as an insular product of Harvard. A graduate of Cambridge Latin School, then Harvard College ('09), he took his Ph.D. in 1912. A Harvard fellowship allowed him to acquire some postdoctoral polish in Germany before he was set to work back at the university as an instructor in chemistry (1913–16). In mid-August of 1916, as Adams prepared for another year's teaching at Harvard, he received a call to an assistant professorship at Illinois. Such an event was normal enough, but Adams's reply was unusual. After ironing out details of teaching and salary, Adams insisted upon getting assurance that after three years he would be promoted or discharged according to the merits of his performance. He telegramed President Edmund James,

> Have learned from reliable sources rapid promotion at Illinois chiefly obtained by receiving calls elsewhere. Unwilling to submit to this plan. Must have absolute assurance from you my success in teaching and research will be recognized by promotion independent of more or less accidental outside offers.

James replied emphatically that he could not "alter the entire system of University management"; that, not knowing what the state legislature might do, he had "no authority to give such assurances"; and that Adams "would have to take his chances along with the rest of us."[35] This Adams did, with very happy results. The episode nevertheless reveals several features of academic recruitment, circa 1920: the prevalence of inbreeding among junior faculty, the strategic importance of the call, and the lack of structure in academic careers.

Faculty inbreeding has been a ubiquitous feature of American colleges and universities, although before 1900 it commonly took the form of schools hiring their own college graduates, and afterward it increasingly meant universities retaining their own Ph.D.'s. Too great a reliance upon one's own graduates was widely frowned upon because, in the case of individuals, it raised the likelihood of narrow training, and in the case of departments, it implied that expediency took precedence over scholarly rigor. The practice nevertheless not only persisted but in all likelihood increased to its maximum extent at the end of the 1920s. Two factors were at work. The use of graduate students as teaching assistants, which became almost universal by 1920, brought them into the teaching ranks even before they received their degrees. The extraordinary expansion of faculty positions in the 1920s then created numerous opportunities for those wishing to pursue an academic career. Departments were more likely to sign on those individuals with whom they were already familiar than to risk bringing in outsiders.

TABLE 10. Percentage of Faculty by Rank at Selected Research Universities Receiving All or Part of Graduate Education at Same Institution, circa 1930.

	Prof.	Assoc.	Asst.	Instr.	All Ranks
California	23.4	35.2	38.3	52.6	33.0
Chicago (Ph.D.'s)	52.7	61.8	62.5	82.9	59.8
Illinois	35.0	46.6	56.0	69.0	54.6
MIT	14.3	30.0	64.3	69.4	44.8
Minnesota	25.3	49.0	53.2	77.4	51.2
Cornell	59.6	n.a.	69.3	83.3	68.7
Wisconsin	60.0	72.7	81.4	84.1	75.1

SOURCES: John H. McNeely, *Faculty Inbreeding in Land-Grant Colleges and Universities* (Washington, D.C.: Department of the Interior, 1932); Floyd W. Reeves et al., *The University Faculty*, University of Chicago Survey, vol. 3 (Chicago: University of Chicago Press, 1933), 27.

Table 10 presents some rare comparable data on the extent of inbreeding at several research universities around 1930. With the exception of the figure for California, these percentages are quite high and rather consistent, at least for the lower ranks. For instructors they vary only from 69 percent to 84 percent. By way of contrast, two decades earlier at Minnesota just 40 percent of instructors were home-trained. Professorial inbreeding reflected Ph.D. production farther in the past. Chicago, Cornell, and Wisconsin—all major prewar Ph.D. producers—each trained more than half of their senior faculty. What seems most certain from these figures is that institutions in the 1920s were most likely to fill their junior faculty positions with their own Ph.D.'s. Penn, where in 1920 more than two-thirds of the faculty were home trained, offered this explanation:

The practice of engaging as instructors young teachers who desire an opportunity to continue their study in the Graduate School is common. By this means, it is believed the staff is filled up at a lower rate of salary than a staff of equal merit could be obtained by any other means. However, when these instructors complete their study . . . it is then very easy for the department to drift into the practice of retaining them as permanent members of the staff without due regard for all the educational questions involved.[36]

California seems to be a significant exception to this pattern, not only because of its relatively low degree of inbreeding but also because California significantly raised its standing among research universities during the 1920s. The evidence suggests that California's ambition for academic distinction caused it to pursue a rather different recruitment strategy. Lacking the resources to outbid the endowed universities for academic stars, departments like physics aggressively sought out promising junior faculty. They also refused to appoint their own Ph.D.'s to more than one-year instructorships. The market for young faculty seems to have been relatively untapped, in contrast to the ongoing competition for recognized scientists. California may also have benefited from the fact that departments like chemistry chose not to ultilize graduate teaching fellows and consequently had to hire a greater number of full instructors.[37] In consciously recruiting promising young faculty members, California clearly applied more-stringent criteria than those universities that were engaging and promoting their own graduates. The rise of Berkeley in the hierarchy of research universities thus stands as an implicit rebuke to prevailing practices of faculty inbreeding.

The high degree of inbreeding, however, was due less to complacency or myopia than to the immaturity of the academic labor market. Consider the plight of an aspiring young academic after receiving a Ph.D. from a research university. His initial position was likely to depend entirely upon the personal contacts of the professors with whom he worked.[38] To accept a position at a lesser institution outside of the university research system would make the chances for productive scholarship rather bleak. Except for the few postdoctoral fellowships available in the sciences, the best alternative under the circumstances was to be retained in the department as an instructor. Young instructors then faced the situation that Roger Adams had feared: they had to strive to earn merit through scholarly works without any assurance that merit would be rewarded. Getting promoted within one's institution, or finding a better position elsewhere, depended heavily upon receiving an outside call.[39]

Well into the 1920s faculty careers lacked a recognized progressive structure, even at leading universities. A faculty member might remain indefinitely as an instructor or assistant professor unless deemed worthy of advancement. In the absence of criteria concerning length of service and accomplishment, the clearest indication that a teacher had earned a better position came when another institution offered one. This system, widely deplored even before the war, was difficult to escape as long as university budgets were under pressure. By the 1920s it had been somewhat improved at most universities by the establishment of fixed salary ranges for each rank and by the widespread adoption of the associate professor level as an intermediate tenured rank. But the call still remained crucial to academic advancement. For example, James B. Conant, who took Roger Adams's position at Harvard, ironically fell victim to the situation that Adams had feared at Illinois: he became an eminent chemist while still an assistant professor at Harvard (1919–27), but he was not promoted to full professor until he was about to accept a generous offer from Caltech.[40]

Princeton in 1920 was the first university specifically to reject dependence on outside calls. It adopted a policy of up-or-out for instructors (after four annual appointments) and assistant professors (after two three-year appointments). In addition, it committed itself to regular reviews of senior faculty salaries at five-year intervals.[41] Other universities tended to praise the Princeton system but hesitated to adopt it. The career prospects of faculty nevertheless improved during the decade. The prosperity of the golden age brought an unprecedented amount of movement between institutions, and the general demand for active scholars also produced a healthy amount of advancement in rank. By 1930 something like the Princeton standard was becoming the tacit expectation at most research universities. Still, Conant found it to be "evident from the record . . . that in the early 1930s the academic world was far from ready to accept wholeheartedly the doctrine of "up-or-out.'"[42] The failure to resolve this critical issue eventually caused overt problems.

The increase in faculty members during the golden age filled the academic pipeline with an abnormally large number of junior faculty, but the impact of the Depression then rather abruptly constricted the outflow into the tenured ranks. The result was a substantial buildup in the junior ranks at most research universities during the 1930s. At Harvard, for example, tenured and untenured teachers had been in approximate balance in the mid-1920s, but by 1933 the number of untenured had risen to more than twice that of tenured.[43] Since wholesale promotions were financially out of the question, attempts to rectify this unhealthy situation were fraught with difficulty. When Yale maladroitly dismissed an untenured associate professor with twelve years of service, it provoked first an AAUP investigation and then an internal effort to standardize promotion policy.[44] The most conspicuous crisis over this matter, however, occurred at Harvard.

President Conant was concerned about the preponderance of junior faculty when he assumed office in 1933, but he was also constrained by the difficulties—for individuals and departments—that any action would entail. When he finally attempted to implement a rigorous up-or-out policy in 1937, its first victims were two assistant professors of economics, Alan Sweezy and Raymond Walsh, who were also leaders of a teachers' union and active supporters of the labor movement. Controversy inevitably swirled around the issue of academic freedom. Although Conant was officially absolved on this score, the Walsh-Sweezy affair heightened faculty suspicions about his policy.[45] These pressures forced the formulation of a comprehensive personnel policy for Harvard. It was agreed that a maximum of eight years of temporary appointments would be allowed before a decision on tenure would have to be reached. This then raised the question of how many tenured positions the university would have. A formula was devised, one based upon the number of existing tenured positions in a department and the average duration of their occupancy, for determining how often each department might propose additional appointments. Finally, these procedures focused intense scrutiny upon the tenure decision itself. Beginning in the early 1940s each potential tenure appointment was reviewed by an ad hoc committee charged with determining whether the person in question was the most qualified available candidate for the position.

Developments at Yale paralleled those at Harvard and led to the adoption of a formal policy on appointments, promotion, and tenure in 1939. In 1941 the AAUP officially amended its position to state that after a probationary period of not more than seven years a decision should be taken upon promotion to tenure.[46] Notwithstanding the discrepancies in pre-tenure probation (seven years for the AAUP, eight for Harvard, nine for Yale, and ten for Princeton), by the early 1940s a standard had come into existence for the American academic career that was significantly different from the practices prevailing two decades earlier. Instead of depending upon the uncertainties of a call, junior faculty could henceforth count on being systematically evaluated, chiefly on the basis of their published work. "Publish or perish" may strike many as a harsh dictum, but it was generally more dynamic and more just than the conditions of "luck or languish" for junior faculty that the new regime replaced.

The academic career structure as it existed in 1940 still contained significant imperfections, but it reflected more faithfully and more widely the universalistic values to which the research universities were committed. Hiring decisions still usually depended upon personal contacts, but this type of influence was less sufficient than formerly. Faculty inbreeding was still evident, but the clearer definition of junior faculty status created greater incentives for the careful choice of appointments. "Deadwood" could still be found in tenured positions, but the keener competition made it less likely that new additions would be similarly complacent. Although the academic marketplace was still comparatively unorganized, a market did exist at national disciplinary meetings and the like where potential employers could scrutinize numerous candidates.[47] Even more significant, those academics who secured a position at one of the research universities were largely assured of the opportunity to conduct research.

University Research. At the beginning of the 1920s the prospects for university research were rather discouraging. As a result of war-induced inflation the research universities were considerably poorer than they had been before the conflict (see Appendix C). The ad hoc system of funding university research that was described in Chapter 2 was inadequate in the aggregate and hopelessly checkered in its incidence. In their financially weakened condition the universities seemed incapable of keeping pace with the proliferation of applied industrial research on one side and the superior conditions of independent research institutes on the other. The opinion was widely expressed that these trends might soon reverse the considerable progress that American universities had recently achieved in fostering research. These fears reached a kind of a crescendo by the middle of the decade. They helped to inspire the launching of the National Research Fund in 1925, conferences in 1926 on the crisis of university research, an AAUP inquiry into conditions for university research, and an American Council of Learned Societies investigation of research in the humanities and social sciences.[48] This last document offers a summary of what had come to be regarded, according to the conventional wisdom, as the "obstacles to university research."[49]

The list compiled by the author, Frederick Ogg, can be boiled down to four fundamental complaints:

1. A weakness in research personnel: since the war many scholars and scientists seemed to have been drawn away from university research to private industry, research institutes, or even university administration, while doubt was widespread that the ablest students were being attracted to university careers.

2. The burden of excessive teaching, especially in introductory courses: it seemed to handicap the American professor in comparison with his European counterpart and to diminish the possibilities for productive research.

3. Inadequate financial support: university budgets were constructed almost solely with regard to teaching, so that research had to "live on the crumbs that fall from the table."

4. Lack of appreciation for research and scholarship: not only on the part of the philistine public but also among the trustees, presidents, and alumni who were crucial to the support of academic inquiry.

If it were a question of American higher education as a whole, much of Ogg's indictment would ring true, not just for the 1920s but also for the decades before and since. For the small group of institutions responsible for most university research, however, the timing of this critique was rather ironic. In the late 1920s the research universities were entering into a golden age in which the combination of foundation support for research and unusually bounteous financing from traditional sources combined to accelerate the development of their research capacities. Ogg's list is nevertheless useful because, by reflecting contemporary perceptions of the problems of the research universities in the early 1920s, it provides a valuable checklist for gauging the progress made during the interwar years.

In retrospect the notion that academe was losing its attractiveness for the most able scientists and scholars seems to have been belied by the powerful advance of American social and natural sciences during the interwar years. Yet, the perceptions of contemporaries were not mistaken. The dislocations of the war and the new opportunities created in its aftermath caused considerable movement among academic personnel, precisely when the competitiveness of academic salaries was at its lowest point in this century. Faculty salaries measured in constant dollars bottomed out in 1919 and 1920, as did per-student university income. Little wonder that there were conspicuous departures. Data on Ph.D.'s in physics show a smaller percentage of them entering academic life in these years than at any time before World War II.[50]

When the interwar period is viewed as a whole, the personnel problem of universities stands out as a temporary phenomenon. University salaries recovered rapidly in the first part of the decade and then kept advancing regularly thereafter. By the end of the decade the median faculty salary had risen by 50 percent in terms of purchasing power. Moreover, faculty were not greatly penalized by the Depression: a decline in average salaries was largely balanced by deflation, so that purchasing power remained fairly constant.[51] More important, however, in light of the tenuous connection between economic motivation and academic careers, was the consistently strong recruitment into the academic profession. The number of Ph.D.'s awarded rose by 280 percent in the 1920s and by another 38 percent during the 1930s. Academic positions continued to be the preferred destination of the majority.[52] The crucial matter from the perspective of university research was that the major universities chose from the best of the new Ph.D.'s by retaining their most qualified students as instructors. The careers of some outstanding young scientists were also given the extraordinary impetus of postdoctoral fellowships. The new blood that flowed into the universities was all the more valuable in light of the dynamism of faculty careers described in the preceding section. In addition, from the late 1920s onward American universities benefited from the inflow of some of Europe's most renowned scholars. Far from losing human capital, the research universities turned it into their greatest asset.

Faculty in the research universities early in the 1920s had nevertheless not yet resolved the perennial problem of American higher education—the conflicting demands of teaching and research. But in this matter, too, considerable progress seems to have been made, with changes affecting both the quality of teaching and the time available for research.

The trends discussed above had a bearing on this issue. Better undergraduate students, more graduate students, and the use of graduate teaching fellows all permitted research university faculty to do more teaching at an advanced level, proximate to their specialized interests. These qualitative changes in teaching responsibilities undoubtedly reinforced some measurable quantitative changes that indicated a lightening of the teaching burden.

By the late 1930s there was a general perception that teaching loads had fallen in the research universities.[53] Student/faculty ratios, crude as they may be, show no discernible trend for the 1920s, although the more widespread use of graduate teaching fellows is not reflected in these figures. At the end of the 1930s, however, they are almost universally lower. By this time, too, the numbers of actual hours of classroom teaching, at least at the top universities, seem to have been significantly lower than the figures reported for 1920. By 1940 Harvard, Columbia, Yale, Caltech, and California could report that they expected their faculty to devote about half of their time to research. Teaching loads could be as low as two to three hours per week, although they varied greatly according to department and rank. The other state research universities, however, ostensibly had average teaching loads of close to twelve hours and expected their faculty to devote one-quarter of their time to research. Princeton, Cornell, and MIT fell between these two extremes.[54]

In addition, the opportunities for faculty to take time off for research generally increased during the interwar years. By the end of this period a policy of granting regular sabbatical leaves for all faculty, rather than just for established scholars, had become the expected practice at research universities. There were still a few laggards, however. Chicago and Johns Hopkins clung to their traditional practices—"vacation credit" earned by teaching summer quarters in the former case, and a liberal leave policy in the latter. Cornell joined the others only at the end of the period, and both Wisconsin and Penn gave no sabbaticals.[55] Harvard under Conant took the additional step of granting research leaves to assistant professors after three years of service—an important concomitant to the up-or-out policy.[56] In general, then, by 1940 the faculty of most of the research universities had separated themselves from their colleagues in the remainder of American higher education with respect to the burdens of teaching. They spent fewer hours in the classroom, their classes were closer to their research interests, and they were able periodically to devote themselves wholly to research. At these institutions at least the teaching-research conflict had been mitigated, but it required ample resources to accomplish this.

The growing financial strength of the research universities during the 1920s allowed them to support a considerable expansion of embedded research expenditures. Most universities did not account for separately budgeted research expenditures until 1930, and even then this category varied widely from institution to institution. It reflected chiefly the potpourri of funds and gifts earmarked for various research purposes, and a large proportion of such funds were designated for medical research. Harvard was far in front, claiming close to one thousand research-related funds.[57] With that single exception, however, these restricted funds could not generally satisfy the ongoing needs of the bulk of university researchers. There was consequently a basic need for "fluid" research funds. As developed at California, the fluid research fund consisted of a budgetary appropriation that was distributed by a faculty committee to assist numerous faculty projects. By the end of the 1920s most research universities had established fluid research funds of one kind or another.

Fluid research funds were indispensable to the state universities as a counterpart to the philanthropic support given to their private rivals. California remained far in the lead, distributing $112,000 in 1927–28. Wisconsin appropriated $55,000 for 1928, followed by Michigan ($30,000) and Minnesota ($25,000). Illinois was able to parcel out only $10,000 to its departments for graduate education and research.[58] The private universities were generally unable to set aside such large sums in a fluid fund. The Heckscher Research Foundation at Cornell was a promising prototype for this, but Cornell was unable to augment it. Harvard's Milton Fund, established by a bequest in 1923, was twice as large as Cornell's research fund, but few other schools received such unrestricted funds. More typically, Stanford's research committee had only $3,300 to award, while Columbia had a publishing fund of $7,800 (1928). In general, the private universities relied instead upon the foundations to provide fluid research funds, though in these cases they were restricted to one or more disciplines. Caltech and Chicago were most conspicuously successful in this respect, and Princeton's gift for natural science research from the GEB has already been discussed. Harvard, Yale, and Johns Hopkins also benefited from such grants. MIT was alone in making a large appropriation from its general budget for departmental research ($200,000).[59]

The difficulty with separately budgeted fluid research funds was that they became vulnerable when cutbacks had to be made. All the figures given above for the state universities were, with the exception of Minnesota, considerably lower by 1934; and the MIT appropriation had dropped to just $50,000.[60]

There was another dimension of university support for research—that embodied in the treatment of faculty. When this is factored in, aggregate university spending for research assumed impressive levels. Estimates of total university expenditures for research made on this basis in the late 1930s arrived at the following sums:[61]

more than $2,000,000	*$1,000,000–$1,500,000*
California	MIT
Chicago	Pennsylvania
Columbia	
Harvard	
Illinois	
Michigan	

$1,500,000–$2,000,000	*under $1,000,000*
Cornell	Johns Hopkins
Minnesota	Princeton
Wisconsin	Stanford
Yale	Caltech

By this date research no longer depended upon the crumbs that fell from the table. All of these universities had to varying degrees made substantial commitments to sustain the research enterprise with "hard" budgetary allocations. The financing of research at these schools had been greatly expanded since the early 1920s, but the needs of research had progressed as well. The need by the late 1930s for the "soft" funds that could finance individual research projects was more pressing than ever. This disparity consititued a fundamental issue for the privately funded system of university research, and it will be considered further in the next chapter. Nevertheless, the shortfall of research funds reflected the economic difficulties of the times and the limitations of existing arrangements more than any lack of appreciation for research on the part of university leaders.

With regard to this last of Ogg's obstacles to university research, it is necessary to distinguish between the oscillations in public perceptions of the value of science and the attitudes of presidents and trustees who actually determined the priorities of universities. On the first score, the public enthusiasm for science that followed in the wake of the First World War had a decidedly practical cast. Science was lauded as the handmaiden of material progress, but the true agents of that progress were usually seen to be businessmen rather than science professors. Perhaps because of this practical emphasis, a current of reaction became evident in the late 1920s.

Antiscientific sentiments then became widespread during the Depression, as progress seemed illusory and technology was blamed for the loss of jobs.[62] Within the research universities, however, the fortunes of science became increasingly insulated from these tides of opinion.

The leadership at most of these universities was consistently favorable to research throughout the interwar years. It is noteworthy that many of the new presidents installed during the 1920s were conspicuously associated with the research side of universities. They would include Angell of Yale, Campbell of California, and both Little and Ruthven of Michigan. More significant, several key appointments in the next decade were explicit efforts to give greater prominence to the research function. The circumstances behind the appointments of Compton at MIT and Conant at Harvard have already been discussed. In both cases the trustees backed this change of course.[63] At Cornell, too, Edmund E. Day of the Rockefeller Foundation became president in 1937, committed to rejuvenating the school's neglected research efforts.[64] On the other side of the ledger, probably only at Wisconsin did regents and presidents consistently slight research in favor of other university tasks.[65] On the whole, though, university research in these institutions tended to gain increased administrative backing during the course of these two decades.

The basic problems that Ogg aired had already been present in American research universities since the beginning of the century, and they still loomed large in the first half of the 1920s. Within a few years, however, they had been largely transcended at the front-ranking institutions by a rapid evolution of the university research system. By 1930 the American research universities had moved to the forefront of the most competitive areas of international science and had furthermore become magnets for advanced scholars of other nations. The progress of the 1920s, capped by the golden age, had achieved a transformation of the position of American science.

4. The Ascendancy of American Science

Before the First World War the United States was all too often regarded as a provincial outpost in the international world of science. The mobilization of American science during the war, together with the enforced isolation from much of European science, hastened the maturation of numerous fields, that of chemistry probably being the most notable. With the return to normalcy, however, the old patterns recurred; during the first half of the 1920s Americans still went to Europe to learn, and European scientists who traveled to the United States did so to teach. This situation had changed markedly by the end of the decade: increasing numbers of American scientists were now to be found working at the frontiers of science. The United States thus attained a rough parity with other leading scientific nations well before events in Europe forced the intellectual migration of the 1930s. The disintegration of learning in Central Europe and the reinforcement of American institutions with leading foreign scientists only accentuated this process. By the outbreak of the Second World War the United States was clearly the foremost center of science in the world.

The "ascendancy of American science" is something of an abstraction when set against the myriad achievements of individual scientists. For them the meaningful context was their own specialty, and each field has a history of its own. With regard to the institutional basis of science, however, such aggregated national comparisons have greater validity. In the university research system of each country, conditions tend to be roughly analogous for different areas of science. In the United States it was largely the foundations and the research universities that created the conditions for the rapid advance of American science.

Before the First World War, American scientists made notable contributions to many fields, but their international stature was probably highest in the fields of genetics, geology, and astronomy.[1] Each of these areas was also, for different reasons, unusually well supported. The Carnegie Institution of Washington funded research in all three of these areas, but its backing of genetics was especially decisive for accelerating its development in this country. The topography of the American West was a particular asset to the science of geology, and this was one of the areas of science that received regular federal support. American astronomy, finally, was a prime beneficiary of science philanthropy. Construction of the Yerkes, Lick, and Mount Wilson observatories gave U.S. astronomers the technological means for making significant discoveries. These fields, though accepted university subjects, owed at least part of their development to extra-academic financing. By way of contrast, the subjects in which the United States gained parity in the 1920s were integral to research universities. Of these none was more fateful than nuclear physics.

The events that led from the unlocking of the secrets of the atom to the harnessing of nuclear energy make one of the most dramatic stories in the history of science. The institutional dimension of this story, while admittedly less dramatic, is nonetheless remarkable in a number of respects. The theoretical physicists who pursued this subject formed a very cosmopolitan scientific community—and a very competitive one as well. As they worked to uncover the basic structure of matter, all were well aware of the scientific significance of their endeavor. The success of Americans in entering this field and the ability of American institutions to attract leading foreign-trained scientists stand as notable achievements in the maturation of the American system of university research.

In the 1920s there were at least eight important centers of theoretical physics in the world—Berlin, Munich, Leipzig, and Göttingen in Germany, as well as Copenhangen, Leiden, Zurich, and the University of Cambridge.[2] The leading physicists in these locations and their numerous assistants were in remarkably close touch with one another. Newly minted Ph.D.'s circulated readily between physics institutes, and the directors of these respective groups met frequently in international meetings. Charles Weiner has called this community a traveling seminar, and its chief concern in the 1920s was the elaboration of atomic theory.[3] Exciting developments had been cumulating in this field for decades, but the decisive intellectual breakthroughs for the interwar generation began to occur about 1925.[4] It was then that quantum mechanics, first suggested by Max Planck at the beginning of the century, finally coalesced into a comprehensive explanation of atomic phenomena. For the relatively few physicists who comprehended these developments, the implications were vast, and so were the incentives. John Slater, then at Harvard and later at MIT, found it "the most competitive situation that has ever been seen in physical science":

> Here was a decade in which the most momentous physics discoveries in a century were being made, and here were fifty or more ambitious young men, entering a field with a smaller number of older and very distinguished workers, all trying to be in on the exciting discoveries that all were convinced were going to be made.[5]

At first it was not easy to enter such a fast-moving field: at least three young Americans made significant contributions, only to find themselves scooped by Europeans.[6] In the long run, however, the timing of the breakthrough was propitious for American science. By 1925 the American research universities were about to enter upon their golden age.

During the first half of the 1920s quantum mechanics was a disputed and incomplete theory not actively followed in all physics departments. For schools like Caltech, which wished to keep abreast of the latest developments, the best expedient was to arrange for visits from the great European physicists. At least one major European theorist spent some time there each year beginning in 1921.[7] Still, for the building of American physics it was the emerging generation that was critical—hence, the crucial role played by foundation fellowships. Although the NRC Fellowships were primarily intended for domestic study, in the period 1926–30 fifteen American physicists were funded for study in European universities. About the same time the Guggenheim program went into operation, allowing another twenty-one American physicists to work in Europe between 1926 and 1932. In addition, the fellowships of the International Education Board greatly facilitated international exchanges. Primarily, this program brought Europeans to the United States, where they often pursued topics in experimental physics—the forte of American physics— in the generally superior American laboratories.[8] As a result of these exchanges several young European theorists were persuaded to remain in the United States. Thus, during the most critical years of the elaboration of quantum theory, American physics was enriched both by advanced European training for native American phsyicists and by the recruitment of promising European scientists. To evaluate the results it is necessary to examine what happened in actual university physics departments.

During the 1920s strong centers of atomic physics were established at just six institutions.[9] Good theorists were few in number and difficult to attract. The development of such centers consequently required conscious commitment and leadership, as well as discretionary resources. The men who built these departments—Robert Millikan at Caltech, Harrison Randall at Michigan, Raymond Birge at California, Percy Bridgman at Harvard, Karl Compton at Princeton, and his brother Arthur Holly Compton at Chicago—were all basically experimental physicists, but they appreciated the ongoing revolution in quantum mechanics and were determined that their departments would be participants. To do so they not only had to identify and hire one of the few able quantum theorists, which was no small feat, but also had to keep them content after they arrived. The problem was both intellectual and institutional. Removed from the rapid pace of discoveries taking place in Europe, a quantum physicist in an American department risked isolation and ultimately obsolescence. Then, too, the knowledge for which they were hired was accessible to only a small number of highly advanced students or postdoctoral fellows. A quantum theorist contributed little to the teaching load of a department. Moreover, these prodigies were not content to toil as assistant professors for six or eight years. The proponents of the new physics did not readily conform to the prevailing patterns in American universities: they required some special treatment.

The exertions of the Michigan physics department illustrate this situation. Eager to develop theoretical physics, Randall succeeded in hiring a promising assistant from Niels Bohr's seminal group. After only two years of relative isolation in Ann Arbor, however, he returned to Copenhagen. Next, while attempting to hire a young physicist from Leiden, the Michigan representative was advised that he ought to bring in two—or, better, more—so that the theorists would have someone to talk to. The advice was taken to heart. Successful offers were made to both Samuel Goudsmit and George Uhlenbeck of the Leiden Institute. A third European theorist, the Munich-trained Otto La Porte, was hired from the National Bureau of Standards, where he was visiting on an IEB Fellowship. The fourth theorist in the cluster was a Michigan Ph.D., David Dennison, who managed to spend three critical years (1924–27) in Europe, on fellowships from the IEB and the Michigan department. A system of paid leaves was then established to allow Michigan physicists to work periodically at other important centers. Finally, Michigan made itself into one of the world centers of atomic physics. Beginning in 1928 the department sponsored summer symposia in theoretical physics, with lectures given by department members and both European and American invited guests. From that year until World War II the Michigan symposia were attended by most of the world's great physicists at one time or another. Without any external funding Michigan was able to develop into an important center for training in quantum physics.[10]

Michigan's accomplishment can be better appreciated in light of the experience of other midwestern state universities. At Minnesota the department head John Tate was not only a proponent of the new physics but, as editor of *Physical Review,* a strategically positioned leader of the profession as well. During the 1920s he managed to hire successively three of the most accomplished young American theorists, but each soon moved on, in part because of intellectual isolation. Wisconsin did somewhat better by bringing in important physicists as guest lecturers or visiting faculty. It managed to become a respectable training center for theoretical physics, but had difficulty retaining renowned scientists in this field. Illinois began to develop as a center of theoretical physics only in the 1930s, after the arrival of F. Wheeler Loomis (1929) and later Maurice Goldhaber (1938).[11]

A second determined effort to build a center of theoretical physics occurred at Princeton. Unlike Michigan, Princeton had considerable outside financial help from the General Education Board (see above, Section 2). These funds allowed Princeton to bring in some eminent scientists and also placed the university under an implicit obligation to succeed. After a discouraging start, for example, the head of the mathematics department wrote Karl Compton that it was time to make "all this money do the job it was intended for."[12] Princeton expanded its staff by hiring European scientists with established reputations as well as promising young Americans with European postdoctoral training. Even so, Princeton at first had a difficult time establishing a critical mass of theoretical physicists. Three of its recruits departed soon after they arrived. It is testimony to the growing strength of the Princeton group that they all subsequently returned.[13] In 1929 Princeton was fortunate to attract from Berlin the mathematician John von Neumann and the physicist Eugene Wigner, two brilliant and versatile scientists still in their twenties. As inducement, the terms of their appointments allowed them to spend half of each year in Berlin. The

Princeton group soon received additional external impetus with the organization of the Institute for Advanced Study in 1932. Although not a part of Princeton University, the mathematical section of the institute at first occupied the same quarters as the mathematics department. When Albert Einstein made the institute his permanent home, in 1933, he became the crowning jewel for arguably the leading center of mathematical physics in the world.[14]

The other major centers of quantum physics in the United States were developed largely with American physicists—albeit with European training. As these young physicists returned from their European stays at the end of the twenties, several departments blossomed. Caltech, despite its concentration of mathematical and theoretical physicists, became active in quantum theory only during the last half of the 1920s through the work of neophytes, considerably encouraged by the visits of important European theorists. Not until 1928 did these young physicists complete their European sojourns and take up permanent residence in Pasadena.[15] At Chicago, Frank Hoyt felt isolated as the lone theorist from 1923 to 1928, but in that year the additions of Robert Mulliken (Chicago Ph.D., NRC Fellow, Guggenheim Fellow) and of Carl Eckart (Princeton Ph.D., NRC Fellow at Caltech, Guggenheim Fellow) formed the nucleus of a strong center.[16]

Only at Harvard does the development of quantum physics appear to have been fairly "normal," in the sense of not having required extraordinary exertions. Harvard's Edwin Kemble was America's first quantum theorist (Ph.D., Harvard, 1917), and he was responsible for keeping a new generation of Harvard physicists in touch with developments during the 1920s. His task was made easier by the fact that Cambridge was a natural stopover for all visiting Europeans. Harvard students also benefited from the availability of institutional as well as national fellowships. Further assistance came from the GEB in the form of a matching grant for a new physics research laboratory. Harvard nevertheless seems to have maintained one of the leading centers of quantum physics without altering its usual pattern of appointments. John Van Vleck, for example, was Kemble's first student in quantum physics (Ph.D., Harvard, 1922), then taught at Harvard, Minnesota, and Wisconsin, held a Guggenheim Fellowship, and was called back to the Harvard physics department in 1934.[17]

The success of both Chicago and Harvard underscores the preponderant role played by Americans in the rise of American physics. Indeed, the university that became the foremost center for atomic theory, the University of California at Berkeley, also relied upon native physicists. Berkeley's renown in theoretical physics was due chiefly to J. Robert Oppenheimer. To be sure, he owed a debt to the Europeans: from 1925 to 1929 he was in Europe almost continually, and unlike others of his generation he took his Ph.D. there as well (Göttingen, 1927). When he returned for good, Oppenheimer accepted a joint position at Caltech and Berkeley, in itself an unusual arrangement; but over the next several years his teaching emphasis came to be at Berkeley. There he was brilliantly complemented by the experimentalist E. O. Lawrence and his ever-larger cyclotrons. When Oppenheimer came to Berkeley, he considered it "a desert, there was no theoretical physics there." His first class was so advanced that only one student among the numerous auditors could be persuaded to take it for credit. Within five years, however, he had become the foremost teacher of his subject in the country.[18]

In 1932 no fewer than five Nobel Prize-winning discoveries were made, which together opened the way to understanding and ultimately utilizing nuclear energy. Remarkably, all took place in the English-speaking world, three in the United States. At Columbia, Harold Urey discovered deuterium (an isotope of hydrogen); at Caltech, Carl Anderson established the existence of the positron (the positively charged counterpart of the electron); and at Berkeley, E. O. Lawrence achieved one million electron volts in his latest cyclotron.[19] During the same year a more symbolic event occurred when Abraham Flexner persuaded Albert Einstein to make the Institute for Advanced Study his new home. Einstein, of course, had numerous offers from which to choose. To Paul Langevin of the Collège de France his choice signified that the United States had become "the new center of the natural sciences."[20]

The achievements of these and other individual physicists should not be allowed to obscure the institutional factors that made American universities the "new site for the seminar."[21] The extraordinary degree of communication with Europeans that the foundations made possible was certainly an important initial factor that helped American physics realize its potential. Only a few universities—Harvard, Caltech, and Berkeley—had institutional funds to encourage such travel or visits on their own. The extensive foundation-supported exchanges of the 1920s allowed American scientists to catch up, much as they had during the late nineteenth century through study in Germany. But in the 1920s the new trainees did not leave European science behind them when they returned. The recruitment of some European scientists into American universities and the foundation-sponsored visits of others permanently linked leading European scientists with the ongoing development of science in the United States.

When European physicists came to the United States, they encountered not only an indigenous tradition in experimental physics but also laboratories that were considerably superior to those in their home institutes. In addition, the American universities had an organizational advantage: the departmental system possessed the flexibility to accommodate numerous

physicists without relegating them to subordinate roles. This factor operated at two levels. It was remarkable that young scientists like Goudsmit,
von Neumann, and Wigner, who already had substantial achievements to
their credit, should choose to relocate outside of the orbit of European
physics. For each of them, however, the possibility for promotion was
exceedingly poor in the Old World. Von Neumann, for example, could
foresee three vacant professorships in the coming years and forty aspiring
docents.[22] For other young physicists who managed to visit the United
States on an IEB Fellowship, career prospects in a system in which every
physicist could become an assistant professor were even more alluring.

The flexibility of American departments was probably a greater advantage for developing the research potential of American physicists. The
departments just discussed were able to add theoretical physicists virtually without instructional considerations. This created a strong demand
for those who had learned the new physics. E. U. Condon had to weigh
offers from six research universities before he chose to go to Princeton in
1928. There, although a beginning assistant professor, he was promised
that he would teach only one seminar in quantum mechanics.[23] The treatment received by Oppenheimer was similar. The competition for theoretical physicists forced the research universities to offer them optimal
conditions for their research, and these conditions then became a boon to
the further development of American physics.

The growth of atomic physics in the United States probably provides
the clearest example of how the wealth that was channeled into the research universities during the golden age of the late 1920s was translated
into actual scientific achievement. By the early 1930s the first phase in the
institutional development of this subject had run its course. Almost all the
American theorists had returned from Europe; a young and exceedingly
vigorous community of atomic physicists was already in place in American research universities. Then, early in 1933, Hitler came to power in
Germany. In April of that year the first dismissals of non-Aryans from
German universities occurred. A new phase in the international relations
of American research universities abruptly commenced. Once again, the
impact of these developments was most apparent and most dramatic in
the physics community, but the intellectual migration had broader effects
on the American university system.

5. The Intellectual Migration

During the golden age of the research universities, conditions favored a
"brain drain" from Europe to the United States, as has just been seen in

the case of physics.[1] By 1933, however, these conditions had been attenuated by the effects of the Depression. The academic profession temporarily ceased to expand, and funds for research were tight. American science may have appeared more attractive than ever for foreign visitors, but American institutions were in a poor position to permit them to stay. Just at this point the international intellectual exchange came to be dominated not by the attractiveness of conditions for scientific work in the United States but by the large number of scholars uprooted from German universities by Nazi racial policies. On May 19, 1933, the *Manchester Guardian* published the names of 196 German academics dismissed from universities in the first wave of Nazi purges. Within a few years the total number of those forced out surpassed 1,600.[2] Comparatively few emigrated directly to the United States at this stage. Most found temporary positions in neighboring countries through their own academic connections, and the special efforts of assistance by the British provided many with a haven there. Throughout the remainder of the decade many of these uprooted scientists and scholars drifted into the United States as their temporary positions became untenable, or as better opportunities beckoned. In 1938 the situation worsened drastically with Hitler's annexation of Austria, Mussolini's adoption of Nazi racial policies, and then the Munich crisis. The slide toward war gradually changed the victims of political persecution into increasingly desperate refugees.[3]

The precise magnitude of the "academic migration" probably cannot be determined. A postwar survey identified 707 former faculty members of European universities who had settled in the United States, and 424 nonuniversity scientists or scholars. Of the first group 523 managed to attain an academic affiliation in America at one time or another, and 130 of the second group did so as well. Considering that academics are more traceable than people in most occupations, this total may be fairly complete. If so, it represents at most one-half of one percent of all American faculty members at the end of the 1930s.[4] Moreover, their distribution was not very representative of the academic profession as a whole. A large number of the newcomers were clustered in New York City, especially in the New School for Social Research, which energetically assisted persecuted academics. Many had to settle for marginal positions in research or part-time teaching. Additional clusters could be found in Chicago and in California, but the remainder were scattered rather widely across the country's numerous colleges and universities. Subsidies by the Rockefeller Foundation, the Carnegie Corporation, and several other agencies helped to induce many of these institutions to find places for the refugees. The Emergency Committee in Aid of Displaced Foreign Scholars worked to arrange these positions, often as the surest way of surmounting legal barriers to immigration. But a degree of underlying anti-Semitism in American colleges and universities and uncertainties about the pedagogical effectiveness of foreigners tended to limit the number accepted by most American colleges and universities.[5]

Scientists were especially well represented among the academic immigrants, and, perhaps because their skills were less culturally grounded, they probably had an easier entrée into American academic life. Chemists were the largest single category of immigrant scientists, but physicists composed the largest number who gained university affiliations.[6] Their placement in universities provides a good example of how immigrant scientists were integrated into the American research community.

Three distant career patterns are evident in this list of Central European physicists (or physical chemists) who emigrated permanently to the United States between 1933 and 1940. Only four of these physicists moved directly from their European professorships into similar positions at leading American research universities, and all of them were Nobel laureates upon arrival (Debye, Einstein, Fermi, and Franck). For the rest the date of arrival seems to have been the critical factor. Early immigrants (1933–37) secured regular faculty positions chiefly at those research universities that were striving to become centers of theoretical physics (Cornell, Stanford, Illinois) or at other developing universities in the tier below the research universities (Rochester, George Washington, Carnegie Tech, Purdue). By the time the latecomers arrived (1938–40), the regular ranks of the major physics departments seem to have been full. They consequently had to settle for makeshift appointments as research associates or visiting fellows.

The addition of so many outstanding individuals obviously could not help but enrich the American physics community. In institutional terms the relative abundance of physics talent permitted new centers of atomic physics to emerge. Hans Bethe, through his encyclopedic grasp of quantum physics, brought Cornell to the forefront of atomic research. Bloch and Goldhaber brought familiarity with the latest research to Stanford and Illinois, respectively, although for research purposes Bloch largely associated with Oppenheimer and the Berkeley group. Probably more important, they added to the density of existing physics research groups in Cambridge, Massachusetts, New York City (Columbia and NYU), Washington, D.C. (George Washington University, the CIW, the Bureau of Standards), Chicago, and Berkeley.

It might be argued that the contribution of the immigrant physicists to the development of the atomic bomb exceeded what they did to augment academic physics. The Hungarian Leo Szilard was the first in this country to grasp the significance of the fission of the uranium atom that was accomplished by a German research team. Working together with his fellow countrymen Edward Teller and Eugene Wigner, he prevailed upon Albert

TABLE 11. Important Immigrant Physicists, 1933–1940[7]

Name	Prof.	Former Institution		to U.S.	New Institution
Hans Bethe		Tübingen	1932–33	1935	Cornell
Felix Bloch		Leipzig	1928–33	1934	Stanford
Sergio deBenedetti	P	Padua	1934–38	1940	Swarthmore*
Peter Debye		Max Planck Inst.	1934–38	1940	Cornell
Max Delbrück	P	Kaiser Wilhelm Inst.	1932–37	1937	Caltech*
Albert Einstein	P	Kaiser Wilhelm Inst.	1914–33	1933	Inst. Adv. Study
Enrico Fermi	P	Rome	1927–38	1939	Columbia
James Franck	P	Göttingen	1920–33	1935	Johns Hopkins
Philipp Frank	P	Prague	1912–38	1938	Harvard*
George Gamow		USSR		1934	George Wash. U.
Maurice Goldhaber		Cambridge	1936–38	1938	Illinois
Victor Hess	P	Vienna	1919–38	1938	Fordham
Fritz London		Munich	1928–33	1939	Duke
Lothar Nordheim		Göttingen	1928–33	1935	Purdue
Eugene Rabinowitz		Göttingen	1929–33	1939	MIT*
Bruno Rossi	P	Padua	1932–38	1939	Chicago*
Marcel Schein		Zurich	1931–35	1938	Chicago*
Emilio Segrè	P	Palermo	1936–38	1938	California*
Otto Stern	P	Hamburg	1923–33	1933	Carnegie Tech
Leo Szilard		Berlin	1925–32	1937	Columbia*
Edward Teller		Göttingen	1931–33	1935	George Wash. U.
Victor Weisskopf		Zurich	1934–37	1937	Rochester

P = professorial rank
* = research associate or visiting fellow

Einstein to write President Roosevelt in order to apprise him of the significance of the splitting of the atom. Other Europeans, such as Enrico Fermi
and Hans Bethe, figured prominently in each stage of the harnessing of
atomic energy. Indeed, the concentration of European scientific talent at
Los Alamos for the actual building of the bomb was probably greater
than on any American campus.[8]

It may be self-defeating to seek definite conclusions about a phenomenon as diverse as the migration of European scholars and scientists to
America. One might note the enrichment of American academic life by
the additions of numerous outstanding individuals. By 1969, twenty-four
of them had been honored as Nobel laureates, to acknowledge only the
tip of this iceberg. Others, of course, had accomplishments of equal distinction in fields not covered by these awards. Somewhat less tangibly,
one might signal the positive effects of cross-fertilization that the intellectual migration seemed to bring. Many displaced Europeans felt that they
were able to achieve far more in an American institutional setting than
they could have in the Old World. Another type of creative mating took
place when individuals vaulted disciplinary boundaries to facilitate major
scientific breakthroughs, the best example being the transfer of European
physicists into molecular biology to form the seminal phase group.[9]

When viewed from an institutional perspective, however, the major
effects of the intellectual migration seem to be somewhat out of the American academic mainstream. The atomic physicists were probably integrated most completely into American universities, but even this took
some time. It was largely after their extraordinary wartime efforts that
many, especially the latecomers, found regular university posts. In purely
intellectual terms the Europeans may have had the greatest impact in
mathematics. In 1965, for example, fourteen of fifty-one members of the
mathematics section of the National Academy of Science were European-
born émigrés.[10] Nevertheless, it was a non-university institution—the Institute for Advanced Study, at Princeton—that can claim most responsibility for this. The institute itself became the greatest concentration of
mathematical talent in the United States, and probably in the world.
Many other prominent mathematicians entered the United States through
the auspices of the institute and later found permanent academic posts
elsewhere. Outside of the institute the next two clusters of outstanding
émigré mathematicians formed in developing, rather than in established,
research universities—Brown and New York University. The other areas
in which émigrés had an important effect upon American academic life
were to be found in those subjects that were not institutionalized in universities (psychoanalysis) or were relatively undeveloped (art history).[11]

The intellectual migration tended to confirm rather than cause the ascendancy of American science. The principal institutional beneficiaries

were less the research universities—which had done most of their recruitment of European scholars during the golden age, that is, before the political crisis struck—than the developing universities that increasingly sought to emulate them. These institutions were able to move to the forefront in selected fields by taking advantage of the abundance of academic talent. Thus, the ultimate effect of the academic migration may well have been to broaden the base of academic research during an era of comparative scarcity.

6

The Research Universities
in the 1930s

1. Effects of the Depression

The impact of the Depression upon the research universities was initially cushioned by the extraordinary surge of prosperity that they experienced in the late 1920s and that persisted even while the country's financial system was deteriorating. When the effects of the economic collapse did penetrate, all but the most favored institutions experienced a period of considerable hardship. These difficulties then receded only grudgingly through the remainder of the 1930s. During the preceding golden age the scope of university research had significantly expanded. Just as important, university commitments to research were irrevocably enhanced. No longer a frill accompanying the educational enterprise, research was now fully rooted in university departments. The rapid pace of scientific advance and the latent competition between institutions further assured that university research would continue to expand despite persistent financial difficulties. The result was a paradox of a sort: university research tended to prosper during the 1930s despite the severe pressures felt elsewhere in the universities.[1] Over time this divergence produced increasing strain between the limited resources available in the university research system and the burgeoning demands of research itself.

The research universities were comparatively unscathed by the effects of the Depression until 1932, almost three years after the initial crash in the stock market. The factors determining university budgets were well

246

insulated from short-term economic fluctuations. Enrollments, for example, continued to climb through 1930–31 and then did not decline precipitously until two years later. Budgets for state universities were passed well in advance and usually for a two-year period. The state appropriations to Michigan for the 1929–31 academic years, for example, were set early in 1929. The endowments of the private universities were invested conservatively in bonds and preferred stocks that continued to yield the expected income until the depths of the crisis. As a result general and educational expenditures for 1931–32 were either equivalent to or greater than those for 1929–30 for all the research universities except Wisconsin.[2]

The financial situation at private universities was buoyed by a timely surge in voluntary support. Individual philanthropy in general in American society peaked in 1928, and declined sharply after 1929. For the research universities, however, 1929–30 was the year of highest giving, and 1930–31 was only slightly less lucrative. Moreover, the peak level was about double the giving level of the mid-twenties.[3] Some of these funds represented commitments made by Beardsley Ruml and Wickliffe Rose before the 1929 reorganization of the Rockefeller Foundation (see Chapter 4). Also, Harvard, Yale, and Princeton had concluded major fundraising efforts in the late 1920s, the pledges for which were still flowing in during these years. Almost all of these universities received infusions of capital as the economy was sinking, and a significant part of these funds were designated for research-related purposes.

The research universities largely ignored the onset of the Depression by expanding many of their research commitments in ways that have been described in the preceding pages. At Chicago the Social Science Research Building was opened, and at Yale the Institute for Human Relations began operations; Harvard constructed a new physics laboratory, Princeton hired additional scientists and mathematicians, and MIT made a commitment to expand basic research. But the widely expected economic recovery failed to materialize, and soon the Depression overtook the research universities.

The same factors that had insulated the research universities in the short run ensured that they would be considerably affected by a prolonged economic downturn. Beginning in the fall of 1932 financial circumstances prevented an increasing number of former and would-be students from attending. Many universities responded to their income shortfall by raising tuition—in effect defying both the sinking price index and the law of supply and demand—although they also did what they could to help students in financial difficulties. Tuition revenues were nevertheless flat at best and were lower at all the state universities. State legislatures faced with emergency conditions had little recourse but to slash university budgets. The year 1932 was when the ax first fell in California, Michigan, Minnesota, and Wisconsin. In most cases the nadir was reached in 1933–34. For Michigan that year's state appropriation was 44 percent lower than that for 1929; cuts in other states ranged from 30 percent in Wisconsin to 15 percent in California. With numerous companies defaulting on interest or dividend payments, the decline in investment income at the private universities was almost as severe. Harvard's 18 percent shrinkage in endowment income was probably typical. Yale's investment income, however, fell 30 percent from peak to trough (1931– 35).[4] General and educational expenditures everywhere were down considerably in 1933–34 from the levels of two years earlier, but at most private research universities they still exceeded the 1929–30 budget. At the state universities, by contrast, expenditures fell significantly below 1929–30 levels.

The relative fortunes of the two sectors were reversed in the last half of the 1930s. At the state research universities expenditures increased considerably and soon surpassed the previous peaks. State appropriations to these schools remained under pressure, but an additional twelve thousand (21 percent) students in the last half of the decade increased tuition revenues. Income from other sources tended to rise as well, particularly external support for research.[5] The private research universities managed to increase their tuition income only modestly, if at all. Their chief problem, however, was the falling rate of return on invested capital. This condition persisted throughout the decade because of the low prevailing interest rates. As the bonds in their endowment portfolios matured or were called, they were replaced with lower-yielding issues. As a consequence the return on endowment for private universities sank from near 5 percent at the beginning of the decade to near 4 percent at the end. For Yale an endowment of just over $100 million yielded $4.7 million in income in 1931, but nearly the same amount produced just $3.5 million in 1936.[6] Such income limitations did not cripple the operations of the private universities, but they did constrain further development. Even Harvard and Yale felt at the end of the 1930s that they were facing an era of persistent retrenchment in which any new commitments would have to be carefully limited and judiciously planned.[7]

The pattern of financial effects produced by the Depression set the framework within which the research universities had to operate. If there was one consolation in this dreary scenario, it was that the general price index declined along with university incomes. By 1933 the cost of living had fallen to 76 percent of the 1929 level, and in 1938 it was still at just 81 percent.[8] Graduate students, temporary research assistants, and the like could live very cheaply indeed during these years. In the absence of competing demands for such academic labor, universities were comparatively well manned with highly qualified personnel. Universities could stretch their budgets considerably once they brought their principal expenditures into line with their reduced incomes.

When the major shortfalls in income began to occur, in 1932, the universities had little recourse but to reduce the payrolls that accounted for close to half of their budgets. Although there were some dismissals among junior faculty, and a tendency not to fill vacant positions, the general approach taken was that of sharing the misery. Like most other American colleges and universities, the research universities resorted to across-the-board reductions in salaries. Only Harvard, Princeton, and Yale had the financial strength to resist this trend. For American higher education as a whole, faculty salary cuts averaged 15 percent (1931–33), and by the end of the decade less than half of that loss had been recouped. The cuts at the research universities varied considerably. Stanford imposed a 10 percent reduction but subsequently paid back half of that loss. At the hard-pressed University of Wisconsin graduated "salary waivers" ranged from 12 to 25 percent. The Michigan faculty accepted a 6 to 10 percent graduated reduction for 1932–33, and then a second cut of from 8 to 20 percent the following year.[9] In general, these cuts were not formally restored but only gradually made up through subsequent promotions and raises. Because of the depressed cost of living, however, the average college teacher in the last half of the 1930s enjoyed the highest sustained level of real income in a generation.[10]

The policy of across-the-board salary cuts served to preserve the faculties of the research universities. Some cutbacks, of course, were inevitable. Chicago chose to force the retirements of professors over sixty-five. Michigan reduced its teaching staff by one hundred positions, or 12 percent, from 1931 to 1933, but it was clearly the exception. More typical was the approach at Wisconsin, where an attempt was made to preserve the normal terms of appointment, promotion, and salary advance, while the budget was reduced through salary reductions and limited staff curtailment.[11] In general, positions that fell vacant were not filled during the worst years, and beginning instructors were particularly vulnerable to the budget ax.

How the adaptation to reduced income was made at the level of the department was ultimately crucial to the health of university research. The chairman of the California physics department provided a rare description of the steps taken to meet a budget reduction of more than 20 percent from 1932 to 1933. All faculty accepted a 10 percent "voluntary" salary cut; the position of a recently deceased professor was not filled; temporary instructors had their wages cut considerably and six of twenty-four teaching fellows were eliminated. Departmental funds for visiting lecturers were entirely eliminated; the budget for contingencies was cut by 30 percent; and the research budget (voted by the university research committee) was reduced by a third.[12] These actions sacrificed much that was desirable, but retained the core that was essential for current needs and for future development. Multiplied by several hundred, it probably typified the reaction to the Depression at the lowest administrative level of the research universities.

Once this painful readjustment had been made, university departments soon found ways to renew their development. The graduate schools were full of recent, highly qualified Ph.D.'s who could be hired very cheaply. As conditions began to improve, universities were eager to replace the losses that they had incurred. Already by 1935 the leading graduate schools were reporting that their finishing Ph.D.'s were nearly all finding teaching positions.[13] This rebuilding process may help to explain one of the more puzzling features of the era.

There were widespread perceptions that numerous faculty had lost their positions during the Depression, and it was reported that teaching loads had been increased [14] (as the steps taken at California would tend to do). Insofar as this view was correct, however, it pertained only to the crisis years. For the 1930s as a whole quite the opposite seems to have been true. The total number of teaching faculty in American higher education actually grew by 36 percent during the 1930s. The contraction of faculty from 1931 to 1933 was only 1.5 percent, whereas the expansion of the last four years (1935–39) was 20 percent.[15] The increase in faculty numbers reported by the research universities was considerably greater— 45 percent from 1929 to 1939—and student/faculty ratios actually declined during the decade everywhere but at Michigan and California. This vigorous expansion of faculty relative to teaching requirements suggests that the financial picture painted above by university income and expenditure figures was by itself too bleak.

In general the research universities seem to have been forced between 1932 and 1934 to make a rapid and painful adjustment in order to exist on reduced means. After these steps had been taken, however, the gradual improvement in economic conditions coupled with the low prevailing costs allowed them to maintain or even improve upon pre-Depression levels of activity. If this pattern was evident in the expansion of faculty ranks and in the lowering of teaching burdens, it was even more pronounced in the case of research.

As was noted earlier, the impact of th Depression on university research was considerably cushioned by the large commitments that foundations made before the downturn as well as by the general prosperity of the golden age. Even after these funds were exhausted, a certain amount of equipment and material remained to be utilized during the leanest period. Depression conditions were actually propitious for research that was labor intensive. Graduate students and postdoctoral assistants were in plentiful supply. Several New Deal programs supplied wages to under-graduate and graduate students wishing to work, in effect serving to sub-sidize many university research projects.[16] The specially designated research funds of individual universities suffered the same fate as other university funds: yields from invested funds declined with the market, and research appropriations in the regular budget were frequently slashed. These developments occurred, however, within a secular trend of increas-ing external support for university research. Most of the research univer-sities reported a larger number of special funds designated for scientific research in 1934 than they had reported five years earlier. Those that existed in 1929 were usually worth less in 1934, but in many cases the differences were more than made up by new funds. Gifts and bequests for medical research were increasingly in evidence, and grants from founda-tions and corporations were also more numerous.[17]

During the last half of the 1930s external funds for university research expanded at a consistent rate. At Yale, for example, where research fi-nanced by special gifts had fallen from $450,000 in 1931–32 to $350,000 for the next two years, these research funds had climbed back to $450,000 by 1935–36. Three years later they had risen to $650,000.[18] At a few universities research budgets received quantum increases during the mid-1930s. The greatest windfall for research occurred at the University of Wisconsin. Harry Steenbock, a Wisconsin biochemist, donated his patent for the manufacture of vitamin D to the Wisconsin Alumni Research Foundation (WARF), the proceeds to be used to promote research at the university. In 1933–34, when the university's own faculty research fund had been reduced from $55,000 to $35,000, WARF provided $120,000 in research support. Some of these funds were used to protect faculty posi-tions during the worst years of the Depression. By the end of the 1930s WARF's annual co tribution exceeded $160,000, and it was given credit for "saving Wisconsin as a great university."[19] The Rackham Funds had a similar impact upon Michigan. By 1938 they were providing more than $200,000 in support for a wide variety of faculty research projects.[20] Still, for most universities ampler research funds seemed merely to whet inves-tigators' appetites. Increasingly during the decade serious doubts were expressed about the adequacy of the existing arrangements for funding university research.

Part of the problem stemmed from the Depression's impact on univer-sity capital. It was here that economic circumstances were most damaging to the private universities. Voluntary support, which had fueled their ex-pansion during the golden age, was greatly curtailed by the decline in national wealth, especially by the shrinking fortunes of potential large benefactors. Moreover, the tax policies of the later New Deal appeared to some to threaten the existence of the kinds of large private fortunes from which the research universities had so handsomely benefited. Gifts to the private research universities reached a low point in 1933 and 1934, and for the rest of the decade they were slightly under the level of giving during the first half of the 1920s. Worse yet, donors tended to earmark most large gifts for specific purposes. It was thus exceedingly difficult for private universities to undertake new initiatives requiring significant capital expenditures. Capital spending in fact almost disappeared in the 1930s once previously funded projects were completed. The trend of university endowment provides further evidence of capital erosion. Caltech, Columbia, Johns Hopkins, MIT, and Stanford reported endowment gains of 10 percent or less for the decade. Only Cornell, Princeton, and Harvard could show significant endowment growth from their 1931 peaks. For many of these institutions the surge of prosperity during the golden age may have satisfied their immediate needs, but by the end of the 1930s they began to hunger for additional capital.

The situation was fundamentally the same at state universities, even though they were relatively better off. California, Minnesota, and Michigan had developed rather broad networks of support in their states, which to varying extents continued to provide contributions during the 1930s. All three increased their endowments, and Michigan's total voluntary support for the decade (including the Rackman Fund gifts) lagged behind only the wealthiest four private universities. The state universities were able to take advantage of federal unemployment relief funds to finance some construction. Such funds tended to be utilized for self-supporting structures like dormitories rather than for facilities that would add to permanent budgetary obligations.[21] The fact remained that state governments, which had been quite magnanimous in augmenting university facilities during the 1920s, were still constrained by the depressed economy. For the state universities, too, capital for the purposes of expanding research activities was thus essentially unavailable in the 1930s.

The foundations had by this time become an integral part of university research funding, but their activities were also curtailed by the effects of the Depression. It would, of course, have been unrealistic to expect the foundations to continue to supply research capital to universities at the rate attained in the late 1920s. The limitations of their resources would have compelled them to reduce appropriations even if the economic crisis had not affected their income. The figures in Table 12, taken from the principal monitor of foundation activities of the period, show the general trend of foundation giving in areas involving university research. The years indicated are not necessarily identical with foundation grant-making years, but the intervals do correspond to the peak of foundation giving, to the trough of the Depression, to the recovery period, and, finally, to the situation at the end of the decade.

TABLE 12. Foundation Grants in the 1930s (in thousands of dollars)

	1931	1934	1937	1940
Number of foundations monitored	122	123	121	162
Total value of grants	52,476	34,212	38,478	40,390
Medicine and public health	18,627	9,167	13,496	12,274
Natural sciences	4,847	1,760	2,253	3,784
Social science and economics	4,031	4,238	2,322	2,278

SOURCES: *American Foundations and Their Fields*, vols. 2–5 (New York: Twentieth Century Fund, 1931, 1935; Raymond Rich Associates, 1939, 1942).

A few general conclusions may be drawn from these data, imperfect as they are. First, an increase in the number of major foundations in the last years of the decade seems to have had only a modest impact on the total value of grants. Actually, the enlargement of the foundation world did little more than compensate for the gradual liquidation of several major funds. Nevertheless, the significant fact remains that the total foundation pie was only 18 percent larger in 1940 than in 1934, during the depths of the Depression. The universities were probably able to claim a somewhat greater share of that pie in 1940, although these data do not make such a breakdown; but the situation nevertheless differed from field to field. Medicine and health claimed almost one-third of each foundation dollar for the decade. In 1931 (the only year it was recorded) about 10 percent of this total was earmarked for medical research, but that proportion almost certainly increased during the decade. With the likes of the Rockefeller Foundation heavily committed to this area, medical research must have been more immune to cutbacks than other programs in this category. Also, new foundation programs were often oriented toward medicine. Among the larger foundations, for example, this was true for the Kellogg and Macy foundations (both f. 1930), and in 1935 the Markle Foundation devoted itself exclusively to medical research. It appears likely, then, that medicine and health were the most generously supported areas of university research during the 1930s.[22]

The next-most-favored group seems to have been the natural sciences. After a precipitous drop from 1931 to 1934, the funding for research increased considerably by 1940. To a large extent this indicated the foundations' appreciation of the opportunities for important research in a number of fields. This was not true of the social sciences, however, despite the manifold social problems of the era.

These basic trends can be amplified to some degree by an examination of the programs of the Rockefeller Foundation.[23] Although less dominant than in the 1920s, it still provided a substantial part of total foundation giving for university science. Rockefeller grants for medical science increased through 1938, before falling off. These funds went largely to American and foreign universities, Harvard and Johns Hopkins being particularly frequent recipients. Funding for natural science research accelerated late in the decade. It tended to be spread rather widely among research universities. In both these areas, however, the Rockefeller policy of concentration was evident. Medical grants went predominantly to promote psychiatry and neurological research; the natural science program was centered on molecular biology. These program interests could sometimes be broadly interpreted, and in this manner some significant physics research managed to qualify for Rockefeller funding. The fact nevertheless remains that because the bulk of natural science research funds were concentrated on one set of problems, research funding for the rest of the natural sciences was decidedly scarce.

The situation was worse in the social sciences. There no other agency could compensate for the withdrawal of Rockefeller support. As the foundation became more concerned with practical results, moreover, the grants that it did make went largely to non-university agencies like the National Bureau of Economic Research and the Brookings Institution. Thus, the shrinkage in outside funding for university social science during the late 1930s was greater than the figures in the table indicate. University social scientists could probably adapt to reduced funding more readily than their collegues in the natural sciences, but they had few resources to fall back upon. The Rockefeller Foundation president Raymond Fosdick himself observed that all the research universities together had only $3 million in endowment to support social science research, equivalent to less than $7,500 per institution in annual income.[24] In light of the considerable work that needed to be done, Fosdick found, university social scientists were under a significant handicap in pursuing research.

The emerging picture of the university research system at the end of the 1930s is at once mixed and consistent. Essentially, conditions for investigators at research universities had never been better. Facilities, though largely erected in the preceding decade, were on the whole the finest in the world; teaching burdens, the perennial lament of American professors, had sunk to their lowest point, and assistance in teaching and research was readily available from abundant numbers of graduate assistants. External support for research, though more easily obtainable than in 1933 or 1934, was still rather tight. American scientists seem nevertheless to have adapted to Depression conditions by making the most of limited resources. The basic problem, however, was precisely the limitations of those resources.

The privately financed system of university research had served admirably since the First World War to develop numerous centers of academic research of the highest order. By the mid-1930s, however, a serious question could be posed as to whether the kinds of funds that had built this system would continue to be available in the needed magnitude. The private-university presidents who gathered at the 1937 AAU meeting found it axiomatic that private sources of research funds were "drying up."[25] The great fortunes of the Gilded Age, many of which had been instrumental in the development of the research universities, were now largely committed. It seemed unlikely that anything similar would soon become available again. The Depression had taken a toll upon the country's millionaires, and New Deal policies promised to restrict further both their numbers and their philanthropic potential. University leaders even complained that the few remaining fortunes were too often entrusted to small, inefficient foundations, instead of being left to universities.[26] The decline in interest rates brought the whole economics of endowments into question: a 4 percent yield instead of 5 percent meant that 25 percent more capital was needed to produce the same amount of income. The inputs of the foundations to university research had leveled off and were now being directed toward rather specialized purposes. Moreover, there was no hope, considering past experience, that private industry could be persuaded to support basic research in the universities. By the last half of the 1930s, then, university researchers had to content themselves with a barely adequate income that had little capacity for expansion and with very dim prospects for additional university capital. Not surprisingly, they were led to contemplate a new patron.

2. The Federal Government and University Research

Well before the 1930s the federal government without doubt constituted one of the principal estates of American science. Annual federal expenditures for research, although impossible to isolate precisely, were estimated in the late 1930s to exceed $100 million. The very vigor of the privately funded research system, however, had effectively precluded government involvement in much of basic science.[1] Federal bureaus were responsible for largely applied research in such fields as agricultural sciences, meteorology, geology, and conservation. Other scientific activities were for all practical purpose dominated by the other three estates—universities, foundations, and industry. This entrenched pattern made it difficult to establish the kind of national government role in basic research that was common in other advanced countries. To begin with, a fundamental antipathy to government involvement with science had become rooted in the leadership of the scientific community. For the government's part, perhaps a deeper hindrance was the lack of consensus on a federal

interest in the advancement of science, combined with the absence of administrative mechanisms for implementing a government role.

The opposition of scientific and educational leaders to government intrusion into the domain of research had its origins in the privately funded
research system that emerged from World War I. Its capstone, the National Research Council, formally brought together the elite of university
science, industrial research, and the foundation world. They generally
shared an ideological commitment to the private stewardship of the nation's scientific research. These arrangements were fully endorsed by the
ascendant Republican establishment of the 1920s. The one political figure
who was conspicuously associated with science and research was Herbert
Hoover: as secretary of commerce he had enthusiastically administered
most nonagricultural government research; he had been the figurehead
for the campaign to raise the National Research Fund; and to the end of
his unsuccessful 1932 reelection campaign he had presented scientific research as a means of rekindling economic growth.[2] Thus, to the extent
that science became a partisan issue in the early 1930s, it was associated
with the losing side.

Franklin Delano Roosevelt, for his part, was not above invoking anti-
science rhetoric when it suited his purposes;[3] but fundamentally he simply accorded a higher priority to political expediency and immediate
social issues than to the alleged long-range benefits of science. Beyond
this, a New Dealer like Henry Wallace, who was sympathetic to an enlarged federal role, had to contend with scientific and engineering professions that instinctively favored laissez-faire economics. Wallace correctly
perceived that they could be "a handicap rather than a help" for any
government science policy.[4] American science, it would seem, was Republican, but after 1932 the Democrats held power in Washington.

Realistically, the possibility that the federal government might become
a significant patron of university science during the 1930s was probably
slight. The subject was nevertheless seriously raised, and it was then that
fundamental differences in outlook between the Roosevelt administration
and the nation's scientific community assured that no constructive science
policy would emerge from the New Deal. Instead, the federal relationship
with nongovernmental science developed along more-predictable lines:
one program brought some support for university research, though for
reasons that were unconnected with science; another sought to delineate
the role of the federal government within the total national research system, but in itself brought no tangible results. Taken together, though,
these episodes defined the politics of science from the New Deal to the
Second World War.

The issue of a federal science policy was first broached by the Science
Advisory Board—a temporary (1933–35) New Deal creation charged

with providing the government with expert advice from civilian scientists.[5] The board was first suggested by the NRC chairman Isaiah Bowman and was intended as an official channel through which government might consult with the networks of scientists represented in the NRC. Its explicit purpose was to review the operations of federal scientific bureaus—to resolve certain controversies, provide timely advice, and generally discourage further budget cuts. The reason for its creation at this juncture, however, was the hope of insinuating science into the terms of the National Industrial Recovery Act.[6] Thus, its ultimate purpose was to secure federal support for nongovernmental scientific research, and it was this issue that divided the leaders of American science.

Science Advisory Board members largely represented the "old guard" of the NRC, including Robert Millikan, Frank Jewett of AT&T, and W. W. Campbell, former president of the University of California and current president of the National Academy of Sciences. They tended to fear government interference with the autonomy of science more than they welcomed its succor. They also zealously guarded the prerogatives of the National Academy of Sciences as the true spokesman for American science. The chairman of the SAB, Karl Compton of MIT, was of a somewhat different mind. Fearful above all of the toll that the Depression was taking of the potential of American science, he soon became the champion of an active federal science policy.

One of Compton's first acts was to propose a "Recovery Program of Science Progress"—an overt attempt to create a New Deal for science. It asked that $16 million be expended, in declining annual appropriations over six years, to fund a variety of research projects in the natural sciences and in engineering. The program was to be administered by the NRC, and the research would be undertaken largely in universities and engineering schools. "The present time," Compton wrote,

> with its subnormal employment of scientifically and technically trained men and diminished resources of universities and foundations . . . is *the* time, if ever, for the Government to step in and support a temporary program which will give employment and at the same time will give results of immediate and permanent general value.[7]

The timing, the phrasing, and the rationale of this program were all designed to attain inclusion in the National Industrial Recovery Act, but it soon became apparent that this legislation could not permit funds to be expended for research. Compton nevertheless succeeded in placing the whole issue of government support for external scientific research onto the political docket, where it would remain for the rest of the decade. For a time, at least, prospects for positive action seemed promising.

In 1934 Compton took his campaign for federal support of science to the public with an article in the *New York Times*: "Put Science to Work! The Public Welfare Demands a National Scientific Program" eloquently argued that thesis. Compared with the investments in research made by major corporations and by foreign countries, the U.S. science budget was niggardly.[8] Furthermore, emergency measures for economic recovery had ignored the longer-term benefits of scientific progress. To remedy this, he advocated that Congress appropriate $5 million annually for scientific research outside of government bureaus. Compton's logic was at points unanswerable: it hardly made sense, for example, to have young scientists dismissed from university posts and then employed on public-works projects at a similar wage. President Roosevelt was sufficiently impressed to instruct Compton "to have the Science Advisory Board give consideration to the subject and submit a program with a budget."[9]

Compton first had to overcome opposition within the board itself, where conservatives worried that government involvement with academic science carried more dangers than benefits. Compton, too, warned that if political or geographical considerations dominated the distribution of aid, "governmental financial support of science would be definitely harmful." But if they were administered by the National Academy of Sciences and the National Research Council, such funds could be directed to the most competent scientists. The ultimate payoff from this research would then be a material contribution to the national welfare. Compton in time won over the board; it authorized him to prepare "A Program for Putting Science to Work for the National Welfare." Although the program called for substantial government spending for research related to public-works construction and increased appropriations for federal scientific bureaus, its key feature was the same $5 million in annual appropriations for research outside of government.[10]

Having overcome one cleavage in the scientific community in order to formulate his proposal, Compton's program was soon wrecked by a second one—the split between natural and social scientists. The National Academy of Sciences and its associated organizations were the exclusive preserve of the natural sciences. This community in general tended to have a rather low opinion of the intellectual technology of the social sciences. In any case, social science seemed irrelevant to their preoccupation with linkages between science, technology, and industrial application. This was especially true of Compton's projects. Social scientists, like their colleagues in the hard sciences, had benefited substantially from the privately funded university research system. But unlike the natural scientists, they also found the basic themes of the New Deal professionally congenial—the primacy of questions of distribution over those of production, the need to assess the social impact of technological advancement, and the desire for greater social planning. Moreover, social scientists did not resist direct involvement with federal activities. The economist Wesley Mitchell and the political scientist Charles Merriam, both distinguished figures and power brokers in their field, were able to work with Hoover and with Roosevelt.[11] They were key members of the National Resources Board, to which Roosevelt turned for an evaluation of Compton's "Program for Putting Science to Work."

It was not that these eminent social scientists were incapable of fair judgment of a proposal for stimulating research in the natural sciences, but rather that their interpretations of the country's ills and what might best remedy them were quite different from the ideas of the SAB. Anyone not sharing Compton's faith in the efficacy of science might raise reasonable doubts about the probable results of allowing the nation's scientific elite to dispense large amounts of research funds. In addition, the National Resources Board was considering other meliorative proposals submitted by the Social Science Research Council and by the American Council on Education. From the board's point of view they could not advise undertaking "the program for pure and applied science without considering the merits of similar but doubtless ambitious programs of the social sciences, of economics, and of education in general." With this logic they reached the somewhat self-serving conclusion that these issues involved "planning for the full use of the research resources of the country." The National Resources Board thus advised against establishing a "large 'free' fund to any Science Research Committee for unspecified projects," but it did encourage federal funding for planned research projects and better funding for government scientific bureaus.[12]

The report of the National Resources Board effectively torpedoed Compton's ambitious plan for a major federal contribution to university science. It also signaled the ascendancy of the National Resources Board, which had ties to the White House and an underlying sympathy with the New Deal, as the spokesman for federal interest in nongovernmental research. The SAB went out of existence shortly after its original two-year appointment lapsed, while the National Resources Board began work on several studies bearing on national policy toward science and technology. It soon embarked upon an extensive survey of the nation's research resources (which will be considered below). Karl Compton remained throughout the 1930s a staunch advocate of federal support for science, but his experience with the SAB seems to have alienated him to a certain extent from the Roosevelt administration. His basic argument that the results of fundamental research would trickle down to benefit the public welfare was soon equated in Washington with "Mr. Hoover's point of view"; and Compton himself would later excoriate the antibusiness policies of the New Deal as portending the impoverishment of the country.[13] But Compton's campaign through the SAB was not entirely barren. His advocacy of the cause of science undoubtedly helped bring the one sop that was thrown to nongovernmental research.

Roosevelt responded to the agitation of the SAB and the National Resources Board by authorizing the newly formed Works Progress Administration to make provision for the support of research (1935). The essential purpose of the WPA was to relieve unemployment by creating jobs in which people could use their skills. For this reason it was stipulated that 90 percent of the labor costs were to be used to employ individuals taken from the relief rolls. This approach was almost the antithesis of the best-science policy advocated by the SAB. Nevertheless, during the last half of the 1930s thousands of projects at tax-supported colleges and universities benefited from the use of WPA-supported labor. The nation's most able scientists were not to be found on the welfare rolls, but now and again their assistants apparently were. For example, among the many products of these projects can be found papers in *Physical Review* co-authored by E. O. Lawrence or Glenn Seaborg from the Berkeley Radiation Lab.[14] Still, it is doubtful that these WPA funds contributed significantly to the advancement of science, although they did, in part, make a marginal contribution to university research. More definitely, the general situation highlighted the absence of a federal policy toward science per se.

Subsequent efforts to fill this void, in this case through Congress, confronted problems similar to those faced by Compton's campaign.[15] In 1937 legislation was introduced that would have substantially increased the research budget of the Bureau of Standards, half the funds to be expended in-house and the other half used to support basic research in nonprofit institutions. This initiative soon prompted competing legislative proposals that sought the same ends—support for scientific research—by funding engineering research stations in each state. Although a number of political issues became ensnarled in the consideration of these bills, the alternatives for a federal science policy could hardly be starker: either the bureau would selectively fund research on the basis of its scientific merit, in which case the support would flow heavily into the research universities, or funds would be distributed on a geographical basis that assured each state of a share. The arguments for federal support were again reviewed, and again a favorable consensus seemed to exist. But once again the community of academic science was divided by these prospects. The land-grant schools naturally favored the dispersion of research funds to each state, as was done with agricultural research funds, while the research universities and the scientific leadership continued to push for a best-science policy. Burdened with such a lack of agreement, these legislative alternatives were considered by successive sessions of Congress until the war. The entire effort nevertheless indicates both the desire for and the obstacles to a coherent federal science policy.

Why, then, did every endeavor to formulate a best-science policy of federal support for university research founder on conflicts within the scientific and academic communities? The basic reason seems to be that the existing research system was built upon tacit relationships that could not be readily transposed into the arena of government.

The leaders of American science perceived the privately funded system of university research as functioning in a best-science manner, but in fact this was only partly true. Their view conveniently ignored that the Rockefeller boards pursued explicitly regional policies, particularly in their efforts to provide special assistance to southern institutions. And the idiosyncratic purposes of many small foundations and individual donors inevitably produced a significant degree of randomness in the private provision of research resources. Nevertheless, at the center of this research system was a network of institutions—the major foundations, endowed research institutes, national councils, and the research universities themselves—that were essentially committed to best-science practices. They did not necessarily conduct formal meritocratic competitions for research grants. Rather, the distribution of research resources was controlled in a collegial and patriarchal manner by an elite of eminent scientists and science managers. On the whole these men were remarkably conscientious in the discharge of their responsibilities, and the attainments of American science attest to their effectiveness.

Those accustomed to this system consequenty demanded that any federal distribution of research funds be done through these established channels. The Columbia psychologist Edward L. Thorndike urged somewhat naively that the National Resources Board simply grant research funds to these scientists and ask them afterward what they had done.[16] Compton's projects in their various permutations merely represented this same approach in a more sophisticated guise. Conservatives in the National Academy of Sciences, however, sensed that federal science policy could not be so benign. Not only did federal intrusion into academic science threaten the autonomy of scientific decisions, particularly in choosing problems, but it also implicitly jeopardized the control that they collectively exercised—hence, the jurisdictional disputes that had plagued the Science Advisory Board. Just as these differences were papered over, however, the rather narrow vision of this group was challenged from without. Neither the social scientists nor the representatives of would-be research universities would accede to the formulation of a federal science policy dominated by the National Academy of Sciences elite. Moreover, they possessed sufficient influence, the former in the Roosevelt administration and the latter in Congress, to assure that this did not come about. The result was that federal patronage for university science could not be grafted onto the privately supported university research system. It then fell to the Science Resources Board to try to find another alternative.

In 1935 the board was first enlarged and then rechristened as the National Resources Committee. Its compositon and its preoccupations nevertheless continued to reflect the interests of the social sciences. Not until 1937 did it focus its attention on the issue of a federal science policy. It then received presidential instructions to study "Federal Aids to Research and the place of research (including natural and social science) in the Federal Government." [17] The resulting document, *Research—A National Resource*, was a comprehensive description of research in industry, government, and universities. In the style of the era, it was a blend of social science and intended social reform—an objective, factual depiction of the research system and an implicit case for new federal policies.[18] Both of these aspects of the section on university research are of interest here.[19]

On the whole, *Research—A National Resource* conveyed the impression that university research was a huge and flourishing enterprise. The data also indicated that it was dominated by a small group of universities. Only a handful of institutions, the author pointed out, "are in every sense universities: the staffs of all departments are selected with a view to research ability, [and] facilities and time are specifically available for research."[20] Essentially, these were the sixteen research universities that have been monitored in this study.

Quantitatively and qualitatively, the research universities claimed the lion's share of university research. They graduated 58 percent of the country's Ph.D.'s, and they were responsible for at least 50 percent of the expenditures for university research. Some 48 percent of the distinguished scientists starred in *American Men of Science* were located in the research universities, and fully 55 percent of those aged sixty-five and under.[21] Various facts that the report failed to mention might have further underlined the dominance of this group. When one compares this with the first such survey of distinguished scientists, done in 1906, it becomes evident that the concentration of leading scientists in the research universities was increasing.[22] An earlier study of the quality of academic departments by the same author had found that 208 of 226 distinguished departments were in the research universities.[23] But such a view was not necessarily conducive toward federal intervention in university research.

Like those of many government reports, the general conclusions of *Research—A National Resource* were implicit in the assignment. In particular, the findings concerning the importance of universities to the total national research effort were in effect the rationale for enlarged federal support. Using some imaginative extrapolations, the study estimated that universities accounted for 30 percent of the research workers in the country and 20 percent of the total dollar volume of national research and development. But the universities' contribution was more strategic than these figures indicate. As training grounds for research workers, as repositories of expertise, and as centers of pure research, the universities formed a crucial component of the national research system. Furthermore, "anything that the Government may do to stimulate and finance pure research in our universities and colleges will probably pay a high return on the investment." [24] Once again it was a question of how the federal government might best channel research aid to the campuses.

The general approach endorsed by *Research—A National Resource* was the integration of federal forms of support with the privately financed system through the existing network of organizations. To improve research personnel, the report proposed a system of federal scholarships and fellowships extending from the undergraduate to the postdoctoral level. It also suggested that the government encourage and support the councils to draw up lists of active scholars in areas not covered by *American Men of Science*. Of particular importance was the need for additional fluid research funds in universities. Here the report recommended that federal activities be coordinated with foundation grants through the assistance of the councils. In recognition of the egalitarian demands of the land-grant institutions, it endorsed federal support for business research and engineering research stations in each state. [25] Like Compton's programs, then, the *Research* report would inject federal funds into university science without altering the existing system. It would preserve the essentials of a best-science policy by granting a large role to the councils, whose functions would be invigorated by a steady federal income. In addition, it proffered benefits to all the disciplines and the gamut of higher educational institutions interested in research. Thus, unlike Compton's schemes, it would leave no one out.

When *Research—A National Resource* appeared in 1938, the immediate economic crisis was long past. The new rationale for federal action, a valid but vague sense of national interest, was scarcely sufficient to launch a major federal program. As a blueprint for a federal science policy, the *Research* report overcame previous obstacles by mollifying all potential opponents, but it was not compelling enough to win additional friends. For all its prolonged fact gathering and comprehensive perspective, *Research—A National Resource* had no immediate effect upon the development of national science policy. [26] By contrast, one other small initiative during the Roosevelt administration helps to indicate why.

In 1937 Congress passed legislation creating the National Cancer Institute as a division of the National Institutes of Health. Although NIH and its parent, the Public Health Service, had traditionally conducted only intramural research, the National Cancer Institute was organized on a different basis. Perhaps because several university medical schools already had well-established programs of cancer research, the new institute was authorized to award grants-in-aid and fellowships to researchers outside of government. It also established an advisory council to assist in the selection of projects and fellows. It thus served in a modest way as a federal grant-making agency; and since its goal was the most effective research on cancer, it functioned in a best-science manner.[27]

What distinguished the procedures of the National Cancer Institute from those proposed for a federal science policy was the relationship of ends to means. Where the scientific end itself had an overriding importance, there could be no question of seeking the best scientific talent as the means. This principle soon became axiomatic in research for the war effort. On the other hand, where research was proposed as an end in itself, as it essentially was by the Science Advisory Board and the National Resources Committee, then any number of means became comparably plausible. In the former case both the politics of disciplines and the politics of regions were clearly subordinated to the scientific goal, but in the latter situation they invariably became dominant. At this juncture a viable federal research policy was rooted better in the actual research needs of the nation than in the aspirations of the research community.

3. Retrospect and Prospect

Federal grants became a significant part of the university research system during World War II. Under pressure of the wartime emergency, Washington began to contract for massive amounts of university research. By 1943–44 the university contracts let by the Office of Scientific Research and Development were approximately triple the level of all prewar university scientific research. It was only after an extensive federal role in support of university research had become an accomplished fact that it was possible to formulate a policy to rationalize and legitimate it. To this end President Roosevelt in 1944 directed the OSRD's director, Vannevar Bush, to advise him on how the wartime government experience in sponsoring scientific research could be applied after the cessation of hostilities. The resulting report, *Science—The Endless Frontier*, is rightly taken as the charter for postwar federal science policy.[1] Indeed, its principal recommendation was fulfilled with the creation of the National Science Foundation in 1950. As a policy document, however, it attempted to build upon the lessons of the past. Accepting implicitly the desirability of fed-

eral support for science, it took as its point of reference the status quo
ante bellum—the university research system of 1940.

Science—The Endless Frontier embodied a familiar perspective on university research.[2] Vannevar Bush came to government service from MIT
(via the CIW) and shared the essential outlook of its president, Karl
Compton. The committee that reported on university research was led by
Isaiah Bowman, president of Johns Hopkins and a partisan in the policy
debate of the 1930s. Both sought to reconcile public support for university
science with the private direction of a best-science research policy.

The report sought to rationalize a permanent federal role in support of
science by demonstrating the inadequacy of the former privately funded
system. Starting from the premise that the universities provide the home
of basic science in the United States, it attempted to document that basic
science had failed to keep pace with technological research based upon
fundamental science. According to the best available figures (actually,
rough estimates derived from *Research—A National Resource*), between
1930 and 1940 spending on applied research in government and industry
far surpassed expenditures for basic research in universities: federal research outlays increased by 200 percent and industry spending by 100
percent, while university expenditures grew by just 50 percent. As a result,
the ratio of applied to basic research in the hypothetical national research
budget increased from 4.5:1 to 6:1. Given that "governmental and industrial expenditure is growing so rapidly, relative to that of the universities,
generous support of university research is essential if the proportion of
pure to applied research is to be maintained at anything like the previous
relationship." [3]

The report collected some rough data of its own in order to argue that
university researchers were markedly underfunded. Using as a standard
the amount of direct operating costs for research compared with salary
costs for research staff, it found that prewar universities generally spent
between fifteen and twenty cents for every salary dollar, while industrial
research laboratories reported expenditures of one to three dollars per
salary dollar. This seemed to indicate that universities contained "many
men with research ability whose productivity could be significantly increased by the provision of more adequate research funds." [4]

Science—The Endless Frontier also stressed the dearth of private capital available for research purposes. In particular, the report found "the
great decline in capital outlays of privately supported institutions ... very
striking." At the same time, "the increasing importance of large and
highly expensive pieces of equipment" made the capital needs of scientific
research far more critical. The basic problem of the astronomer had now
become common to many scientific specialties:

the physicist wishes to work with a cyclotron or betatron, and the biochemist with an ultracentrifuge or mass spectrograph; and workers in many fields have need . . . for the use of complicated computing equipment, such as the differential analyzer[; and] much of present-day engineering research requires large installations of a semi-industrial nature.

Federal aid was thus needed to meet the capital needs of university research as well.[5]

A finer-grained inquiry into conditions in scientific departments confirmed the irregularity of the incidence of the prewar private research system: "time and funds for research varied substantially between departments in the same university and between universities"; and "extraordinary variations" were noted "in the extent to which direct research expenditures are met from outside sources—especially grants from industry or the foundations." The inquiry found only five universities at which research conditions in the science departments seemed satisfactory. At these unidentified institutions—apparently, California, Caltech, Columbia, Harvard, and Yale—teaching loads were relatively light, and "most members of the staff [were] expected to devote more than half of their time to research." The report warned that beyond these relatively fortunate institutions, however, there existed an acute need for supplemental research resources among the twenty-five universities just below these leaders.[6]

Science—The Endless Frontier, notwithstanding its partisan intent and its uncertain data, effectively demonstrated that the privately funded university research system had failed during the 1930s to keep pace with the burgeoning needs of university research. No matter that those needs were themselves to a considerable extent generated by the remarkable expansion of the system that culminated in the short-lived golden age. For the remainder of the 1930s the increasing potential of university-based research was in general not fully realized, because of a paucity of available resources. This contention may have been debatable in 1940, but it was no longer so in 1945. By then the volume of war research conducted on the nation's campuses had demonstrated a vastly greater productive capacity than had previousy been utilized. From this came the implicit premise of the Bush report—that the era of private philanthropy in the development of American research universities had passed.

Foreseeing what might take its place was a more hazardous task. The genius of the Bush report derives from its linking of the ideal of enhancing human welfare through endless scientific discovery with practical institutional arrangements. But in this respect Bush and the members of the committees identified closely with the established research universities and the existing authority structure in the privately funded system. They consequently wished in essence to superimpose a federal funding agency on the existing system without substantially altering its operation. Above all, they sought to avoid a situation in which federal support would bring some degree of federal control, or one in which federal assistance would simply displace existing state and private research resources.[7] In particular, freedom of scientific research, peer control, and the autonomy of the universities were the principles they hoped to preserve. Their ultimate aim was thus to protect what they deemed the strength and the integrity of American research universities. They nevertheless recognized that "no matter on what conditions money is given to universities, the very existence of such support will, of course, modify university policy."[8]

The truth of this observation transcends the historical situation. The research universities had been profoundly modified by the sources from which they had received resources in the past. In the first two decades of the century they had shaped themselves to serve the needs of the different constituencies that supported their ambitions. In the next twenty years they had adapted, in addition, to the disbursement of research resources by a national network of private agencies. The result was a research system that was at once unitary with regard to the scientific communities composing it and pluralistic in the way in which universities fulfilled their varied tasks and drew resources from different portions of American society. From this perspective the viability of the ideals that Bush and his collaborators cherished depended little upon the mechanisms chosen to distribute federal funds for university research. Rather, the pluralism and the independence of the university research system rested in part upon the continued involvement of its numerous components.

Judging from the difficult experience of the 1930s, it could hardly have been foreseen that private voluntary support for universities would soon be reinvigorated by the robust expansion of the American economy: that the postwar decades would witness a flood of new foundations as well as a persistent foundation interest in higher education; that individual gifts, especially to the private research universities, would not only grow with the economy but also continue to make a vital contribution to their research capacities; or that corporate contributions to higher education would acquire new rationales and new legitimacy. The growing federal contribution to university research consequently mingled in complex ways with the continued provision of private resources. The federal presence may have modified university behavior at times, as had been predicted, but it did not become so overbearing as to smother those manifold linkages between the research universities and American society. The stature of the research universities in the postwar world has derived in no small measure from this deeply rooted pluralism. Thus, the diverse social linkages that the research universities forged during the first four decades of the century have served to safeguard their independent initiative and to enhance their continued development during the succeeding era of federally funded university research.

Appendices

APPENDIX A. Full-time Fall Enrollments in Research Universities, 1894–1939

	1894	1899	1904	1909	1914	1919
Small private universities						
Caltech (a)	n/a					386
Johns Hopkins	589	645	746	725	1,058	1,300e
MIT (a)	1,183	1,178	1,561	1,530	1,893	2,884
Princeton	1,109	1,194	1,374	1,400	1,641	1,850
Stanford	1,100	1,331	1,568	1,747	1,888	2,441
Yale	2,350	2,517	2,992	3,297	3,289	3,326
SUBTOTAL	6,331	6,865	8,241	8,699	9,769	12,187
National %	4.5	4.1	4.4	3.3	3.2	2.6
Comprehensive private universities						
Chicago	1,546(b)	3,183(b)	2,347	2,690	3,887	4,682
Columbia (c)	1,942	2,452	3,377	3,664	5,248	5,331
Cornell	1,689	2,299	3,318	4,103	5,078	5,718
Harvard	3,295	4,103	4,152	4,054	4,534	5,273
Pennsylvania	2,398	2,673	2,838	4,599	5,736	7,094
SUBTOTAL	10,899	15,465	16,032	19,110	24,483	28,098
National %	7.8	9.2	8.5	7.2	8.1	6.1
State research universities						
Cal.-Berkeley (d)	1,124	1,987	2,699	3,352	5,848	9,967
Illinois	602	1,907	3,222	4,783	5,137	8,052
Michigan	2,818	3,303	3,832	4,755	5,522	8,255
Minnesota	1,928	2,934	3,604	4,121	3,940	7,451
Wisconsin	1,530	2,285	3,175	4,295	4,874	6,875
SUBTOTAL	8,002	12,416	16,532	21,306	25,321	40,600
National %	5.7	7.4	8.8	8.0	8.4	8.8
NATIONAL TOTAL	139,826	167,999	187,726	266,654	303,223	462,445

Small private universities			
Caltech	559(f)	695	789(g)	921
Johns Hopkins	1,380	1,468	1,798	1,653
MIT	2,949(f)	3,066	2,606(g)	3,100
Princeton	2,392	2,459	2,622	2,694
Stanford	2,949	3,535	3,670	4,345
Yale	4,731	5,084	5,036	5,367
SUBTOTAL	14,960	16,307	16,521	18,080
National %	2.1	1.8	1.7	1.4
Comprehensive private universities			
Chicago	4,989	5,867	5,950	6,011
Columbia	7,640	8,886	7,981	8,008
Cornell	5,232	5,500	5,717	6,949
Harvard	7,035	8,377	7,671	8,209
Pennsylvania	7,626	7,119	6,115	7,347
SUBTOTAL	32,522	35,749	33,434	36,524
National %	4.5	3.9	3.4	2.8
State research universities			
Cal.-Berkeley	10,476	11,383	13,218	17,744
Illinois	10,089	12,413	10,747	13,510
Michigan	8,856	9,688	9,005	12,098
Minnesota	9,417	10,657	12,188	15,301
Wisconsin	7,643	9,468	8,053	11,268
SUBTOTAL	46,481	53,609	53,211	69,921
National %	6.5	5.8	5.5	5.3
NATIONAL TOTAL	716,000e	924,275	975,000e	1,317,158

SOURCES: Edwin E. Slosson, *Great American Universities* (New York: Macmillan, 1910) (1894–1909 unless otherwise noted); *Science* 65 (1915): 92: *School and Society* 12 (1920): 110–13; 21(1925): 154: 30 (1929): 794–95: 40 (1934): 793–94; 50 (1939): 778–79. Totals from Bureau of Education, *Report of the Commissioner of Education* (1895. 1905. 1915); and *Biennial Survey of Education.*

(a) From Bureau of Education, *Commissioner's Report,* and *Biennial Survey of Education.* (b) Enrollment for four quarters. (c) Not including Barnard College and Teachers College; from Columbia University, *President's Report.* (d) From Verne A. Stadtman, ed., *The Centennial Record of the University of California* (Berkeley: University of California Press, 1967). (e) Estimated. (f) 1923–24. (g) 1933–34.

APPENDIX B. Faculty and Student/Faculty Ratios at Research Universities 1899–1939

	1899		1909		1919		1929		1939	
	Fac.	S/F	Fac.	S/F	Fac.	S/F	Fac.	S/F	Fac.	S/F
Cal.-Berkeley	108	18.4	213	15.7	390	25.5	521	21.8	633	28.0
Illinois	217	8.8	548	8.7	948	8.5	1,098	12.3	1,617	8.4
Michigan	207	16.0	317	15.0	454	18.2	827	11.7	889	13.6
Minnesota	208	14.1	324	12.7	814	9.2	952	11.2	1,524	10.0
Wisconsin	161	14.2	486	8.8	518	13.3	704	13.4	917	12.3
Caltech							100	7.0	230	4.0
Chicago	211	11.3	334	8.1	413	11.3	772	7.6	871	6.9
Columbia	350	(7.0)	513	(7.1)	725	(7.4)	1,265	(7.0)	1,633	(4.9)
Cornell	321	7.2	636	6.5	876	6.5	803	6.8	1,629	4.3
Harvard	448	9.2	618	6.6	783	6.5	928	9.0	1,978	4.2
Johns Hopkins	141	4.6	218	3.3	341	3.8	640	2.3	735	2.2
MIT	135	8.7	223	6.9	269	10.7	397	7.7	694	4.5
Pennsylvania	260	10.3	454	10.1	827	8.6	1,374	5.2	1,680	4.4
Princeton	80	16.6	169	8.3	192	9.6	308	8.0	360	7.5
Stanford	131	10.2	160	10.9	298	8.2	477	7.4	661	6.6
Yale	258	9.8	404	8.2	410	8.1	598	8.5	1,024	5.2

SOURCES: Faculty: from Bureau of Education, *Commissioner's Report*, and *Biennial Survey of Education*; Students: from Appendix A; all Cal.-Berkeley from *Centennial Record*.

( ) Incommensurate units.

APPENDIX C. Research University Income, 1900–1937

State Universities	1899	1909	1919	1929	1937
CALIFORNIA*					
a) Student tuition ($000)	9	82	594	1,748	2,618
b) State approp. ($000)	173	776	2,622	6,984	8,221
c) ratio, (b/a + b)	.95	.90	.81	.80	.76
d) enrollment	2,553	3,788	13,860	19,723	29,767
e) inc./stud. (a + b/d)	71	226	232	443	364
f) inc./stud. (1938$)	114	361	172	359	364
ILLINOIS					
a)	112	203	354	879	1,261
b)	267	693	2,447	5,024	5,044
c)	.70	.77	.87	.85	.80
d)	1,907	4,783	8,052	12,413	13,647
e)	199	187	349	475	462
f)	318	299	258	385	462
MICHIGAN					
a)	192	327	682	1,200	1,501
b)	294	585	2,022	4,873	4,687
c)	.61	.64	.75	.80	.76
d)	3,303	4,755	8,255	9,688	10,952
e)	147	192	328	627	565
f)	235	307	242	508	565
MINNESOTA					
a)	98	164	501	1,168	1,516
b)	136	667	2,406	4,882	5,318
c)	.58	.80	.83	.81	.78
d)	2,934	4,121	7,451	10,657	13,691
e)	80	202	390	568	499
f)	128	323	288	460	499
WISCONSIN					
a)	36	213	716	1,463	1,391
b)	268	949	1,859	4,086	3,652
c)	.88	.82	.72	.74	.72
d)	2,285	4,295	6,875	9,468	10,864
e)	133	271	375	586	464
f)	213	433	277	475	464

APPENDIX C. Research University Income, 1900–1937 (*continued*)

Private Universities	1899	1909	1919	1929	1937
CALTECH					
a) student tuition				148	239
b) endow. income				382	377
c) ratio (b/a + b)				.28	.39
d) enrollment			386	695	877
e) income/student				763	702
f) inc./stud. (1938$)				565	702
CHICAGO					
a) student tuition	294	589	1,095	2,410	2,300
b) endow. income	208	774	1,372	3,053	3,169
c) ratio (b/a + b)	.41	.57	.56	.56	.58
d) enrollment	3,183	2,690	4,682	5,867	6,035
e) income/student	158	507	527	931	906
f) inc./stud. (1938$)	252	811	390	754	906
COLUMBIA					
a)	420	564	1,669	4,376	3,109
b)	501	705	1,564	3,528	4,553
c)	.54	.56	.48	.45	.59
d)	2,452	3,664	5,331	5,500	8,000e
e) #					
f)					
CORNELL					
a)	234	483	975	1,631	1,907
b)	386	440	738	1,280	1,257
b′) state approp.	0	231	1,089	2,629	2,802
c) b + b′/a + b + b	.62	.58	.65	.71	.68
d)	2,299	4,103	5,718	5,500	6,439
e)	270	281	490	1,007	927
f)	431	450	363	816	927
HARVARD					
a)	669	641	1,187	3,276	3,517
b)	542	730	2,022	5,293	5,243
c)	.45	.53	.63	.62	.60
d)	4,103	4,054	5,273	8,377	8,138
e)	295	338	609	1,023	1,076
f)	472	541	450	829	1,076
JOHNS HOPKINS					
a)	38	86	186	680	799
b)	109	219	468	1,319	1,271
c)	.74	.72	.72	.66	.61
d)	645	725	1,300	1,468	1,507
e)	228	421	503	1,362	1,374
f)	365	673	372	1,103	1,374

MIT

a)	207	341	750	1,268	1,459
b)	104	80	526	1,703	1,551
c)	.33	.19	.41	.57	.52
d)	1,178	1,530	2,884	3,066	2,966
e)	264	275	442	969	1,015
f)	422	440	327	785	1,015

PENNSYLVANIA

a)	355	558	1,148	2,818	2,629
b)	144	447	575	965	699
c)	.29	.45	.33	.26	.21
d)	2,673	4,599	7,094	7,119	7,015
e)	187	219	243	531	474
f)	299	350	180	430	474

PRINCETON

a)	158	201	429	1,147	1,212
b)	114	189	370	932	1,195
c)	.42	.49	.46	.45	.50
d)	1,194	1,400	1,850	2,459	2,647
e)	228	279	432	845	909
f)	364	446	320	685	909

STANFORD

a)	31	45	326	1,091	1,602
b)	200	825	1,090	1,485	1,183
c)	.87	.95	.77	.58	.42
d)	1,331	1,717	2,441	3,535	4,161
e)	158	498	580	729	669
f)	253	797	429	590	669

YALE

a)	487	516	705	1,900	2,164
b)	256	592	1,388	4,123	3,825
c)	.35	.53	.66	.69	.64
d)	2,517	3,297	3,326	5,084	5,221
e)	295	336	629	1,185	1,147
f)	472	538	466	960	1,147

SOURCES: Bureau of Education, *Commissioner's Report*, and *Biennial Survey of Education*.

* All campuses; 1939 instead of 1937; from *Centennial Record*.
# Incommensurate units.

APPENDIX D. Endowment Value, Library Volumes, and Ph.D.'s Awarded for
Research Universities, 1899–1939

	1899	1909	1919	1929	1939
CALIFORNIA*					
a) endowment ($000)	2,828	4,463	7,254	15,223	24,214
b) library volumes (000)	79	248	479	1,119*	1,074*
c) Ph.D.'s awarded	2	6	33	86	94
ILLINOIS					
a)	502	647	649	1,137	1,341
b)	44	158	462	836	1,176
c)	—	12	32	69	106
MICHIGAN					
a)	542	309	1,329	3,978	14,356
b)	140	271	432	749	1,061
c)	4	9	28	82	89
MINNESOTA					
a)	1,369	1,450	3,860	8,755	16,058
b)	60	145	300	654	1,062
c)	3	—	26	67	88
WISCONSIN					
a)	530	626	717	995	1,510
b)	62	152	276	796	472
c)	5	18	52	129	147
CALTECH					
a)			640	10,795	11,456
b)				25	49
c)			2	18	32
CHICAGO					
a)	5,726	14,902	28,364	59,615	70,944
b)	303	500	599	916	1,271
c)	43	45	96	184	179
COLUMBIA					
a)	13,265	25,846	39,602	73,376	70,714
b)	300	449	747	1,223	1,665
c)	21	44	81	182	203
CORNELL					
a)	6,756	8,687	16,000	24,709	30,872
b)	239	384	631	810	1,036
c)	19	35	47	129	130
HARVARD					
a)	12,615	21,989	44,569	108,087	135,032
b)	549	850	2,028	2,972	4,080
c)	35	41	173	115	107

JOHNS HOPKINS

a)	3,250	4,558	9,135	26,827	30,387
b)	94	142	225	377	553
c)	35	25	36	84	65

MIT

a)	3,099	1,872	14,989	33,221	36,230
b)	50	87	141	260	340
c)	—	2	5	29	66

PENNSYLVANIA

a)	3,092	3,770	9,035	17,448	22,323
b)	145	294	509	712	901
c)	15	35	27	89	54

PRINCETON

a)	2,317		10,313	23,000	31,532
b)	144	270	444		940
c)	3	9	17	31	55

STANFORD

a)	18,000	24,000	33,260	27,846	30,503
b)	45	174	320	530	740
c)	2	5	9	43	56

YALE

a)	4,942	12,532	24,050	82,857	100,448
b)	310	575	1,250	1,983	2,151
c)	21	27	39	83	132

SOURCES: Bureau of Education; American Council on Education, *American Universities and Colleges* (Washington, D.C.; 1940). For Ph.D.'s, 1921–22 instead of 1919–20; 1938–39 instead of 1939–40.

* All campuses.

APPENDIX E. Biannual Gifts and Bequests to Fourteen Research Universities, 1921–1938 (in thousands of dollars)

	1921–23	'23–25	'25–27	'27–29	'29–31	'31–33	'33–35	'35–37	'37–39
California	2,602	2,426	5,447	4,120	5,512	2,780	2,345	3,326	2,840
Illinois	938	872	419	286	541	345	358	384	810
Michigan								9,561	5,265
Minnesota	593	3,968	1,311	2,752	1,234	870	1,247	850	1,091
Chicago	1,248	5,261	9,706	13,785	22,537	8,930	3,892	13,246	7,964
Columbia	13,476	2,526	6,133	7,059	4,668	3,859	3,920	7,049	3,364
Cornell	2,706	1,600	2,099	8,478	4,077	3,728	1,829	2,255	2,347
Harvard	9,715	19,134	17,237	20,384	27,691	12,164	5,860	14,547	9,812
Johns Hopkins						3,515	1,287	2,129	2,854
MIT	2,477	5,616	1,911	1,729	1,992	2,087	790	1,242	3,699
Pennsylvania	1,473	1,525	3,973	6,313	3,585	1,538	1,228	3,375	4,158
Princeton	3,023	2,024	2,543	3,455	5,872	1,745	959	1,177	3,597
Stanford	1,300	1,082	954	1,165	1,618	1,803	906	1,085	1,758
Yale	14,209	9,062	10,663	27,785	50,926	15,571	15,417	10,048	7,891

SOURCE: Adapted from John Price Jones, ed., *The Yearbook of Philanthropy, 1940* (New York: Inter-River Press, 1940); Michigan totals from *Annual Report*.

Notes

Chapter 1. The Shaping of the American Research University, 1865–1920

Section 1. Toward a National System of Universities

1. Robert Wiebe, *The Search for Order, 1877–1920* (New York: Hill and Wang, 1968), 111–32; Thomas L. Haskell, *The Emergence of Professional Social Science* (Urbana: University of Illinois Press, 1977), 24–47.

2. Laurence R. Veysey, *The Emergence of the American University* (Chicago: University of Chicago Press, 1965); Alexandra Oleson and John Voss, eds., *The Organization of Knowledge in Modern America, 1860–1920* (Baltimore: Johns Hopkins University Press, 1979). Studies of individual institutions will be cited as these are discussed.

3. In subsequent chapters Caltech, founded in 1920, will be added to this group of research universities.

4. James Axtell, "The Death of the Liberal Arts College," *History of Education Quarterly* 11 (1971): 339–52; and below, n. 8. The most thoroughgoing recent defense of the nineteenth-century college is Colin B. Burke, *American Collegiate Populations: A Test of the Traditional View* (New York: Columbia University Press, 1982); but see also Walter P. Metzger, "The Academic Profession in the United States," in Burton R. Clark, ed., *The Academic Profession in Europe and America* (Los Angeles: University of California Press, 1986).

5. Richard Hofstadter and Walter Metzger, *The Development of Academic Freedom in the United States* (New York: Columbia University Press, 1955), 222–38; Frederick Rudolph, *The American College and University: A History* (New York: Knopf, 1962), 201–20; Richard Storr, *The Beginnings of Graduate Education in America* (Chicago: University of Chicago Press, 1953), 1–6; Veysey, *Emergence*, 22–56. "The Yale Report of 1828," in Richard Hofstadter and Wilson Smith, eds. *American Higher*

Education: A Documentary History, 2 vols. (Chicago: University of Chicago Press, 1961), 1:275–91.

6. David B. Potts, "American Colleges in the Nineteenth Century: From Localism to Denominationalism," *History of Education Quarterly* 11 (1971): 363–80; idem, "'College Enthusiasm!' as Public response, 1800–60," *Harvard Education Review* 47 (1977): 28–42; Natalie A. Naylor, "The Ante-Bellum College Movement: A Reappraisal of Tewksbury's Founding of American Colleges and Universities," *History of Education Quarterly* 13 (1973): 261–74; Stanley M. Guralnick, *Science and the Ante-Bellum American College*, Memoirs of the American Philosophical Society, vol. 109, (Philadelphia: 1975); and Burke, *Collegiate Populations*.

7. For the antecedents of graduate education before the establishment of the Ph.D., see Storr, *Beginnings of Graduate Education*.

8. Rudolph, *American College and University*, 23–40; Francis Wayland, *Report to the Corporation of Brown University, on Changes in the System of Collegiate Education, Read March 28, 1850 (Providence, 1850)*; Henry Tappan, *University Education* (New York, 1851).

9. Veysey, *Emergence*, 57–120. Practical higher education antedated the Morrill Act in such "deviant" institutions as the United States Military Academy at West Point (f. 1802) and the Rensselaer Polytechnic Institute (f. 1824). See Rudolph, *American College and University*, 228–31.

10. Hofstadter and Smith, *American Higher Education*, 2:568–69.

11. Rudolph, *American College and University*, 247–63; Earle D. Ross, *Democracy's College: The Land-Grant Movement in the Formative Stage* (Ames: Iowa State College Press, 1942)

12. Merle Curti and Vernon Carstensen, *The University of Wisconsin: A History*, 2 vols. (Madison: University of Wisconsin Press, 1949), 1:296f.; James Gray, *The University of Minnesota, 1851–1951*; (Minneapolis: University of Minnesota Press, 1951), 55–61; Winston U. Solberg, *The University of Illinois, 1867–1894* (Urbana: University of Illinois Press, 1968), 59f. and passim; Verne Stadtman, *The University of California* (New York: McGraw-Hill, 1970), 24–34.

13. Veysey, *Emergence*, 113; Burke, *Collegiate Populations*, 254–60.

14. Veysey, *Emergence*, 82–86; Morris Bishop, *A History of Cornell* (Ithaca: Cornell University Press, 1962), 8–90.

15. Hugh Hawkins, *Between Harvard and America: The Educational Leadership of Charles W. Eliot* (New York: Oxford University Press, 1973); Veysey, *Emergence*, 86–98.

16. At Yale the university grew around the college, leaving the school "in sentiment still a great College with university appurtenances": George W. Pierson, *Yale College: An Educational History, 1871–1921* (New Haven: Yale University Press, 1952), 44–65. At Princeton the appointment of scholarly faculty kept the university abreast, despite little presidential leadership in this direction: J. David Hoeveler, Jr., *James McCosh and the Scottish Intellectual Tradition: From Glasgow to Princeton* (Princeton: Princeton University Press, 1978), 14–43.

17. Edward Shils, "The Order of Learning in the United States: The Ascendency of the University," in Oleson and Voss, *Organization of Knowledge*, 19–47, quotation on 28.

18. Hugh Hawkins, *Pioneer: A History of the Johns Hopkins University, 1874–1889* (Ithaca: Cornell University Press, 1960), 3–93.

19. Ibid., 21–25, 107–13, 122–24, 238–43; and see below, Section 2.

20. Hugh Hawkins, "Three University Presidents Testify," *American Quarterly* 11 (1959): 99–119; idem, *Between Harvard*.

21. Hawkins, *Pioneer*, 38–62; idem, *Between Harvard*, 56–58, 77; Robert A. McCaughey, "The Transformation of American Academic Life: Harvard University, 1821–92," *Perspectives in American History* 8 (1974): 239–332, esp. 287–91, 297–98.

22. The influence of Hopkins is extensively entangled with that of German universities. Veysey writes, "The Hopkins immediately symbolized German research, and its existence so near at hand imparted a new and dramatic sense of accessibility to the Germany of science." The influence of both Hopkins and German universities peaked during the 1880s; it subsequently declined, as the pattern of American universities crystallized after 1890: *Emergence*, 128–30.

23. Talcott Parsons and Gerald M. Platt, *The American University* (Cambridge: Harvard University Press, 1973).

24. Veysey, *Emergence*, 264–68.

25. For example, in 1894 President Francis Walker of MIT, noting that "not less than one hundred colleges and universities in the United States are today offering technical instruction," could exult "that the battle of the New Education is won": MIT, *President's Report*, 1894, 6–7.

26. These benefits accrued chiefly to the most successful academics who achieved professorial rank in a university. Much teaching was still done, even at the best universities, by a proletariat of instructors whose numbers were adjusted annually according to enrollments.

27. University of Michigan, *President's Report, 1892*, 22. Angell's comments attest that the competition for faculty was exerting upward pressure on professorial salaries during this period.

28. Hawkins, *Pioneer*, 38–62; Rudolph, *American College and University*, 350–51. Examples of Chicago's recruitment are given in Thomas Wakefield Goodspeed, *A History of the University of Chicago: The First Quarter-Century* (Chicago: University of Chicago Press, 1972; 1st ed. 1916), 189–217; and Richard J. Storr, *Harper's University: The Beginnings* (Chicago: University of Chicago Press, 1966), 68–75. Storr gives the original faculty size as 147, with 77 in grades of instructor or higher.

29. William F. Russell, ed., *The Rise of a University: The Latter Days of Columbia College, from the Annual Reports of Frederick A. P. Barnard* (New York: Columbia University Press, 1937), 339–86.

30. Columbia University, *President's Report*, 1890, 10; Munroe Smith, "The Development of the University," in *A History of Columbia University, 1754–1904* (New York: Columbia University Press, 1904), 199–266.

31. Low's methods of faculty building were sometimes unique: on at least three occasions he secured trustee approval for appointments in the Faculty of Political Science by paying their salaries out of his own pocket: Joseph Dorfman, "The Department of Economics," in R. Gordon Hoxie et al., *A History of the Faculty of Political Science, Columbia University* (New York: Columbia University Press, 1955), 176–77.

32. Edwin E. Slosson, *Great American Universities* (New York: Macmillan, 1910), x, 9, 473, 474–85. In 1872 Columbia College had only 116 students.

33. Joseph Ben-David, *Trends in American Higher Education* (Chicago: University of Chicago Press, 1972); idem, *The Scientist's Role in Society: A Comparative Study*, 2d ed. (Chicago: University of Chicago Press, 1984).

34. See Appendix A. The growth rate of the research unviersities would be greater if summer school enrollments were taken into account.

35. Percentages estimated from annual treasurer's reports. Payrolls constitute the

bulk of actual instructional expenditures, and they are the most comparable figure between institutions with quite different budget categories. For Harvard at this time, despite its great wealth, tuition revenues exceeded the payroll by about 10 percent.

36. See Appendix C; also cf. Slosson, *Great American Universities*, x.

37. Veysey, *Emergence*, 356–57.

38. Ibid., 265–67.

39. These and the following enrollment figures are based on the institutional tables in Slosson, *Great American Universities*, and on data from MIT, *President's Report*.

40. MIT, *President's Report*, 1894, 5.

41. Harvard University, *President's Report*, 1904, 24–29.

42. Ibid.

43. University of Michigan, *President's Report*, 1905, 28.

44. Slosson, *Great American Universities*. A more typical figure for a summer session would be half regular students and half new students.

45. Calculated from Slosson, *Great American Universities*.

46. Veysey, *Emergence*, 269; Slosson, *Great American Universities*.

47. Veysey, *Emergence*, 338.

48. Charles W. Eliot, *University Administration* (New York, 1908), 124.

49. James Cattell, ed., *University Control* (New York, 1913); Joseph A. Leighton, "University Government," *Education Review* 60 (1920): 363–75; and the famous critique by Thorstein Veblen, *The Higher Learning in America* (New York, 1918).

50. Mark Beach, "Professional versus Professorial Control of Higher Education," *Educational Record* 49 (1968): 263–73; Veysey, *Emergence*, 346–56; Hofstadter and Metzger, *Academic Freedom*, 453–60.

51. The importance of the competitive, decentralized structure of American higher education for the spread of innovation is far more evident in comparative perspective and has accordingly been emphasized by scholars like Joseph Ben-David: "Universities and the Growth of Science in Germany and the United States," *Minerva* 7 (1968): 1–35, esp. 18–25. Similarly, the "dull standardization of the whole" perceived by Veysey, *Emergence*, 330–31, is "dull" only in comparison with the almost anarchic conditions existing before 1890, and hardly "standardized" at all in comparison with other systems.

52. Slosson, *Great American Universities*, 75.

53. Edith R. Mirrielees, *Stanford: The Story of a University* (New York: Putnam's, 1959), 168–97.

54. Slosson, *Great American Universities*, 34–74; Brooks Mather Kelley, *Yale: A History* (New Haven: Yale University Press, 1974), 369–92; George W. Pierson, *Yale: The University College, 1921–37* (New Haven: Yale University Press, 1955).

55. Willard Thorp, Minor Myers, Jr., and Jeremiah Finch, *The Princeton Graduate School: A History* (Princeton: Princeton University, 1978), 52–61; Henry W. Bragdon, *Woodrow Wilson: The Academic Years* (Cambridge: Harvard University Press, 1967), 291–93, 406–7.

56. Thorp, Myers, and Finch, *Princeton Graduate School*, 75, 79, 101–2, 105, 152–75; Bragdon, *Woodrow Wilson*, 281–82 and passim.

57. MIT, *President's Report*, 1902, 12; 1903, 15–16.

58. Slosson, *Great American Universities*, 382–83.

59. Association of American Universities, *Journal of Proceedings and Addresses* (hereafter *JAAU*) 1–2 (1901): 11. A few of the German universities were decidedly lax in the Ph.D. requirements for foreigners (Veysey, *Emergence*, 131); and the newly organized French universities created a *doctorat d'université*, largely for foreigners,

which was inferior to the government-sanctioned *doctorat d'état*: George Weisz, *The Emergence of Modern Universities in France, 1863–1914* (Princeton: Princeton University Press, 1983), 260–63.

60. *JAAU* 3 (1902): 28–38; *JAAU* 4 (1903): 13–14. New members proposed by the executive committee of the AAU had to be approved by three-quarters of the membership.

61. William K. Selden, "The Association of American Universities: An Enigma in Higher Education," *Graduate Journal* 8 (1968): 199–209. The AAU discontinued accreditation in 1948 because it threatened to overwhelm all other AAU activities.

62. Cf. what has been called the "master matrix" of higher education: Burton R. Clark, ed., *Perspectives on Higher Education: Eight Disciplinary and Comparative Views* (Berkeley: University of California Press, 1984).

Section 2. Academic Disciplines

1. William J. Goode, "Encroachment, Charlatanism, and the Emerging Profession: Psychology, Sociology, and Medicine," *American Sociological Review* 25 (1960): 901–14. However, see also Eliot Freidson, *Profession of Medicine: A Study of the Sociology of Applied Knowledge* (New York: Dodd, Mead, 1970), 71–84; and Magali Sarfatti Larson, *The Rise of Professionalism: A Sociological Analysis* (Berkeley: University of California Press, 1977).

2. The concerns that brought the AAUP into being were typical of professionalizing groups: there was a widespread desire to raise standards in the academic profession and to achieve greater autonomy, and there was also a serious effort to draft a code of ethics for professors. However, the activities of the association gravitated instead toward self-defense, virtually to the exclusion of these other professionalizing concerns: Walter P. Metzger, "Origins of the Association," *AAUP Bulletin* 51 (1965): 229–37.

3. Burton R. Clark, *The Higher Education System: Academic Organization in Cross-National Perspective* (Berkeley: University of California Press, 1983), 76–81, 91–95.

4. Freidson, *Medicine*, 71–72.

5. The following discussion is based upon the stages of professionalization detailed in Harold L. Wilensky, "The Professionalization of Everyone?" *American Journal of Sociology* 70 (1964): 137–58.

6. Information on associations and journals has been taken chiefly from J. David Thompson, ed., *Handbook of Learned Societies and Institutions: America* (Washington, D.C.: Carnegie Institution, 1980). Also helpful are Joseph C. Kiger, ed., *Research Institutions and Learned Societies* (Westport, Conn.: Greenwood, 1982); and Ralph S. Bates, *Scientific Societies in the United States*, 3d ed. (Cambridge: MIT Press, 1965).

7. Cf. A. Hunter Dupree, "The National Pattern of American Learned Societies, 1769–1863," in Alexandra Oleson and Sanborn C. Brown, eds., *The Pursuit of Knowledge in the Early American Republic* (Baltimore: Johns Hopkins University Press, 1976), 21–32.

8. Laurence R. Veysey, "The Plural Organized Worlds of the Humanities," in Alexandra Oleson and John Voss, eds., *The Organization of Knowledge in Modern America, 1860–1920* (Baltimore: Johns Hopkins University Press, 1979), 51–106; Frank Gardner Moore, "A History of the American Philological Association," *American Philological Association Transactions* 50 (1919): 5–32; William Riley Parker, "The

MLA, 1885–1953," *Proceedings of the Modern Language Association* 68, pt. 2 (1953): 3–39.

9. Veysey, "Humanities."

10. Daniel J. Kevles, *The Physicists: The History of a Scientific Community in Modern America* (New York: Knopf, 1978), 40; idem, "The Physics, Mathematics, and Chemistry Communities: A Comparative Analysis," in Oleson and Voss, *Organization of Knowledge*, 139–72. A longtime editor of the *AJS* admitted that the result of scientific specialization had "been of necessity to narrow, little by little, the sphere of a general scientific periodical such as the Journal": Edward S. Dana et al. *A Century of Science in America, with Special Reference to the American Journal of Science, 1818–1918* (New Haven, 1918), 54–56.

11. Sally G. Kohlstedt, *The Formation of the American Scientific Community: The American Association for the Advancement of Science, 1848–60* (Urbana: University of Illinois Press, 1976); also, Nathan Reingold, "Definitions and Speculations: Professionalization of Science in the Nineteenth Century," in Oleson and Brown, *Pursuit of Knowledge*, 33–69.

12. By 1895 the AAAS contained the following sections (to which more have since been added): A. Mathematics and Astronomy; B. Physics; C. Chemistry; D. Engineering; E. Geology and Geography; F. Zoology; G. Botany; H. Anthropology and Psychology; I. Social and Economic Science; J. Physiology and Experimental Medicine; and K. Education.

13. Kevles, "Physics, Mathematics, and Chemistry," 139–72 (quotation on 148). However, the formation of national scientific communities could also diminish the vitality of local scientific communities. See Douglas Sloan, "Science in New York City, 1867–1907," *Isis* 71 (1980): 35–76.

14. Kevles, "Physics, Mathematics, and Chemistry," 157–58.

15. Frank Sanborn's description of the objects of the proposed ASSA (1865), quoted in Thomas L. Haskell, *The Emergence of Professional Social Science* (Urbana: University of Illinois Press, 1977), 97–98.

16. Ibid., 190–95.

17. Another field with heavy amateur involvement developed quite differently from history. The amateur pitch of the American Geographical Society and the National Geographic Society (f. 1888) caused academic geographers to defect to their own, strictly professional, Association of American Geographers in 1904. See Bates, *Scientific Societies*, 102–3.

18. John Higham et al., *History* (Englewood Cliffs, N.J.: Prentice-Hall, 1965), 10–40; Veysey, "Humanities"; Haskell, *Social Science*, 168–77. Perhaps the historians never felt threatened enough to sound the professional tocsin: the AHA at first consisted mostly of American historians who were largely spared the competitive stimulus of European scholarship; the methodologically rigorous ancient historians gravitated toward classics and archaeology; and history experienced little difficulty in securing a niche in the elective curriculum.

19. Three useful studies come to different conclusions about the professionalization of economists. Mary Furner argues that wide acceptance of the professional norm of objectivity drew economists away from advocacy of social policy; Robert Church feels that professionalization was pursued primarily to allow economists to continue social advocacy behind the cloak of expertise; and Thomas Haskell stresses the necessary causes and continuous operation of the imperatives of professionalization: Mary O. Furner, *Advocacy and Objectivity: A Crisis in the Professionalization of American Social Science, 1865–1905* (Lexington: University of Kentucky Press, 1975); Robert

L. Church, "Economists as Experts: The Rise of an Academic Profession in America, 1870–1917" in Lawrence Stone, ed., *The University in Society*, 2 vols. (Princeton: Princeton University Press, 1974), 2:571–610; Haskell, *Social Science*.

20. Dorothy Ross, "The Development of the Social Sciences," in Oleson and Voss, *Organization of Knowledge*, 107–38; Barry D. Karl, *Charles E. Merriam and the Study of Politics* (Chicago: University of Chicago Press, 1974), 118–21.

21. See the discussion in Haskell, *Social Science*, 18–23.

22. Thus, the social relations within disciplines depend heavily upon the cognitive structure of the particular subject, despite the great similarity in social organization. One practical effect of this is that the normative structure of science imposes itself more slowly, less completely, and with greater attendant controversy in disciplines with weak paradigms than in those strong-paradigm "hard" sciences about which Thomas Kuhn originally theorized. See Kuhn, *The Structure of Scientific Revolutions*, 2d ed. (Chicago: University of Chicago Press, 1970); and the interpretation offered by Haskell, *Social Science*, 18–23. The few works touching on this subject include Tony Becher, "The Cultural View [of Higher Education]," in Clark, *Perspective*; Janice B. Lodahl and Gerald Gordon, "The Structure of Scientific Fields and the Functioning of University Graduate Departments," *American Sociological Review* 37 (1972): 57–72; and Roger Geiger, "The Institutionalization of Sociological Paradigms: Three Examples from Early French Sociology," *Journal of the History of the Behavioral Sciences* 9 (1975): 235–45.

23. Scholarship on the professions in recent years has tended to take a cynical perspective, as if determined to demonstrate the truth of George Bernard Shaw's dictum that "any profession is a conspiracy against the laity": Burton J. Bledstein, *The Culture of Professionalism* (New York: Norton, 1976); Church, "Economists"; and Larson, *Professionalism*. The danger in this view lies in overlooking the functional importance of professional arrangements for the activities in question, in favor of emphisizing the undeniable benefits that accrue to many professional individuals. See Thomas L. Haskell, "Power to the Experts," *New York Review of Books*, October 13, 1977, 28–34.

24. Freidson, *Medicine*, 72; Goode, "Encroachment"; Wilensky, "Professionalization."

25. Ross, "Social Sciences," 113–21.

26. Robert Silverman and Mark Beach, "A National University for Upstate New York," *American Quarterly* 22 (1979): 701–13; David Madsen, *The National University: Enduring Dream of the USA* (Detroit: Wayne State University Press, 1966); Kohlstedt, *Scientific Community*, 224–33; Haskell, *Social Science*, 63–90.

27. See e.g., Mark Beach, "Was There a Scientific Lazzaroni?" in George H. Daniels, ed., *Nineteenth-Century American Science: A Reappraisal* (Evanston: Northwestern University Press, 1972), 115–32; see also Benjamin Peirce's notion of merging the ASSA with Johns Hopkins University, discussed in Haskell, *Social Science*, 144–67.

28. Cf. the argument in Martin Trow, "Aspects of Diversity in American Higher Education" in Herbert J. Gans, ed., *On the Making of Americans: Essays in Honor of David Riesman*, (Philadelphia: University of Pennsylvania Press, 1979), 272–77.

29. It has been repeatedly argued in the twentieth century that American scientific efforts have been *too* broad, in that they have included much shoddy and valueless work, or the cultivation of pseudoscientific fields. While it can be argued that such breadth is wasteful of resources, a counterargument would be that attempts to restrict the growth of science ultimately do harm to valid and vital scientific activities. The

success of American science compared with that of other countries, despite this inefficiency and redundancy, lends weight to this argument. See Roger L. Geiger, "The Home of Scientists: Perspectives on University Research," in Bjorn Wittrock and Aant Elzinga, eds., *The University Research System: The Public Policies of the Home of Scientists* (Stockholm: Almquist and Wiksell International, 1985).

30. Haskell considers Gilman "the single most important figure in the professionalization of the American academic world": *Social Science*, 159. Also see below, n. 33.

31. Hugh Hawkins, *Pioneer: A History of the Johns Hopkins University, 1874–1889* (Ithaca: Cornell University Press, 1960), 107–10; Haskell, *Social Science*, 168–72, 177–83.

32. Quoted in Haskell, *Social Science*, 182.

33. The Hopkins mathematics pioneer J. J. Sylvester reported that "Gilman had badgered him to found the [*American Journal of Mathermatics*] almost from the moment of his arrival": Hawkins, *Pioneer*, 74–75.

34. Thompson, *Handbook of Learned Societies.*

35. Charles M. Bakewell, "The Administration, Financial Support, and Distribution of University Publications, Including Journals and Doctoral Dissertations," *JAAU* 5 (1904): 42–52; Hawkins, *Pioneer*, 109; Floyd W. Reeves et al., *The University Faculty*, University of Chicago Survey, vol. 3 (Chicago: University of Chicago Press, 1933), 238–64; Samuel E. Morison, ed., *The Development of Harvard University, 1869–1929* (Cambridge: Harvard University Press, 1930).

36. Burton R. Clark, *Academic Power in Italy: Bureaucracy and Oligarchy in a National University System* (Chicago: University of Chicago Press, 1977), 81; Joseph Ben-David, "Universities and the Growth of Science in Germany and the United States," *Minerva* 7 (1968): 1–35.

37. Henry James, *Charles W. Eliot*, 2 vols. (New York: Houghton Mifflin, 1930), 2:12.

38. Cf. Edwin E. Slosson, *Great American Universities* (New York: Macmillan, 1910), 4–10.

39. Robert A. McCaughey, "The Transformation of American Academic Life: Harvard University, 1821–92," *Perspectives in American History* 8 (1974): 239–332.

40. William Rainey Harper, "The President's Annual Report: Administration," *University of Chicago Decennial Publications*, 10 vols. (Chicago: University of Chicago Press, 1903–4), 1:xix. See also Hugh Hawkins, "University Identity: The Teaching and Research Functions," in Oleson and Voss, *Organization of Knowledge*, 285–312, esp. 239–94.

41. Guido H. Marx, "The Problem of the Assistant Professor," *JAAU* 11 (1910): 17–46 (quotation on 26).

42. James McKeen Cattell, *University Control* (New York, 1913).

43. Robert E. Kohler, *From Medical Chemistry to Biochemistry: The Making of a Biomedical Discipline* (New York: Cambridge University Press, 1982), 255–59, 269–71 (quotation on 271).

44. James McKeen Cattell, "A Statistical Study of American Men of Science," *Science*, 24 (1906): esp. 732–43.

45. Ibid., 739.

46. See below, Chapter 6.

Section 3. The Wealth of Universities

1. Bureau of the Census, *Historical Statistics of the United States: Colonial Times to 1970* (Washington, D.C.: Dept. of Commerce, 1975), 302.

2. *The General Education Board: An Account of Its Activities, 1902–1914* (New York: General Education Board, 1915), 113–16.

3. See Appendix C.

4. See Appendix D.

5. See Appendix C.

6. See Appendix C.

7. Richard Rees Price, *The Financial Support of the University of Michigan: Its Origin and Development* (Cambridge: Harvard University Press, 1923), 36.

8. Ibid., 52–54; Richard Rees Price, *The Financial Support of State Universities* (Cambridge: Harvard University Press, 1924), 114–15, 126, 160–61.

9. Merle Curti and Vernon Carstensen, *The University of Wisconsin: A History*, 2 vols. (Madison: University of Wisconsin Press, 1949), 2:206–23.

10. Jesse B. Sears, *Philanthropy in the History of American Higher Education*, U.S. Bureau of Education, Bulletin 26 (Washington, D.C.: 1922), 58; Merle Curti et al., "Anatomy of Giving: Millionaires in the late 19th Century," *American Quarterly* 15 (1963): 416–35. This situation is perhaps epitomized by Andrew Carnegie's "gospel of wealth": Robert H. Bremner, *American Philanthropy* (Chicago: University of Chicago Press, 1960), 105–9.

11. Sears comments, "Charity is education's great competitor, and we may be fairly sure that wars, famines, earthquakes and other great disasters which appeal to human sympathy for help will be costly to education" (*Philanthropy*, 60–61).

12. Ibid., 60; F. Emerson Andrews, *Philanthropic Giving* (New York: Russell Sage Foundation, 1950).

13. Sears, *Philanthropy*, 81–102. In keeping with this pattern, the General Education Board was established to aid southern education, but in 1905 it redirected its principal efforts to higher education.

14. For Carnegie, see Robert M. Lester, *Forty Years of Carnegie Giving* (New York: Scribner's, 1941); Raymond B. Fosdick has chronicled the two largest Rockefeller philanthropies: *Adventure in Giving: The Story of the General Education Board* (New York: Harper & Row, 1962); and *The Story of the Rockefeller Foundation* (New York: Harper, 1952).

15. Ellen Condliffe Lagemann, *Private Power for the Public Good: A History of the Carnegie Foundation for the Advancement of Teaching* (Middletown, Conn.: Wesleyan University Press, 1983), 3–52; Merle Curti and Roderick Nash, *Philanthropy and the Shaping of American Higher Education* (New Brunswick: Rutgers University Press, 1965).

16. *General Ed. Board*, 103–16; Ernest V. Hollis, *Philanthropic Foundations and Higher Education* (New York: Columbia University Press, 1938), 127–28.

17. *General Ed. Board*, 15.

18. Specifically, the General Education Board, in keeping with Rockefeller's beliefs, was tolerant of religiously affiliated colleges, and it had already acquired much experience in dealing with the relative educational backwardness of the South at this time.

19. Abraham Flexner, *Medical Education in the United States and Canada*, Carnegie Foundation for the Advancement of Teaching, Bulletin no. 4 (New York: CFAT 1910).

20. Curti et al., "Anatomy of Giving."

21. Samuel R. Betts, "General Alumni Gifts to Yale," with introductory matter and addenda by Peter Dobkin Hall (November 1973). I would like to thank Peter Hall for allowing me to use his unpublished expanded version of Betts's 1916 account.

22. Roger L. Geiger, *Private Sectors in Higher Education: Structure, Function and Change in Eight Countries* (Ann Arbor: University of Michigan Press, 1986), 178–79.

23. Trevor Arnett, *College and University Finance* (New York: General Education Board, 1922); Bureau of Education, *Bulletin*, no. 30 (1918): 44.

24. Hugh Hawkins, *Pioneer: A History of the Johns Hopkins University, 1874–1889* (Ithaca: Cornell University Press, 1960), 316–21.

25. Seymour E. Harris, *The Economics of Harvard* (New York: McGraw-Hill, 1970), 297.

26. Harvard University, *Treasurer's Report*, 1901. Harris reports that four of every five dollars donated to Harvard during the nineteenth century were for designated purposes (*Economics*, 293); but figures from the above *Treasurer's Report* show that 90 percent of the permanent gifts for that year were earmarked.

27. Columbia University, *President's Report*, 1914, 5–6.

28. Yale University, *President's Report*, 1921, 21.

29. Horace Coon, *Columbia: The Colossus on the Hudson* (New York: Dutton, 1937).

30. Webster Schultz Stover, *Alumni Stimulation by the American College President* (New York: Columbia Teachers College, 1930). The first alumni associations were formed in the 1820s, at the beginning of what Stover calls the "early organized alumni period" (12–14).

31. Betts, "Alumni Gifts."

32. Yale University, *President's Report*, 1891, 16.

33. Yale University, *President's Report*, 1904, 25.

34. George C. Holt, "The Origins of the Alumni Fund," *Yale Alumni Weekly* (1917): 528–29.

35. Ibid.

36. Yale University, *Treasurer's Report*, 1906, 1918.

37. Curti and Nash, *Philanthropy*, 186–202.

38. Clarence Deming, "Yale's Larger Gifts," *Yale Alumni Weekly* (1910): 634–35; (1917): 535; Yale University, *President's Report*, 1921, 22.

39. *Endowment Funds of Harvard University, June 30, 1947* (Cambridge: Harvard University, 1948).

40. Stover, *Alumni Stimulation*; Betts, "Alumni Giving."

41. Betts reports that the bicentennial fund attained only slightly over $1 million, but official university claims put the total closer to $2 millions. The follow-up was known as the University Endowment and Extension Fund, and that, too, seems to have fallen somewhat short. The General Education Board subscribed $300,000 toward a goal of $2 millions for this fund; however, the GEB granted only $287,000, indicating that the drive was not quite fully subscribed. See *General Ed. Board*, 159; and Yale University, *President's Report*, 1907.

42. Deming, "Yale's Larger Gifts."

43. The head of this campaign, Bishop William Lawrence, commented that "this was . . . long before campaigns for great sums were thought of or the word 'drive' invented": *Memories of a Happy Life* (New York: Houghton Mifflin, 1916), 215–16. See also Harris, *Economics*, 78. The *Endowment Funds of Harvard University* shows only $1,993,181.41 of the projected $2.5 million actually in this fund—another indication of the difficulty of raising large sums before 1905 (p. 78).

44. Harris, *Economics*, 298–99.

45. John Price Jones Corporation, *A Nation-Wide Survey of Fund Raising* (New York: John Price Jones Corp., 1926).

46. *Yale Old and New*, vols. 61–62, Yale University Archives, New Haven.

47. Frederick P. Keppel, *Columbia* (New York: Oxford University Press, 1914), 280–84.

48. Quoted ibid., 68.

49. Columbia University, *President's Report*, 1892, 26; Keppel, *Columbia*, 280–81.

50. Columbia University, *President's Report*, 1898, 308.

51. Columbia University, *President's Report*, 1902, 8; 1903, 11–12.

52. After repeated failures to find donors to reduce this debt, Columbia concluded a mortgage agreement that was paid up in 1939.

53. After receiving gifts of $30 million during the period 1920–26, Columbia still had to go into debt for an additional $4.75 million, and President Butler could report in 1926 that the university was undercapitalized by $60 million: Columbia University *President's Report*, 1926.

54. Roger L. Geiger, "After the Emergence: Voluntary Support and the Building of American Research Universities," *History of Education Quarterly* 25 (1985): 369–81.

55. Stover, *Alumni Stimulation*, 55–56.

56. John Price Jones, ed., *The Yearbook of Philanthropy, 1940* (New York: Inter-River Press, 1940). See Appendix E.

57. Yale University, *President's Report*, 1904, 25.

58. Stover, *Alumni Stimulation*, 76–77.

59. George W. Pierson, *Yale College: An Educational History, 1871–1921* (New Haven: Yale University Press, 1952), 477–93; Brooks Mather Kelley, *Yale: A History* (New Haven: Yale University Press, 1974), 360–66.

60. Edwin Slosson, *The Great American Universities* (New York: Macmillan, 1910), 502–8; see also 317, 329–34.

61. Quoted by George W. Pierson, *Yale: The University College, 1921–37* (New Haven: Yale University Press, 1955), 568.

62. Stover, *Alumni Stimulation*, 65.

63. Slosson, *Great American Universities*, 333–34.

64. Some of these themes have been addressed by David O. Levine, "The Social Functions of American Higher Education between the Wars" (Ph.D. diss., Harvard University, 1981).

65. Harvard University, *President's Report*, 1920, 33.

Chapter 2. The Conditions of University Research, 1900–1920

Section 1. The Research System in 1900

1. Fiscal year 1902; *Report of the Committee of Organization of Government Scientific Work* (1903), cited in A. Hunter Dupree, *Science in the Federal Government: A History of Policies and Activities to 1940* (Cambridge: Harvard University Press, 1957), 294–95.

2. Margaret W. Rossiter, "The Organization of the Agricultural Sciences," in Alexandra Oleson and John Voss, eds., *The Organization of Knoweledge in Modern America, 1860–1920* (Baltimore: Johns Hopkins University Press, 1979), 216–20; Dupree, *Science in the Federal Government*, 181–83.

3. Dupree, *Science in the Federal Government*, 157–61.

4. Ibid. 149–83, 271–92.

5. Ibid. 172–75, 297; Rossiter, "Agricultural Sciences."

6. Charles E. Rosenberg, "Rationalization and Reality in Shaping American Agricultural Research, 1875–1914," in Nathan Reingold, ed., *The Sciences in the American Context: New Perspectives* (Washington, D.C.: Smithsonian Institution Press, 1979), 143–64.

7. Dupree, *Science in the Federal Government*, 296–97.

8. Carl Snyder, "America's Inferior Position in the Scientific World," *North American Review* 174 (1902): 59–72. European medical research institutes created in the 1890s in the waker of the Pasteur Institute seem to have provided direct precedents for the Rockefeller Institute: George W. Corner, *A History of the Rockefeller Institute, 1901–1953* (New York: Rockefeller Institute Press, 1964), 24–28.

9. Corner, *Rockefeller Institute*, 1–55.

10. Howard Miller, *Dollars for Research: Science and Its Patrons in Nineteenth-Century America* (Seattle: University of Washington Press, 1970), 166–81.

11. Snyder, "America's Inferior Position." Snyder's elaboration of these themes seems so patently crafted to influence the undecided Carnegie in favor of a research institute that one must concur with Howard Miller that it may have been deliberately planted (*Dollars for Research*, 173–74).

12. Minutes, Board of Trustees, CIW, January 29, 1902, in Nathan Reingold and Ida H. Reingold, eds., *Science in America: A Documentary History, 1900–1939* (Chicago: University of Chicago Press, 1981), 14–17.

13. Columbia University, *President's Report*, 1902, 26.

14. James McKeen Cattell, "The Carnegie Institution," *Science* 16 (1902): 460–69. Contributions to this discussion appeared in *Science* for the remainder of 1902, but many letters addressed only one of the numerous issues involved.

15. Charles E. Bessey, in *Science* 16 (1902): 605–6.

16. David Madsen, "Daniel Coit Gilman at the Carnegie Institution of Washington," *History of Education Quarterly* 9 (1969) 154–86.

17. Nathan Reingold, "National Science Policy in a Private Foundation: The Carnegie Institution of Washington," in Oleson and Voss, *Organization of Knowledge*, 313–41.

18. Reingold and Reingold, *Science in America*, 8.

19. At close to full operations in 1905, the CIW spent one-third of its research expenditures on the small-grants programs. In the second decade of its existence this figure was nearer to 15 percent. For the first twenty years its existence the CIW spent 76 percent of the research funds on major programs (in house), 17 percent on various small grants, and 7 percent on publications: *CIW Yearbook* 20 (1921); 14.

20. *CIW Yearbook* 4 (1905): 32.

21. Reingold, "National Science Policy," 333–34.

22. Ibid., 322–23; Robert Woodward, "Report of the President, 1905," *CIW Yearbook* 4 (1905); "Report of the President, 1906," *CIW Yearbook* 5 (1906).

23. This tendency is evident in the case of Luther Burbank, whose exceptional talents were anything but unrecognized: Reingold, "National Science Policy," 320–22.

24. Carnegie seemed to endorse this inefficiency when he remarked, "If you have three or four exceptional men, that is a great deal. We do not judge by the number that do not produce, we judge by the number that are successes." But Woodward likened the process to a "Havana Lottery, with monthy drawings, in which the inexperienced and the inexpert man is almost as likely to receive a prize as the expert and the experienced man." Later he summed up the situation as follows: "That happy phrase of our Founder has worked out very unhappily for the Institution." Quoted in Reingold, "National Science Policy," 320, 322–23.

25. William Welch to John Shaw Billings, January 16, 1902, in Reingold and Reingold, *Science in America*, 12.

26. Reingold and Reingold, *Science in America*, 51–55; Reingold, "National Science Policy," 329–30.

27. Woodward paid lip service to the nation that the CIW "ought to sustain close relations with the universities, since they are now the chief centers of research"; but at the same time he felt "the possible methods of effective cooperation remain, essentially, to be discovered." He did little to attempt to discover such methods because of his conviction about the efficacy of full-time research and because of his deep distrust of universities themselves: "since the normal condition of an educational institution too often borders on poverty," he believed that they would use research funds to underwrite other functions. Similarly, he felt that university researchers could not be insulated from other insitutional responsibilities. This attitude does not reflect well on Columbia, where Woodward held his only university appointment, as dean of pure science before joining the CIW. See "President's Report, 1905," *CIW Yearbook* 4 (1905): 31–32.

28. Reingold, "National Science Policy," 322–23. The trustees rejected implementation of this policy in 1906, so the programs to which Woodward objected remained in existence.

29. Garland Allen, "The Transformation of a Science: T. H. Morgan and the Emergence of a New American Biology" in Oleson and Voss, *Organization of Knowledge*, 194–96.

30. Reingold, "National Science Policy," 323.

31. Simon Newcomb, "Conditions Which Discourage Scientific Work in America," *North American Review* 174 (1902): 145–58; for Cattell and others, see above, nn. 14 and 15. The preceding movement to found a national university in Washington had done much to heighten these expectations: Miller, *Dollars for Research*, 167–73. However, Woodward felt that "a wave of popular expectations" followed the establishment of the CIW, peaking only around 1905–6: "President's Report, 1911," *CIW Yearbook* 10 (1911): 12. The RIMR provoked some extravagant hopes as well: Corner, *Rockefeller Institute*, 38–39.

32. The proliferation of independent research institutes after World War I, which was significantly abetted by Rockefeller and Carnegie support, created a very complicated picture. In general, the more practical the aim, the more likely an institute would be to exist without university connections; the more involved in basic research, the more likely that such connections would exist. Nevertheless, independent research did for a time seem to threaten university research hegemony (see below, Chapter 4, Section 1, and Chapter 5, Section 3). See also Frederic A. Ogg, *Research in the Humanistic and Social Sciences* (New York: Century, 1928), 155–63.

Section 2. Resources for University Research: The Treatment of Faculty

1. David Starr Jordan, "To What Extent Should the University Investigator Be Relieved from Teaching?" *Journal of the Association of American Universities (hereafter JAAU)* 7 (1906): 24.

2. Laurence Veysey, "Stability and Change in the American Undergraduate Curriculum," in Carl Kaysen, ed., *Content and Context* (New York: McGraw-Hill, 1973), 23–26.

3. Harvard University, *President's Report*, 1901, 34. The best general discussion of this issue is provided by Hugh Hawkins, "University Identity: The Teaching and Research Functions," in Alexandra Oleson and John Voss, eds., *The Organization of Knowledge in Modern America, 1860–1920* (Baltimore: Johns Hopkins University Press, 285–312).

4. Carnegie Foundation for the Advancement of Teaching, *Third Annual Report* (New York, 1908), 134–43.

5. Ibid., 137.

6. Floyd W. Reeves et al., *The University Faculty*, University of Chicago Survey, vol. 3 (Chicago: University of Chicago Press, 1933), 94. The university's *Official Bulletin*, no. 2 (April 1891), also stipulated that classes were not to exceed thirty students. In fact, the Chicago faculty was inadequate for these standards: Richard J. Storr, *Harper's University* (Chicago: University of Chicago Press, 1966), 61n, 353.

7. "Encouragement of University Research: Report of Committee R," *Bulletin of the American Association of University Professors* 8 (April 1922): 27–39.

8. See Appendix B.

9. Reeves, *University Faculty*, 194–95.

10. *CIW Yearbook* 1 (1902): 15–21, 83, 164, 168, 173, 234. Contributors to the forum in *Science* often made this same point.

11. Ibid., 85.

12. Paul Forman, John L. Heilbron, and Spencer Weart, *Physics circa 1900: Personnel, Funding, and Productivity of the Academic Establishments*, Historical Studies in the Physical Sciences, vol. 5 (Princeton: Princeton University Press, 1975): 120–23; Morris L. Cooke, "Academic and Industrial Efficiency," *CFAT Bulletin* 5 (1910).

13. Guido H. Marx, "The Problem of the Assistant Professor," *JAAU* 11 (1910): 17–46. Comments ranged from "have ideal research position" to "have had almost no time for past five years for research or investigation" (28).

14. William James, "The Ph.D. Octopus," *Harvard Monthly* (1903), reprinted in *Educational Review* 55 (1918): 149–57; Hawkins, "University Identity," 302–5.

15. Cf. Ira Remsen, comments, "University Investigator," *JAAU* 7 (1906): 49.

16. Charles R. Van Hise, "The Opportunities for Higher Instruction and Research in State Universities." *JAAU* 6 (1905): 55.

17. H. B. Hutchins, "Should Men Bearing the Same Title in Any Institution Receive the Same Pay?" *JAAU* 8 (1906): 92–106.

18. Hawkins, "University Identity," 292. The position of postdoctoral fellows would seem to belong to this short-lived tradition. A large gift from the Penn provost Charles Harrison established postdoctoral research fellowships there in 1895, and these funds were enlarged in 1904. This type of position does not seem to have been copied elsewhere before 1920. See University of Pennsylvania, *Annual Report of the Provost*, 1896, 99–102, 175–79; 1904, 91–94.

19. "University Investigator," discussion, *JAAU* 7 (1906): 48–51.

20. Merle Curti and Vernon Carstensen, *The University of Wisconsin: A History*, 2 vols. (Madison: University of Wisconsin Press, 1949), 2:60–61; Morris Bishop, *A History of Cornell* (Itahaca: Cornell University Press, 1962), 358; Nathan Reingold and Ida H. Reingold, eds., *Science in America* (Chicago: University of Chicago Press, 1981), 144–45.

21. Reingold and Reingold, *Science in America*, 144.

22. For example, Titchener had a personality that was certainly comfortable with special treatment, if not demanding of it; Hans Eigenmann, a research professor in ichthyology at Indiana, raised a good eal of research money for the university himself; and Illinois had a research professorship in material engineering, a subject easily justified by its practical usefulness.

23. Hawkins, "University Identity," 303; Cooke, "Efficiency."

24. Edwin Slosson perceived the inherent contradiction in the career situation of preceptors: if they seek to advance in their profession, then "they have the same faults

as younger instructors elsewhere. On the other hand, if a man is contented to remain a preceptor all his life, . . . will he be the most inspiring and profitable of associates for young men?" *Great American Universities* (New York: Macmillan, 1910), 85.

25. Regarding trends in the development of departments, see Evarts B. Greene, "Departmental Administration in American Universities," *JAAU* 13 (1911): 17–35.

26. Hardin Craig, *Woodrow Wilson at Princeton* (Norman: University of Oklahoma Press, 1960), 90–98; Henry W. Bragdon, *Woodrow Wilson: The Academic Years* (Cambridge: Harvard University Press, 1967), 407. In a parallel situation Harvard tutors were integrated into departments in the same mammer.

27. Yale University, *President's Report*, 1910, 22.

28. Hugh Hawkins, *Pioneer: A History of the Johns Hopkins University, 1874–1889* (Ithaca: Cornell University Press, 1960), 156; idem, "University Identity," 292.

20. Yale University, *President's Report*, 1910, 42–43.

30. Eliot commented, "The institution called the 'sabbatical year' has been decidedly useful to the University, having indeed, but one drawback,—namely, that a teacher with a family and no resources but his salary can hardly avail himself of it." Harvard University, *President's Report*, 1901, 13; see also Marx, "Assistant Professor," 19–24.

31. *JAAU* 21 (1919): 50.

32. *JAAU* 17 (1915): 54.

33. Armin O. Leuschner, "The Organization of the Graduate School and Its Relation to the Other Schools of the University," *JAAU* 17 (1915): 41–43. Faculty research committees were advocated as early as 1911: 41–43. Faculty research committees were advocated as early as 1911, and one was apparently created in Minnesota: *JAAU*, 13 (1911): 37, 42. Stanford had by 1920 adopted arrangements identical to California's, but allocated only $2,000 for these purposes: Stanford University, *President's Report*, 1921.

34. *JAAU* 22 (1920): 49–50.

35. "Report of Committee R," *AAUP Bulletin* 8 (April 1922): 27–35.

36. *University of Chicago, Decennial Publications*, 10 vols. (Chicago: University of Chicago Press, 1903–4), 1:41–42.

37. G. Stanley Hall, "The Appointment and Obligations of Graduate Fellows," *JAAU* 8 (1906): 16–38.

38. Leuschner, "Graduate School," 43.

Section 3. Resources for University Research: Capital and Project Funds

1. Harvard University, *President's Report*, 1881, 38; 1884, 43–44; Edwin H. Hall, "Physics, 1869–1928," in Samuel E. Morison, ed., *The Development of Harvard University, 1869–1929 (Cambridge: Harvard University Press*, 1930), 277.

2. Charles L. Jackson and Gregory P. Baxter, "Chemistry, 1865–1929," in Morison, *Development of Harvard*, 271–72.

3. Howard Miller, *Dollars for Research* (Seattle: University of Washington Press, 1970), 159–62.

4. Harvard University, *President's Report*, 1881, 40; William C. Lane, "The Harvard College Library, 1877–1928," in Morison, *Development of Harvard*, 623–24.

5. Harvard University, *President's Report*, 1902, 62.

6. Waterman T. Hewett, *Cornell University: A History*, 4 vols. (New York, 1905) 2:66–101.

7. Solon I. Bailey, "Astronomy, 1877–1927," in Morison, *Development of Harvard*, 292–303; *The Harvard University Catalogue*, 1900, 634.

8. Miller, *Dollars for Research*, 98–118.

9. William M. Wheeler, "The Bussey Institution, 1871–1929," in Morison, *Development of Harvard*, 508–17.

10. Verne A. Stadtman, *University of California, 1868–1968* (New York: McGraw-Hill, 1970) 206–9.

11. Joshua L. Chamberlain, ed., *The University of Pennsylvania* (Boston, 1901), 160–61, 144–46. For the controversy over the Babylonian expedition, see Paul Ritterband and Harold Wechsler, "A Message to Lushtamer: The Hilprecht Controversy and Semitic Scholarship in America," *History of Higher Education Annual* 1 (1981): 5–41.

12. These examples are drawn from the indicated annual reports.

13. E.g., "gifts . . . are obtained by solicitation by the heads of departments . . .": University of Michigan, *President's Report*, 1901, 37.

14. Columbia University, *Treasurer's Report*, 1903; Harvard University, *Treasurer's Reports*. The Harvard Library was not self-supporting either before or after the 1890s. See Lane, "Library," 621.

15. Paul Forman, John L. Heilbron, and Spencer Weart, *Physics circa 1900*, Historical Studies in the Physical Sciences, vol. 5 (Princeton: Princeton University Press, 1975), 83–89.

16. Brigitte Schroeder-Gudehus, "Division of Labor and the Common Good: The International Association of Academics, 1899–1914," in *Science, Technology and Society in the Time of Alfred Nobel* (New York: Pergamon, 1982), 3–20, esp. 12.

17. Yale University, *President's Report*, 1911, 21–27.

18. Harvard University, *President's Report*, 1901, 34–41; substantially the same message is repeated by Eliot in his 1905 *President's Report* (48–49).

19. Charles R. Van Hise, "The Opportunities for Higher Instruction and Research in State Universities," *JAAU* 6 (1905): 57.

20. *Science* 32 (1910): 695–701.

21. Jackson and Baxter, "Chemistry," 272; Lane, "Library," 625–29.

22. See Appendix D.

23. University of California, *President's Report*, 1913; Stadtman, *University of California*, 205, 210.

24. John W. Servos, "Physical Chemistry in America, 1890–1933: Origins, Growth and Definition" (Ph.D. diss., Johns Hopkins University, 1979), 178–92.

25. John W. Servos, "The Industrial Relations of Science: Chemical Engineering at MIT, 1900–1939," *Isis* 71 (1980): 531–49. See below, Chapter 5.

26. This account of the development of research-oriented medical schools is drawn primarily from Robert E. Kohler, *From Medical Chemistry to Biochemistry* (New York: Cambridge University Press, 1982), 114–93. Also useful, for leadership in reform: Richard Shryock, *The Unique Influence of Johns Hopkins University on American Medicine* (Copenhagen: Munksgaard, 1954); on Flexner's study: Ellen Condliffe Lagemann, *Private Power for the Public Good* (Middletown, Conn.: Wesleyan University Press, 1983); and for the coeval medical profession: Paul Starr, *The Social Transformation of American Medicine* (New York: Basic Books, 1982).

27. Yale University, *President's Report*, 1912, 26; Brooks Mather Kelley, *Yale: A History*, (New Haven: Yale University Press, 1974), 374–77.

28. In most cases million-dollar gifts were required to establish the endowments necessary to support these medical schools and their hospitals: Colonel Oliver Payne made the Cornell Medical Center possible, Edward Harkness secured a hospital for Columbia, and it took large gifts from J. P. Morgan, J. D. Rockefeller, Jr., and Mrs. Collis P. Huntington to construct a new medical complex at Harvard after the turn of the century.

29. Orrin Leslie Elliott, *Stanford University: The First 25 Years* (Stanford: Stanford University Press, 1937); Edith R. Mirrielees, *Stanford* (New York: Putnam's 1959).

30. Eliot remarked with characteristic acumen "so long as medical schools are conducted as private ventures for the benefit of a few physicians and surgeons . . . the community ought not to endow them." They would merit gifts only after they became "a constituent department of the University, devoted like other departments to the advancement of science and learning." Quoted in Roger C. Shattuck and J. Lewis Bremer, "The Medical School, 1869–1929," in Morison, *Development of Harvard*, 562.

31. Yale University, *Treasurer's Report*, 1914, 25.

32. Stanford University, *President's Report*, 1921, 35.

33. *Bulletin of the National Research Council*, no. 9 (1921): 21–54.

Chapter 3. Research Universities from World War I to 1930

Section 1. Science and the University Go to War

1. Lillian Hoddeson, "The Emergence of Basic Research in the Bell Telephone System, 1875–1915," *Technology and Culture* 22 (1981): 512–44; David F. Noble, *America by Design: Science Technology and the Rise of Corporate Capitalism* (New York: Oxford University Press, 1979), 110–18.

2. Noble, *America by Design*, 149; Daniel J. Kevles, *The Physicists* (New York: Knopf, 1978), 138.

3. For Hale's multifaceted career, see Helen Wright, *Explorer of the Universe: A Biography of George Ellery Hale* (New York: Dutton, 1966).

4. See Ronald C. Tobey, *The American Ideology of National Science, 1919–1930* (Pittsburgh: University of Pittsburgh Press, 1971), 4–12, for the delining appreciation of science in the United States.

5. A. Hunter Dupree, "The National Academy of Science and the American Definition of Science," in Alexandra Oleson and John Voss, eds., *The Organization of Knowledge in Modern America, 1860 1920* (Baltimore: Johns Hopkins University Press, 1979), 342–63; George E. Hale, *National Academies and the Progress of Research* (Lancaster, Pa., 1915), reprinted from *Science* 38–41 (1913–15).

6. Daniel J. Kevles, "George Ellery Hale, the First World War, and the Advancement of Science in America," *Isis* 59 (1968): 427–37.

7. Ibid.; Kevles, *Physicists*, 139–42; National Research Council, *Third Annual Report*, 1918, 2–3.

8. National Research Council, *Second Annual Report*, 1917.

9. Kevles, *Physicists*, 117–38; Robert M. Yerkes, ed., *The New World of Science* (New York, 1920); also, A. Hunter Dupree, *Science in the Federal Government* (Cambridge: Harvard University Press, 1957), 315–23.

10. Robert H. Kargon, *The Rise of Robert Millikan: Portrait of a Life in American Science)* Ithaca: Cornell University Press, 1982), 83–87.

11. Tobey, *National Science*, 35–47.

12. Noble, *America by Design*, 155–56.

13. "The National Importance of Scientific and Industrial Research," *Bulletin of the National Research Council*, no. 1 (1919), 1–44; Alfred D. Flinn, comp., "Research Laboratories in Industrial Establishments of the United States of America," ibid., no. 2 (1920): 45–130.

14. Tobey, *National Science*, 62–95, 133–98.

15. Robert A. Millikan, "A New Opportunity in Science," *Science* 50 (1919): 285–97 (quotation 292).

16. George E. Hale, "Industrial Research and National Welfare," *Science* 48 (1918): 505–7; Kevles, *Physicists*, 148–49.

17. Kevles, *Physicists*, 111, 149–50; Wright, *Hale*, 305–17; engineering enrollments are discussed below, in Section 2; Caltech, in Chapter 5.

18. William R. Whitney, "Research as a National Duty," *Science* 43 (1916): 629; Kevles, *Physicists*, 150; Tobey, *National Science*, 40.

19. Daniel J. Kevles, "Federal Legislation for Engineering Experiment Stations: The Episode of World War I," *Technology and Culture* 12 (1971): 182–87.

20. Kargon, *Millikan*, 91, 104; Kevles, *Physicists*, 152n.

21. Robert E. Kohler has aptly described the NRC as a "trade association for science: part interest group and lobby, part scientific parliament and communications center, and part service agency": "Foundations and the Community of Science: The 1920s" (Typescript, January, 1985).

22. Kevles, *Physicists*, 152–54.

23. Tobey, *National Science*, 53–55.

24. See below, Chapter 4.

25. Quoted in Kevles, *Physicists*, 152.

26. Kargon, *Millikan*, 105.

27. David Noble considers the interaction of these individuals no less than "industrial sponsorship and direction of university-based scientific research" (*America by Design*, 147). This view would seem to take postwar rhetoric at face value and ignore the actual course of university research in subsequent years. Outside of engineering departments, research universities found relatively little attraction in vocationalism and direct industrial research. The exception was MIT during the 1920s. See John W. Servos, "The Industrial Relations of Science: Chemical Engineering at MIT, 1900–1939," *Isis* 71 (1980): 531–49. Universities, foundations, and industry each had their own vested interests and were not capable of dominating one another. Nor was the NRC a forceful central organization for American science (Dupree, *Science in the Federal Government*, 330). The interaction of these elites facilitated the pursuit of *common* interests. The failure of the National Research Fund demonstrated the limitations of concerted actions. (See below, Chapter 5).

28. George W. Pierson, *Yale College: An Educational History, 1871–1921* (New Haven: Yale University Press, 1952), 435–46.

29. Charles F. Thwing, *The American Colleges and Universities in the Great War, 1914–1919* (New York: Macmillan, 1920), 14–39.

30. Pierson, *Yale College*, 452–67; Princeton University, *Princeton in the World War* (Princeton, 1932), introd.; Morris Bishop, *A History of Cornell* (Ithaca: Cornell University Press, 1962), 425–42; Edith R. Mirrielees, *Stanford* (New York: Putnam's, 1959), 180.

31. Carol S. Gruber, *Mars and Minerva: World War I and the Uses of Higher Learning in America* (Baton Rouge: Louisiana State University Press, 1975), 163–212; William Summerscales, *Affirmation and Dissent: Columbia's Response to the Crisis of World War I* (New York: Teachers College Press, 1970), 42–103; and, more generally, David M. Kennedy, *Over Here: The First World War and American Society* (New York: Oxford University Press, 1980).

32. Gruber, *Mars and Minerva*, 232–38; Howard H. Peckham, *The Making of the University of Michigan, 1817–1967* (Ann Arbor: University of Michigan Press, 1967), 133–36.

33. Quoted in Thwing, *Colleges in the Great War,* 70–72.

34. Richard C. Maclaurin, "Problems Presented by the Students' Army Training Corps, and the Future Military Training of Students," *JAAU* 20 (1918); 113–16.

35. "Colleges after the War," reprinted in *School and Society* 8 (1918): 774–75.

36. Thwing, *Colleges in the Great War,* 245–60; Parke Rexford Kolbe, *The Colleges in Wartime and After* (New York: Appleton, 1919), 183–206.

37. Bishop, *Cornell,* 435; Maclaurin, "Problems Presented by SATC," 119–20; Columbia University, *President's Report,* 1919.

38. Harvard University, *President's Report,* 1918, 10–13, 20; Maclaurin, "Problems Presented by SATC," 121–14.

39. Noble, *America by Design,* 245–56.

40. Samuel Capen, "The Colleges in a Nationalized Educational Scheme," *School and Society* 9 (1919): 613–18.

41. Hugh Hawkins, "Banding Together: Associations in the History of American Higher Education, 1887–1973" (work in progress). I would like to thank Hugh Hawkins for sharing this information.

42. Ibid.; Noble, *America by Design,* 248–56; see also the *Educational Record* for activities of the ACE.

43. Hawkins, "Banding Together."

Section 2. Growth and Differentiation

1. Colin B. Burke, "The Expansion of American Higher Education," in Konrad H. Jarausch, ed., *The Transformation of Higher Learning, 1860–1930* (Stuttgart: Klett-Cotta, 1983), 108–30.

2. U.S. higher-education enrollments for the twenties and thirties, as given in the Bureau of Education's biennial surveys, may be expressed in "minimal" or "maximal" figures, depending on the inclusion of normal schools–teachers colleges, which enter the universe of higher education during this period. The maximal figure readjusts previous totals upward to reach enrollments that are unrealistically high for the years before 1930; the minimal figures, which are used here, probably err in the opposite sense after 1930. They consist of college and university fall enrollments minus the number of preparatory students. This student population is more consistent with research university clienteles. The relative difference between the two figures decreases over time as follows:

	1909	1919	1929	1939
Minimal	266,654	462,445	924,275	1,317,158
Maximal	355,213	597,880	1,100,737	1,494,203

3. Ernest H. Wilkins, "Major Trends in Collegiate Enrollments," *School and Society* 42 (1935): 442–48.

4. Bureau of Education, *Biennial Survey of Education,* 1936–38, 2:8–9; Burke, "Expansion."

5. David O. Levine, "The Functions of Higher Education in American Society between World War I and World War II" (Ph.D. diss., Harvard University, 1981).

6. See Appendix A.

7. See above, no. 2.

8. *Biennial Survey of Education,* 1928–30, 332–33.

9. James H. Bossard and J. Frederic Dewhurst, *University Education for Business* (New York, 1931), 252–56; Levine, "Functions of Higher Education," 17–56.

10. Engineering enrollments from the *Biennial Survey of Education.*
11. *Biennial Survey of Education,* 1932–34, 2:31.
12. *Biennial Survey of Education,* 1934–36, 2:8.
13. *Biennial Survey of Education,* 1928–30, 334, 339.

	1920	*1930*
Law enrollment	3,273	8,874
Other professional	5,501	10,914
Total	8,774	19,788

14. *Biennial Survey of Education,* 1928–30, 339. See Appendix D.
15. Cf. Levine, "Functions of Higher Education," 237–74.
16. Association of Urban Universities, *First Annual Report, 1915,* in the Bureau of Education's *Bulletin,* no. 38 (1915).
17. Richard Angelo, "The Social Transformation of American Higher Education," in Jarausch, *Transformation of Higher Learning,* 261–92.

Section 3. The Collegiate Syndrome

1. Frederick Rudolph, *The American College and University: A History* (New York: Knopf, 1962), 464–65.
2. David Levine makes this point about liberal arts colleges in general: "The Functions of Higher Education in American Society" (Ph.D. diss., Harvard University, 1981).
3. Rudolph, *American College and University,* 443–47.
4. Cf. Laurence R. Veysey, *The Emergence of the American University* (Chicago: Chicago University Press, 1965), 180–251.
5. This pattern, in fact, conformed to two important contemporary developments: the rise of the junior college and the tendency of many professional schools to recruit students after their sophomore year.
6. Edwin Slosson, *Great American Universities* (New York: Macmillan, 1910); Stanford University, *President's Report,* 1921, 37; Kent Sagendorf, *Michigan: The Story of the University* (New York: Dutton, 1948), 295–99; Harold Wechsler, *The Qualified Student: A History of Selective Admissions in America* (New York: Wiley, 1977), 215–32; Harvard University, *President's Report,* 1925, 11; Levine, "Functions of Higher Education," 124–29.
7. William H. Cowley, "European Influences upon American Higher Education," *Educational Record* 20 (1939): 165–90.
8. Yale University, *President's Report,* 1919, 17.
9. Woodrow Wilson, for example, stated that the important effects of the university community were felt "between the hours of 6 P.M. and 9 A.M.": quoted in Marcia Graham Synnott, *The Half-Opened Door: Discrimination and Admissions at Harvard, Yale, and Princeton, 1900–1970* (Westport, Conn.: Greenwood, 1979), 173.
10. Synnott, *Half-Opened Door,* 21–23; 165–70; Henry Aaron Yeomans, *Abbott Lawrence Lowell, 1865–1943* (Cambridge: Harward University Press, 1948), 169, 181; a similar socially stratified residential pattern had developed at Yale: Brooks M. Kelley, *Yale: A History* (New Haven: Yale University Press, 1974), 309.
11. Most of the old colleges of the East maintained dormitories for at least some of their students, but policies were haphazard. Penn built "houses" for its students after 1896, as donated funds became available, and then profited from the rents. Cornell built major dormitories with donations in 1913 and 1914. In the Midwest, concern for

the proper housing of young women prompted the first dormitories at Michigan, Wisconsin, and Illinois before 1920, but Berkeley held off until 1928, in part because the university's Organic Act stated that "the dormitory system shall not be adopted": Verne E. Stadtman, *University of California, 1868–1968* (New York: McGraw-Hill, 1970) 157, 160–61; Edward Cheyney, *History of the University of Pennsylvania, 1740–1940* (Philadelphia: University of Pennsylvania Press, 1940), 355; Morris Bishop, *A History of Cornell* (Ithaca: Cornell University Press, 1962), 359–61. On the other hand, Chicago and Stanford built dormitories at their founding, no doubt because of the absence of student housing in their vicinity.

12. Merle Curti and Vernon Carstensen, *The University of Wisconsin: A History*, 2 vols. (Madison: University of Wisconsin Press, 1949), 2:497–503.

13. Yeomans, *Lawrence*, 180–98; George W. Pierson, *Yale: The University College, 1921–37* (New Haven: Yale University Press, 1955), 207–52.

14. Paula S. Fass, *The Damned and the Beautiful: American Youth in the 1920s* (New York: Oxford University Press, 1977), 119–67, esp. 133.

15. Ibid., 140.

16. Ibid., 170–76.

17. Harvard University, *President's Report*, 1923, 12–13; Yale University, *President's Report*, 1923, 11–12.

18. There was a perceptible decline in the strength of the collegiate syndrome in the late 1920s, according to Fass (*Damned and the Beautiful*, 179–80); and Bishop detected the same phenomenon at Cornell (*Cornell*, 487–89).

19. Fass, *Damned and the Beautiful*, 126–29; Levine, "Functions of Higher Education," 65–68.

20. Richard R. Price, *The Financial Support of the University of Michigan: Its Origins and Development* (Cambridge: Harvard University Graduate School of Education, 1923), 54.

21. See Appendix E.

22. John Price Jones, ed., *The Yearbook of Philanthropy, 1940* (New York: Inter-River Press, 1940).

23. Ibid., 5–10.

24. Eduard C. Lindeman, *Wealth and Culture* (New York: Harcourt, Brace, 1936), 6–7.

25. Raymond B. Fosdick, *Adventure in Giving* (New York: Harper & Row, 1962), 140–49; Ernest V. Hollis, *Philanthropic Foundations and Higher Education* (New York: Columbia University Press, 1938), 199–208.

26. General Education Board, *Annual Report*, 1923–24.

27. Specifically, Bureau of Education figures indicate that in 1904–5, of $16.7 million contributed to higher education, 45 percent was received by nine of the research universities; in 1909–10, eight of these universities claimed 48 percent of $18.7 million.

28. See Appendix E.

29. General Education Board, *Annual Report*, 1924–25.

30. Michigan alumni were for decades the most numerous in the country, and they were organized well before those of other state universities. The *Michigan Alumnus* (f. 1984) was the second alumni magazine established (Yale's was first), and the alumni association was formed in 1898. There fund-raising capacity was rather low until the second decade of the century. An alumni fund was not created until the 1920s: Howard H. Peckham, *The Making of the University of Michigan, 1817–1967* (Ann Arbor: University of Michigan Press, 1967), 56, 92, 155.

31. Peckham, *Michigan*, 120, 123, 162–63, 174; Sagendorf, *Michigan*, 304–8.

32. Bishop, *Cornell*, 454–60, 503.

33. Kelley, *Yale*, 373–76; Peter E. Van de Water, *Alexander Grant Ruthven of Michigan* (Grand Rapids: Eerdmans, 1977), 56.

34. Kelley, *Yale*, 356–66; Cheyney, *Penn*, 382–94.

35. Edith R. Mirrielees, *Stanford* (New York: Putnam's, 1959), 203.

Section 4. Who Shall Go to College?

1. "Too Many Men in College?" *School and Society* 16 (1922): 379–80.

2. David Levine found 150 letters to Hopkins and 129 newspaper editorials concerning this speech in the Hopkins Papers, Dartmouth College Archives: "The Functions of Higher Education in American Society" (Ph.D. diss., Harvard University, 1981), 311 n. 117.

3. Columbia University, *President's Report*, 1921, 43–44; Harvard University, *President's Report*, 1920, 33.

4. Columbia University, *President's Report*, 1920, 199–207; Stanford University, *President's Report*, 1921, 44–47; Bishop, *Cornell*, 444; Marcia Graham Synnott, *The Half-Opened Door* (Westport, Conn.: Greenwood, 1979), 106–10, 147–52, 192–98; Harold Wechsler, *The Qualified Student* (New York: Wiley, 1977), 162–66, 225–26.

5. Wechsler, *Qualified Student*, 131–226; Synnott, *Half-Opened Door*.

6. Wechsler, *Qualified Student*, 221; various unsubstantiated statements after 1932 indicate a policy of discrimination at Chicago, although the university never had a surplus of applicants. During World War II Chicago's president Robert M. Hutchins displayed leadership in condemning discrimination (230, 235–36n).

7. Harvard University, *President's Report*, 1923, 8–9; Yale University, *President's Report*, 1923, 5–6.

8. Ralph Boas, "Who Shall Go to College?" *Atlantic Monthly* 130 (1922): 441–48.

9. Claude M. Fuess, *The College Board: Its First Fifty Years* (New York: Columbia University Press, 1950), 4–11, 79–88; Wechsler, *Qualified Student*, 3–59.

10. James McLachlan, *American Boarding Schools: An Historical Study* (New York: Scribner's, 1970), 223; Synnott, *Half-Opened Door*, 5–8; Jerome Karabel, "Status-Group Struggle, Organizational Interests, and the Limits of Institutional Autonomy," *Theory and Society* 13 (1984).

11. For example, Dartmouth, despite Hopkins's statement about an "aristocracy of brains," gave its alumni a large role in selecting students, and by the 1930s Hopkins himself oversaw a policy of substantial, overt discrimination against Jews: Levine, "Functions of Higher Education," 185–91. Synnott points out that while Dartmouth recruits appeared to be "a fine group of attractive gentlemen and excellent sportsmen," they were a year or more behind Harvard and Yale freshman: *Half-Opened Door*, 154–55.

12. President Wilbur of Stanford noted that "in a list of students who had fine high school records who were eliminated at the end of the first quarter, it was striking to find that five of them were sons of high school principals": Stanford University, *President's Report*, 1925, 15–16.

13. Boas, "Who Shall Go to College?" suggests that elite eastern women's colleges were the first to apply a severe form of selective admissions on the basis of personal and social characteristics. This seems plausible, because they were essentially residential and had limited living accommodations and because social composition was an important consideration.

14. Wechsler, *Qualified Student*, 137–45. Selective admissions applied only to Co-

lumbia College, and subsequently to the medical and the law schools. The rest of Columbia often recruited aggressively: "Columbia University drew men and women into its home-study courses by a system of follow-up letters worthy of a manufacturer of refrigerators, and sent out salesmen to ring the door bells of those who expressed a flicker of interest": Frederick Lewis Allen, *Only Yesterday* (New York: Harper, 1931), 177.

15. Wechsler, *Qualified Student*, 164–65.

16. This conflict is perhaps best exemplified by the contrast between Lowell and Charles Eliot described by Synnott, *Half-Opened Door*, 26–57, 72–80, 110.

17. Ibid., 125–59.

18. Ibid., 192–93.

19. Edward Cheyney, *History of the University of Pennsylvania, 1740–1940* (Philadelphia: University of Pennsylvania Press, 1940), 384–97. The Valley Forge plan "was largely due to the influence of . . . William Otto Miller, Comptroller of the University. He found as he was campaigning for funds that many of the College alumni declared themselves dissatisfied with the city location of the University, and gave that as a reason for sending their sons elsewhere and for feeling such languid interest in its affairs" (395).

20. These figures for Yale and Harvard may be found in their respective annual reports; for Princeton, see Synnott, *Half-Opened Door*, 5.

21. Yale University, *President's Report*, 1925, 7; Synnott, *Half-Opened Door*, 154–57.

22. J. Pearce Mitchell, *Stanford University, 1916–1941* (Stanford: Stanford University Press, 1958), 47–56: in 1930 the trustees raised the quota on women to the same percentage of total enrollment as it had been in 1899.

23. Stanford University, *President's Report*, 1925, 8–17.

24. Ibid.

25. Karabel, "Status-Group Struggle."

26. Christopher Jencks and David Riesman, *The Academic Revolution* (Garden City, N.Y.: Doubleday, 1969).

27. Columbia University, *President's Report*, 1919, 51–62.

Chapter 4. Foundations and University Research

1. Carnegie Corporation of New York, *President's Report*, 1924, 7–10; General Education Board, *Annual Report*, 1924; Robert E. Kohler, "A Policy for the Advancement of Science: The Rockefeller Foundation, 1924–29," *Minerva* 16 (1978): 480–515.

2. Barry D. Karl and Stanley N. Katz, "The American Private Philanthropic Foundation and the Public Sphere, 1890–1930," *Minerva* 19 (1981): 236–70.

3. Carnegie Corporation of New York, *Report of the Acting President*, 1922, 18.

4. Trevor Arnett, *College and University Finance* (New York: General Education Board, 1922), 10–12, 44; idem, "To What Extent Should College Students Pay the Cost of Education?" in Association of University and College Business Officers of the Eastern States, *Minutes of the Eighth Annual Meeting*, 1927, 18–29.

5. Ernest V. Hollis, *Philanthropic Foundations and Higher Education* (New York: Columbia University Press, 1938), 141–55.

Section 1. Ways and Means

1. "Reform trusts" are discussed in Barry D. Karl and Stanley N. Katz, "The American Private Philanthropic Foundation and the Public Sphere, 1890–1930," *Minerva* 19 (1981): 246.

2. Abraham Flexner, *Report on Medical Education in the United States and Canada* (New York: Carnegie Foundation for the Advancement of Teaching, 1910); and Ellen Condliffe Lagemann, *Private Power for the Public Good* (Middletown, Conn.: Wesleyan University Press, 1983), 59–93.

3. John M. Glenn and Lilliam Brandt, *The Russell Sage Foundation, 1907–1946* (New York: Russell Sage Foundation, 1947); James A. Smith, *A Commonwealth of Experts: Public Policy Research Institutions in the United States,* in progress.

4. "American Foundations," *Bulletin of the Russell Sage Foundation* 11 (1915).

5. Raymond B. Fosdick, *The Rockefeller Foundation* (New York: Harper, 1952), 30–43, 80–92.

6. For the following, see David M. Grossman, "American Foundations and the Support of Economic Research, 1913–29," *Minerva* 20 (1982); 59–82; and "Rockefeller Foundation: History" (typescript), vols. 1–6, Rockefeller Archives Center (RAC).

7. Quoted in Grossman, "Foundations and Economic Research," 68; Fosdick later wrote of Gates, "Thirty-five years later, Gates' argument, and particularly the illustrations which he used to point it up, seem like reflections from another world": *Rockefeller Foundation,* 193.

8. Fosdick, *Rockefeller Foundation,* 16–28; "Rockefeller History," RAC.

9. Karl and Katz, "Foundation," 250. See also Raymond B. Fosdick, *John D. Rockefeller, Jr.: A Portrait* (New York: Harper, 1956), 143–66.

10. W. L. Mackenzie King, *Industry and Humanity: A Study of the Principles Underlying Industrial Reconstruction* (Boston: Houghton Mifflin, 1918); Grossman, "Foundations and Economic Research," 72–76.

11. Commonwealth Fund, *Annual Report,* 1919, 14.

12. Carnegie Corporation of New York, *Annual Report,* 1924, 7; Fosdick, *Rockefeller Foundation,* 201; see also below, Section 2. Smaller foundations remained relatively free to advocate partisan views: e.g., the Pollack Foundation.

13. Karl and Katz, "Foundation," 259, 263.

14. Fosdick, *Rockefeller Foundation,* 145–46; Daniel Kevles, *The Physicists* (New York: Knopf, 1979), 149–50. For the complicated prelude, see Nathan Reingold, "The Case of the Disappearing Laboratory," *American Quarterly* 29 (1977): 79–101.

15. See below, Chapter 5; see also Robert E. Kohler, "Foundations and the Community of Science: The 1920s" (typescript).

16. Frederic A. Ogg, *Research in the Humanistic and Social Sciences* (New York: Century, 1928), 281–301; Lawrence K. Frank, "The Status of the Social Sciences in the United States: Appendix," RAC, LSRM, series III, box 63, folder 679; National Research Council. "Funds Available in 1920 in the United States for the Encouragement of Scientific Research," *Bulletin of the National Research Council,* no. 9 (1921).

17. "Rockefeller History," 7:1630–57, RAC.

18. Grossman, "Foundations and Economic Research"; Ogg, *Research,* 183–86; Lucy Sprague Mitchell, *Two Lives: The Story of Wesley Clair Mitchell and Myself* (New York: Simon & Schuster, 1953), 349–62.

19. Grossman, "Foundations and Economic Research."

20. Charles B. Saunders, Jr., *The Brookings Institution: A Fifty-Year History* (Washington, D.C.: Brookings, 1966); Flexner reported that the IGR was engaged in propaganda as well as research, and it thereby seems to have discouraged Rockefeller

support: RAC, LSRM, series III, box 63, folder 678. The IGR's director, Harold Moulton, generated considerable controversy by arguing that the world economic system could not accommodate anything near the full repayment of war debts to the United States (an issue on which events seem to have proved him correct).

21. RAC, LSRM, series III, box 63, folder 677.

22. Ogg, *Research*, 155–63.

23. Ibid., 157; *Science* 63 (1926): 317, 518.

Section 2. Foundations and the Social Sciences

1. Ruml quotations from Joan Bulmer and Martin Bulmer, "Philanthropy and Social Science in the 1920s: Beardsley Ruml and the Laura Spelman Rockefeller Memorial, 1922–29," *Minerva* 19 (1981): 347–407; see also Raymond B. Fosdick, *The Rockefeller Foundation* (New York: Harper, 1952).

2. These three documents are ably summarized in Bulmer and Bulmer, "Ruml and the LSRM." The following draws upon this excellent study.

3. Barry D. Karl, *Charles E. Merriam and the Study of Politics* (Chicago: University of Chicago Press, 1974), 118–39.

4. Social Science Research Council, *Decennial Report, 1923–1933* (New York: SSRC, 1934).

5. Barry Karl describes the "central purpose" of the summer conferences as affording "the opportunity . . . to give the SSRC and its financial backers the means of deciding on the distribution of research funds for the coming year": *Merriam*, 135.

6. Bulmer and Bulmer, "Ruml and the LSRM," 386.

7. Eduard C. Lindeman, *Wealth and Culture* (New York: Harcourt, Brace, 1936).

8. John H. Stanfield, *Philanthropy and Jim Crow in American Social Science* (Westport, Conn.: Greenwood Press, 1985).

9. Merle Curti and Vernon Carstensen, *The University of Wisconsin: A History*, 2 vols. (Madison: University of Wisconsin Press, 1949), 1:223–32; Frederic A. Ogg, *Research in the Humanistic and Social Sciences* (New York: Century, 1928), 188–90.

10. The following account is indebted to Martin Bulmer's admirable study "The Early Institutional Establishment of Social Science Research: The Local Community Research Committee at the University of Chicago, 1923–30," *Minerva* 18 (1980): 51–110.

11. Bulmer, "LCRC," 77.

12. Sufficient local donations were found to qualify for nearly the maximum in matching funds from the LSRM; however, such fund-raising was a perpetual cause for concern because of the active local interests of local donors: Bulmer, "LCRC," 83.

13. Bulmer and Bulmer, "Ruml and the LSRM."

14. Ibid.

15. Priscilla Ellis, "The Institute of Human Relations at Yale: A Study in the Prehistory and Creation of a Setting" (Typescript, Yale University, Institution for Social and Policy Studies, n.d.). I would like to thank Seymour Sarason for making this study available to me.

16. Mark A. May, "A Retrospective View of the Institute of Human Relations at Yale," *Behavior Science Notes* 6 (1971): 141–72 (quotation on 141–42). The IHR was intended to bring together five facets of the study of man. In its own building it was to house the Department of Psychiatry, the Institute of Psychology, the Child Development Clinic, and certain research projects in law, anthropology, sociology, and economics; the fifth (the medical school) was in an adjoining building.

17. Quoted in Brooks Mather Kelley, *Yale: A History* (New Haven: Yale University Press, 1974), 382–83.

18. Ellis, "Institute of Human Relations."

19. Bruce J. Schulman, "Reorganization of the Institute of Human Relations at Yale, 1935–38," (1981), Yale Archives.

20. May, "Retrospective View," 168.

21. For a statement of the IHR's positive achievements, see Mark A. May, *Toward a Science of Human Behavior: A Survey of the Work of the Institute for Human Relations through Two Decades, 1929–49* (New Haven: Yale University Press, 1950).

22. At the time of reorganization, the IHR attempted, and failed, to attain departmental status: see Schulman, "Reorganization."

23. Cf. Nicholas C. Mullins, *Theories and Theory Groups in Contemporary American Sociology* (New York: Harper & Row, 1973), 39–45; and Albert Solnit and Joseph Tanenhaus, *The Development of American Political Science* (New York: Irvington, 1982), 91–133.

24. Bulmer, "LCRC," 67.

25. Ibid., 84–86. A parallel development occurred at the SSRC, also in response to Rockefeller Foundation policies. In 1930 the council concluded that "less diffusion of resources appeared imperative"; and thereafter a series of decisions were taken in favor of greater planning, concentration on a limited number of areas, and emphasis on the solution of practical social problems: *Decennial Report*, 12–14.

26. Bulmer, "LCRC," 108–9.

27. Fosdick, *Rockefeller Foundation*, 202.

28. Ibid., 207–8.

Section 3. Foundations and Universities: The Natural Sciences

1. George W. Gray, *Education on an International Scale: A History of the International Education Board, 1923–1938* (New York: Harcourt, Brace, 1941); Raymond B. Fosdick, *The Rockefeller Foundation* (New York: Harper, 1952), 145–55; Robert E. Kohler, "A Policy for the Advancement of Science: The Rockefeller Foundation, 1924–29," *Minerva* 16 (1978): 480–515.

2. General Education Board, *Annual Report*, 1925, 4–7; 1929, 10–13; Robert E. Kohler, "Science and Philanthropy: Wickliffe Rose and the International Education Board," *Minerva* 13 (1985): 75–95.

3. General Education Board, *Annual Report*, 1926, 24–25.

4. Fosdick, *Rockefeller Foundation*, 154; Kohler, "Wickliffe Rose."

5. The figures are from the annual reports; not included are grants to medical schools, to the National Academy of Sciences, or to the Woods Hole Oceanographic Institute.

6. Substantial gifts in support of the natural sciences were also made to Vanderbilt and Rochester universities. These formed part of a larger effort to develop these institutions.

7. International Education Board, *Annual Report*, 1926, 12–15. The IEB fellowships for Americans were soon terminated, since they duplicated the NRC fellowship program.

8. Gray, *Education*, 44–46, 37–44, 78–82.

9. Kohler, "Advancement of Science"; Fosdick, *Rockefeller Foundation*, 135–44.

10. The details of the reorganization were far more complicated than this outline can convey: the International Health Board was reduced to a division of the founda-

tion, but the China Medical Board was made independent; and remnants of the IEB and the memorial (the Spelman Fund) continued to exist for several years.

11. Rockefeller Foundation, *Annual Reports*, 1929, 1934.

12. Cf. Rockefeller Foundation, *Annual Reports*, 1929–34.

13. Robert E. Kohler, "The Management of Science: The Experience of Warren Weaver and the Rockefeller Foundation Programme in Molecular Biology," *Minerva* 14 (1976): 279–306.

14. Fosdick, *Rockefeller Foundation*, 157.

15. Kohler, "Warren Weaver."

16. Ibid., 298.

17. Rockefeller Foundation, *Annual Report*, 1938: in addition, $1.5 million was given to the University of Chicago in support of biology, demonstrating once again that Chicago remained a special case for the Rockefeller philanthropies.

18. Fosdick, *Rockefeller Foundation*, 156–66.

19. *American Foundations and Their Fields*, 1934, appendix 1.

20. Kohler, "Foundations and the Community of Science: The 1920s" (typescript).

21. E.g., Carnegie Corporation, *Annual Report*, 1932; cf. Frederick P. Keppel, *Philanthropy and Learning* (New York, 1930).

22. Robert M. Lester, *A Thirty Year Catalog of Grants* (New York: Carnegie Corporation, 1942), 11; Joseph C. Kiger, "Frederick P. Keppel," *Dictionary of American Biography*, suppl. 3 (New York: Scribner's, 1973), 414–17.

23. *American Foundations and Their Fields*, 1939, 35.

Section 4. Common Goals and Cross-purposes

1. Harold J. Laski, "Foundations, Universities and Research," *Harper's*, 157 (1928): 295–303.

2. E.g., the vast sums appropriated to the Oriental Institute were later regarded with some ambivalence: Raymond B. Fosdick, *The Rockefeller Foundation* (New York: Harper, 1952), 239.

3. Stanley Coben, "Foundation Officials and Fellowships: Innovation in the Patronage of Science," *Minerva* 14 (1976): 225–40: Robert E. Kohler, "Foundations and the Community of Science: The 1920s" (typescript).

4. Carnegie Corporation, *Annual Report*, 1938, 26–29, 66–67; idem, "The Individual and His Work," *Review Series* 28 (1938).

5. *American Foundations and Their Fields*, 1934, 20.

6. Calculated from Eduard C. Lindeman, *Wealth and Culture* (New York: Harcourt, Brace, 1936), 80–81.

7. Rockefeller Foundation, *Annual Report*, 1929–34.

8. Frederick P. Keppel, "Opportunities and Dangers of Educational Foundations," *Journal of the Association of American Universities* 27 (1925): 64–72 (quotation on 65).

Chapter 5. The Privately Funded University Research System

Section 1. Business and University Research

1. Carl W. Ackerman, *George Eastman* (Boston: Houghton Mifflin, 1930), 326–50; William Lawrence, *Memories of a Happy Life* (Boston: Houghton Mifflin, 1926),

419–20; Richard P. Hallion, *Legacy of Flight: The Guggenheim Contribution to American Aviation* (Seattle: University of Washington Press, 1977); Peter Dobkin Hall, *The Business of America*, in progress.

2. Based upon examination of corporate gifts to Columbia, Harvard, Michigan, Minnesota, and Yale, 1920–1939, as reported in their respective annual treasurer's reports.

3. Columbia University, *Report of the Treasurer*, 1926: University of Minnesota, *President's Report*, 1936–38.

4. Edward S. Mason, "The Harvard Department of Economics," *Quarterly Journal of Economics* 97 (1982): 385–433; University of Michigan, *President's Report*, 1930–31, 91–93; Edward P. Cheyney, *History of the University of Pennsylvania, 1740–1940* (Philadelphia: University of Pennsylvania Press, 1940), 410–13.

5. David F. Noble, *America by Design* (New York: Oxford University Press, 1977), 137–41.

6. John W. Servos, "The Industrial Relations of Science: Chemical Engineering at MIT, 1900–1939," *Isis* 71 (1980): 531–49 (quotations on 533, 535); the argument that follows is indebted to this cogent study.

7. Arthur Lachman, *Borderland of the Unknown: The Life Story of Gilbert Newton Lewis* (New York: Pageant Press, 1955), 43, 66–67; John W. Servos, "Physical Chemistry in America, 1890–1933," (Ph.D. diss., Johns Hopkins University, 1979), 388.

8. Servos, "Industrial Relations of Science," 539.

9. MIT, *President's Report*, 1919.

10. William H. Walker, "The Technology Plan," *Science* 51 (1920): 357–59.

11. MIT, *President's Report*, 1919; *Treasurer's Report*, 1922. David Noble, *America by Design*, 14–44, mistakenly concludes that the Technology Plan was designed to be an ongoing source of revenue, in which case the income would have been placed in the current operating budget. He is also incorrect about the plan's permanence (see below, and n. 15). The Division of Industrial Cooperation (later the Division of Sponsored Research) remained after the plan was abandoned.

12. F. Leroy Foster, "Sponsored Research at MIT, 1900–1968," vol. 1, "1900–1940" (MS, Institute Archives and Special Collections), 187.

13. See Servos, "Industrial Relations of Science," 541, for the RLAC budgets. Besides the RLAC, MIT had the Research Laboratory of Applied Physics, the Division of Municipal and Industrial Research, and the Fuel and Gas Section, all devoted to contract research.

14. Ibid., 540–42.

15. Foster, "Sponsored Research," 78–86.

16. MIT, *Treasurer's Report*, 1920 and 1929.

17. MIT, *President's Report*, 1926, 1928; Norbert Wiener, *I Am a Mathematician: The Later Life of a Prodigy* (Cambridge: MIT Press, 1956), 141.

18. MIT, *President's Report*, 1928, 1929. These were exceptional grants compared with those of the foundations discussed in Chapter 4. In 1927 the Daniel Guggenheim Fund for the Promotion of Aeronautics awarded $230,000 to MIT for the creation of an aeronautical engineering building. The later grants from the Daniel and Florence Guggenheim Foundation (a general-purpose foundation established in 1924) were thus to augment work with which the Guggenheim family name was already associated: Hallion, *Legacy of Flight*, 54–59, 218–21.

19. Servos, "Industrial Relations of Science," 544–45.

20. According to James McKeen Cattell's compilations in *American Men of Science*, MIT declined somewhat in chemistry and considerably in physics between 1910 and 1927 (2d ed., p. 593; 4th ed., p. 1128).

21. Servos, "Industrial Relations of Science," 540–42.

22. G. L. Norton to S. W. Stratton, April 26, 1927, in Foster, "Sponsored Research," 78–85. Even industrialist trustees like Gerard Swope became critical of these arrangements, particularly because they seemed to encourage faculty either to moonlight or to defect to industry: David Loth, *Swope of G.E.* (New York: Simon & Schuster, 1958), 194–95.

23. Karl T. Compton, "Memorandum," in James R. Killian, Jr., *The Education of a College President* (Cambridge: MIT Press, 1985), 421–26; MIT, *President's Report*, 1934, 28–29; K. T. Compton to A. M. Palmer, Sept. 26, 1930, MIT Office of the President, Compton Papers (AC4, box 1, file 2), Institute Archives and Special Collections, MIT Libraries.

24. MIT, *President's Report*, 1935, 19, 23.

25. MIT, *President's Report*, 1931, 19; 1932, 16–17. The "professor's fund" was dissolved in 1934: Servos, "Industrial Relations of Science," 547.

26. "Principles Concerning the Obligations of Full-Time Members of the Staff" (March 13, 1934), MIT Office of the President, Compton Papers (AC4, box 1, file 8), Institute Archives. See also Servos, "Industrial Relations of Science," 547, for Compton's hostility toward "overindulgence in consulting activities."

27. MIT, *President's Report*, 1932, 13–15; Foster, "Sponsored Research," provides a unique and thorough chronicle of these matters.

28. MIT, *President's Report*, 1931, 11; 1935, 19–22; 1936, 11–13; "Proposal to Establish a Graduate School" (1932), MIT Office of the President, Compton Papers (AC4, box 2, file 9.5), Institute Archives.

29. MIT, *President's Report*, 1935, 25; 1937, 20.

30. MIT *President's Report*, 1936, 20–21, 41.

31. National Resource Planning Board, *Research—A National Resource*, vol. 2, *Industrial Research* (Washington, D.C.: GPO, 1940), 174 (rankings based on *American Men of Science*, 6th ed.); Philip M. Morse, *In at the Beginnings: A Physicist's Life* (Cambridge: MIT Press, 1977), 119.

32. On the founding of Caltech, see Helen Wright, *Explorer of the Universe: A Biography of George Ellery Hale* (New York: Dutton, 1966); Robert H. Kargon, *The Rise of Robert Millikan* (Ithaca: Cornell University Press, 1982); Robert A. Millikan, *The Autobiography of Robert A. Millikan* (New York: Prentice-Hall, 1950).

33. Servos, "Physical Chemistry," 363–415; idem, "The Knowledge Corporation: A. A. Noyes and Chemistry at Cal-Tech, 1915–30," *Ambix* 23 (1976): 175–86.

34. Nathan Reingold, "The Case of the Disappearing Laboratory," *American Quarterly* 29 (1977): 79–101; and above, Chapter 4.

35. Robert W. Seidel, "Physics Research in California: The Rise of a Leading Sector in American Physics" (Ph.D. diss., University of California, Berkeley, 1978), 70–73 (quotation on 72); Millikan, *Autobiography*, 207–19; Kargon, *Millikan*, 92–114; Lawrence Shirley, "Two Decades of Caltech Development: Sources for Institute Growth, 1920–1940" (undergraduate thesis, Caltech Archives, 1969).

36. Seidel, "Physics in California," 75; see also Millikan, *Autobiography*, 228–37; Ronald C. Tobey, *The American Ideology of National Science, 1919–30* (Pittsburgh: University of Pittsburgh Press, 1971), 218–19.

37. Seidel, "Physics in California," 319–33; Servos, "Physical Chemistry," 386–89; Hallion, *Legacy of Flight*, 187–206.

38. Seidel, "Physics in California," 319–33.

39. Millikan, *Autobiography*, 239.

40. Ibid., 238–41; Shirley, "Caltech Development."

41. Millikan stated unequivocally, "The definite, tangible interest of the Associates . . . was what sold the Institute to the foundations": *Autobiography*, 250.

42. Millikan asked Frank Jewett and J. J. Carty of AT&T and John C. Merriam of the CIW to intercede with Harry Guggenheim and explain the virtues of Caltech as a site for an aeronautics school: Paul A. Hanle, *Bringing Aerodynamics to America* (Cambridge: MIT Press, 1982), 9–13.

43. Shirley, "Caltech Development."

44. National Resources Planning Board, *Research*, 1:174.

45. Ibid. In this ranking of eminent scientists, Caltech had the highest proportion (twenty-six of twenty-seven) under sixty-five years of age for any research university.

46. National Research Council, *National Research Fellowships, 1919–1938* (Washington, D.C.: NRC, 1938), 81. Caltech ranked third in NRC Fellows in the physical science, behind Princeton and Harvard: see below, Section 4.

47. Wright, *Hale*, 365–66; Tobey, *National Science*, 200–8.

48. "The National Research Endowment," *Science* 63 (1926): 10–11.

49. Tobey, *National Science*, 209–14.

50. G. E. Hale to Harry M. Goodwin, January 31, 1926, in Nathan Reingold and Ida H. Reingold, eds., *Science in America* (Chicago: University of Chicago Press, 1981), 389–92; Tobey, *National Science*, 207–17.

51. Lance E. Davis and Daniel J. Kevles, "The National Research Fund: A Case Study in the Industrial Support of Academic Science," *Minerva* 12 (1974): 207–20.

52. In general, the cases of the most successful cooperation seem to involve costly instruments or facilities that can simultaneously serve the practical needs of industry and the theoretical ends of scientists: e.g., Theodor von Karman's work with the Caltech wind tunnel: Hanle, *Aerodynamics*.

Section 2. Institutional Patterns of University Research

1. A 1925 peer rating of graduate departments rated Harvard first in seven and second in six (N = 19); Chicago rated first in seven and second in four: R. M. Hughes, *A Study of the Graduate Schools of America* (Oxford, Ohio: Miami University, 1925). A decade later a well-informed observer also found Harvard first and Chicago second: Edwin R. Embree, "In Order of Their Eminence: An Appraisal of American Universities," *Atlantic Monthly* 155 (1935): 652–64. Harvard also received the largest number of NRC Fellows between the wars and consistently had the most scientists starred in *American Men of Science*.

2. For three perspectives on Lowell's achievements, see Frederick P. Keppel, "President Lowell and His Influence," *Atlantic Monthly* 151 (1933): 753–63; James B. Conant, *My Serveral Lives: Memoirs of a Social Inventor* (New York: Harper & Row, 1970), 22–23; A. Lawrence Lowell, *At War with Academic Traditions in America* (Cambridge: Harvard University Press, 1934).

3. Because many instructors were graduate students, they were not counted as part of the faculty. In the late 1930s, however, the ranks of junior faculty became much larger than the number of potential promotions and posed a difficult problem for the university: Conant, *My Several Lives*, 157–71. Also see below, Section 3.

4. The Harvard Faculty of Arts and Sciences, by rank:

	1924–25	1929–30	1934–35	1939–40
Professors	109	124	131	143
Associates	24	53	65	52
Assistants	40	53	65	52
Instructors	31	41	73	60
Total	204	253	320	315

SOURCE: Harvard University, *Annual Reports to the President*.

5. Callie Hull and Clarence J. West, "Fellowships and Scholarships for Advanced Work in Science and Technology," *Bulletin of the National Research Council*, no. 94 (1934); idem., "Funds Available in the United States for the Support and Encouragement of Research in Science and its Technologies," *Bulletin of the National Research Council*, no. 95 (1934).

6. Bruce Kuklick, *The Rise of American Philosophy: Cambridge, Massachusetts, 1860–1930* (New Haven: Yale University Press, 1977), 414.

7. Ibid., 407–16. The "new" philosophy department exhibited rather typical Harvard career patterns: James Houghton Woods was a Bostonian, Harvard B.A., European Ph.D. (Strasbourg), who taught only at Harvard (often without pay) before being made professor in 1913; Ralph Barton Perry was a Harvard Ph.D. who taught briefly at Williams and Smith colleges before making a career at Harvard; William Ernest Hocking, also a Harvard Ph.D., spent a decade teaching at Berkeley and Yale before being called back to Cambridge; and Clarence Irving Lewis, Harvard B.A. and Ph.D., taught nine years at Berkeley before returning to Harvard for the rest of his career: Ibid., passim.

8. Edward S. Mason, "The Harvard Department of Economics from the Beginning to World War II," *Quarterly Journal of Economics* 97 (1982): 385–433 (quotation on 409). Sorokin joined the economics department in 1930 to teach sociology. A separate sociology department was formed the following year.

9. Paul A. Samuelson, "Economics in a Golden Age: A Personal Memoir," in Gerald Holton, ed., *The Making of Modern Science* (New York: Norton, 1972), 155–70 (quotation on 162).

10. Keppel, "President Lowell," 759; Seymour Martin Lipset and David Riesman, *Education and Politics at Harvard* (New York: McGraw-Hill, 1975), 153–55.

11. Conant, *My Several Lives*, 82–83.

12. Ibid., 120–79.

13. University of Chicago, *President's Report*, 1929–30, 5.

14. *President's Report*, 1926–27, 7; "Report on the Graduate Schools," President's Papers, 1925–45, 68:6; "Report on Theory of Education," President's Papers, 1925–45, 3:8, Special Collections, University of Chicago Library.

15. General Education Board, *Annual Report*, 1925–30.

16. Caltech and Johns Hopkins resembled Chicago in this regard but lacked the consistent denigration of undergraduates common at Chicago.

17. Robert Maynard Hutchins, "Report of the President to the Board of Trustees, 1938–39" (unpub.), Special Collections, UCL. David Stevens to Harold Swift, January 25, 1928, President's Papers, 1925–45, 3:8, Special Collections, UCL. Harold Wechsler, *The Qualified Student* (New York: Wiley, 1976), 225.

18. Floyd W. Reeves and John D. Russell, *Admission and Retention of Students*, University of Chicago Survey, vol. 5 (Chicago: University of Chicago Press, 1933), 21–26; Hutchins, "Report of the President, 1930–34," Special Collections UCL, 19.

19. Hutchins's iconoclasm is most familiar through *The Higher Learning in America* (New Haven: Yale University Press, 1936).

20. Hutchins, "Report, 1930–34," passim (quotation on 15).

21. Hutchins, "Report, 1934–35," 34, 37–38.

22. Hutchins, "Report, 1930–34," 30–38.

23. Hutchins, "Report, 1935–36," 1, 6; "Report, 1936–37," passim (including AAUP committee reports entitled "Academic Tenure" and "The Organization of Departments").

24. Hutchins, "Report, 1930–34," 34–35; "Report, 1935–36," 29; "Report, 1938–39," 1–8.

25. Hutchins, "Report, 1938–39." Paul Samuelson felt that he personally received

"a great education at the University of Chicago from 1932 to 1935," but he also thought that Hutchins "by the time of his retirement . . . had reduced a thriving college of 5000 undergraduates into a few hundred underage neurotics": "Economics," 169.

26. Hutchins, *Higher Learning in America*.

27. See "The University of Chicago," *Fortune* 16 (1937): 141–57.

28. Princeton University, *President's Report*, 1920, 10.

29. Willard Thorp, Minor Myers, Jr., and Jeremiah Finch, *The Princeton Graduate School: A History* (Princeton: Princeton University, 1978).

30. *President's Report*, 1930–31, 14.

31. *President's Report*, 1924–25, 1–13; 1925–26, 60.

32. "Memorandum of Conversation with Dr. Wickliffe Rose, 5/22/25," "University Research board" file, University Archives, Princeton University. The following account of negotiations with the GEB is drawn from this file. The original faculty delegation consisted of Professors Edwin Conklin, Henry Fine, and Karl Compton. The latter was especially prominent in subsequent negotiations—a fact well known by the MIT trustees, who later chose him to be president. The Rockefeller staff was particularly impressed that the "spirit of industrialism" was absent from the Princeton chemistry department. See also Thorp, Myers, and Finch, *Princeton Graudate School*, 181–84. The GEB granted Princeton an additional $1 million for scientific buildings in 1928.

33. *President's Report*, 1924–25, 6.

34. Princeton had 110, compared with 86 for Harvard and 81 for Caltech: *National Research Fellowships, 1919–38* (Washington, D.C.: NRC, 1938), 81.

35. *President's Report*, 1926–27, 6; 1927–28, 11–14.

36. "Research in the Fundamental Sciences at Princeton" (1926), University Archives, Princeton University.

37. *President's Report*, 1930–31, 12.

38. Yale University, *President's Report*, 1925–26, 12.

39. Edgar S. Furniss, *The Graduate School of Yale: A Brief History* (New Haven: Yale Graduate Schools 1965). See also Brooks Mather Kelley, *Yale: A History* (New Haven: Yale University Press, 1974), 356–66; George W. Pierson, *Yale College: An Educational History, 1871–1921* (New Haven: Yale University Press, 1952), 477–92, 513–34.

40. George W. Pierson, *Yale: The University College, 1921–37* (New Haven: Yale University Press, 1955), 3–19.

41. Ibid., 177–78; *President's Report*, 1925–26, 10–11.

42. Pierson, *Yale: University College*, 186.

43. Ibid., 178, 179, 187.

44. Yale University, *Reports to the President*, 1926–27, 38–62; Furniss, *Graduate School*, 82–87. For faculty budgets, see below, n. 47.

45. Pierson, *Yale: University College*, 672–77.

46. Ibid., 182–83; Furniss, *Graduate School*, 66–67. Wilbur L. Cross, *Connecticut Yankee: An Autobiography* (New Haven: Yale University Press, 1943), 152–59, 172–86.

47. Yale Faculties of Arts and Sciences, Annual Budgets (in thousands of dollars):

	1921–22	1925–26	1930–31
Graduate School	258.9	340.9	537.5
Yale College	228.2	313	425.3
Sheffield School	261.8	380.7	444.8
Freshman Year	170.5	177.6	229
Totals	919.4	1,212.2	1,636.6

SOURCE: Yale University, treasurer's reports.

48. Pierson, *Yale: University College*, 672–77.

49. Ibid., 597–600.

50. Yale University, *Treasurer's Report*, 1926, 44.

51. Furniss, *Graduate School*, 99–100.

52. Ibid., 99.

53. Kelley, *Yale*, 393.

54. Ibid., 393–96; *President's Report*, 1938–39, 3.

55. Howard H. Peckham, *The Making of the University of Michigan, 1817–1967*, (Ann Arbor: University of Michigan Press, 1967), 140.

56. Mark H. Ingraham, "The University of Wisconsin, 1925–50" in Alan G. Bogue and Robert Taylor, eds., *The University of Wisconsin: One-Hundred and Twenty-fife Years* (Madison: University of Wisconsin Press, 1975), 38–78.

57. From Appendix C.

58. University of Michigan Faculty, by rank, 1930 and 1940.

	1930–31		1940–41	
	LS&A	University	LS&A	University
Professors	84	202	102	244
Associate professors	45	99	74	155
Assistant Professors	90	204	80	177
Instructors	158	328	59	220
Total	377	833	315	796

University of Michigan, Resident Enrollment and Degrees, 1925 and 1940

	1925–26	1940–41
University enrollment	9,923	12,875
LS&A enrollment	5,224	4,895
LS&A bachelors degrees	994	937
Graduate school enrollment	822	2,966
Doctorates	51	121

SOURCE: University of Michigan, president's reports.

59. Peter E. Van de Water, *Alexander Grant Ruthven of Michigan* (Grand Rapids: Eerdmans, 1977); Peckham, *Michigan*, 139–99; David B. Laird, Jr., *The Regents of the University of Michigan and the Legislature of the State, 1920–1950* (Ann Arbor: University of Michigan School of Education, 1972).

60. Alexander G. Ruthven, *Naturalist in Two Worlds: Random Recollections of a University President* (Ann Arbor: University of Michigan Press, 1963), 156. Wilfred B. Shaw, "The Support of the University of Michigan from Sources Other than Public Funds or Student Fees, 1817–1931," in *President's Report*, 1932–33, 215–64; idem, "The Support of the University of Michigan . . , 1931–39," in *President's Report*, 1938–39, 383–418.

61. *President's Report*, 1929–30, 84–89; *President's Report*, 1935–36, 132; Van de Water, *Ruthven*, 110–11; Peckham, *Michigan*, 121, 141, 174–75. Although the Cook bequest was comparable in size to Yale's great Sterling bequest, and thus the largest ever given to a public university, its value diminished considerably because of the Depression.

62. The Michigan Department of Engineering Research performed more than $300,000 worth of contract research in 1929–30. This was more industrial research than was done at MIT, but without the negative implications that such work acquired there. The Michigan department, besides employing many engineering students, provided other units in the university with equipment, research assistance, and fellowships. See, e.g., *President's Report*, 1930–31, 91–93.

63. Verne A. Stadtman, *The University of California, 1868–1968* (New York:

McGraw-Hill, 1970), 239–57 (quotation on 256).

64. Ibid., 212–13, 365–68; Robert W. Seidel, "Physics Research in California" (Ph.D. diss., University of California, Berkeley, 1978), 85–96. The Berkeley Research Fund, unlike comparable funds at most other universities, included appropriations for departmental research.

65. E.g., "State-supported institutions, with few exceptions, are not at present able to bid against the salaries paid at the University of Chicago": Floyd W. Reeves et al., *The University Faculty,* University of Chicago Survey, vol. 3 (Chicago: University of Chicago Press, 1933), 67. Indeed, California was not able to lure the physicist Arthur Compton away from Chicago in 1927 (Seidel, "Physics in California," 97–98); but conditions were somewhat different by the late 1930s. In 1938–39 two Chicago department chairmen departed for Berkeley. Hutchins attributed the moves to the attraction of the California climate, but one could surmise that salaries had become competitive: Hutchins, "Report of the President, 1938–39."

66. The following account draws upon Seidel, "Physics in California," 85–106.

67. Ibid., 99–101.

Section 3. Students, Professors, and Research

1. George W. Pierson, *Yale: The University College, 1921–37* (New Haven: Yale University Press, 1955), 144, 149–50, 670.

2. Ibid., 146–47, 670.

3. Ibid., 145; Yale University, *Reports to the President,* "Admissions Department," 1926 (quotation on p. 5); see also 1927, 1928, 1929, and 1930.

4. David Riesman, "Educational Reform at Harvard College: Meritocracy and Its Adversaries," in Seymour Martin Lipset and David Riesman, *Education and Politics at Harvard* (New York: McGraw-Hill, 1975), 296.

5. See, e.g., Pierson, *Yale: University College,* 151–63; Riesman, "Educational Reform at Harvard," 298.

6. Princeton University, *President's Report,* 1923, 1–15. At Yale the departmental major became inextricably combined with the honors course: Pierson, *Yale: University College,* 197–207, 356–65, 381–86.

7. Harvard University, *President's Report,* 1927–28, 7–9. Cf. Pierson, *Yale: University College,* 333–55.

8. University of Michigan, *President's Report,* 1926–27, 173–76; 1927–28, 177–83; 1930–31, 219–23.

9. University of Michigan, *President's Report,* 1928–29, 33.

10. Howard H. Peckham, *The Making of the University of Michigan, 1817–1967* (Ann Arbor: University of Michigan Press, 1967), 158–59; Lotus D. Coffman, "The Growth of State Universities," in John L. Brumm, ed., *Educational Problems in College and University* (Ann Arbor: University of Michigan Press, 1921), 132–47. Minnesota actually incorporated a junior college, named the General College, into the university: Roland L. Guyotte, "Liberal Education and the American Dream: Public Attitudes and the Emergence of Mass Higher Education" (Ph.D. diss., Norhwestern University, 1980), 111–47. For another expression of this view, from the president of the University of Missouri, see Stratton D. Brooks, "Limiting Enrollments, Especially in the Larger Institutions," *Transactions and Proceedings of the National Association of State Universities* (hereafter NASU) 24 (1926): 35–39. However, California's president David Barrows opposed this trend: *President's Report,* 1919–20, 7.

11. Alexander Meiklejohn, *The Experimental College* (New York: Harper, 1932), 278–94; Guyotte, "Liberal Education," 68–110; George C. Sellery, *Some Ferments at Wisconsin, 1901–1947* (Madison: Wisconsin University Press, 1960), 9–34; Mark H.

Ingraham, "The University of Wisconsin, 1925–50," in Alan G. Bogue and Robert Taylor, eds., *The University of Wisconsin* (Madison: University of Wisconsin Press, 1975), 40. Michigan established an honors program in 1957; Wisconsin, in 1960.

12. E.g., applicants to the Yale freshman class declined from 4,166 in 1930 to 3,086 in 1934. The percentage of Yale freshmen from private schools peaked at 78 percent in the early thirties, then declined. See Yale University, *Reports to the President*, "Admissions Department," 1930 through 1934. The number of transfers and repeaters also increased modestly: Pierson, *Yale: University College*, 670.

13. James B. Conant, *My Several Lives* (New York: Harper & Row, 1970) 129.

14. Riesman, "Educational Reform at Harvard," 288–89.

15. When Yale established its university regional scholarships, in 1928, it based the criteria of selection on those of the Rhodes Scholarships—character, scholarship, and physical vigor: Pierson, *Yale: University College*, 489–90. According to David Riesman, the Rhodes Scholarships epitomize "the aristocratic style of selection," which relies upon "the unarticulated judgement of men who are satisfying each other and their own consciences": "Educational Reform at Harvard," 289.

16. Conant, *My Several Lives*, 122; Pierson, *Yale: University College*, 501.

17. Cornell University, *President's Report*, 1920–21, iv–vi. Large teaching loads for graduate students were long viewed with alarm at Cornell.

18. Charles S. Slichter, "Selective Admission of Graduate Students," *Journal of the Association of American Universities* (hereafter *JAAU*) 32 (1930): 60–65; Frederick J. E. Woodbridge, "Maintaining Standards without Excessive Standardization," *JAAU* 26 (1924): 51–59.

19. Columbia University, *President's Report*, 1925–26, 162.

20. University of Michigan, *President's Report*, 1925–26, 112; Harvard University, *President's Report*, 1925–26, 102. Harvard's graduate school undoubtedly had more national appeal than did that of any other American university, yet its recruitment was highly localized. From 1910 to 1925, 10.3 percent of its graduate students came from just six liberal arts colleges—Amherst, Brown, Bowdoin, Dartmouth, Haverford, and Williams. The six best-represented research universities, in contrast, supplied just 9.4 percent (ibid., 100). By 1925 all of the research universities were supplying 18 percent of Harvard's graduate students, while the six colleges produced 11 percent. These percentages were unchanged in 1939–40.

21. Slichter, "Selective Admission"; James Baxter, "Student Selection for Graduate Work in the Social Sciences," *JAAU* 35 (1933): 45–49; Harvard University, *President's Report*, 1925–26, 101.

22. These issues were thoroughly aired in the annual meetings of the Association of American Universities, particularly from 1924 to 1929. See *JAAU;* also, cf. R. M. Hughes, *A Study of Graduate Schools of America* (Oxford, Ohio: Miami University, 1925), 7–9.

23. Henry Suzzallo, "Discussion of Graduate Work in American Universities," *NASU* 25 (1927): 83–96. Suzzallo's language belies the impulse for a Flexner-styrle rationalization of graduate study: he was dismayed by "the poor distribution of our product"; and he aspired to establish "how many we ought to train," and "how we can control the situation." More generally, critics who, like Suzzallo, attempted to comprehend the totality of American graduate education were invariably frustrated: enrollments seemed too large, the motivations and abilities of students too varied, the degrees from nonresearch universities too numerous, and the disjunction between the formal requirements and the essential purpose too great. In contrast to the issues that dominated the twenties (above, n. 22), this general critique became more widespread during the 1930s: e.g., David Allan Robertson, "Graduate Study in the United States," *JAAU* 19 (1927): 49–75; Laurence Foster, *The Functions of a Graduate*

School in a Democratic Society (New York: Huxley House, 1936); Ernest V. Hollis, *Toward Improving Ph.D. Programs* (Washington, D.C.: American Council on Education, 1945). Robert M. Hutchins's *Higher Learning in America* (1934) is also germane. As the research universities dealt with their own, specific problems, they seemed to lose interest in these broad-brush critiques. In a survey of institutional gripes, four of five state research universities contravened the majority by finding "no general indictment" of graduate work: John J. Tigert, "What Is the Matter with Graduate Work?" *NASU* 34 (1936): 183–97.

24. Examples of the give-and-take between graduate schools and departments may be found in Edgar S. Furniss, *The Graduate School of Yale* (New Haven: Yale Graduate School, 1965), 104–9; and Willard Thorp, Minor Myers, Jr., and Jeremiah Finch, *The Princeton Graduate School: A History* (Princeton: Princeton University Press, 1978) 187–205.

25. Floyd W. Reeves and John D. Russell, *Admission and Retention of Students*, University of Chicago Survey, vol. 5 (Chicago: University of Chicago Press, 1933), 236–44; Cornell University, *President's Report*, 1931–32, 15; Yale University, *Reports to the President*, 1933–34, 57–59; Harvard University, *President's Report*, 1928–29, 15–16.

26. Baxter, "Studet Selection for Graduate Work."

27. Furniss, *Graduate School*, 109.

28. Carnegie Foundation for the Advancement of Teaching, *The Graduate Record Examination* (New York: CFAT, 1941); Thorp, Myers, and Finch, *Princeton Graduate School*, 201–3.

29. Malcolm D. Willey, *Depression and Recovery in Higher Education* (New York: McGraw-Hill, 1937), 268–80.

30. "In the personnel of its student body as well as in the nature of its studies the [Harvard] Graduate School of Arts and Sciences shades almost imperceptibly into the Faculty": Charles H. Haskins, "The Graduate School of Arts and Sciences," in Samuel Eliot Morison, ed., *The Development of Harvard University, 1869–1929* (Cambridge: Harvard University Press, 1930), 451–62 (quotation on 461). Conant, *My Several Lives*, 74.

31. Robert A. Millikan, *The Autobiography of Robert A. Millikan* (New York: Prentice-Hall, 1950), 184.

32. National Research Council, *Consolidated Report upon the Activities of the National Research Council, 1919 to 1932* (Washington, D.C.: NRC, 1932).

33. Suzzallo, "Graduate Work," 91–92.

34. Hollis, *Improving Ph.D. Programs*, 56.

35. D. Stanley Tarbell and Ann T. Tarbell, *Roger Adams: Scientist and Statesman* (Washington, D.C.: American Chemical Society, 1981), 42–47.

36. University of Minnesota, *President's Report*, 1911–12, 19; University of Pennsylvania, *Report of the Committee on Educational Survey of the University of Pennsylvania* (Philadelphia: University of Pennsylvania Press, 1924), 55–56.

37. Raymond T. Birge, "History of the Physics Department: (Typescript, University of California, Berkeley, n.d.), 10:6;12:5–7; Robert W. Seidel, "Physics Research in California" (Ph.D. diss., University of California, Berkeley, 1978), 93–103; Conant, *My Several Lives*, 65–66.

38. A. B. Hollingshead, "Ingroup Membership and Academic Selction," *American Sociological Review* 3 (1938): 826–33; Logan Wilson, *The Academic Man: A Study in the Sociology of a Profession* (New York: Oxford University Press, 1942), 49–56. If the new Ph.D. happened to be female, she faced more-formidable obstacles. See Margaret W. Rossiter, *Women Scientists in America: Struggles and Strategies to 1940* (Baltimore: Johns Hopkins University Press, 1982), esp. 160–217, 267–96.

39. The effect of a call obviously depended upon the relative status of the employing institution and the one issuing the call. Hollingshead reported that Indiana University did not ordinarily try to match outside offers ("Climbing the Academic Ladder," *American Sociological Review* 5 (1940): 384–94); and a Minnesota dean, commenting on 138 faculty departures over twenty years, testified, "In practically all cases these persons have gone to positions with rank and salary higher than were in prospect for them here" (University of Minnesota, *President's Report*, 1934–36, 177).

40. Conant, *My Several Lives*, 73–75.

41. Princeton University, *President's Report*, 1920, 31–33.

42. Conant, *My Several Lives*, 173.

43. Ibid., 160.

44. Ibid., 172–73.

45. The Walsh-Sweezy affair and its aftermath are described in ibid., 157–76; and in Edward S. Mason, "The Harvard Department of Economics," *Quarterly Journal of Economics* 97 (1982): 385–433. See also Special Committee appointed by the President of Harvard University, *Report on the Terminating Appointments of Dr. J. R. Walsh and Dr. A. R. Sweezy* (Cambridge: Harvard University Press, 1938).

46. Yale University, *President's Report*, 1938–39, 13–14; Conant, *My Several Lives*, 173.

47. Wilson, *Academic Man*.

48. Frederic A. Ogg, *Research in the Humanistic and Social Sciences* (New York: Century, 1928), 155–63; *Science* 63 (1926): 317, 518.

49. Ogg, *Research*, 63–70.

50. George J. Stigler, *Employment and Compensation in Education*, National Bureau of Economic Research, Occasional Paper 33 (New York: NBER, 1950), 42–44; Spencer R. Weart, "The Physics Business in America, 1919–1940," in Nathan Reingold, ed., *The Sciences in the American Context* (Washington, D.C.: Smithsonian Institution Press, 1979), 295–358.

51. Stigler, *Employment and Compensation*, 42.

52. Hollis, *Improving Ph.D. Programs*, 56.

53. National Resources Committee, *Research—A National Resource*, vol. 1, *Relation of the Federal Government to Research* (Washington, D.C.: GPO, 1938) 179.

54. "Report on the Committee on Science and the Public Welfare," in Vannevar Bush, *Science—The Endless Frontier* (Washington, D.C.: National Science Foundation, 1960), 125–34.

55. This information is from an inquiry on sabbatical practices made by the president's office at Cornell in 1938: Edmund Ezra Day Papers, series 1, box 47, file 62, Cornell University Archives.

56. "Leaves of Absence for Research at Harvard University," *School and Society* 39 (1934): 743.

57. "Funds Available in the United States for the Support and Encouragement of Research in Science and Its Technologies," *Bulletin of the National Research Council*, 2d ed., no. 66 (1928); 3d ed. no. 95 (1934).

58. Ibid. Also see above, Chapter 2.

59. All figures from "Funds," 2d ed., 1928.

60. All figures from "Funds," 3d ed., 1934.

61. National Resources Committee, *Resources*, 190–91.

62. On the "revolt against science," see Daniel J. Kevles, *The Physicists* (New York: Knopf, 1978), 236–79; and Carroll W. Purcell, Jr., "'A Savage Struck by Lightning': The Idea of a Research Moratorium, 1927–37," *Lex et Scientia* 10 (1974): 146–58.

63. Conant, *My Several Lives*, 81–89; David Loth, *Swope of G.E.* (New York: Simon & Schuster, 1958), 194–95.

316 NOTES

64. Cornell University, *President's Report*, 1938–39, 16–19; 1939–40, v.

65. The trustee vote to refuse all foundation grants and the absence of sabbatical leaves are indicative of this policy. The vitality of research at Wisconsin owes much to the existence of the Wisconsin Alumni Research Foundation (see below).

Section 4. The Ascendancy of American Science

1. See above, Chapter 2; Stanley Coben, "The Scientific Establishment and the Transmission of Quantum Mechanics to the United States, 1919–32," *American Historical Review* 76 (1971): 442–66.

2. These were the principal stops for the many American physicists who visited Europe during the 1920s. Rome became an important center under Enrico Fermi late in the decade; significant work was done in Paris, but it was not part of the theoretical-physics circuit. See Katherine R. Sopka, *Quantum Physics in America, 1920–35* (New York: Arno Press, 1980), 3.40–42.

3. Charles Weiner, "New Site for the Seminar: The Refugees and American Physics in the Thirties," in Donald Fleming and Bernard Bailyn, eds., *The Intellectual Migration: Europe and America, 1930–1960* (Cambridge: Harvard University Press, 1969), 190–234.

4. Jagdish Mehra and Helmut Rechenberg, *The Historical Development of Quantum Theory*, vol. 4 (New York: Springer-Verlag, 1982); Daniel J. Kevles, *The Physicists* (New York: Knopf, 1978), 155–69; Coban, "Quantum Mechanics," 450–51.

5. John C. Slater, "Quantum Physics in America between the Wars," *Physics Today*, January 1968, 43–51; also quoted in Weiner, "New Site for the Seminar," 193–94.

6. Coban, "Quantum Mechanics," 457–58.

7. Sopka, *Quantum Physics*, A.17–27; Robert W. Seidel, "Physics Research in California" (Ph.D. diss., University of California, Berkeley, 1978), 518–20.

8. Sopka, *Quantum Physics*, 3.11–13, 3.39–43; Seidel, "Physics in California," 520–21.

9. Coban, "Quantum Mechanics," 458; Sopka, *Quantum Physics* 3.54–63, 4.51–73. Coban does not include Harvard as a center of quantum theory in the 1920s, but Sopka makes a strong case that it was.

10. Weiner, "New Site for the Seminar," 197–99; Coban, "Quantum Mechanics," 460–61; Sopka, *Quantum Physics*, 2.42–44; David M. Dennison, "Physics and the Department of Physics since 1900," in Donald E. Thackrey, ed., *Research—Definitions and Reflections* (Ann Arbor: University of Michigan Press, 1967), 120–36; Wilfred B. Shaw, *The University of Michigan: An Encyclopedic Survey*, 4 vols. (Ann Arbor: University of Michigan Press, 1942–58), 692–701.

11. Coban, "Quantum Mechanics," 455; Sopka, *Quantum Physics* 4.58–63. John Van Vleck taught at Wisconsin from 1928 to 1934 and then returned to Harvard; Eugene Wigner joined the Wisconsin department in 1937 but returned to Princeton the next year.

12. Quoted in Coban, "Quantum Mechanics," 462.

13. Herman Weyl (Princeton-Zurich-Institute for Advanced Study); E. U. Condon (Princeton-Minnesota-Princeton); and Wigner (above, no. 11): ibid., 461–65.

14. Gerald Holton, "The Migration of Physicists to the United States," in Jarrel C. Jackman and Carla M. Borden, eds., *The Muses Flee Hitler* (Washington, D.C.: Smithsonian Institution Press, 1983), 169–88.

15. Seidel, "Physics in California," 516–31.

16. Sopka, *Quantum Physics*, 4.61–62, A.4, A.6.

17. Ibid., 1.62–67, 4.55, 4.67–69.

18. Seidel, "Physics in California," 102, 532–53.

19. Kevles, *Physicists*, 222–35. The other two Nobel Prize-winning accomplishments were the discovery of the neutron and the creation of a linear proton accelerator—both done in Ernest Rutherford's laboratory at the University of Cambridge.

20. Ibid., 221.

21. Weiner, "New Site for the Seminar."

22. S. Ulam et al., "John von Neumann, 1903–57,"in Fleming and Bailyn *Intellectual Migration*, 235–69.

23. Coban, "Quantum Mechanics," 463. Coban suggests that there was conflict over so light a teaching load, but Condon seems to have prevailed.

Section 5. The Intellectual Migration

1. Charles Weiner, "New Site for the Seminar," in Donald Fleming and Bernard Bailyn, eds., *The Intellectual Migration* (Cambridge: Harvard University Press, 1969), 226–27n.

2. Ibid., 202–6, 234; Maurice R. Davie, *Refugees in America* (New York: Harper, 1947), 300.

3. Laura Fermi, *Illustrious Immigrants: The Intellectual Migration from Europe, 1930–41,* 2d ed. (Chicago: University of Chicago Press, 1971), 39–53, 84.

4. Davie, *Refugees,* 315–18, 320–22.

5. Ibid., 301–14; Fermi, *Immigrants,* 71–82.

6. The 231 immigrants are listed in Davie, *Refugees,* 435–40.

7. Information compiled from Fleming and Bailyn, *Intellectual Migration,* 675–718.

8. Fermi, *Immigrants,* 195–97.

9. Ibid., 16; Donald Fleming, "Emigré Physicists and the Biological Revolution," in Fleming and Bailyn, *Intellectual Migration,* 152–89.

10. Fermi, *Immigrants,* 283–95.

11. Ibid., 139–74, 247–53; Maria Jahoda, "The Migration of Psychoanalysis: Its Impact on American Psychology," in Fleming and Bailyn, *Intellectual Migration,* 420–45.

Chapter 6: The Research Universities in the 1930s.

Section 1. Effects of the Depression

1. Cf. the paradox Spencer Weart perceives in the rapid advance of physics during the depths of the Depression: "The Physics Business in America, 1919–1940: A Statistical Reconnaissance," in Nathan Reingold, ed., *The Sciences in the American Context* (Washington, D.C.: Smithsonian Institution Press, 1979), 295–358.

2. Department of Education, *Biennial Survey of Education,* 1929–30 and 1931–32 (Washington, D.C.: GPO, 1931, 1933). See Appendix C.

3. John Price Jones, ed., *The Yearbook of Philanthropy, 1940* (New York: Inter-River Press, 1940), 49. See Appendix E.

4. From $4.68 million in 1930–31 to $3.27 million in 1934–35: Yale University, *Treasurer's Report,* 1931, 1935.

5. Beginning with the academic year 1929–30 the Education Department's *Biennial Survey of Education* included separately budgeted university income for organized research. These figures are incomplete and inconsistent from year to year for private

universities but somewhat more meaningful for the state research universities. Nevertheless, the bulk of these reported funds represent federal support for agricultural research. Each of these five universities reported higher totals for 1939–40, and the aggregate increase for the decade was 78 percent.

6. For the Yale endowment the rate of return on investments declined from 5.2 percent in fiscal year 1929 to 3.97 percent in 1939. For Stanford, by way of comparison, the return sank from 4.9 percent in 1928 to 3.9 percent in 1936: Yale University, *Treasurer's Report*, 1930–31, 49; 1938–39, 31; Stanford University, *President's Report*, 1935–36, 64. See also Karl T. Compton, "Income from Endowment as Affected by Conditions of the Investment Market," *Journal of the Association of American Universities* (hereafter *JAAU*) 39 (1937): 63–77; and Trevor Arnett, *Recent Trends in Higher Education in the United States*, General Education Board, Occasional Paper no. 13 (New York: GEB, 1940), 61.

7. Harvard University, *President's Report*, 1939, 7; Yale University, *President's Report*, 1939, 2.

8. Calculated from George J. Stigler, *Employment and Compensation in Education*, National Bureau of Economics, Occasional Paper no. 33 (New York: NBER, 1950), 34.

9. Stanford University, *President's Report*, 1936, 17–18; Peter E. Van de Water, *Alexander Grant Ruthven of Michigan* (Grand Rapids: Eerdmans, 1977), 104–5; Mark H. Ingraham, "The University of Wisconsin, 1925–50," in Allan G. Bogue and Robert Taylor, eds., *The University of Wisconsin* (Madison: University of Wisconsin Press, 1975), 72–73.

10. Stigler, *Employment and Compensation*, 42–44.

11. Ingraham, "Wisconsin," 72–73.

12. Raymond T. Birge, "History of the Physics Department" (Typescript, University of California, n.d. [1966]), 11:12–13.

13. Remarks by Edgar Furniss, *JAAU* 36 (1934): 105–7; see also Weart, "Physics Business."

14. Princeton University, *President's Report*, 1936, 26; Verne A. Stadtman, *The University of California, 1868–1968* (New York: McGraw-Hill, 1970), 266; S. H. Slichter, "A Survey of Economic Conditions of the Academic Profession," *JAAU* 36 (1934): 97–101; Malcolm M. Willey, *Depression, Recovery and Higher Education* (New York: McGraw Hill, 1937), 118–23.

15. The total numbers of college and university faculty for 1928–40 are as follows:

1927–28	76,080	1935–36	92,580
1929–30	82,386	1937–38	102,895
1931–32	88,172	1939–40	110,885
1933–34	86,914	1941–42	114,693

Department of Education, *Biennial Survey of Education*, 1938–40, (Washington, D.C.: GPO, 1944), 7.

16. Weart, "Physics Business," 310–12.

17. Cf. National Research Council, "Funds Available in the United States for the Support and Encouragement of Research in Science and Its Technologies," *Bulletin of the National Research Council*, 2d ed., no. 66 (1928); 3d ed., no. 95 (1934). Strict comparisons between universities for these two years are not always possible, because of irregularities in reporting.

18. Yale University, *Treasurer's Report*, 1932, 1934, 1936, 1939.

19. National Research Council, *Funds for Research*, 1934, 126; Ingraham, "Wis-

consin," 73–74; quotation from Daniel J. Kevles, *The Physicists* (New York: Knopf, 1978), 268.

20. University of Michigan, *President's Report*, 1939, 159–60.

21. E.g., in 1939 Michigan reported receiving $2.54 million from the Federal Emergency Administration of Public Works, primarily for dormitory construction: ibid., 369.

22. *American Foundations and Their Fields*, 1935, 1939.

23. Rockefeller Foundation, *Annual Report*, 1936–1940.

24. Rockefeller Foundation, *Annual Report*, 1939, 43.

25. Compton, "Income from Endowment," 79; Harold W. Dodds, "Problems Arising from the Relationships of Educational Institutions with the Government," *JAAU* 39 (1937): 82–85.

26. Dodds, "Problems," 85.

Section 2. The Federal Government and University Research

1. Cf. A. Hunter Dupree, *Science in the Federal Government* (Cambridge: Harvard University Press, 1957), 296–99; estimated government research expenditures, 331. A somewhat higher estimate for the late 1930s is found in National Resources Committee, *Research—A National Resource*, vol. 1, *Relation of the Federal Government to Research* (Washington, D.C.: GPO, 1938), 65. This document is discussed below.

2. Dupree, *Science in the Federal Government*, 346.

3. Carroll W. Purcell, Jr., "'A Savage Struck by Lightning': The Idea of a Research Moratorium," *Lex et Scientia* 10 (1974): 146–58.

4. Dupree, *Science in the Federal Government*, 349; Daniel J. Kevles, *The Physicists* (New York: Knopf, 1978), 261–66.

5. The following shed light upon the Science Advisory Board from somewhat different perspectives: Lewis E. Auerbach, "Scientists in the New Deal: A Pre-War Episode in the Relations between Science and the Government in the United States," *Minerva* 4 (1965): 457–82; Carroll W. Purcell, Jr., "Anatomy of a Failure: The Science Advisory Board, 1933–35," *Proceedings of the American Philosophical Society* 109 (1965): 342–51; Dupree, *Science in the Federal Government*, 350–58; and Kevles, *Physicists*, 252–58.

6. The National Industrial Recovery Program spawned advisory boards for industry, labor, and consumers, and the SAB seems to have been originally conceived to become part of this framework: Auerbach, "Scientists in the New Deal," 459–60.

7. Science Advisory Board, *Annual Report*, vol. 1 (Washington, D.C.: SAB, 1934), 271.

8. Karl T. Compton, "Put Science to Work!" *Technology Review* 37 (1935): 133–35, 152–58; see also *New York Times Magazine*, December 16, 1934.

9. Quoted in Auerbach, "Scientists in the New Deal," 473.

10. Compton, "Put Science to Work!" 158; Dupree, *Science in the Federal Government*, 55–56.

11. Cf. Barry N. Karl, "The Power of Intellect and the Politics of Ideas," *Daedalus* 97 (1968): 1002–35; Kevles, *Physicists*, 254–55.

12. Dupree, *Science in the Federal Government*, 356–57; Kevles, *Physicists*, 255.

13. Kevles, *Physicists*, 266; Karl T. Compton, "Income from Endowment as Affected by Conditions of the Investment Market," *JAAU* (1937): 77.

14. Works Progress Administration, *Index of Research Projects*, vol. 1 (Washington, D.C.: WPA, 1938).

15. Kevles, *Physicists*, 258–60.

16. Quoted ibid., 257–58.

17. Dupree, *Science in the Federal Government*, 358–60.

18. Cf. Barry N. Karl, "Presidential Planning and Social Science Research: Mr. Hoover's Experts," *Perspectives in American History* 5 (1971): 347–409.

19. National Resources Committee, *Research*, 1:167–93.

20. Ibid., 175.

21. Ibid., 172–74; 190–91.

22. Cf. Chapter 1, Table 3.

23. [Raymond M. Hughes,] American Council on Education, *Report of Committee on Graduate Instruction* (Washington, D.C., ACE, 1934).

24. National Resources Committee, *Research*, 169.

25. Ibid., 183–190.

26. Dupree, *Science in the Federal Government*, 360–61. *Research* did, however, become a basic source for the authors of *Science—The Endless Frontier*, the influential postwar report written by Vannevar Bush: see below.

27. Daniel C. Swain, "The Rise of a Research Empire: NIH, 1930 to 1950," *Science* 138 (1962): 1233–37; Dupree, *Science in the Federal Government*, 365–66: The National Advisory Committee for Aeronautics also let contracts for outside research: "in 1939 NACA had contracts for twelve special investigations at ten universities" (ibid., 365).

Section 3. Retrospect and Prospect

1. Vannevar Bush, *Science—The Endless Frontier* (Washington, D.C.: National Science Foundation, 1960); J. Merton England, *A Patron for Pure Science: The National Science Foundation's Formative Years, 1945–57* (Washington, D.C.: National Science Foundation, 1982), 3–7.

2. Daniel J. Kevles, "The National Science Foundation and the Debate over Postwar Research Policy, 1942–1945," *Isis* 68 (1977): 5–26; see also England, *Patron for Pure Science*, 9–23.

3. Bush, *Endless Frontier*, 85–89.

4. Ibid., 125–26, 133–34.

5. Ibid., 87, 122–23; postwar capital needs of American colleges and universities were estimated to total $130 million (p. 123).

6. Ibid., 126–32.

7. Ibid., 31–33; 77–80.

8. Ibid., 94.

Index